SECRETS

OF

HEAVEN

SECRETS

OF

HEAVEN

The Portable New Century Edition

EMANUEL SWEDENBORG

Volume 9

Translated from the Latin by Lisa Hyatt Cooper

SWEDENBORG FOUNDATION

Royersford, Pennsylvania

Originally published in Latin as *Arcana Coelestia,* London, 1749–1756. The volume contents of this and the original Latin edition, along with ISBNs of the annotated version, are as follows:

Volume number in this edition	Text treated	Volume number in the Latin first edition	Section numbers	ISBN (hardcover)
1	Genesis 1–8	1	§§1–946	978-0-87785-486-9
2	Genesis 9–15	1	§§947–1885	978-0-87785-487-6
3	Genesis 16–21	2 (in 6 fascicles)	§§1886–2759	978-0-87785-488-3
4	Genesis 22–26	3	§§2760–3485	978-0-87785-489-0
5	Genesis 27–30	3	§§3486–4055	978-0-87785-490-6
6	Genesis 31–35	4	§§4056–4634	978-0-87785-491-3
7	Genesis 36–40	4	§§4635–5190	978-0-87785-492-0
8	Genesis 41–44	5	§§5191–5866	978-0-87785-493-7
9	Genesis 45–50	5	§§5867–6626	978-0-87785-494-4
10	Exodus 1–8	6	§§6627–7487	978-0-87785-495-1
11	Exodus 9–15	6	§§7488–8386	978-0-87785-496-8
12	Exodus 16–21	7	§§8387–9111	978-0-87785-497-5
13	Exodus 22–24	7	§§9112–9442	978-0-87785-498-2
14	Exodus 25–29	8	§§9443–10166	978-0-87785-499-9
15	Exodus 30–40	8	§§10167–10837	978-0-87785-500-2

ISBN of e-book of library edition, vol. 9: 978-0-87785-738-9
ISBN of Portable Edition, vol. 9, containing translation only: 978-0-87785-436-4
ISBN of e-book of Portable Edition, vol. 9: 978-0-87785-732-7

(The ISBN in the Library of Congress data shown below is that of volume 1.)

Library of Congress Cataloging-in-Publication Data

Swedenborg, Emanuel, 1688–1772.
    [Arcana coelestia. English]
    Secrets of heaven / Emanuel Swedenborg ; translated from the Latin by
Lisa Hyatt Cooper. — Portable New Century ed.
    p. cm.
    Includes bibliographical references and indexes.
    ISBN 978-0-87785-408-1 (alk. paper)
    1. New Jerusalem Church—Doctrines. 2. Bible. O.T. Genesis—Commentaries—Early works to 1800. 3. Bible. O.T. Exodus—Commentaries—Early works to 1800. I. Title.
    BX8712.A8 2010
    230'.94—dc22

2009054171

Ornaments from the first Latin edition, 1749–1756
Text designed by Joanna V. Hill
Senior copy editor, Alicia L. Dole
Typesetting by Mary M. Wachsmann and Sarah Dole
Cover design by Karen Connor
Cover photograph by Magda Indigo

Further information about the New Century Edition of the Works of Emanuel Swedenborg can be obtained directly from the Swedenborg Foundation, 70 Buckwalter Road, Suite 900 PMB 405, Royersford, PA 19468 U.S.A.
Telephone: (610) 430-3222 • Web: www.swedenborg.com • E-mail: info@swedenborg.com

Contents

Volume 9

Conventions Used in This Work

MOST of the following conventions apply generally to the translations in the New Century Edition Portable series. For introductory material on the content and history of *Secrets of Heaven,* and for annotations on the subject matter, including obscure or problematic content, and extensive indexes, the reader is referred to the Deluxe New Century Edition volumes.

Volume designation *Secrets of Heaven* was originally published in eight volumes; in this edition all but the second original volume have been divided into two. Thus Swedenborg's eight volumes now fill fifteen volumes, of which this is the ninth. It corresponds to approximately the second half of Swedenborg's volume 5.

Section numbers Following a practice common in his time, Swedenborg divided his published theological works into sections numbered in sequence from beginning to end. His original section numbers have been preserved in this edition; they appear in boxes in the outside margins. Traditionally, these sections have been referred to as "numbers" and designated by the abbreviation "n." In this edition, however, the more common section symbol (§) is used to designate the section numbers, and the sections are referred to as such.

Subsection numbers Because many sections throughout Swedenborg's works are too long for precise cross-referencing, Swedenborgian scholar John Faulkner Potts (1838–1923) further divided them into subsections; these have since become standard, though minor variations occur from one edition to another. These subsections are indicated by bracketed numbers that appear in the text itself: [2], [3], and so on. Because the beginning of the first *subsection* always coincides with the beginning of the *section* proper, it is not labeled in the text.

Citations of Swedenborg's text As is common in Swedenborgian studies, text citations of Swedenborg's works refer not to page numbers but to section numbers, which unlike page numbers are uniform in most editions.

In citations the section symbol (§) is generally omitted after the title of a work by Swedenborg. Thus "*Secrets of Heaven* 29" refers to section 29 (§29) of Swedenborg's *Secrets of Heaven,* not to page 29 of any edition. Subsection numbers are given after a colon; a reference such as "29:2" indicates subsection 2 of section 29. The reference "29:1" would indicate the first subsection of section 29, though that subsection is not in fact labeled in the text. Where section numbers stand alone without titles, their function is indicated by the prefixed section symbol; for example, "§29:2".

Citations of Swedenborg's unnumbered sections Some material in *Secrets of Heaven* was not given a section number. Swedenborg assigns no section numbers to his quoting of a biblical chapter before he takes up each verse in turn. He also gives no section numbers to occasional prefatory material, such as his author's table of contents in *Secrets of Heaven* (before §1), his prefaces to Genesis 16 and 18 (before §§1886 and 2135, respectively), and his preface to Genesis 22 (before §2760). The biblical material needs no section number, as it is referred to simply by chapter and verse. In this edition, references to the author's unnumbered prefaces follow these models: "(preface to Genesis 22)"; "see the preface to Genesis 18."

Citations of the Bible Biblical citations in this edition follow the accepted standard: a semicolon is used between book references and between chapter references, and a comma between verse references. Therefore "Matthew 5:11, 12; 6:1; 10:41, 42; Luke 6:23, 35" would refer to Matthew chapter 5, verses 11 and 12; Matthew chapter 6, verse 1; Matthew chapter 10, verses 41 and 42; and Luke chapter 6, verses 23 and 35. Swedenborg often incorporated the numbers of verses not actually represented in his text when listing verse numbers for a passage he quoted; these apparently constitute a kind of "see also" reference to other material he felt was relevant. This edition includes these extra verses and also follows Swedenborg where he cites contiguous verses individually (for example, John 14:8, 9, 10, 11), rather than as a range (John 14:8–11). Occasionally this edition supplies a full, conventional Bible reference where Swedenborg omits one after a quotation.

Quotations in Swedenborg's works Some features of the original Latin text of *Secrets of Heaven* have been modernized in this edition. For example, Swedenborg's first edition generally relies on context or italics rather than on quotation marks to indicate passages taken from the Bible or from other works. The manner in which these conventions are used in the original suggests that Swedenborg did not belabor the distinction between direct quotation and paraphrase; but in this edition, directly quoted material is indicated by either block quotations or quotation marks, and paraphrased material is usually presented without such indicators. In passages of dialog as well, quotation marks have been introduced that were not present as such in the original. Furthermore, Swedenborg did not mark his omissions from or changes to material he quoted, a practice in which this edition generally follows him. One exception consists of those instances in which Swedenborg did not include a complete sentence at the beginning or end of a Bible quotation. The omission in such cases has been marked in this edition with added points of ellipsis.

Grammatical anomalies Swedenborg sometimes uses a singular verb with certain dual subjects such as love and wisdom, goodness and truth, and love and charity. The wider context of his works indicates that his reason for doing so is that he understands the two given subjects as forming a unity. This translation generally preserves such singular verbs.

Italicized terms Any words in indented scriptural extracts that are here set in italics reflect a similar emphasis in the first edition.

Special use of vertical rule The opening passages of the early chapters of *Secrets of Heaven,* as well as the ends of all chapters, contain material that derives in some way from Swedenborg's experiences in the spiritual world. Swedenborg specified that the text of these and similar passages be set in continuous italics to distinguish it from exegetical and other material. For this edition, the heavy use of italic text was felt to be antithetical to modern tastes, as well as difficult to read, and so such passages are instead marked by a vertical rule in the margin.

Changes to and insertions in the text This translation is based on the first Latin edition, published by Swedenborg himself (1749–1756); it also reflects emendations in the third Latin edition, edited by P. H. Johnson, John E. Elliott, and others, and published by the Swedenborg Society (1949–1973). It incorporates the silent correction of minor errors, not only in the text proper but in Bible verse references and in section references to this and other volumes of *Secrets of Heaven.* The text has usually been changed without notice where the verse numbering of the Latin Bible cited by Swedenborg differs from that of modern English Bibles. Throughout the translation, references or cross-references that were implied but not stated have been inserted in brackets; for example, [John 3:27]. In many cases, it is very difficult to determine what Swedenborg had in mind when he referred to other passages giving evidence for a statement or providing further discussion on a topic. Because of this difficulty, the missing references that are occasionally supplied in this edition should not be considered definitive or exhaustive. In contrast to such references in square brackets, references that occur in parentheses are those that appear in the first edition; for example, (1 Samuel 30:16), (see §42 above). Occasionally square brackets signal an insertion of other material that was not present in the first edition. These insertions fall into two classes: words likely to have been deleted through a copying or typesetting error, and words supplied by the translator as necessary for the understanding of the English text, though they have no direct parallel in the Latin. The latter device has been used sparingly, however, even at the risk of some inconsistency in its application. Unfortunately, no annotations concerning these insertions can be supplied in this Portable edition.

Biblical titles Swedenborg refers to the Hebrew Scriptures as the Old Testament and to the Greek Scriptures as the New Testament; his terminology has been adopted in this edition. As was the custom in his day, he refers to the Pentateuch (Genesis, Exodus, Leviticus, Numbers, and Deuteronomy) simply as "Moses"; for example, in §6394 he writes, "It can be seen in Moses," and then quotes a passage from Deuteronomy. Similarly, in sentences or phrases introducing quotations he sometimes refers to the Psalms as "David," to Lamentations as "Jeremiah," and to the Gospel of John, the Epistles of John, and the Book of Revelation as simply "John." Conventional references supplied in parentheses after such quotations specify their sources more precisely.

Problematic content Occasionally Swedenborg makes statements that, although mild by the standards of eighteenth-century theological discourse, now read as harsh, dismissive, or insensitive. The most problematic are assertions about or criticisms of various religious traditions and their adherents—including Judaism, ancient or contemporary; Roman Catholicism; Islam; and the Protestantism in which Swedenborg himself grew up. These statements are far outweighed in size and importance by other passages in Swedenborg's works earnestly maintaining the value of every individual and of all religions. This wider context is discussed in the introductions and annotations of the Deluxe edition mentioned above. In the present format, however, problematic statements must be retained without comment. The other option—to omit them—would obscure some aspects of Swedenborg's presentation and in any case compromise its historicity.

Allusive References in Expositional Material

Swedenborg's use of pronouns that refer back to vague or distant antecedents may cause confusion for readers. Such allusive references occur in two situations in his expositions:

In mentions of Jesus If the pronoun *he* without a nearby antecedent appears in a proposition, the reader can assume that it refers to Jesus, the main topic of the exegesis as a whole.

In preview material Swedenborg's preview sections (see the Deluxe edition of *Secrets of Heaven,* vol. 1, pages 30–35) feature a series of propositions, each of which consists of a phrase of biblical text followed by a brief assertion of its inner meaning. These glimpses of the inner meaning quite often use pronouns that point back to other inner meanings mentioned earlier in the preview section. For instance, in *Secrets of Heaven* volume 7, §4962, a preview section, we read this:

> *And Joseph* symbolizes spiritual heavenliness drawing on rationality. *Was taken down to Egypt* means to religious learning. *And Potiphar, Pharaoh's chamberlain, bought him* means that **it** had a place among items of inner knowledge. *The chief of the bodyguards* means **that** were of primary importance in interpretation. *An Egyptian man* symbolizes earthly truth.

The words "it" and "that" (shown here in boldface) are confusing: *What* had a place among items of inner knowledge? *What things* were of primary importance in interpretation? The answers lie in the fragments of inner meaning given in propositions earlier in the preview section: The "it" refers back to the "spiritual heavenliness" mentioned in the first proposition. The referent of "that" is the "items of inner knowledge" mentioned at the end of the immediately preceding proposition. Thus Swedenborg has laid the propositions out in such a way that if put together, the five statements might read as follows:

> *And Joseph was taken down to Egypt, and Potiphar, Pharaoh's chamberlain, the chief of the bodyguards, an Egyptian man, bought him* means that spiritual heavenliness drawing on rationality was brought to religious learning and given a place among items of inner knowledge and earthly truth that were of primary importance in interpretation.

SECRETS
OF
HEAVEN

Genesis 45

1. And Joseph could not restrain himself before all those standing with him, and he shouted, "Make every man go out from beside me!" And no one stood with him in Joseph's making himself known to his brothers.

2. And he gave his voice up to weeping, and the Egyptians heard, and Pharaoh's household heard.

3. And Joseph said to his brothers, "I am Joseph. Is my father still alive?" And his brothers could not answer him, because they were in shock before him.

4. And Joseph said to his brothers, "Please come close to me," and they came close, and he said, "I am Joseph, your brother, whom you sold into Egypt.

5. And now, don't let it grieve you and don't let it be cause for anger in your eyes that you sold me here, because for preservation of life God sent me before you.

6. Because there is this: two years [now] of famine in the middle of the land, and five years to come in which there will be no plowing or harvest.

7. And God sent me before you to establish survivors for you in the land and to keep you alive for a great rescue.

8. And now, it was not you who sent me here but God, and he has made me like a father to Pharaoh and like a master to all his household, and I rule in all the land of Egypt.

9. Hurry and go up to my father, and you are to say to him, 'This is what your son Joseph has said: "God has made me like a master to all Egypt. Come down to me; you are not to stay there.

10. And you will settle in the land of Goshen and be near me, you and your sons and your sons' sons and your flocks and your herds and everything that is yours.

11. And I will sustain you there (since there are still five years of famine) so that you will not be wiped out, you and your household and everything that is yours."'

12. And look: your eyes see—and the eyes of my brother Benjamin—that with my own mouth I am speaking to you.

13. And you are to tell my father all the glory I have in Egypt, and everything that you are seeing, and you are to hurry and bring my father down here."

14. And he fell on the neck of Benjamin his brother and wept, and Benjamin wept on his neck.

15. And he kissed all his brothers and wept on them. And after that his brothers spoke with him.

16. And the voice was heard in Pharaoh's house, saying, "Joseph's brothers have come," and it was good in the eyes of Pharaoh and in the eyes of his servants.

17. And Pharaoh said to Joseph, "Say to your brothers, 'Do this: load your beasts of burden and come, go to the land of Canaan.

18. And take your father and your households and come to me, and I will give you the best of the land of Egypt, and you will eat the fat of the land.

19. And now, do this command: take yourselves wagons from the land of Egypt for your little children and for your women, and you are to bear your father and come.

20. And your eye is to be merciless over your household effects, because the best of all the land of Egypt is yours.'"

21. And Israel's sons did so, and Joseph gave them wagons, according to Pharaoh's word. And he gave them provisions for the road.

22. And to them all he gave changes of clothes, [one] each. And to Benjamin he gave three hundred pieces of silver and five changes of clothes.

23. And to his father he sent as follows: ten male donkeys carrying some of the best of Egypt, and ten female donkeys carrying grain and bread, and sustenance for his father for the road.

24. And he sent his brothers off, and they went. And he said to them, "You are not to quarrel on the way."

25. And they went up from Egypt and came to the land of Canaan, to Jacob their father.

26. And they told him, saying, "Joseph is still alive," and that he was ruling in all the land of Egypt. And his heart failed, because he did not believe them.

27. And they spoke to him all Joseph's words that he had spoken to them. And he saw the wagons that Joseph had sent to bear him, and the spirit of Jacob their father revived.

28. And Israel said, "A great thing! Joseph my son is still alive; I will go and see him before I die."

Summary

THE previous chapter dealt with the way the [Lord's] inner self (Joseph) introduced his outer, earthly self (Jacob's ten sons) to union with itself **5867** through the middle ground (Benjamin).

This chapter now deals with the way the inner self united itself with the outer, earthly self. Union with the outer, earthly self, though, is possible only by means of spiritual goodness on the earthly plane (Israel), so the inner self first prepares to attach that goodness to itself.

Inner Meaning

GENESIS 45:1, 2. *And Joseph could not restrain himself before all those* **5868** *standing with him, and he shouted, "Make every man go out from beside me!" And no one stood with him in Joseph's making himself known to his brothers. And he gave his voice up to weeping, and the Egyptians heard, and Pharaoh's household heard.*

And Joseph could not restrain himself before all those standing with him means that the inner, heavenly self had now made everything ready for union. *And he shouted* means that it was about to happen. *Make every man go out from beside me* means that discordant and contradictory items of knowledge were cast out from the center. *And no one stood [with him] in Joseph's making himself known to his brothers* means that none of them were present when the inner, heavenly self united with truth on the earthly level by means of a middle ground. *And he gave his voice up to weeping* symbolizes mercy and joy. *And the Egyptians heard* means down to the lowest, outermost level. *And Pharaoh's household heard* means throughout the earthly level.

5869   *And Joseph could not restrain himself before all those standing with him* means that the inner, heavenly self had now made everything ready for union, as the following shows: *Joseph* represents inner goodness, as discussed in §§5805, 5826, 5827, so he represents inner heavenliness, since "heavenliness" means goodness that comes from the Lord. And *not being able to restrain himself* means that everything was ready for union. When we work as hard as we can to prepare ourselves for some goal or outcome, gathering and arranging the necessary means, then once everything is ready, we can no longer hold back. That is what these words mean. The previous chapter was about being introduced to union, but the current chapter is about union itself; see §5867.

All those standing with him symbolizes anything that blocks union, which is why it was cast out, as explained below [§5871].

5870   *And he shouted* means that it was about to happen. This can be seen from the symbolism of *shouting,* after the words "he could not restrain himself," as the imminent event.

5871   *Make every man go out from beside me* means that discordant and contradictory items of knowledge were cast out from the center. This is established by the meaning of *every man from beside him* as items of knowledge, since they were Egyptians, who symbolize knowledge; see §§1164, 1165, 1186, 1462, 5700, 5702. It follows that they were discordant and contradictory, because they were cast out.

Let me explain this situation, which arises when union takes place between truth in the outer or earthly self and goodness in the inner self, or when religious truth unites with neighborly kindness. Under those circumstances, any items of knowledge that fail to harmonize and especially those that clash are cast off from the middle to the sides and so from the light at the center to the shadows at the edges. They are then partly ignored, partly dismissed. However, from the compatible, harmonious information that remains, an essence is drawn out and refined, so to speak, producing a deeper understanding. As long as we are in the body we do not perceive it except as a kind of cheerfulness, such as the mind feels at break of day.

That is how the truth taught by faith unites with the goodness urged by neighborly love.

5872   *And no one stood with him in his making himself known to his brothers* means that none of them were present when the inner, heavenly self united with truth on the earthly level by means of a middle ground. This can be seen from the explanation just above at §5871 without further commentary.

And he gave his voice up to weeping symbolizes mercy and joy. This can be seen from the symbolism of *weeping* as the effect of mercy, [or compassion] (as discussed in §5480). *Weeping* also symbolizes the effect of love (§3801) just as much as it symbolizes the effect of sorrow, so it symbolizes joy.   **5873**

And the Egyptians heard means down to the lowest, outermost level, as the following shows: *Hearing,* when a weeping voice is the thing heard, symbolizes an awareness of mercy and joy. And the *Egyptians* represent items of knowledge, as discussed in §§1164, 1165, 1186, 1462, so they symbolize the lowest, outermost level, since what we know forms that level.   **5874**

Items of knowledge form our lowest, outermost level, at least in respect to our memory and thinking, but this is not easy to see. It seems to us as though they constitute all our understanding and wisdom, but they do not. They are only containers *holding* concepts of understanding and wisdom, and the lowest, outermost containers at that, since they are tied to the body's sense impressions.

Any who reflect on their own thought process can see that items of knowledge are the outermost containers. When we look into a truth, they are present but not in a visible way. Our mind draws out the contents of many pieces of information, widely scattered and perhaps even submerged, and uses them to draw a conclusion, and the deeper our thinking penetrates, the farther away from that information we move.

One piece of evidence is this: When we go to the other world and become spirits, we keep the things we know but for many reasons (§§2476, 2477, 2479) are not allowed to use them. Nonetheless we think and talk about truth and goodness much more clearly and fully than in this world. Plainly, then, items of knowledge serve to form our intellect, but once the intellect has been fashioned, they form its outermost foundation. It is no longer on that lowest level but above it that we do our thinking.

And Pharaoh's household heard means throughout the earthly level. This is established by the representation of *Pharaoh* as the earthly level in general, as mentioned in §§5160, 5799. His *household* therefore means the whole earthly level.   **5875**

Genesis 45:3, 4, 5. *And Joseph said to his brothers, "I am Joseph. Is my father still alive?" And his brothers could not answer him, because they were in shock before him. And Joseph said to his brothers, "Please come close to me," and they came close, and he said, "I am Joseph, your brother, whom you sold into Egypt. And now, don't let it grieve you and don't let it be cause for*   **5876** *anger in your eyes that you sold me here, because for preservation of life God sent me before you.*"

And Joseph said to his brothers means that inner heavenliness gave truth on the earthly plane an ability to perceive. *I am Joseph* symbolizes self-revelation. *Is my father still alive?* symbolizes the presence of earthly-level spiritual goodness. *And his brothers could not answer him* means that truths on the earthly plane had not yet reached a stage at which they could speak. *Because they were in shock before him* symbolizes upheaval among them. *And Joseph said to his brothers* symbolizes a perception on the new earthly plane. *Please come close to me* symbolizes deeper communication. *And they came close* means that it was brought about. *And he said, "I am Joseph, your brother,"* symbolizes [the inner dimension's] revealing itself by an inflow. *Whom you sold into Egypt* means that [earthly-level truth] had banished the inner dimension. *And now, don't let it grieve you* symbolizes distress of heart, or of the will. *And don't let it be cause for anger in your eyes* symbolizes dejection of spirit, or of the intellect. *That you sold me here* means that they had banished it to the lowest level. *Because for preservation of life God sent me before you* symbolizes consequent spiritual life for them as a result of providence.

5877   *And Joseph said to his brothers* means that inner heavenliness gave truth on the earthly plane an ability to perceive, as the following shows: *Saying,* in the Word's narratives, symbolizes perception, as discussed in §§1898, 1919, 2080, 2619, 2862, 3395, 3509, 5687, 5743. Here it means granting an ability to perceive, as discussed below. *Joseph* represents inner heavenliness, as noted just above at §5869. And Jacob's ten sons—the *brothers* here—represent truth on the earthly plane, as noted at §§5403, 5419, 5458, 5512. The resulting inner meaning is that inner heavenliness gave truth on the earthly plane an ability to perceive.

The reason *saying* in this case means granting an ability to perceive is that the verses directly following are about union between inner heavenliness (Joseph) and truth on the earthly plane (Jacob's sons). When this union takes place, an ability to perceive develops, made possible by a desire for truth and consequently for goodness.

5878   *I am Joseph* symbolizes self-revelation, as can be seen without explanation.

5879   *Is my father still alive?* symbolizes the presence of earthly-level spiritual goodness, as the following indicates: Israel, the *father,* represents spiritual goodness on the earthly level. (This is discussed in §§5801, 5803, 5807, 5812, 5817, 5819, 5826, 5833; and the fact that it is on the earthly level, in §4286.) And *is he still alive?* symbolizes its presence. When Joseph revealed himself, his first thought was of his father. He knew his father was alive, so his father was present in his mind right at the start and is present afterward as well, the whole time he talks to his brothers. The reason is that inner heavenliness, which is Joseph, cannot unite with truth on the earthly plane, which is Jacob's sons, except through spiritual goodness on the earthly plane, which is Israel. Once they have been united, Jacob's sons are no longer Jacob's but Israel's sons, these being spiritual truth on the earthly plane.

And his brothers could not answer him means that truths on the earthly plane had not yet reached a stage at which they could speak. This can be seen from the representation of Jacob's sons, here called Joseph's *brothers,* as truth on the earthly plane (as explained above in §5877) and from the symbolism of *being unable to answer* as not yet having reached a stage at which it could speak. That is, truth could not yet speak to the inner dimension. 5880

Here is the situation: When an inner level is uniting with an outer level, or goodness with truth, at first the inner level communicates with the outer, but the communication is not yet two-way. When it is two-way, the union is complete. So after Joseph had cried on Benjamin's neck and kissed all his brothers, that is the point (verse 15) at which the text first says his brothers spoke with him. The meaning is that after union was complete, shared communication took place because of acceptance [by truth on the earthly plane].

Because they were in shock before him symbolizes upheaval among them. This can be seen from the symbolism of *shock* as upheaval. Shock is nothing else. By upheaval I mean a rearrangement and reorganization of truth on the earthly level. About this reorganization, be aware that we do not know the pattern in which items of knowledge and truths are arranged in our memory, but angels do know, if the Lord wants them to. The pattern is amazing. The items of knowledge and truths form bundles, and the bundles themselves form further bundles, in accordance with the connections our mind had drawn among them. The way these bundles are structured is more wonderful than anyone could ever believe. In the other life one can actually see them sometimes, because such things can be presented to the sight of the eye in heaven's light, which is spiritual, but never in the world's light. 5881

The only agents organizing knowledge and truths into these bundled forms are the different kinds of love we have. Love for ourselves and love of worldly advantages give them a hellish shape, but love for our neighbor and love for God give them a heavenly shape. When we are being reborn, then, and goodness in our inner self is uniting with truths in our outer self, upheaval arises among the truths, because they are being reorganized. This upheaval is what is meant and symbolized by *they were in shock*.

The upheaval that then occurs reveals itself as anxiety rising out of change from the previous state, specifically out of loss of the pleasure we felt during that state. The upheaval also reveals itself as anxiety over the life we have so far lived, since we have made inner goodness and the whole inner dimension our lowest priority. Such anxiety is the subject in what follows.

5882   *And Joseph said to his brothers* symbolizes a perception on the new earthly plane. This can be seen from the symbolism of *saying* as a perception (noted above at §5877) and from the representation of Jacob's sons as truth on the earthly plane (also noted above at §5877). Here they represent the earthly plane itself, because anyone who represents truth on the earthly plane also represents the earthly plane itself. Take Pharaoh, who as monarch of Egypt represents knowledge in general; he therefore represents the earthly level itself in general as well (§§5160, 5799). Truth on that level is essentially one with the earthly level itself, or a person's earthly self, because the earthly plane is a container, and truth is the content. In an inner sense, then, it is sometimes the content and sometimes the container that is symbolized, depending on the flow of ideas.

[2] The reason Jacob's sons represent a new earthly level here is that the inner meaning describes the process of union. That process follows the outline given in the running explanation here. To be specific: When a union exists between our inner and outer levels, or between goodness and truth, then for the first time we gain the ability to perceive that we are being affected by truth and consequently by goodness. Next we experience upheaval. Afterward, deeper communication takes place by means of an inflow. And so on.

Clearly, then, the earthly plane that Jacob's sons now represent is a new one, since its previous state has changed (§5881).

5883   *Please come close to me* symbolizes deeper communication. This can be seen from the symbolism of *coming closer* as communicating more *directly*. When an outer level is said to come closer to an inner level, though, it means communicating more *deeply*.

People do not realize that there is an inner and an outer type of communication with the earthly or outer self, because they have formed no idea of an inner self or of its life as something different from the life of the outer self. Their only notion of the inner self is that it lies within them but is entirely indistinguishable from the outer self. In reality the two are so distinct that the inner dimension can separate from the outer and still live a life that is the same as before, only purer. [2] That is exactly what happens when we die: the inner dimension separates from the outer. The inner part that lives on after separating is what is then called the spirit, but is the actual person who lived inside the body. To itself and to others in the next life the inner part even looks like a person in the world, with a person's whole shape, from head to toe. It is also equipped with the same abilities as a person in the world: touch, smell, sight, hearing, speech, and thought. The similarity is so strong that, as I have heard spirits say a number of times, they think they are in their body in the world unless they reflect on the fact that they are in the other life.

This information shows what a person's inner and outer parts are. If you glean some idea of them from it, the numerous statements about the inner and outer self in the explanation will become somewhat clearer. It will also become clearer what deeper communication means, as symbolized here by *please come close to me.*

And they came close means that it was brought about. That is, deeper **5884** communication took place. This is self-evident.

And he said, "I am Joseph, your brother," symbolizes [the inner dimen- **5885** sion's] revealing itself by an inflow. This is established by the symbolism of *saying, "I am Joseph, your brother,"* as self-revelation, as above in §5878. It follows that the self-revelation took place through [spiritual] inflow, because the only way the inner plane acts on the outer plane is by flowing into it, especially now that deeper communication has been brought about (§5883). When goodness reveals itself by an inflow, it appears as an awareness of what is good, brought about by a desire for truth, and as neighborly love. When truth reveals itself by an inflow, it appears as an acknowledgment of what is true and as faith.

Whom you sold into Egypt means that [earthly-level truth] had ban- **5886** ished the inner dimension. This is clear from the representation of Joseph, the one *whom they sold,* as what is inward (discussed at §§5805, 5826, 5827), and from that of *selling* as banishing, [or disowning] (discussed at §§4752, 4758). *Egypt* here symbolizes the lowest level, as below in §5889, because to categorize something as a mere item of information without acknowledging it is to cast it off to the sides and so to the last and lowest level. That is the situation today with the inner dimension of a human being. People do count its existence as information, because they know from doctrine that there is an inner self, but they toss the concept to the bottom level, because they do not acknowledge or believe in it. This means that they banish it not from their memory but from their faith.

The evidence that *selling* in an inner sense means banishing, [or disowning,] anything of faith or neighborly love—anything that makes up a person belonging to the inner part of the church—is this: In the spiritual world there is no buying and selling of the type that takes place on earth. Instead, people adopt goodness and truth (which is what buying symbolizes) or disown it (which is what selling symbolizes). Selling also symbolizes communication of knowledge about goodness and truth, because business dealings symbolize the acquisition and sharing of such knowledge (§§2967, 4453). In that case, though, the sale is described as being "not for silver."

[2] The meaning of selling as banishing, [or disowning,] is also plain from the following passages in the Word. In Isaiah:

> This is what Jehovah has said: "Where is the document of divorce for your mother, whom I supposedly sent away? Or who is the one of my moneylenders *to whom I supposedly sold you?* Here, now, it is because of your sins that *you have been sold* and because of your transgressions that your mother has been sent away." (Isaiah 50:1)

A mother stands for the church; selling stands for disowning. In Ezekiel:

> The time has come; the day has arrived. The *buyer* is not to rejoice, and the *seller* should not mourn, because my wrath is on its whole throng. For the *seller* will not return to the *property sold,* even if there still is life among the living. (Ezekiel 7:12, 13)

This is about the land of Israel, or a spiritual religion. The seller stands for someone who has banished truth and instilled falsity. [3] In Joel:

> The children of Judah and the children of Jerusalem *you have sold* to the children of the Greeks, to move them far away from their own borders. Watch: I myself will stir them up from the place to which *you sold* them. And *I will sell* your sons and your daughters into the hand of the children of Judah, who *will sell* them to the Sabeans, a distant people. (Joel 3:6, 7, 8)

This is about Tyre and Sidon. Once again the selling stands for banishment. In Moses:

> Their Rock *sold* them, and Jehovah shut them in. (Deuteronomy 32:30)

The selling obviously stands for disowning. In the highest sense, their Rock is the Lord in regard to truth, while in a representative sense, a rock is faith. "Jehovah" is the Lord in regard to goodness.

[4] Since in a spiritual sense buying means obtaining, and selling means banishing, in Matthew the Lord compares the kingdom of the heavens to a person selling and buying:

> The kingdom of the heavens is like treasure hidden in a field, which, when someone discovered it, he hides, and because of his joy he goes and *sells absolutely everything he has* and *buys* that field. Again, the kingdom of the heavens is like a merchant looking for beautiful pearls, who, when he had found a precious pearl, went and *sold everything that he had* and bought it. (Matthew 13:44, 45, 46)

The kingdom of the heavens stands for goodness and truth in us and consequently for heaven in us. The field stands for goodness and the pearl for truth. Buying stands for acquiring and adopting them. Selling everything that one has stands for banishing what used to be one's own and consequently for banishing evil and falsity, since these are one's own. [5] In Luke:

> Jesus [said] to the young leader: "One thing you still lack: *sell everything that you have* and distribute it to the poor. Then you will have treasure in heaven; and come, follow me." (Luke 18:22)

These words in an inner sense mean that we ought to banish everything of our own, which is nothing but evil and falsity, because that is "everything we have." We will then receive goodness and truth from the Lord, these being "treasure in heaven." [6] Other words in the same author have a similar meaning:

> *Sell your resources,* and give money to the poor; make for yourselves purses that do not age, treasure in the heavens that does not fail. (Luke 12:33)

Anyone can see that this passage carries some other meaning. After all, selling one's resources today would mean becoming a beggar and robbing oneself of all remaining ability to practice neighborly kindness. Besides, it is impossible not to be self-righteous about such an act; and it is a reliable truth that there are both rich and poor in heaven. The alternate meaning of the passage is the one stated just above.

[7] The symbolism of *selling* as banishing the attributes that characterize the church led to the law that if a female captive taken as a wife did not please [her husband], she was to be sent off all by herself *but was absolutely not to be sold* for silver. No money was to be made on her, because he had afflicted her (Deuteronomy 21:14). A female captive as wife stands for a foreign kind of truth, truth of illegitimate stock, that can nonetheless be connected in some fashion with the goodness that characterizes the church, as that goodness exists inside a person. If that truth fails to match on numerous counts, it can be put aside but not banished, because it has been internalized to some degree. That is the spiritual thrust of this law. [8] The following law has the same source:

> If a man is found who has stolen a soul from among his brothers and sisters, from among the children of Israel, and if he has made a profit on that person and *sold that person,* this thief shall be killed, so that you can remove the evil from your midst. (Deuteronomy 24:7)

Thieves who steal the children of Israel stand for people who garner religious truth not for the purpose of living by it and therefore teaching it from their heart but of making a profit on it. They are damned, as is symbolized by the order that they be killed.

5887   *And now, don't let it grieve you* symbolizes distress of heart, or of the will. This can be seen from the symbolism of *grief* as distress. Specifically, it symbolizes distress of heart, or of the will, because the next phrase, "don't let it be cause for anger in your eyes," symbolizes dejection of spirit, or of the intellect.

I equate the heart with the will, and the spirit with the intellect, because these pairs relate by correspondence. The heart relates to matters of the will because it relates to what is heavenly, that is, to the goodness urged by love. The spirit, [or breath,] which belongs to the lungs, relates to matters of intellect because it relates to what is spiritual, that is, to the truth that leads to faith. See §§3635, 3883–3896.

5888   *And don't let it be cause for anger in your eyes* symbolizes dejection of spirit, or of the intellect, as the following shows: *Anger* here symbolizes dejection, because it virtually repeats the phrase it follows, "don't let it grieve you," which symbolizes distress of heart, or of the will. Wherever something in the Word seems redundant, one element relates to the will and the other to the intellect. In other words, one element relates to the goodness urged by love and the other to the truth that leads to faith. This is because of the heavenly marriage, the marriage of goodness and truth, in every detail of the Word, as discussed in §§683, 793, 801, 2173, 2516, 2712, 5502. And *eyes* symbolize the intellect, as discussed in §§2701, 4403–4421, 4523–4534.

That you sold me here means that they had banished [the inner dimension] to the lowest level, as the explanation above at §5886 shows.

5889

Because for preservation of life God sent me before you symbolizes spiritual life for them as a result of providence. This can be seen from the symbolism of *preservation of life* as spiritual life (discussed below) and from that of *God sent me before you* as something providential.

5890

The providential nature of the event can be seen from Joseph's dreams, which predicted that his brothers would bow down to him, as would his father [Genesis 37:5–10]. If this had not been provided, it also would not have been foreseen.

One argument is enough to show that *preservation of life* (or keeping someone alive) symbolizes spiritual life (or a new life through rebirth): only such a meaning can make the Word spiritual. There is such a thing as physical life and spiritual life. Physical life is meant in the Word's literal sense, but spiritual life is meant in its inner sense; and even in the literal sense spiritual life is quite often meant by life and preservation of life. In Ezekiel, for instance:

> When I say to the ungodly, "*You shall surely die,*" and you do not warn them or speak to urge the ungodly away from their evil path, *to keep them alive . . .* (Ezekiel 3:18)

In the same author:

> You profaned me among my people for handfuls of barleycorns and for crumbs of bread, *to kill souls that should not die* and to *keep* souls *alive* that should not *live.* You strengthen the hands of the ungodly so that they will not turn from their evil way, [and by doing so you are] *keeping them alive.* (Ezekiel 13:19, 22)

In Hosea:

> Jehovah *will bring us to life* after two days, and on the third day he will raise us up, so that *we may live* before him. (Hosea 6:2)

In David:

> If I did not believe I would see goodness in the *land of life,* . . . ! (Psalms 27:13)

In John:

> To those who conquer I will grant to eat from the *tree of life* that is in the middle of God's paradise. (Revelation 2:7)

In the Gospel of John:

> As the Father raises the *dead* and *gives them life,* so also the Son *gives life* to whomever he wishes. (John 5:21)

In the same author:

> The spirit is what *gives life;* the flesh is of no benefit. The words that I am speaking are spirit and are *life.* (John 6:63)

In these passages, life, giving life, and keeping someone alive plainly stand for spiritual life, which is life in heaven. Life there is also called simply life, as in Matthew:

> Narrow and restricted is the way that *leads to life,* and there are few who find it. (Matthew 7:14)

In other passages, entering *life* stands for going to heaven (Matthew 18:8, 9; 19:17; Mark 9:43, 45, 47; John 5:24).

5891   Genesis 45:6, 7, 8. *"Because there is this: two years [now] of famine in the middle of the land, and five years to come in which there will be no plowing or harvest. And God sent me before you to establish survivors for you in the land and to keep you alive for a great rescue. And now, it was not you who sent me here but God, and he has made me like a father to Pharaoh and like a master to all his household, and I rule in all the land of Egypt."*

Because there is this means that such is the situation. *Two years [now] of famine in the middle of the land* symbolizes a state in which goodness is lacking in the earthly mind. *And five years to come* is a symbol for the length of time that state lasts, until a remnant shines out. *In which there will be no plowing or harvest* means that goodness and the truth it leads to will not be visible in the meantime. *And God sent me before you* means that divine providence took care of it. *To establish survivors for you in the land* symbolizes the central, inmost part of the church. *And to keep you alive* symbolizes spiritual life for truth on the earthly plane as a result. *For a great rescue* symbolizes deliverance from damnation. *And now, it was not you who sent me here* means that they were not the ones who thrust [inner heavenliness] down onto the same plane as earthly-level knowledge. *But God* means that the Divine did this. *And he has made me like a father to Pharaoh* means that [the Lord as Joseph] was now the source of the earthly plane. *And like a master to all his household* means that he was the source of everything present on the earthly plane. *And I rule in all the land of Egypt* means that he arranges the information there.

Because there is this means that such is the situation. This can be seen without explanation, since it is a phrase that refers to what precedes and what follows.

[5892]

Two years [now] of famine in the middle of the land symbolizes states in which goodness is lacking in the earthly mind, as the following shows: *Years* symbolize states, as mentioned in §§487, 488, 493, 893. *Famine* symbolizes a lack of what is good, since bread in a spiritual sense means the goodness that springs from love and food symbolizes the goodness that springs from truth. Famine, [or hunger,] is therefore a lack of goodness, while thirst is a lack of truth. And *in the middle of the land*—the land of Egypt—symbolizes the earthly mind, as mentioned in §§5276, 5278, 5280, 5288, 5301. The text says *in the middle* because the middle is the core (1074, 2940, 2973), where goodness resides. *Two years* means states in which goodness and truth unite, since *two* symbolizes union (5194). Here it means that there is not yet union, since the two years are years of famine.

[5893]

[2] To expand: The earthly mind has to contain truth, if goodness is to accomplish anything, and what introduces the truth has to be a desire rising out of some genuine kind of love. Absolutely all information in a person's memory was once introduced through some type of love, and the two remain there united. This includes religious truth, if it was introduced through a love for truth; such truth remains united with this love.

When they are united, here is what happens: if the desire is brought back, the true ideas bound up with it also come out into the open, and if the true ideas are brought back, the desire with which they are bound up also comes out.

When we are being reborn, then, the Lord governs us through angels. (Rebirth happens in adulthood, because not until then do people think for themselves about religious truth.) The angels' method is to anchor us in concepts that we have engraved on our minds as true, and through these true concepts to anchor us in the desire with which the concepts are so closely joined. Because the desire—a desire for truth—originates in goodness, it gradually leads to goodness.

[3] Much experience has proved to me that this is the case. Evil spirits have sometimes pushed evil and falsity on me, and at those times I have sensed angels, empowered by the Lord, holding me to the truth that had been planted in me. In this way they withheld me from the evil and falsity.

The experience also showed me that religious truth that is rooted in us by a desire for truth is the plane angels operate in. As a consequence, people without this plane cannot be led by angels but allow themselves to be led by hell instead. The angels' efforts cannot become established anywhere but pass right on through. However, we cannot acquire this plane unless we have acted on religious truth, which grounds it in our will and by this means in our life.

It is also worth mentioning that angels' activity surrounding the religious truth we know is rarely noticeable. Rarely do they stir explicit thoughts about the concept at issue. Rather, they inspire a general awareness of notions that buttress that concept, along with the connected desire. The angels work by an imperceptible inflow that, when presented in visual form, looks like a stream of light. The light consists of countless truths-within-goodness that encircle a single concept we possess, maintaining us in the truth and at the same time in the love that goes with it. So angels lift our minds out of falsity and protect us from evil.

But the person knows nothing at all of what is happening.

5894 *And five years to come* is a symbol for the length of time that state lasts, until a remnant shines out. This can be seen from the symbolism of *five* as a remnant (discussed at §5291) and from the symbolism of *years* as states (as just above at §5893). The length of time it lasts is symbolized by so many years *to come*. This shows that the phrase is a symbol for the length of time that state lasts, until a remnant shines out.

A remnant is truth and goodness hidden away by the Lord in our inner self; see §§468, 530, 560, 561, 660, 1050, 1738, 1906, 2284, 5135, 5342. The remnant consists of acknowledgments of truth and desires for it stored up in us before goodness reveals itself. When accompanied by goodness, they shine out. Until then, only the amount useful for our lives is brought out of storage. That is how the Lord's providence works, and works constantly, although we know nothing whatever about it and do not even want to know. After all, we deny that providence is in the details, when in reality it is in the smallest details of all, from the first thread of our life to its end and beyond to eternity. More efforts of providence come together in every single moment for every person than could ever be assigned a number. This I know from heaven.

In which there will be no plowing or harvest means that goodness and **5895** the truth it leads to will not be visible in the meantime. This can be seen from the symbolism of *plowing* as being prepared by goodness to receive truth (discussed below) and from that of *harvest* as truth that grows out of goodness. A harvest is a ripened crop that is being gathered in, so it means truth arising from goodness. Before this kind of truth comes into being, one can admittedly see truth, but only the truth that leads to goodness, not truth that arises out of goodness. People who act on truth have the kind that leads to goodness, but people who act on goodness have the truth that grows out of goodness.

The reason for equating *plowing* with goodness is that a field, the thing plowed, symbolizes the church in regard to goodness (§2971) and therefore the goodness in a church (§§3310, 3317, 4982). Plowing, then, means being prepared by goodness to receive truth. What is more, the oxen that were used in plowing symbolize goodness on the earthly level (§§2180, 2566, 2781).

[2] Since this was the symbolism of plowing, the representative church had a prohibition against *plowing with an ox* and a donkey together (Deuteronomy 22:10). This would never have been forbidden if not for some deeper-lying reason and accordingly for some reason in the spiritual world. Otherwise, what harm would it do if the two plowed together? What value would there be to such a law in the Word? The deeper-lying cause in the spiritual world is that plowing with an ox symbolizes goodness on the earthly plane, and plowing with a donkey symbolizes truth there. For the symbolism of a donkey as truth in the form of knowledge and therefore truth on the earthly plane, see §§5492, 5741. The inner, spiritual reason for the command was that angels could not picture goodness and truth separately. The two must unite into a single whole, so they had no wish to see this kind of plowing, by an ox and donkey together. Heavenly angels do not even want to think about truth separate from goodness. In them, all truth resides within goodness, so truth *is* goodness for them.

For the same reason, there was also a prohibition against wearing a mixed garment of wool and linen together (Deuteronomy 22:11). Wool symbolized goodness, and linen, truth.

[3] The symbolism of plowing—and of harrowing, sowing, and reaping—as processes involving goodness and its related truth can be seen in Hosea:

> I will ride Ephraim, Judah will *plow,* Jacob will *harrow* for him. *Sow* for yourselves in accordance with righteousness; *reap* in accordance with devout duty; *till untilled ground* for yourselves. And it is time to seek Jehovah, until he comes and teaches righteousness. (Hosea 10:11, 12)

The riding is associated with Ephraim because to ride is to make use of one's intellect, and Ephraim is the church's intellect. The plowing is associated with Judah because Judah is the goodness in a church. [4] In Amos:

> Will horses run on rock? Will anyone *plow it with oxen?* Because you have turned integrity into poison, and the fruit of righteousness into wormwood. (Amos 6:11, 12)

"Will horses run on rock?" asks whether anyone is going to understand religious truth. Rock in a spiritual sense means faith (preface to Genesis 22), and horses mean the contents of the intellect (§§2761, 2762, 3217, 5321). "Will anyone plow it with oxen?" asks whether anyone is going to do good. Oxen mean what is good on the earthly level (see §§2180, 2566, 2781). Neither of these propositions is a possibility, which is symbolized by the next phrases, "Because you have turned integrity into poison, and the fruit of righteousness into wormwood." [5] In Luke:

> Jesus said, "None who put their hand *onto the plow* but look back are fit for the kingdom of God." (Luke 9:62)

The symbolism here is the same as that of the Lord's words in Matthew:

> Those who are on top of the house should not go down to take anything from their house. And those in the field should not turn back behind to take their clothes. (Matthew 24:17, 18)

The meaning of these words is that people motivated by goodness must not turn from that to matters of religious doctrine. See §3652, where these verses are explained. Those who put their hand onto the plow, then, are people motivated by goodness, whereas those who look back are people who then turn to religious doctrines, abandoning goodness. [6] As a result, Elijah was displeased that when he called Elisha, who was plowing in a field, Elisha asked to kiss his father and his mother first. Elijah indicated his displeasure by saying, "Leave; go back, for *what have I done to you?"* (1 Kings 19:19, 20, 21).

In a negative sense plowing symbolizes evil that annihilates goodness and therefore symbolizes spiritual devastation, as in Jeremiah:

> Zion *will be plowed like a field,* and Jerusalem will be mere heaps, and the mountain of the house will become a hilltop forest. (Jeremiah 26:18; Micah 3:12)

And God sent me before you means that divine providence took care of it. This can be seen from the discussion above in §5890 of the symbolism of *God sent me before you* as divine providence.

5896

To establish survivors for you in the land symbolizes the central, inmost part of the church. This can be seen from the symbolism of *survivors,* [or a remnant,] as good impulses united with true ideas, hidden deep within us by the Lord, as discussed in §§468, 530, 560, 561, 660, 1050, 1906, 2284, 5135, 5342. Here it symbolizes the central, inmost part of the church. I describe it as central and inmost because what is inmost is at the center of the earthly plane. On the earthly plane, inmost qualities coexist with other inner qualities. As a rule, whatever is inmost in a consecutive series is at the center or in the middle of the resulting simultaneous arrangement (of which the earthly level is an example). The center is where the inmost parts position themselves in relation to more outward parts.

5897

To establish survivors for you in the land holds inside it the idea that the inmost depths of the church were to exist among Jacob's offspring. The meaning is not that his offspring would actually be in the inmost depths but that a representation of the church in its entirety would be set up among them and that the Word would exist there. That is what "survivors" means in relation to the church and in isolation from the nation.

[2] The Word often mentions survivors and a remainder, but both have been understood literally, as meaning only survivors and a remainder of the people, or of the nation. Until now it has been completely unknown that on a spiritual level the words symbolize goodness and truth hidden away by the Lord in a person's inner self. Take for example the following passages. In Isaiah:

> On that day Jehovah's offshoot will become the honor and glory—and the earth's fruit will become the excellence and adornment—of Israel's refugees. And it will happen that the one *left* in Zion and the one *remaining*

in Jerusalem will be called holy—everyone in Jerusalem assigned to life.
(Isaiah 4:2, 3)

The people left in Zion and remaining in Jerusalem had not by any means
become holy and were no more "assigned to life" than anyone else. Obviously, then, the people left and remaining stand for what is holy, what is
assigned to life, which is goodness united to truth, hidden away by the
Lord in a person's inner self. [3] In the same author:

> On that day the *survivors of Israel* and the refugees of Jacob's house will
> no longer continue to lean on the one that strikes them but will lean
> on Jehovah, the Holy One of Israel, in truthfulness. The *survivors* will
> return, the *survivors of Jacob,* to the mighty God. (Isaiah 10:20, 21, 22)

The survivors are plainly not survivors of any people or nation, because
in the Word, especially the prophetic books, Israel did not mean Israel,
and Jacob did not mean Jacob. Both meant religion and religious attributes. So survivors do not mean survivors of Israel and Jacob but truth
and goodness, which are religious. In fact, when the text mentions survivors of the people and a remainder of the nation, not even these mean the
survivors of any people or a remainder of any nation. On an inner level a
people symbolizes truth (§§1259, 1260, 3295, 3581) and a nation goodness
(§§1259, 1260, 1416). The symbolism of survivors as truth and goodness has been unknown and seems outlandish because the literal meaning, especially when it is telling a story, distracts and powerfully withholds
us from such thinking. [4] In the same author:

> Then there will be a path for the *survivors of the people* who *will remain*
> from Assyria, as there was [a path] for Israel through the sea when he
> went up from the land of Egypt. (Isaiah 11:16)

The same ideas apply here. The individuals remaining from Assyria are
people who have not been destroyed by twisted reasoning. For this meaning of Assyria, see §1186. In the same author:

> On that day, Jehovah Sabaoth will serve as a crown of beauty and a
> diadem of glory *to the survivors of his people.* (Isaiah 28:5)

In the same author:

> Moreover, the *remaining* refugees of Judah's house will put new root
> downward and produce fruit upward, because from Jerusalem will issue

survivors, and from Mount Zion, those who have been rescued. (Isaiah 37:31, 32)

In the same author:

Butter and honey are what everyone who is *left* in the middle of the land will eat. (Isaiah 7:22)

In Jeremiah:

I will gather the *survivors of my flock* out of all the lands to which I scattered them, and I will bring them back to their fold, so that they may breed and multiply. (Jeremiah 23:3)

In the same author:

The population of *those left* by the sword found favor in the wilderness as they went to give rest to Israel. (Jeremiah 31:2)

The population of those left by the sword in the wilderness meant the people referred to as little children who were brought into the land of Canaan when everyone else had died. These children were left, and they symbolized innocent goodness. Their introduction into the land of Canaan represented admission into the Lord's kingdom. [5] In Ezekiel:

I will leave a remainder when those of you rescued from the sword are living among the nations, when you have been scattered in the land. Then your refugees will remember me among the nations where they are held captive. (Ezekiel 6:8, 9)

The remainder and survivors among the nations where they had been scattered and captured represented goodness and truth hidden away by the Lord in a person's inner depths. The reason for the representation is that we are always living in the midst of evil and falsity, which hold us captive. Evil and falsity are what the nations symbolize. When the outer self detaches from the inner, it is completely engrossed in evil and falsity, so if the Lord did not gather up the goodness and truth instilled in us from time to time during the course of our life, we could never be saved. Without a remnant there is no salvation. [6] In Joel:

It will happen that everyone who calls on the name of Jehovah will escape, because on Mount Zion and in Jerusalem there will be rescue, as

Jehovah has said, and among the *remainder* will be those whom Jehovah is calling. (Joel 2:32)

In Micah:

The *survivors of Jacob* will live among the nations, in the middle of many peoples, like a lion among the animals of the forest. (Micah 5:8)

In Zephaniah:

The *survivors of Israel* will not do wrong or speak a lie, nor will a deceitful tongue be found in their mouth. They will graze and lie down, and none will terrify them. (Zephaniah 3:13)

This passage tells what a surviving remnant is like. The quality depicted did not exist at all in the people called Israel, as is known, which shows that something else is meant by survivors. This something else is goodness and truth, of course, since these are what do not do wrong, do not speak a lie, and do not have a deceitful tongue found in their mouth. [7] In Zechariah:

The city's streets will be filled with boys and girls playing in its streets, which will be amazing in the eyes of the *survivors of my people.* I will not now be to the *survivors of this people* as I was in the earlier days, because they will be the *seed of peace;* the grapevine will yield its fruit, and the earth will yield its produce, and the heavens will yield their dew. I will make the *survivors* of this people heir to all those things. (Zechariah 8:5, 6, 11, 12)

The survivors here are called the seed of peace, and they are people dedicated to truth that rises out of goodness. The fruitfulness of such truth is depicted in the promise that the grapevine would yield its fruit, the earth its produce, and the heavens their dew.

[8] A remnant in its spiritual sense is so tightly closed off by an evil life and distorted convictions that it disappears. It is even obliterated by a denial of such truth as one has previously acknowledged, when both the acknowledgment and the denial are sincere. The combination mixes truth and falsity, and this is called profanation.

Here is how the Word speaks of such situations. In Isaiah:

He will take humankind away, and deserted [territory] will multiply in the middle of the land; hardly a *tenth* will remain there, yet they are destined for expulsion. (Isaiah 6:12, 13)

For the meaning of ten as a remnant, see §§576, 1906, 2284. In the same author:

> I will kill your root, and *those remaining to you* will be killed. (Isaiah 14:30)

This is about Philistines, who stand for people who know religious concepts but do not live by them (§§1197, 1198, 3412, 3413). The remainder is called a root because it functions as one; the goodness and truth that make a person human sprout from it. "He will take humankind away," then (in the previous quotation from Isaiah above), means destroying the remnant. [9] In Jeremiah:

> The young people will die by the sword, their sons and their daughters will die of famine, and *they will not have survivors.* (Jeremiah 11:22, 23)

This is about the men of Anathoth. In the same author:

> I will take hold of the *survivors of Judah*—who turned their faces to come into the land of Egypt, to stay as immigrants there—so as to have them all consumed. And there will not be anyone escaping or anyone *remaining to the survivors of Judah* who came to settle in the land of Egypt. (Jeremiah 44:12, 14, 28)

The reason people from Judah were not to stay as immigrants in Egypt or settle there, and the reason it was so strictly forbidden, was that the tribe of Judah represented the Lord's heavenly church. Heavenly people have no desire whatever to learn the type of knowledge symbolized by Egypt. The heavenly goodness they are immersed in teaches them everything, and this goodness would die out if they turned to worldly knowledge. Indeed, individuals from the Lord's heavenly kingdom do not want to even mention faith. They dwell in heavenly goodness, and the heavenly form of truth is neighborly love, whereas the spiritual form is faith. They fear that if they talked about faith, they would fall away from goodness and be looking backward; see §§202, 337, 2715, 3246, 4448. The same thing is meant by the command for those on the house not to go down to take anything from the house and for those in the field not to turn back behind to take their clothes (Matthew 24:17, 18); see just above at §5895. The same thing is also meant by "Remember Lot's wife" (Luke 17:32), who looked back and turned into a pillar of salt. About looking back and turning back, see §§2454, 3652.

[10] Some nations were so completely destroyed that not even a few survivors were left to them. This represented the extent of their wickedness, which was so complete that no goodness or truth—and therefore no remnant—was left. In Moses, for instance:

> They struck Og, king of Bashan, and all his sons, and all his people, *until they left no survivors.* (Numbers 21:35; Deuteronomy 3:3)

In the same author:

> They seized all the cities of Sihon and exterminated every inhabited city and the women and the toddler; *they did not leave a survivor.* (Deuteronomy 2:34)

Likewise in other passages saying people were destroyed.

[11] To say more about the remnant, or goodness and truth hidden away by the Lord in our inner depths: When we choose goodness and truth out of desire, and therefore in freedom, they are grafted onto us. When that happens, angels from heaven move closer and bind themselves to us. This bond is what causes goodness, joined to truth, to arise in our inner depths. However, when we live for what is external, such as worldly and body-driven concerns, the angels withdraw, and once they have withdrawn, absolutely none of the goodness and truth remains visible. Still, since the bond was created at one point, we have the ability to unite with angels and consequently with the goodness and truth they possess. Union takes place only so often and so far as it pleases the Lord, though, who makes sure the arrangement will be entirely useful to our life.

5898   *And to keep you alive* symbolizes spiritual life for truth on the earthly plane as a result. This is established by the symbolism of *keeping someone alive* as spiritual life, discussed above at §5890. All spiritual life comes from the remnant, which is why I speak of it as resulting. It is because of this cause and effect that what the text says about survivors is followed immediately by the phrase *to keep you alive.* This is talking about preservation of the life in earthly-level truth, which is represented by Jacob's sons (§§5403, 5419, 5427, 5458, 5512).

5899   *For a great rescue* symbolizes deliverance from damnation. This can be seen from the symbolism of a *rescue* as a deliverance from damnation that is accomplished through the remnant, or goodness and truth hidden away in us by the Lord. People who accept such goodness and truth— that is, who let it be planted in their inner depths—escape damnation and are counted among the survivors.

That is why the Word often mentions a rescue in connection with a remnant or survivors. Joseph himself does so here, and there are other places too, such as Isaiah:

> On that day the fruit of the earth will become the excellence and adornment of *those of Israel who have been rescued,* and it will happen that the one *left* in Zion and the one *remaining* in Jerusalem will be called holy. (Isaiah 4:2, 3)

In the same author:

> On that day the *survivors of Israel* and *those of Jacob's house who have been rescued* will no longer continue to lean on the one that strikes them. (Isaiah 10:20, 21, 22)

In the same author:

> Moreover, the *remaining refugees of Judah's house* will put new root downward and produce fruit upward, because from Jerusalem will issue *survivors,* and from Mount Zion, *those who have been rescued.* (Isaiah 37:31, 32)

In Ezekiel:

> I will leave a *remnant* when those of you *rescued* from the sword are living among the nations, when you have been scattered in the land. Then your *refugees* will remember me. (Ezekiel 6:8, 9)

In Joel:

> It will happen that everyone who calls on the name of Jehovah *will be rescued.* Because on Mount Zion and in Jerusalem there will be a *rescue,* as Jehovah has said, and among the *remnant* will be those whom Jehovah is calling. (Joel 2:32)

In Jeremiah:

> There will not be a *refugee* or *survivor remaining to Judah.* (Jeremiah 44:12, 14)

These passages show what rescue means; the people who are rescued are the ones who have a remnant, and the rescue is deliverance from damnation.

And now, it was not you who sent me here means that they were not the ones who thrust [inner heavenliness] down onto the same plane as earthly-level knowledge. This can be seen from the symbolism of Egypt,

5900

the *here* to which Joseph was sent, as knowledge on the earthly level (discussed in §§1164, 1165, 1186, 1462, 4749, 4964, 4966, 5700). *You did not send me* clearly means that they were not the ones who thrust [inner heavenliness onto that plane].

5901   *But God* means that the Divine did this, as is self-explanatory.

How matters stand in all this was explained where I dealt with Joseph's being sold into Egypt and starting his life there by serving in Potiphar's house. The explanation was that items of knowledge are what need to be learned first. This is because Joseph in the highest sense represented the Lord, and in a lower sense, people whom the Lord regenerates. It is from knowledge that truth must be drawn as a conclusion and on knowledge as its foundation that truth must then rest. Later it deepens.

This is the situation Joseph represented, and because it is such [that items of knowledge are needed first], the Divine was what sent him there.

5902   *And he has made me like a father to Pharaoh* means that [the Lord as Joseph] was now the source of the earthly plane. This can be seen from the representation of *Pharaoh* as the earthly plane in general (mentioned at §§5160, 5799). The idea of [the Lord under the figure of Joseph] as a source is symbolized by his being *made like a father,* because children descend from their father.

A *father* properly symbolizes goodness (§§2803, 3703, 3704, 5581), and goodness is the source of everything in both the inner and the outer self. So *God made him like a father to Pharaoh* means that as goodness, he was the source of the earthly level. Joseph represents inner heavenliness, or inner goodness (§§5805, 5826, 5827, 5869, 5877), the inflow of which organizes everything on the earthly level and eventually makes him the source of the earthly level.

5903   *And like a master to all his household* means that he was the source of everything present on the earthly plane. This is indicated by the symbolism of *all Pharaoh's household* as everything on the earthly plane. The idea of [the Lord under the figure of Joseph] as the source of everything on that plane is symbolized by his being made *like a master* over that household.

The Word uses the term *master* too in connection with goodness.

5904   *And I rule in all the land of Egypt* means that he arranges the information there, as the following shows: *Ruling* symbolizes organizing. And the *land of Egypt* symbolizes the earthly mind (dealt with in §§5276, 5278, 5280, 5288, 5301), so it also symbolizes all types of knowledge, since they exist in the earthly mind. Knowledge makes up the intellectual side of

that mind, but goodness, which by an inflow organizes the knowledge
there, creates a kind of will in that mind.

Genesis 45:9, 10, 11, 12, 13. *"Hurry and go up to my father, and you are* **5905**
to say to him, 'This is what your son Joseph has said: "God has made me like
a master to all Egypt. Come down to me; you are not to stay there. And you
will settle in the land of Goshen and be near me, you and your sons and your
sons' sons and your flocks and your herds and everything that is yours. And I
will sustain you there (since there are still five years of famine) so that you will
not be wiped out, you and your household and everything that is yours."' And
look: your eyes see—and the eyes of my brother Benjamin—that with my own
mouth I am speaking to you. And you are to tell my father all the glory I have
in Egypt, and everything that you are seeing, and you are to hurry and bring
my father down here."

Hurry and go up to my father means to spiritual goodness. *And you are*
to say to him, "This is what your son Joseph has said," symbolizes a perception spiritual goodness had about inner heavenliness. *God has made me*
like a master to all Egypt means that [inner heavenliness] determines how
everything on the earthly level is arranged, in whole and in part. *Come*
down to me; you are not to stay there symbolizes a sure union. *And you will*
settle in the land of Goshen symbolizes the center of the earthly level. *And*
be near me symbolizes lasting union. *You and your sons and your sons' sons*
symbolizes spiritual goodness, and everything that grows out of it, and
everything that grows out of that in turn. *And your flocks and your herds*
symbolizes earthly goodness, both inner and outer. *And everything that*
is yours symbolizes whatever grows out of it. *And I will sustain you there*
symbolizes a constant inflow of spiritual life from inner heavenliness.
Since there are still five years of famine is a symbol for the length of time
during which goodness is lacking. *So that you will not be wiped out* means
so that it will not die out. *You and your household and everything that is*
yours symbolizes spiritual goodness and everything that goes with it. *And*
look: your eyes see symbolizes the testimony offered by perception. *And the*
eyes of my brother Benjamin means by the middle ground's perception.
That with my own mouth I am speaking to you symbolizes self-revelation.
And you are to tell my father all the glory I have in Egypt symbolizes a message for spiritual goodness from the spiritual heaven on the earthly level.
And everything that you are seeing symbolizes whatever is sensed and perceived on that level. *And you are to hurry and bring my father down here*
symbolizes a close bond.

5906   *Hurry and go up to my father* means to spiritual goodness. This is established by the representation of Israel, the *father* here, as spiritual goodness on the earthly plane (dealt with at §§5801, 5803, 5807, 5812, 5817, 5819, 5826, 5833).

How can spiritual goodness be the father of inner heavenliness, when spiritual goodness, being on the earthly plane, is shallower? The answer is that we are necessarily shallow until our inner self comes into being. We advance step by step from shallow to deep, as, for instance, from knowledge to concepts truly understood. The shallower traits then serve as a foundation for something deeper. Because this is how our capacities develop, or are born, the shallower attribute is called the father of the deeper attribute. Spiritual goodness on the earthly plane, or Israel, is therefore called the father of inner heavenliness, or Joseph.

5907   *And you are to say to him, "This is what your son Joseph has said,"* symbolizes a perception spiritual goodness had about inner heavenliness. This can be seen from the symbolism of *saying* in the Word's narratives as perception (discussed often) and from the representation of *Joseph* as inner heavenliness (discussed in §§5869, 5877).

The reason these phrases symbolize a perception by spiritual goodness (Israel) about inner heavenliness (Joseph) is that in an inner sense *your son Joseph has said* means an ability to perceive the inflow of inner heavenliness into spiritual goodness.

5908   *God has made me like a master to all Egypt* means that [inner heavenliness] determines how everything on the earthly level is arranged, in whole and in part, as the following shows: Being *made like a master* means arranging, as above in §§5903, 5904. And *all Egypt* symbolizes knowledge on the earthly level, so it symbolizes everything on that level, in whole and in part, since the earthly level is made up of knowledge. The meaning of Egypt as knowledge has been demonstrated many times before.

5909   *Come down to me; you are not to stay there* symbolizes a sure union. This can be seen from the symbolism of *coming (down) to me* as union and from that of *you are not to stay there* as what is sure.

5910   *And you will settle in the land of Goshen* stands for the center of the earthly level. This can be seen from the symbolism of *settling* as living (discussed in §§1293, 3384, 3613, 4451) and from that of the *land of Goshen* as the central, inmost part. As the land of Goshen is in Egypt, and Egypt symbolizes knowledge on the earthly level, Goshen is the central, inmost part of that level. After all, it was the best territory in the land of Egypt, and on the earthly plane, where knowledge resides, what is best stands in the center or middle. Real goodness is there as a kind of sunlike object, radiating light to truth at the sides.

And be near me symbolizes lasting union. This can be seen from the symbolism of *being near,* which means lasting union, because coming to Joseph symbolizes union (§5909), so being near him and therefore constantly close to him means lasting union.

5911

You and your sons and your sons' sons symbolizes spiritual goodness, and everything that grows out of it, and everything that grows out of that in turn, as the following shows: Israel—the *you* here—represents spiritual goodness (referred to above in §5906). *His sons* symbolize what grows out of spiritual goodness, that is, earthly-level truth, which is what they represent. And *his sons' sons* symbolize what grows out of this truth in turn, namely, another generation or further development of truth.

5912

When goodness stands in first place and has control, it is constantly producing truth. Goodness makes truth multiply around itself and also around each true concept. It turns each true idea into a little star that glows at its center. Goodness not only makes truth multiply around itself; it also produces truth from truth in cycle after cycle. These are the sons' sons, or grandsons, and further generations.

Joseph does not invite his brothers to join him except through his father, asking the father to come with his sons and sons' sons. The reason is that inner heavenliness unites with earthly-level truth only through a middle ground.

And your flocks and your herds symbolizes earthly goodness, both inner and outer, as the following indicates: A *flock* symbolizes inner goodness (mentioned at §2566). Here it symbolizes inner earthly goodness because the flocks belonged to Israel, who represents spiritual goodness *on the earthly plane* (§5906). And a *herd* symbolizes outer earthly goodness.

5913

A herd symbolizes outer goodness and flocks inner goodness because in sacrifices, the animals that made up a herd, such as full-grown cattle and young cattle, symbolized the outward goodness of neighborly love, and the goodness of the outer self; but the animals that made up flocks, such as lambs, sheep, and goats, symbolized a more inward kind of charitable goodness, and the goodness of the inner self. People with both kinds of goodness are referred to in the Word by the inclusive term *flock,* and one who leads them is called a shepherd.

And everything that is yours symbolizes whatever grows out of it. This can be seen from the symbolism of *everything that is yours* as what grows out of [spiritual goodness]. Goodness and truth on the earthly plane come

5914

from spiritual goodness as their father, and since they come from it, they belong to it.

5915   *And I will sustain you there* symbolizes a constant inflow of spiritual life from inner heavenliness. This can be seen from the symbolism of *sustaining*. When Joseph, who represents inner heavenliness, uses the term, it symbolizes an inflow of spiritual life from inner heavenliness. In a spiritual sense, sustenance is nothing but an inflow of goodness and truth from the Lord through heaven. This is what sustains angels, and this is what sustains the human soul, or a person's inner self.

What corresponds to inner sustenance is sustenance of the outer self by food and drink, so food symbolizes goodness, and drink, truth. The correspondence is such that when we eat food, the angels with us think about goodness and truth. Surprisingly, they think different thoughts depending on the particular kind of food.

When we take bread and wine during the Holy Supper, then, the angels with us think about goodness based on love and goodness based on faith (§§3464, 3735). They do so because bread corresponds to goodness based on love and wine to goodness based on faith. Since that is what these substances correspond to, it is also what they symbolize in the Word.

[2] The Lord's words in Moses make it clear that the human soul, or the inner self, is sustained by spiritual food and drink, or goodness and truth:

> Humankind does not live by bread alone; rather by every utterance of Jehovah's mouth does humankind live. (Deuteronomy 8:3; Matthew 4:4)

The utterance of Jehovah's mouth is goodness and truth that come from him. In John:

> Work, not for the food that perishes, but for the food that lasts to eternal life, which the Son of Humankind will give you. (John 6:27)

In the same author:

> The disciples asked Jesus, saying, "Teacher, eat!" He said to them, "I have food to eat that you do not know of." (John 4:31, 32)

Concerning drink, in the same author:

> Jesus said, "If any are thirsty, let them come to me and drink. Any who believe in me, as the scripture said, from their belly will flow rivers of living water." (John 7:37, 38)

Since there are still five years of famine is a symbol for the length of time during which goodness is lacking. This can be seen from statements above at §§5893, 5894 explaining *famine* and *five*.

§5916

So that you will not be wiped out means so that it will not die out, as is self-explanatory.

§5917

You and your household and everything that is yours symbolizes spiritual goodness and everything that goes with it. This can be seen from the representation of Israel—the *you* here—as spiritual goodness (explained before). *Your household and everything that is yours* plainly means everything that goes with it.

§5918

And look: your eyes see symbolizes the testimony offered by perception. This can be seen from the symbolism of *eyes* and *seeing* as perception (discussed in §§2150, 3764, 4567, 4723, 5400). It is obvious that testimony is being offered.

§5919

And the eyes of my brother Benjamin means especially by the middle ground's perception. This is established by the symbolism of *eyes* and seeing as understanding and therefore perceiving (as above in §5919) and from the representation of *Benjamin* as a middle ground (discussed in §§5411, 5413, 5443, 5639, 5688, 5822).

§5920

Here is how the case stands: Benjamin represented a middle ground, and this middle ground consisted in inner truth (§§5600, 5631), which stems directly from the inner goodness that is Joseph. It therefore perceives more clearly and keenly than does the outer truth below it, which is represented by his ten brothers. The more inward the position of truth and goodness, the more complete the perceptive ability they bring with them. Internally they stand in heaven's light, fairly close to the Lord. The inflow of divine goodness and truth from the Lord is constantly being mediated as it flows along, so it undergoes a succession of changes. People standing upstream at its head consequently receive the inflow with clearer perception, because they receive it more directly than people halfway down or at the end. The goodness and truth gradually grow dimmer at a distance, just as light does, because accumulating imperfections blunt it along the way.

This shows how to understand the phrase "testimony offered . . . especially by the middle ground's perception." The middle ground is within, and the truth represented by Jacob's sons is outside it.

That with my own mouth I am speaking to you symbolizes self-revelation, as the following shows: The first piece of evidence was that their eyes saw him, the second that Benjamin's eyes did, and now the third that *with*

§5921

his own mouth he was speaking to them. By this means he removed all doubt that he was Joseph, so he revealed himself fully. His words, then, imply self-revelation.

5922   *And you are to tell my father all the glory I have in Egypt* symbolizes a message for spiritual goodness from the spiritual heaven on the earthly level, as the following shows: *Telling* symbolizes a message. *Glory* symbolizes the spiritual heaven, as treated of below. *Egypt* symbolizes knowledge on the earthly level and so the earthly level itself, as above at §5908. And Israel, the *father* being communicated with here, represents spiritual goodness, as mentioned above at §5906. Clearly, then, *you are to tell my father all the glory I have in Egypt* symbolizes a message for spiritual goodness from the spiritual heaven on the earthly level.

[2] Concerning the idea that *glory* means the spiritual heaven: Heaven is made up of two kingdoms, the heavenly and the spiritual. The heavenly kingdom is the third or inmost heaven. The spiritual kingdom is the second or middle heaven. The goodness to which the heavenly are devoted is called heavenly goodness, and the goodness to which the spiritual are devoted is called spiritual goodness. Heavenly goodness is goodness growing out of love for the Lord, and spiritual goodness is goodness growing out of love for one's neighbor. What unites the two kingdoms? The goodness that springs from charitable feelings toward one's neighbor. People in the heavenly kingdom, you see, have love for the Lord at their core and charitable feelings toward their neighbor on the outside. People in the spiritual kingdom, though, have charitable feelings toward their neighbor at their core and a faith resulting from charity on the outside. Clearly, then, charity toward one's neighbor forms the bond between the two kingdoms. The heavenly kingdom ends with it, and the spiritual kingdom begins with it. The termination of one is the start of the other. So each takes up where the other leaves off.

[3] Now let me define glory. In the highest sense, glory is the Lord in regard to divine truth, so it is divine truth coming from the Lord. In a representative sense, glory is the good done by neighborly love, and this good is charity. Charity is the outward goodness of the Lord's heavenly kingdom and the inward goodness of his spiritual kingdom. This form of goodness is actually the same as the divine truth that exists in heaven.

The current verse talks about Israel, who stands for spiritual goodness, or charity, which constitutes the spiritual kingdom in the heavens and the spiritual church on earth. The glory of Joseph that the brothers were to tell Israel about, then, means the spiritual heaven.

The spiritual heaven is called glory because objects there appear in light, in brilliance, in radiance.

[4] Glory comes up in connection with divine truth originating in the Lord's divine humanity and is attributed to the Lord as king. (Monarchy on an inner level means divine truth; §§1728, 2015, 2069, 3009, 3670, 4581, 4966, 5044, 5068.) This is evident in John:

> But the Word became flesh and resided among us, and we saw his *glory: glory* like that of the Only-Born of the Father, who was full of grace and *truth.* (John 1:14)

The Word is divine truth. Because divine truth comes from the Lord, it is the Lord himself. So glory refers to divine truth. [5] In Luke:

> When Jesus was transfigured on the mountain, here, two men conversed with him, and they were Moses and Elijah, *who appeared in glory.* (Luke 9:30, 31)

The Lord was showing Peter, James, and John his divine humanity as it really was and as it appeared in divine light. The form in which he was then seen presented an image of the Word as it is in its inner meaning and consequently of the divine truth that exists in heaven. (After all, the Word is divine truth for the use of the church.) For this reason the vision included Moses and Elijah speaking with the Lord, since Moses represents the Law (meaning the books he wrote, along with the narrative books), and Elijah represents the Prophets (that is, the prophetical part of the Word). To see that Moses represents the one set of books, see the preface to Genesis 18, and §4859 at the end. To see that Elijah represents the other set, see the same preface and §§2762, 5247 at the end. [6] In Matthew:

> They will see the Son of Humankind coming in the *clouds of heaven* with power and *glory.* (Matthew 24:30)

The Word's literal meaning is the clouds, and the inner meaning is the glory, which is therefore divine truth as it exists in heaven (see the preface to Genesis 18). Glory also means the understanding and wisdom inherent in divine truth (§4809). Cloud surrounds the Word's outward meaning because human minds are in the dark, so that if the Word were not beclouded, hardly anyone would understand it. The holy content of the inner meaning would also be profaned by evil people in the world. That is why the Lord says in Isaiah:

> Jehovah will create over the whole dwelling place of Mount Zion and over its convocations a *cloud* by day and the radiance of a fiery flame by night. For *over all the glory there will be a canopy,* and a *shelter* will serve *as shade* by day. (Isaiah 4:5, 6)

[7] For the same reason, cloud appeared over the tabernacle by day, and fire by night [Exodus 40:34–38; Numbers 9:15–23]. The tabernacle represented the Lord's divine humanity, so it represented the divine truth that comes from him and consequently the Word, which is divine truth for the church (see §§3210, 3439). The following passage in Moses has the same symbolism:

> The *cloud* covered the meeting tent, and the *glory of Jehovah* filled the dwelling place. (Exodus 40:34)

In the same author:

> The *glory of Jehovah* appeared in the meeting tent before all the children of Israel. (Numbers 14:10)

And elsewhere [in the same book]:

> The *cloud* covered the tent, and the *glory of Jehovah* appeared. (Numbers 16:42)

[8] It is similar with the cloud and glory on Mount Sinai described this way in Moses:

> When Moses went up onto the mountain, the *cloud* covered the mountain, and the *glory of Jehovah* resided on Mount Sinai six days. (Exodus 24:15, 16)

Another reason these representations took place is that the Law, which is divine truth, was issued from that mountain. The cloud and Jehovah's glory appeared when Moses went up there because on the mountain he represented the Law, or the narrative part of the Word. That is why Scripture speaks numerous times of Moses and the Prophets, or the Law and the Prophets. "The Law" means the books of Moses, along with the other narrative books, but not the Prophets, because that part of the Word was represented by Elijah and Elisha. The Word has a narrative part and a prophetical part, as is known, so when it is called the Law and the Prophets, the Law means the narrative part, and the Prophets means the prophetical part.

[9] Divine truth was also represented in Ezekiel by a brilliance resembling a rainbow in a cloud, around and over some guardian beings. This is what the passage says about them:

> I saw an appearance of fire; it was like a brilliance all around, like the appearance of the *rainbow* that is *in a cloud* on a rainy day. This was the appearance of the likeness of *Jehovah's glory.* (Ezekiel 1:26, 27, 28)

Other names are the *glory of Jehovah* and the *glory of Israel's God,* used in Ezekiel 8:4; 10:18, 19; 11:22, 23. "The glory of Jehovah" is used in respect to the inmost heaven, and "the glory of Israel's God" in respect to the middle, spiritual heaven. Divine truth appears in glory in the heavens because in the spiritual heaven, truth itself appears before the inhabitants' eyes as a white cloud (which I have been allowed to see a number of times), and the goodness within that truth appears as something fiery in the cloud. The appearance of the cloud shifts with the firelight in marvelous ways. These variegations are what glory is in a superficial sense. In an inner sense, though, glory is understanding and wisdom, which is also what such sights represent.

[10] The following passages give further evidence that glory consists in divine truth, the source of all understanding and wisdom, and in the colorful appearance of the cloud as seen by the outer eye. In Moses:

> Jehovah said, "As I live, the whole earth will be filled with the *glory of Jehovah.*" (Numbers 14:21)

Jehovah said this when he was rejecting the Israelite people and saying that only their little children would enter the land of Canaan. The symbolism of the statement then that the whole earth would be filled with the glory of Jehovah had to do with two things. One was the Israelites' observance of practices representing a church. The other was the Word, which was mostly about them. These two things would hold the glory of Jehovah, which would fill all of heaven and would therefore fill whatever was holy in the religion. [11] In Isaiah:

> The seraphs shouted, "Holy, holy, holy is Jehovah Sabaoth! *The fullness of all the earth is his glory.*" (Isaiah 6:3)

In the same author:

> The *glory of Jehovah* will be revealed, and all flesh will see it together. (Isaiah 40:5)

In the same author:

> Therefore *give glory to Jehovah* in the Urim, to the name of Jehovah, God of Israel, in the islands of the sea. (Isaiah 24:15)

The Urim stand for the light shed by divine truth coming from the Lord. The islands of the sea stand for people somewhat isolated from this truth (§1158). [12] In the same author:

> The *glory of Lebanon* has been given to it, the *honor* of Carmel and Sharon. They will see the *glory of Jehovah,* the *honor* of our God. (Isaiah 35:2)

Lebanon stands for a spiritual religion, Carmel and Sharon for a heavenly one. The glory of Jehovah is mentioned in relation to a heavenly religion when this religion is understood to consist in heavenly truth, which is charity. The honor of Israel's God is mentioned in relation to a spiritual religion when this is understood to consist in spiritual goodness, which is also charity. [13] In the same author:

> Rise, shine, because *your light* has come, and the *glory of Jehovah* has dawned over you, for look: shadows cover the earth, and darkness, the peoples. But Jehovah will dawn above you, and *his glory* will be seen above you. (Isaiah 60:1, 2)

This is about the Lord, who is called the light, as in John 1:4, 9. The passage also says that the glory of Jehovah will dawn over him, meaning that he will have divine truth. Likewise in the same author:

> For my own sake, for my own sake I will act, because why should there be profanation? *My glory I do not give to another.* (Isaiah 48:11)

This too is about the Lord. Glory in the highest sense stands for his divine humanity and consequently for divine truth as well, since the latter comes from the former. Not giving his glory to another means giving it only to his divine humanity, which is identical with himself. [14] In John:

> The holy city Jerusalem was coming down out of heaven, *having the glory of God,* and its light was like a very precious stone. (Revelation 21:10, 11)

The holy city Jerusalem is the Lord's spiritual kingdom in the heavens and his spiritual church on earth, which are described as having glory. Its light is truth from the Divine.

[15] Divine truth is what monarchy represents in the Word, since the Lord was represented as to his divine truth by monarchs; see the passages cited just above. So glory is attributed to him in his role as monarch, as in David:

> Gates, raise your heads, and be lifted up, doorways of the world, so that a *glorious monarch* can march in. Who is this *glorious monarch?* Jehovah, mighty and a hero; Jehovah, a war hero. Gates, raise your heads, and raise the doorways of the world, *so that a glorious monarch can march in.* Who is this *glorious monarch?* Jehovah *Sabaoth*—he is the *glorious monarch.* (Psalms 24:7, 8, 9, 10)

In Isaiah:

> Jehovah *Sabaoth will rule* on Mount Zion and in Jerusalem, and before his elders his *glory* will rule. (Isaiah 24:23)

The glory stands for divine truth. Jehovah is called Jehovah Sabaoth, or Jehovah of Armies, when the text is dealing with divine truth, because an army symbolizes truth (§3448).

[16] Since monarchy represented divine truth, the throne on which monarchs sat to pass judgment was called a *glorious throne* (Isaiah 22:23; Jeremiah 14:21; 17:12). And in Matthew:

> The Son of Humankind will sit *on his glorious throne.* (Matthew 19:28)

In the same author:

> When the Son of Humankind comes *in his glory,* and all the holy angels with him, then he will sit *on his glorious throne.* And the *King* will say to them, . . . (Matthew 25:31, 34, 40)

Another reason the throne was called a glorious throne was that judgment was carried out on the basis of truth. In the same author:

> The Son of Humankind will come *in the glory of his Father,* with his angels, and then he will repay every person according to that person's deeds. (Matthew 16:27)

[17] The above considerations also show what glory means in the Lord's Prayer:

Yours is the kingdom, the power, and the glory, forever. (Matthew 6:13)

The Lord's spiritual kingdom in the heavens and his spiritual church on earth is also called an *ornament,* [or *beauty*] (Isaiah 60:7; 63:15; 64:11; Daniel 8:9, 10, 11; 11:16, 41, 45).

It is for the same reason that Joseph mentions his glory, because in the highest sense he too represents the Lord's divine spirituality, or divine truth. In a [less exalted] inner sense he represents the Lord's spiritual kingdom and the goodness that comes of faith (see §§3969, 4669, 4723, 4727).

5923 *And everything that you are seeing* symbolizes whatever is sensed and perceived on that level. This is established by the symbolism of *seeing* as understanding and therefore as perceiving and sensing (discussed in §§2150, 2325, 2807, 3764, 3863, 4403–4421, 4567, 4723, 5400).

5924 *And you are to hurry and bring my father down here* symbolizes a close bond. This can be seen from the discussion above at §5909. Because the same thing is said again here, and said with desire and love, it means a close bond.

5925 Genesis 45:14, 15. *And he fell on the neck of Benjamin his brother and wept, and Benjamin wept on his neck. And he kissed all his brothers and wept on them. And after that his brothers spoke with him.*

And he fell on the neck of Benjamin symbolizes a very deep bond with the middle ground. *And wept* symbolizes the effect of mercy. *And Benjamin wept on his neck* symbolizes acceptance and so a response in kind. *And he kissed all his brothers* symbolizes attachment as a matter of favor. *And wept on them* symbolizes the outcome of affection. *And after that his brothers spoke with him* symbolizes communication in both directions as a result of acceptance.

5926 *And he fell on the neck of Benjamin* symbolizes a very deep bond with the middle ground, as the following shows: A *neck* symbolizes an inflow, communication, and connection (discussed at §§3542, 3695, 3725). Strictly speaking, it means a connection between the heavenly and spiritual dimensions (§§5320, 5328), so it means a connection between inner heavenliness (Joseph) and heavenly spirituality (Benjamin). *Falling on his neck,* then, means creating a tight connection, which means creating a very deep bond. And *Benjamin* represents a middle ground (discussed in §§5411, 5413, 5443, 5639, 5686, 5688, 5689).

And wept symbolizes the effect of mercy. This can be seen from the symbolism of *weeping,* which, since it results from mercy, means the effect of mercy, [or compassion] (dealt with in §§5480, 5873).

And Benjamin wept on his neck symbolizes acceptance and so a response in kind. This can be seen from the fact that the gesture was mutual, which is why it means acceptance and so a response in kind.

Here is what needs to be known about the connection of goodness to truth, and of truth to goodness in response: When goodness flows into true ideas and binds them to itself, it pours its own goodness into them and through this goodness claims ownership of them. The result is union. The true ideas receive life in the process, so when they then respond, or react, they seem to be acting on their own. In reality, though, truth does not act on its own. It acts under the power of goodness, which flows into the goodness that it itself imparted to truth.

The case resembles that of blood vessels in a living body. Truth is like vessels empty of blood; goodness is like blood. When blood flows into vessels that have been empty, it makes them active. The activity is only a response, because the vessels have received their ability to move—and life, so to speak—from the blood.

This discussion shows how matters stand regarding the connection of goodness with truth and the answering connection of truth with goodness.

And he kissed all his brothers symbolizes attachment as a matter of favor. This can be seen from the symbolism of *kissing* as union based on desire (discussed in §§3573, 3574, 4353). Here it symbolizes attachment as a matter of favor, because earthly-level truth known to the church (represented by Jacob's sons) is relatively distant from inner goodness (Joseph). Truth that is relatively distant does unite with inner goodness through a middle ground, admittedly, but for a long time it nonetheless retains qualities that fail to correspond with that goodness. So *kissing his brothers* symbolizes attachment as a matter of favor.

[2] The attachment is said to be a matter of favor rather than of mercy because remote attributes that are not in full correspondence are not humble enough to beg for mercy or even to speak of it from the heart. They substitute favor instead. The reason is that the traits that do not correspond, which are tenacious, arise out of self-love. People who love themselves can never humble themselves sincerely. They swagger, because they see themselves in everything they look at, and they dismiss anything outside themselves.

5930   *And wept on them* symbolizes the outcome of affection. This can be seen from the symbolism of *weeping* as the outcome of mercy (mentioned just above at §§5927, 5928). Here it symbolizes the outcome of affection, for the same reason given just above in §5929.

5931   *And after that his brothers spoke with him* symbolizes communication in both directions as a result of acceptance. This can be seen from the explanation above at §5880. The explanation above at §5928 shows what two-way communication resulting from acceptance is.

5932   Genesis 45:16, 17, 18, 19, 20. *And the voice was heard in Pharaoh's house, saying, "Joseph's brothers have come," and it was good in the eyes of Pharaoh and in the eyes of his servants. And Pharaoh said to Joseph, "Say to your brothers, 'Do this: load your beasts of burden and come, go to the land of Canaan. And take your father and your households and come to me, and I will give you the best of the land of Egypt, and you will eat the fat of the land. And now, do this command: take yourselves wagons from the land of Egypt for your little children and for your women, and you are to bear your father and come. And your eye is to be merciless over your household effects, because the best of all the land of Egypt is yours.'"*

And the voice was heard in Pharaoh's house means that this message filled the entire earthly level. *Saying, "Joseph's brothers have come,"* symbolizes a perception that earthly-level truth known to the church was present. *And it was good in the eyes of Pharaoh* symbolizes joy throughout that level. *And in the eyes of his servants* means down to the lowest part of that level. *And Pharaoh said to Joseph* symbolizes a perception on the earthly plane received from inner heavenliness. *Say to your brothers* means concerning earthly-level truth known to the church. *Do this: load your beasts of burden* means that they filled every bit of truth with goodness. *And come, go to the land of Canaan* symbolizes the place where they lived. *And take your father and your households and come to me* symbolizes bringing spiritual goodness and the church's truth into contact with earthly-level learning. *And I will give you the best of the land of Egypt* symbolizes possession of knowledge. *And you will eat the fat of the land* symbolizes adoption of the goodness on that level. *And now, do this command* symbolizes the will. *Take yourselves wagons from the land of Egypt* symbolizes teachings in the form of knowledge. *For your little children and for your women* means for people who do not yet know. *And you are to bear your father and come* symbolizes the service they owed, and closer contact. *And your eye is to be merciless over your household effects* means that the means are unimportant. *Because the best of all the land of Egypt is yours* means that they have first claim on the earthly mind.

And the voice was heard in Pharaoh's house means that this message **5933** filled the entire earthly level, as the following shows: When a *voice* heard elsewhere, at a distance, is being attributed to a spiritual inflow, it symbolizes being filled. Just as an audible voice fills an area, an inflow does likewise. And *Pharaoh's house* symbolizes the entire earthly level, since Pharaoh represents the earthly plane in general (§§5160, 5799).

Saying, "Joseph's brothers have come," means that earthly-level truth **5934** known to the church was present. This is indicated by the symbolism of *having come* as presence and by the representation of Jacob's sons, or *Joseph's brothers,* as earthly-level truth known to the church (treated of in §§5403, 5419, 5458, 5512).

The earthly level holds knowledge of various kinds. There is knowledge about earthly, bodily, and worldly matters, which is the lowliest kind, since it comes directly from the evidence of the outward, physical senses. There is knowledge about the civil realm and the government, statutes, and laws of the state; and this is a little deeper. There is knowledge about the issues of moral life, which is even deeper. But knowledge about spiritual life is deeper than all the other types. This is the church's truths. As long as we know them only from theology, they are mere items of knowledge, but when they come from a loving goodness, they soar above knowledge, because they then dwell in spiritual light. From that vantage point they see items of knowledge laid out in order below them.

By these steps—different levels of knowledge—we climb to a point of understanding, because types of knowledge on their different levels open our mind, enabling light from the spiritual world to flow in.

This description now shows what is meant by the presence of earthly-level truth.

And it was good in the eyes of Pharaoh symbolizes joy throughout that **5935** level—the earthly level. This can be seen from the symbolism of *being good in the eyes of* someone as being a joy to that person and from the representation of *Pharaoh* as the earthly level in general (mentioned just above in §5933).

And in the eyes of his servants means down to the lowest part of that **5936** level. This can be seen from the symbolism of *servants* as something lowly (discussed in §§2541, 5161, 5164, 5305) and therefore as what is lowest.

For the identification of the lowlier and lowliest types of knowledge on the earthly plane, see just above at §5934.

5937   *And Pharaoh said to Joseph* symbolizes a perception on the earthly plane received from inner heavenliness, as the following shows: *Saying,* in Scripture narrative, symbolizes perception (mentioned many times). *Pharaoh* represents the earthly plane in general (dealt with at §§5160, 5799). And *Joseph* represents inner heavenliness (dealt with in §§5869, 5877). The heavenliness that Joseph represents is inward, and the earthliness that Pharaoh represents is outward, so perception on the earthly plane comes from inner heavenliness. All perception comes from within; inner levels never perceive anything from outer levels. Perception comes from the same place as all inflow.

[2] I should briefly define this "perception" I have mentioned so often. Everyone has an ability to perceive whether an idea is so or not so. The capacity to decide inwardly, in our own mind, causes the idea to be perceived. This ability is completely impossible without inflow from the spiritual world.

Some people have more of this gift than others. The less skilled are those who inwardly, in their own minds, draw few conclusions and consequently have few perceptions. Instead they say, "This is true because people I trust say so." The more skilled are those who see that it is true on their own rather than relying on others.

However, the kind of perception that everyone has relates to worldly affairs; no one today has perception concerning spiritual matters. This is because the inflowing spiritual force that makes perception possible has been dimmed and almost quenched by the pleasures of materialism and self-love. People therefore have no interest in spiritual concerns except as a result of duty and habit. If they lost the fear associated with duty and the pleasure associated with habit, they would scorn what is spiritual, turn their back on it, and even deny it.

[3] People who are to have perception in spiritual matters must have a desire for truth based on goodness and will always be longing to know truth. This illuminates their intellect, and when their intellect has been illuminated, they are able to perceive something inwardly. People without a desire for truth, on the other hand, know what truth they know from the religious teachings they choose to believe in, and from the fact that a priest, elder, or monk has called it true.

This discussion shows what perception is and demonstrates that we have perception on worldly subjects but not on spiritual ones. For more evidence, consider the fact that everyone remains in the dogma that she or he was born into. That includes people born as Jews and people born outside the church, even if they live inside it. Also included are people who subscribe to heresy. If you presented them with absolute truth and went on to prove it, they still would not perceive it as true at all. To them it will seem false.

Say to your brothers means concerning earthly-level truth known to the church—that is, a perception concerning it. This is established by the representation of Joseph's *brothers* as earthly-level truth known to the church (mentioned in §§5403, 5419, 5458, 5512).   **5938**

Pharaoh here invites Jacob's sons to come to Egypt with their little children and women and to bear their father with them. "Say to your brothers," says Pharaoh, "'Do this, and take your father. And take yourselves wagons from the land of Egypt for your little children and your women. And you are to bear your father and come.'" A little earlier, though, Joseph invites his father without inviting his brothers, except as belonging to his father. "Go up to my father," he says, "and you are to say to him, 'Come down to me; you are not to stay there. And you will settle in the land of Goshen and be near me, you and your sons and your sons' sons and everything that is yours.' Hurry, and you are to bring my father down here" [Genesis 45:9, 10, 13].

The reason Pharaoh invited Jacob's sons, and Joseph invited his father, is clear only from the inner meaning, which is this: The earthly level in general, represented by Pharaoh, communicates directly with earthly-level truth known to the church, represented by Jacob's sons. That is why Pharaoh talks about them. Inner heavenliness, represented by Joseph, does not communicate directly with earthly-level truth known to the church, which is Jacob's sons, but instead communicates through spiritual goodness, which is Israel their father. That is why Joseph talks about his father.

Do this: load your beasts of burden means that they filled every bit of truth with goodness. This can be seen from the symbolism of *loading beasts of burden* as filling truth up and from that of the grain loaded onto the beasts as goodness based on truth (mentioned in §§5295, 5410). Beasts of burden in this case mean truth because they were donkeys (Genesis 42:26, 27; 43:18, 24; 44:3), which symbolize knowledge (§5741). Since donkeys symbolize knowledge, and union with inner goodness through a middle ground has now been achieved, the knowledge is now truths. As a result, the donkeys are being called beasts of burden.   **5939**

5940   *And come, go to the land of Canaan* symbolizes the place where they—
earthly-level truths known to the church—lived. This can be seen from
the symbolism of the *land of Canaan* as the place where the people of the
church lived (discussed in §§3686, 3705, 4447, 4454, 4517, 5136). Because
of this symbolism, the land of Canaan symbolizes the place where the
church's truth lived alongside goodness, since these two go to make up
the church.

5941   *And take your father and your households and come to me* symbolizes bringing spiritual goodness and the church's truth into contact with
earthly-level learning, as the following shows: Israel, the *father*, represents spiritual goodness (as in §§5801, 5803, 5807, 5812, 5817, 5819, 5826,
5833). His sons represent the church's truth on the earthly plane (discussed in §§5414, 5879), which in its entirety is *their households. Coming*
means making contact. And Pharaoh, the *me* to whom they were to
come, represents earthly-level learning in general. All of this evidence
shows that *take your father and your households and come to me* symbolizes bringing spiritual goodness and the church's truth into contact with
earthly-level learning.

5942   *And I will give you the best of the land of Egypt* symbolizes possession of knowledge. This can be seen from the symbolism of the *land of
Egypt* as knowledge (discussed at §§1164, 1165, 1186, 1462, 4749, 4964,
4966, 5700) and from that of *giving the best of its land* as giving possession. One who gives possession of something gives the best of it, and
the reverse.

5943   *And you will eat the fat of the land* symbolizes adoption of the goodness on that level. This is established by the symbolism of *eating* as being
communicated, united, and adopted (discussed in §§2187, 2343, 3168, 3513
at the end, 3832, 4745) and by that of the *fat of the land*—the land of
Egypt—as what is good on the earthly level.

The symbolism of *fat* as something heavenly, or good, can be seen
from many Scripture passages. This applies not only to the fat on an
animal but also to fat of other kinds, such as butter and oil, and to anything with fatlike qualities, such as milk, honey, and resin. The more they
resemble fat, the more they symbolize goodness.

[2] The role fat played in representing heavenly goodness and therefore
love from the Lord is clear in the burnt offerings and sacrifices. Consider
that all the fat was burned on the altar, that this gave off a restful smell
to Jehovah, and that the children of Israel were accordingly forbidden
to eat it. These facts and all the others [concerning the fat of a sacrifice]

demonstrate that the rituals established among the Israelites represented heavenly and spiritual qualities and consequently meant something holy. Otherwise there would have been no divine purpose in sacrificing all of an animal's fat, in its being a restful smell to Jehovah, or in forbidding the eating of fat, like the eating of blood. To believe that the Divine would be pleased by fat, or that Jehovah would create a statute that hid no other meaning inside it, would certainly be to think very coarsely about him. A person would have to be excessively caught up in the earth and the body not to care what such rules symbolize. It would be a sign that the person had no desire to know about the Word or eternal life.

[3] This is what Moses says about fat:

You shall take all the *fat* sheathing the intestines, and the *omentum* over the liver, and the *fat* over the kidneys and burn it on the altar. (Exodus 29:13, 22; Leviticus 3:4, 5, 9, 10, 14, 15; 4:8, 9, 19, 26, 31, 35; 7:3, 4)

The *fat of the breast* was also to be sacrificed. (Leviticus 7:30, 31)

This is what is said about the sacrifice of fat as a restful smell to Jehovah:

This is the bread of the fire offering to Jehovah *as a restful smell.* (Leviticus 3:16)

The priest shall spatter blood on Jehovah's altar and *offer the fat as a restful smell to Jehovah.* (Leviticus 17:6)

And in another place:

The *fat* of a firstborn ox or sheep shall be burned on the altar *as a restful smell to Jehovah.* (Numbers 18:17)

A restful smell symbolizes the pleasing quality of a loving goodness.

[4] Statements that the children of Israel were not to eat fat:

Let all the *fat* be Jehovah's. Therefore it is an eternal statute throughout your generations, everywhere you live: *you shall not eat any fat* or any blood. (Leviticus 3:16, 17)

And in another place:

Speak to the children of Israel, saying, "*You shall not eat any fat of ox or sheep or goat.* All *who eat fat* from the animal from which a fire offering to Jehovah has been offered—the souls eating it will be cut off from their people. And you shall not eat any blood." (Leviticus 7:23, 24, 25, 26)

[5] Burnt offerings and sacrifices were the main feature of divine worship among that people (§§923, 2180), so burnt offerings and sacrifices as a whole symbolize worship. The items sacrificed and the entire procedure used symbolize the nature of the worship. The fat and its burning symbolize heavenly divinity itself, which is a loving goodness from the Lord, as is apparent in the following passages. In Isaiah:

Jacob, you have not bought calamus for me with silver, and with the *fat of sacrifices* you have not filled me. You have only subjected me to work, by your sins. (Isaiah 43:24)

"You have not bought calamus with silver" means you have not acquired religious truth. "And with the fat of sacrifices you have not filled me" means you have not acquired a loving goodness. [6] In David:

Burnt offerings of fat animals I will offer to you, along with the incense of rams. (Psalms 66:15)

The burnt offerings of fat animals stand for worship from love. In Moses:

. . . at which point it will be said, "Where are their gods—the rock they trusted in—who ate the *fat* of their *sacrifices,* [who] drank the wine of their libation?" (Deuteronomy 32:37, 38)

The passage predicts that this would be said by people outside the church, who imagined that gods needed food, especially these kinds of food. They had no idea at all that the fat of sacrifices meant heavenliness (which is to say a loving goodness) expressed in worship, or that the wine of a libation meant the resulting religious truth. This goodness and truth touched angels' hearts when there was a sacrifice, so the actions were commanded in order to bring heaven and humankind close together through deeds carrying representation and correspondence. [7] In David:

Jehovah will remember all your offerings and *make your burnt offering fat.* (Psalms 20:3)

Making a burnt offering fat stands for making worship good. In Isaiah:

Jehovah Sabaoth will make for all peoples on this mountain a *banquet of fatty foods,* a banquet of mellow wines, of *fatty foods full of marrow,* of wine free of dregs. He will swallow death up forever, and the Lord Jehovih will wipe away the tear from all faces. (Isaiah 25:6, 8)

The banquet stands for heaven and union there with angels through love and charity (§§3596, 3832, 5161). The fatty foods mean the goodness that comes of love and charity. In the same author:

Why do you weigh out silver for that which is not bread and your labor for that which does not satisfy? Pay wholehearted attention to me and *eat what is good,* and let your soul revel *in the fat.* (Isaiah 55:2)

[8] And in Jeremiah:

I will turn their mourning into joy and comfort them and cheer them out of their sorrow, *and I will fill the soul of the priests with fat,* and my people will receive fully of *my goodness.* (Jeremiah 31:13, 14)

The fat plainly stands for goodness, because it is said to satisfy the soul and is called Jehovah's goodness, which is actually his heavenliness. In David:

My soul will be filled, as with *fat* and *grease,* and my mouth will give praise with lips of song. (Psalms 63:5)

The same applies here. In the same author:

You have crowned the year of your *goodness,* and your course drips with *fat.* (Psalms 65:11)

In the same author:

The children of humankind trust in the shade of your wings, *they are filled with the fat* of your house, and you slake their thirst with a river of pleasures. (Psalms 36:7, 8)

In Isaiah:

Then Jehovah will give rain for the seed with which you will sow the land, and bread from the produce of the land. And there will be *fat* and richness. (Isaiah 30:23)

[9] In John:

All things *fat* and resplendent have left, and you will no longer find them. (Revelation 18:14)

This is about Babylon. "All things fat and resplendent have left" means that all loving goodness and religious truth have left. In Moses:

> He made them suck *honey* from a crag, and *oil* from a boulder of rock; the *butter* of the herd and the *milk* of the flock, together with the *fat* of lambs and of rams—the sons of Bashan—and of goats, together with the *fat of the kidneys of wheat;* and the blood of the grape you drink as unmixed wine. (Deuteronomy 32:13, 14)

This is about the ancient church, a spiritual religion. The passage lists its different types of goodness, which are symbolized by honey, oil, butter, milk, and fat.

[10] Because fat stood for what was good, the word is also applied to substances that are not actually fatty; but they still symbolize the best part. "Fat" and "good," then, meant virtually the same thing. There is an example in the last quotation: "the fat of wheat." Likewise in David:

> I would feed them *from the fat of the wheat.* (Psalms 81:16)

In another place:

> . . . who makes your border peaceful and satisfies you with the *fat of the wheat.* (Psalms 147:14)

And in Moses:

> All the *fat of* pristine *oil* and all the *fat of new wine* and *grain,* which were first fruits, were Jehovah's, so they were given to Aaron. (Numbers 18:12)

5944   *And now, do this command* symbolizes the will, as is self-evident.

5945   *Take yourselves wagons from the land of Egypt* symbolizes teachings in the form of knowledge. This can be seen from the symbolism of the *land of Egypt* as knowledge, as mentioned before, and from that of *wagons* as teachings.

Where the Word talks about Egypt it often mentions chariots and horses. The chariots in those passages mean teachings, whether false or true, and the horses mean matters of intellect, again in both senses. For the meaning of chariots as teachings, see §5321. Wagons in the Word have a similar meaning but symbolize teachings in the form of knowledge. Teachings in the form of knowledge are teachings from the Word's literal meaning. They are especially useful to people who are first being introduced to the church's inner truth. Such teachings include the idea that above all we ought to help widows, orphans, and the poor on the streets. They also include the Ten Commandments. These concepts and others like them are teachings in the form of knowledge and are symbolized by Egypt's wagons.

Teachings of this kind are the first we learn, so they afterward serve as a foundation for us. As we make inward progress, they become our lowest plane.

In addition, the heavenly and spiritual dimensions actually have their grounding in such teachings, because they stand on those teachings and rest their weight on them, so to speak. The spiritual world has its legs and feet in the physical world. In us, so far as our spiritual life is concerned, it has its legs and feet in the teachings we know. It is the same as the grounding the Word's inner meaning has in its literal meaning.

Wagons, which symbolize these teachings, are mentioned in only a few places in the Word. The same word in the original language is used in a passage on the ark [of the covenant] to refer to a wagon on which the ark was placed (1 Samuel 6:7; 2 Samuel 6:3). The word is also used when the dwelling place [of the tabernacle] was being consecrated (Numbers 7:3). The reason it was used there is that the ark represented heaven (§3478), which stands on and rests its weight on teachings that are known, as just mentioned.

For your little children and for your women means for people who do **5946** not yet know, that is, who do not yet know the church's inner depths. This is established by the symbolism of *little children* as people who do not yet know such things and from that of *women* as desires for truth. Where men symbolize truth (as Jacob's sons do here), their women symbolize desires for truth. When men symbolize goodness, on the other hand, their women symbolize truth; but in that case the men are called husbands (§§3236, 4510, 4823).

What is more, desires for truth, meant by the women here, cannot know the church's inner depths except through truth, meant by men. Desires without truth are like the will without the intellect. If the will is to see and know anything, it must use the intellect. The intellect is what supplies it with eyes, or vision.

And you are to bear your father and come symbolizes the service they **5947** owed, and closer contact. This is established by the symbolism of *bearing their father* as the service they owed, discussed below, and from that of *coming* as making contact, as above in §5941.

About the service symbolized by *bearing their father:* What is lower ought to serve what is inner. Earthly-level truth known to the church, which Jacob's sons represent, is lower. Spiritual goodness, which Israel their father represents, is inner. Because this goodness is inner—in other words, higher—it ought to be served by what is outer, or lower. Lowly attributes, you see, are designed specifically for service, because they are designed to have something within, living and acting in them and through them. In fact, they are designed in such a way that if the inner element is removed from them, they become mere vessels, devoid of life and activity. They become completely dead.

The relationship between a body and its spirit is the same, so when the spirit withdraws, the body immediately falls dead. The relationship between the outer and inner selves is also the same, and so is the relationship between the inner self and the Lord. The inner self is designed to receive life from the Lord and is actually an instrument of his life. So it is designed to serve the Lord in all the functions demanded by love for him and charity toward one's neighbor, first in the physical world and then in the spiritual world.

5948   *And your eye is to be merciless over your household effects* means that the means are unimportant. This can be seen from the symbolism of *household effects,* or implements, as means. Their lack of importance is symbolized by *your eye is to be merciless.*

There are essential elements and there are means. In order for something essential to bring about an effect anywhere, it must have a means through which to act. Its activity depends on the formation of the means.

For example, the body is a means for its spirit. The outer self is a means for the inner self. Knowledge is a means for truth, and truth is a means for goodness (§§3068, 3079). And so on.

[2] Means are referred to in the Word as vessels. Here they are called household effects, because the term is used in connection with the move that [Jacob's sons] are making and so in connection with the contents of their houses.

Essential elements, on the other hand, are referred to in the Word as "matters" and are what act through the means. Inner elements, then, are more essential, since they act through outer elements.

In saying that means must be unimportant, I mean that they should not be the goal. Essentials should be the goal. To the extent that we make the means our goal, what is essential withdraws and vanishes. If we make knowledge our aim, for instance, and have no interest in truth, truth eventually fades to the point where we cannot tell whether it is true. If we make truth our aim and have no interest in goodness, goodness eventually fades to the point where it ceases to exist. If we make earthly, body-driven, or worldly concerns our aim, so that we care only about them, not about heavenly concerns, the latter fade to the point where we eventually acknowledge almost nothing heavenly.

These ideas and others like them are what is symbolized by *your eye is to be merciless over your household effects.*

[3] However, bear in mind that essential elements and means are relative. An entity is described as essential because it acts through some other entity as its means or instrument. But when a third entity acts through what was formerly essential, it becomes a means; and so on.

Besides, nothing that is essential in an absolute sense exists anywhere in creation, only in the Supreme Being, that is, in the Lord. Because he is existence itself, or the absolute essential, he is called Jehovah, from [the Hebrew word for] being. Everything else is just a means.

From this thought it now follows that since we should aim at essentials rather than means (as just mentioned), the Lord alone should be our goal.

Because the best of all the land of Egypt is yours means that they have first claim on the earthly mind. This can be seen from the symbolism of the *land of Egypt* as the earthly mind (discussed in §§5276, 5278, 5280, 5288, 5301). The *best of all that land* symbolizes a first claim.

These words also mean that if we focus on what is essential rather than on the means, we will have abundant means. For instance, if we focus on truth, we will have knowledge—the best of the land of Egypt—in abundance. Likewise, if we focus on goodness, we will have abundant truth.

We do need to care about knowledge and truth, but these must look to goodness as their purpose. When we keep our eye on goodness as a goal, we are able to see what follows from it; we are aware of the ramifications. That never happens unless goodness is the goal, unless it is dominant throughout the whole and all the individual parts.

[2] The situation is like the relationship between the body and its soul. We have every obligation to take care of our body, making sure it is nourished and clothed and has worldly pleasure to enjoy. The whole point, though, is the soul, not the body. The point is for the soul to function in a healthy body that responds properly, and to have the body as its fully obedient instrument. The soul will then be our purpose. Except that the soul will not be a final but only an intermediate purpose. We will take care of our soul not for its own sake but for the sake of services

5949

we then perform in both worlds. And when being useful is our goal, the Lord is our goal, because he disposes us to be useful and oversees the useful activity itself.

[3] Few know what having a final purpose is, so this needs explaining. Having something for a final purpose means loving it above all else. What we love, we have as our purpose.

What we take as our purpose is easy to recognize, because it has overall control in us. It is constantly present, even when we seem to ourselves not to be thinking at all about it. It takes up residence in us and composes our inner life, so it secretly governs each and every thing in us. When people honor their parents at heart, for example, that honor is present in every single thing they do in their parents' presence and think in their parents' absence. Not only is it present, it is perceptible in their deeds and words. For people who fear and honor God from the heart, then, that fear and honor is present in everything they think, say, and do. It is present because it exists inside them even when it does not seem present, as for instance when they are engaged in unrelated business. It has control overall and therefore in every detail. What controls us is sensed plainly in the other world, because the whole aura of our life, wafting from us, originates in it.

[4] This shows how to understand the idea that we ought to have God before our eyes at all times. It does not mean that we need to think about him constantly but that fear of him or else love for him must reign supreme throughout our being. Under those circumstances we have God before our eyes every step of the way, and when we do, we do not think, speak, or do anything against him or anything displeasing to him. If we do transgress, that deeply hidden, universally reigning principle reveals itself and warns us.

5950   Genesis 45:21, 22, 23. *And Israel's sons did so, and Joseph gave them wagons, according to Pharaoh's word. And he gave them provisions for the road. And to them all he gave changes of clothes, [one] each. And to Benjamin he gave three hundred pieces of silver and five changes of clothes. And to his father he sent as follows: ten male donkeys carrying some of the best of Egypt, and ten female donkeys carrying grain and bread, and sustenance for his father for the road.*

And Israel's sons did so symbolizes what was accomplished by spiritual truth on the earthly plane. *And he gave them wagons, according to Pharaoh's word* means that they received teachings from the inner dimension, as was pleasing. *And he gave them provisions for the road* symbolizes being nourished by goodness and truth in the meanwhile. *And to them all he gave changes of clothes, [one each]* symbolizes truth introduced to goodness. *And to Benjamin he gave three hundred pieces of silver* means that the middle ground received a full amount of truth based on goodness. *And five changes of clothes* symbolizes a great deal of earthly-level truth. *And to his father he sent as follows* symbolizes something given for free to spiritual goodness. *Ten male donkeys carrying some of the best of Egypt* symbolizes better knowledge, along with a great deal of subservient information. *And ten female donkeys carrying grain and bread* symbolizes truth-from-goodness and goodness-from-truth, also with a great deal of subservient information. *And sustenance for his father for the road* symbolizes inner truth for spiritual goodness in the meantime.

And Israel's sons did so symbolizes what was accomplished by spiritual truth on the earthly plane. This can be seen from the symbolism of *they did* as accomplishment and from the representation of *Israel's sons* as spiritual truth on the earthly plane, as discussed in §§5414, 5879.

5951

Spiritual truth on the earthly plane needs to be defined. Religious truth outside a person, spirit, or angel is not religious truth, because it has not been attached to anyone capable of believing it, which turns it into truth. However, when it is attached to a person, spirit, or angel capable of believing, it does become religious truth, with differences according to everyone's state of life. In people who are first learning this kind of truth, it consists of mere knowledge. In people who later develop awed respect for such truth, it advances further and becomes the church's truth. In people who are touched by it and live by it, though, it becomes spiritual truth. A loving, charitable goodness, which comes only from the spiritual world, then permeates it and brings it alive. The capacity to be touched by truth and live by it comes from this goodness.

[2] I was shown what the kind of truth called religious truth is like in people who do and do not live by it. In people who do not live by this truth, it looked like white threads. In people who had this truth but no goodness, the threads looked breakable. In people who live by it, on the other hand, it looked like fibers from the brain, filled with fluid, and soft. The latter kind of truth consequently was animated, but the former kind was lifeless. This shows that the quality of truth in people depends on each individual's state of life.

The truth represented by Jacob's sons is truth that is not yet spiritual because it has not yet become part of life. The truth represented by them as Israel's sons, though, is spiritual, because it has become a part of life and is therefore imbued with a loving, charitable goodness.

Such truth is meant here, because by now the text has dealt with the introduction of truth on the earthly level (Jacob's sons) to union with inner goodness (Joseph) through a middle ground (Benjamin) and also through spiritual goodness (Israel).

5952 *And he gave them wagons, according to Pharaoh's word* means that [they received] teachings from the inner dimension, as was pleasing, which the following shows: Joseph, the one who *gave,* represents inner goodness, as noted before. *Wagons* symbolize teachings, as discussed above in §5945. And *according to Pharaoh's word* means as was pleasing—pleasing to spiritual truth (Israel's sons), since this truth lies on the earthly level, represented by *Pharaoh* (§§5160, 5799), and since the wagons, symbolizing teachings, were given to them to use as they wished.

Here is the reason for saying "as was pleasing": The teachings symbolized by Egypt's wagons come from the Word's literal meaning (§5945), which can be adapted to any good endeavor, without reference to the inner meaning. The Lord never teaches us the truth openly but uses goodness to lead us to wonder what is true. Although we are unaware of it, he also inspires us to sense that something is true and then to adopt it because the Word says so and because it makes sense. In this way the Lord matches truth to the acceptance of goodness in every individual. The level of acceptance depends on everyone's preferences and therefore on freedom, which is the reason for saying "as was pleasing" here.

5953 *And he gave them provisions for the road* symbolizes being nourished by goodness and truth in the meanwhile. This is indicated by the symbolism of *provisions* as nourishment by goodness and truth, discussed at §5490.

5954 *And to them all he gave changes of clothes, [one] each* symbolizes truth introduced to goodness. This is established by the symbolism of *clothes* as truth, discussed below. *Changes of clothes,* then, are truth that is new, and truth becomes new when it is introduced to goodness, because it then receives life. The subject here is the union of the earthly and spiritual selves, or outer and inner selves. When they unite, truth changes into something new, because it receives life from an inflow of goodness; see just above at §5951. Changing clothes was an act representing the need to put on sacred truth, which gave rise to ceremonial clothes, [or "clothes for changing"]; see §4545.

[2] Clothes in the Word symbolize truth because truth clothes goodness, in almost the same way as blood vessels sheathe their blood, or as nerve fibers sheathe their fluid.

The reason clothing is a symbol for truth is that spirits and even angels appear wearing clothes that match the truth they individually possess. Those intent on the religious truth that leads to goodness appear in white. Those intent on the religious truth that *grows out of* goodness, though, appear in radiant, dazzling white, because the goodness gleams out through the truth, creating radiance; see §5248.

[3] The Word, where it mentions angels who are seen, also shows that spirits and angels appear wearing clothes. In Matthew, for instance:

> The appearance of the angel sitting at the Lord's tomb was like lightning, and his *clothing, white as snow.* (Matthew 28:3)

In John:

> On the thrones I saw twenty-four elders sitting, *dressed in white clothes.* (Revelation 4:4)

In the same author:

> The one sitting on the white horse *was dressed in a garment dyed with blood,* and his name is called God's Word. His armies in heaven followed him on white horses, *dressed in fine linen, white* and *clean.* (Revelation 19:11, 13, 14)

Clothes as white as snow and fine, white linen symbolize sacred truth, because white is used to describe truth (§§3301, 3993, 4007, 5319). After all, white comes close to the color of light, and light from the Lord is divine truth. That is why the Lord's clothes looked like the light when he was transfigured, as described in Matthew:

> When Jesus was transfigured, his face shone like the sun, and *his clothes became like the light.* (Matthew 17:2)

The fact that light is divine truth is known in the church, but the fact that light is equated with clothing can be seen in David:

> Jehovah covers himself with the *light* as *clothing.* (Psalms 104:2)

[4] The meaning of clothes as truth is plain from many passages in the Word, as for example in Matthew:

> The king, having gone in to look at the people reclining, sees there a person *not dressed in a wedding garment.* And he said to the person,

"Friend, how did you come in here *not having a wedding garment?*" So the person was cast out into outer darkness. (Matthew 22:11, 12, 13)

For who is meant by a person not dressed in a wedding garment, see §2132. In Isaiah:

Wake up! Wake up! Put on your strength, Zion! *Put on your finest clothes,* Jerusalem, you holy city, because the uncircumcised and unclean will not come into you any longer. (Isaiah 52:1)

The "finest clothes" stand for truth rising out of goodness. [5] In Ezekiel:

I clothed you with embroidery and gave you shoes of badger and *swathed you in fine linen* and *covered you in silk. Your clothes were fine linen and silk* and *embroidery.* Flour, honey, and oil you ate. (Ezekiel 16:10, 13)

This is about Jerusalem. In this case Jerusalem means the ancient church, a spiritual religion established by the Lord after the earliest church, which was a heavenly religion, had breathed its last. The truth with which that church was gifted is depicted as clothes. The embroidery means knowledge, and when the knowledge is sound, it even appears in the other world as embroidery and lace, as I was allowed to see. Fine linen and silk mean truth rising out of goodness, but in heaven, where heavenly light shines on it, this truth is even shinier than usual, and transparent. [6] In the same author:

Fine linen with embroidery from Egypt was what you spread out, and *blue-violet* and *red-violet fabric* from the islands of Elishah were *your covering.* (Ezekiel 27:7)

This is about Tyre, which represents inner knowledge, the knowledge of what is true and good (§1201). Sound knowledge of this type is the fine linen with embroidery from Egypt. The resulting goodness—truth-based goodness—is the blue-violet and red-violet fabric. [7] In David:

All glorious is the king's daughter; *her clothing is made of gold braid.* In *embroidery* she will be brought to the *king.* (Psalms 45:13, 14)

The king's daughter stands for a desire for truth. "Her clothing is made of gold braid" stands for truth that contains goodness. The embroidery stands for the lowliest kind of truth. In John:

You have a few names in Sardis *who have not defiled their clothes* and will walk with me *in white* because they are worthy. Those who conquer *will be dressed in white clothes.* (Revelation 3:4, 5)

Not defiling one's clothes stands for not contaminating truth with falsity. [8] In the same author:

> Fortunate are those who are watchful and *keep their clothes,* to avoid walking naked and letting others see their shame. (Revelation 16:15)

Again the clothes stand for truth. Strictly speaking, it is religious truth from the Word that clothes symbolize. People need to acquire truth from the Word—or something resembling truth from their religion, as non-Christians do—and apply it to life, or they do not have goodness, no matter how much they think they do. Because they have no truth from the Word or from their religion, they let themselves be led as readily by the reasonings of evil spirits as by those of good spirits. Angels cannot protect them then. That is what is meant by the need to be watchful and keep one's clothes, to avoid walking naked and letting others see one's shame. [9] In Zechariah:

> Joshua was *in defiled garments;* he was standing in them before the angel, who said to those standing before him, "*Take the defiled garments off him.*" But to [Joshua] he said, "Look! I have made your wickedness pass from you, *dressing you in ceremonial clothing.*" (Zechariah 3:3, 4)

Defiled garments stand for truth sullied by the falsity that comes of evil. So when those clothes had been removed and other clothes had been put on him, it says, "Look! I have made your wickedness pass from you." Anyone can see that changing clothes does not make wickedness pass away, so anyone can also draw the conclusion that changing clothes was a representational act. It was like the *washing of clothes* that was commanded when people were being purified, as for instance when they approached Mount Sinai (Exodus 19:14) or when they were being cleansed of various taints (Leviticus 11:25, 40; 14:8, 9; Numbers 8:6, 7; 19:21; 31:19–24).

[10] Religious truth is what cleanses us of contamination, because it teaches us what goodness, neighborly love, the neighbor, and faith are, and that the Lord, heaven, and eternal life exist. Without the truth to teach us, we cannot know what these are, or even that they exist. On our own, we cannot help thinking that only the goodness of self-love and the goodness of materialism benefit us, because both kinds of goodness are the central pleasures of our life. Without religious truth, how can we see that we are capable of other kinds of goodness, the goodness of love for God and the goodness of charity toward our neighbor? How can we see that these kinds of goodness hold heavenly life? That they flow into

us from the Lord through heaven only to the extent that we do not love ourselves above others or love the world above heaven?

This discussion shows that the purification once represented by the washing of clothes takes place by means of religious truth.

5955 *And to Benjamin he gave three hundred pieces of silver* means that the middle ground received a full amount of truth based on goodness, as the following shows: *Benjamin* represents the middle ground, as mentioned in §§[5411, 5413, 5443,] 5639, 5688, 5822. Joseph, who *gave* the money, represents inner goodness, as discussed in §§5826, 5827, 5869, 5877. *Three hundred* symbolizes a full amount, as discussed below. And *silver* symbolizes truth, as treated of in §§1551, 2954, 5658. This makes it plain that *to Benjamin he gave three hundred pieces of silver* means that he bestowed on the middle ground a full amount of truth based on goodness. The middle ground, represented by Benjamin, consists in inner truth received by an inflow from inner heavenliness (§§5600, 5631).

The reason *three hundred* means a full amount is that it is the product of three times one hundred, and three symbolizes what is complete (§§2788, 4495), while one hundred symbolizes a large amount (§4400). The significance of a multiple number can be seen from its factors.

[2] Three hundred has the same meaning when it is mentioned elsewhere in the Word. Noah's ark, for example, was three hundred cubits long (Genesis 6:15), and Gideon struck Midian with three hundred men, as told in Judges:

> The number of those lapping with their hand to their mouth was *three hundred men.* Jehovah said to Gideon, "By the *three hundred men* who were lapping I will give Midian into your hand." Gideon divided the *three hundred men* into *three companies* and put a horn into the hand of each of them, and empty water jugs, and torches in the middle of the jugs. When they blew on the *three hundred horns,* Jehovah set the sword of a man against his companion and against the whole camp. (Judges 7:6, 7, 8, 16, 22)

The three hundred men here also symbolize a full amount, as do the three companies into which the three hundred were divided. The hundred that made up each company symbolizes a large amount, and enough, and therefore means that they had sufficient numbers against Midian.

Furthermore, all the details there represent something—the fact that the men who were accepted were the ones who lapped water with their hand, that each had a horn, that they had water jugs with torches inside.

This was because Midian, their opponent, represented truth that is actually untrue because it is unaccompanied by active goodness. These details will be discussed elsewhere, however, with the Lord's divine mercy. The fact that numbers were also representational is clear in many other passages. For example, the number seven represented something in the Book of Joshua at the point where the Israelites seized Jericho. It was commanded then that *seven priests* carry *seven horns* of jubilee before the ark, and that on the *seventh day* they were to circle the city *seven times* (Joshua 6:4).

And five changes of clothes symbolizes a great deal of earthly-level truth. This can be seen from the symbolism of *five* as much (discussed at §5708) and from that of *changes of clothes* as truth introduced to goodness. The reason it is truth on the earthly plane is that clothes have to do with what is earthly.

5956

The middle ground, represented by Benjamin, received *earthly*-level truth because in order to be a middle ground it has to partake of the inner plane and the outer plane (§5822). The influence of the inner plane is meant by the middle ground's receiving a full amount of truth-from-goodness, as symbolized by the three hundred pieces of silver discussed just above at §5955. The influence of the outer plane is meant by its receiving a great deal of earthly-level truth, as symbolized by the five changes of clothes.

And to his father he sent as follows symbolizes something given for free to spiritual goodness. This is clear from the representation of Israel, the *father,* as spiritual goodness on the earthly level (as in §§5801, 5803, 5807, 5812, 5817, 5819, 5826, 5833) and from the symbolism of *sending* as giving for free. Everything that flows from the Lord through the inner dimension into the outer, earthly dimension is given for free. Likewise everything that flows the same way into the spiritual goodness that is Israel, since this kind of goodness is on the earthly level.

5957

It is true that the Lord demands humility, worship, gratitude, and so on from us. These look like repayment, so the gift does not seem free. But it is not for his sake that the Lord demands these things. Our humility, worship, and gratitude add no glory to one who is divine. Any trace of the self-love that seeks such gestures on its own behalf is unthinkable in the Divine. No, it is for our own sake. When we are humble, we can accept goodness from the Lord, because we are then detached from self-love and the evil it spawns, which stand in the way. The Lord therefore desires a humble attitude in us on our behalf, because when we have that attitude, the Lord can flow in with heavenly goodness. The same applies to worship and gratitude.

5958   *Ten male donkeys carrying some of the best of Egypt* symbolizes knowledge, along with a great deal of subservient information, as the following shows: *Ten* symbolizes a large amount, as noted in §§3107, 4638, 5708. *Donkeys* symbolize knowledge, as noted in §5741, and here they symbolize the lowliest types of knowledge, described in §5934. Because they "carry" what is inner, they are subservient. And the *best of Egypt* symbolizes knowledge, as above at §§5942, 5949, but religious knowledge, since this is the knowledge Egypt properly symbolizes (§§4749, 4964, 4966). Knowledge is the best of Egypt because Joseph sent it to Israel; that is, inner heavenliness sent it to spiritual goodness.

5959   *And ten female donkeys carrying grain and bread* symbolizes truth-from-goodness and goodness-from-truth, also with a great deal of subservient information, as the following shows. *Ten* symbolizes a large amount, as above at §5958. *Donkeys* symbolize subservient information, again as above at §5958. *Grain* symbolizes goodness-from-truth, as discussed in §§5295, 5410, but here it symbolizes truth-from-goodness, because it comes from inner heavenliness, or Joseph. And *bread* symbolizes goodness belonging to that truth, as discussed in §§276, 680, 2165, 2177, 3478, 3735, 4211, 4217, 4735, 4976.

Why does grain symbolize truth-from-goodness in one place and goodness-from-truth in another? Symbolism differs, depending on whether the text is dealing with the inflow of the heavenly level or of the spiritual level. From the heavenly level flows nothing but goodness. The goodness does contain truth, but this truth is a form of goodness. From the spiritual level, on the other hand, flows nothing but truth. When this truth becomes part of a person's life, it is called goodness-from-truth. That is why grain sometimes symbolizes goodness-from-truth and sometimes truth-from-goodness. It symbolizes truth-from-goodness here because it is coming from inner heavenliness, which is Joseph.

Why did the female donkeys carry grain and bread and the male donkeys carry the best of Egypt? Male donkeys symbolize subservient information of a kind that relates to truth, while female donkeys symbolize subservient information of a kind that relates to goodness. The male donkeys' load therefore suited them, and the female donkeys' load suited them. Otherwise there would have been no point in mentioning that there were male and female donkeys and identifying what each carried.

And sustenance for his father for the road symbolizes inner truth for **5960**
spiritual goodness in the meantime, as the following shows: *Sustenance*
symbolizes inner truth, which rises out of the truth-from-goodness and
goodness-from-truth symbolized by the grain and bread (just above in
§5959). Besides which, inner truth is the sustenance of spiritual goodness.
Israel, the *father,* represents spiritual goodness, as noted above at §5957.
And *for the road* means in the meantime, before Israel arrived—that is,
before full union took place.

    Genesis 45:24, 25, 26, 27, 28. *And he sent his brothers off, and they went.* **5961**
And he said to them, "You are not to quarrel on the way." And they went up
from Egypt and came to the land of Canaan, to Jacob their father. And they
told him, saying, "Joseph is still alive," and that he was ruling in all the land
of Egypt. And his heart failed, because he did not believe them. And they
spoke to him all Joseph's words that he had spoken to them. And he saw the
wagons that Joseph had sent to bear him, and the spirit of Jacob their father
revived. And Israel said, "A great thing! Joseph my son is still alive; I will go
and see him before I die."

    And he sent his brothers off, and they went symbolizes concealment. *And*
he said to them, "You are not to quarrel on the way," symbolizes a perception granted, leaving them calm. *And they went up from Egypt* symbolizes
withdrawal from religious knowledge. *And came to the land of Canaan, to*
Jacob their father, symbolizes a dwelling place alongside earthly goodness,
not spiritual goodness. *And they told him, saying,* symbolizes an inflow
and awareness. *Joseph is still alive* means that the inner dimension had not
been rejected. *And that he was ruling in all the land of Egypt* means that
the earthly mind is under its authority. *And his heart failed, because he*
did not believe them symbolizes faintness of earthly life and consequently
of the intellect. *And they spoke to him all Joseph's words that he had spoken*
to them symbolizes an inflow of spiritual heavenliness. *And he saw the*
wagons that Joseph had sent to bear him symbolizes teachings from that
source, which were persuasive. *And the spirit of Jacob their father revived*
symbolizes fresh life. *And Israel said,* symbolizes spiritual goodness at this
point. *A great thing! Joseph my son is still alive* symbolizes joy that the inner
dimension had not been destroyed. *I will go and see him before I die* symbolizes a longing for union before a new state begins.

    And he sent his brothers off, and they went symbolizes concealment, as **5962**
the following shows: *Sending them off* symbolizes removing them from
himself and in consequence no longer being present in the same way with

them. *Going,* or leaving, symbolizes living, living at a distance from, and abandoning (as discussed at §§3335, 3416, 3690, 4882, 5493, 5605), so it symbolizes being concealed.

The inner meaning of what follows shows that the current theme is removal from inner heavenliness and accordingly its concealment.

[2] If you do not know what the conditions of life are like for spirits and angels in the heavens, you also cannot know why the text is now talking about the concealment of truth and goodness, when these had just been shedding their light on everything. Conditions in heaven are that spirits and angels there have morning, afternoon, and evening, then twilight and morning again, over and over. Their morning comes when the Lord is present and blesses them with obvious happiness, at which time they dwell in a perception of what is good. Their afternoon comes when they enjoy the light of truth. Their evening comes when they are separated from these boons, because it then looks to them as though the Lord is farther away and hidden from them. All who are in heaven undergo and pass through these cycles; otherwise they could not constantly improve. The cycles provide them with contrasts, which provide them with better powers of perception, because from the experience they know what is less than happy, having discovered what is less than good and less than true.

[3] What is remarkable is that one state is never exactly the same as another to eternity. Neither does one spirit or angel run through the same changes of state as another, because none has the same goodness and truth as another, any more than one person has the same face as another. Still, the Lord brings unity out of this variety. It is a universal rule that any unified whole with its own characteristics is made up of varied parts, these parts being reduced to such complete unison by harmonious agreement that the whole range of individuals appears as one. In the heavens the resulting oneness or unity is brought about by love and charity. See also §§3241, 3267, 3744, 3745, 3986, 4005, 4149, 5598.

[4] The concealment symbolized by *Joseph sent his brothers off, and they went* is referred to in the Word as evening. For angels, evening falls when they do not sense the Lord as present. Heaven has a constant awareness of the Lord. When angels are in a state devoid of awareness, they do not feel touched by goodness or see truth, as they did before, and this distresses them. A half-light dawns shortly afterward, though, and morning follows.

5963   *And he said to them, "You are not to quarrel on the way,"* symbolizes a perception granted, leaving them calm. This can be seen from the symbolism of *saying to them* as a perception granted by the inner dimension, which is Joseph (as discussed many times), and from the symbolism of *not quarreling on the way* as a resulting calmness. Strife with others is anything but calm, since it is emotional turbulence.

Varying conditions in the other world, described just above in §5962, depend on the inhabitants' perception of goodness and truth and so depend on a perception of the Lord's presence. The inhabitants have serenity in the same measure they have that perception, because people with a perception of the Lord's presence perceive that all events in their life without exception contribute to their welfare. They also perceive that evil does not touch them. So they are tranquil. Without this faith or trust in the Lord no one can possibly achieve peace and calm, or consequently joy and bliss, since joy and bliss reside in peace and calm.

And they went up from Egypt symbolizes withdrawal from religious knowledge, as the following shows: *Going up* from there symbolizes withdrawing. People are said to go up from Egypt to the land of Canaan and to go down from Canaan to Egypt for the reason given several times before. In this case going up means leaving. And strictly speaking, *Egypt* symbolizes religious knowledge, as discussed in §§4749, 4964, 4966. That is the kind of knowledge symbolized here because that is what [the brothers] had when they were with Joseph in Egypt (§5958).

5964

What the chapter is talking about from here to the final verse is detachment from any concern with goodness and truth, or from religious considerations. Such detachment is meant by the concealment above at §5962 and the withdrawal here. The state is symbolized in the Word by evening. When people are in this state, they move away from what is heavenly and spiritual and move toward interests devoid of anything heavenly or spiritual. The concealment or withdrawal is brought about not by the Lord's hiding or withdrawing but by the withdrawing or hiding of the people themselves. It is impossible—because it is inappropriate—for them to be held back from self-centeredness any longer. This stage therefore arrives when people are left to themselves and their own devices. The more they are abandoned to or immersed in self-direction, the more they find that the qualities of heaven withdraw, goodness becomes imperceptible, and truth grows dim. Clearly, then, it is not the Lord who hides, but the person, spirit, or angel.

And came to the land of Canaan, to Jacob their father, symbolizes a dwelling place alongside earthly goodness, not spiritual goodness, as the following shows: The *land of Canaan* symbolizes the church (as stated

5965

in §§3686, 3705, 4447, 4517, 5136) and accordingly the dwelling place of the people who represented the church. That means Jacob's descendants, as everyone knows. And *Jacob* represents earthly goodness, as stated in §§3305, 3659, 3775, 4009, 4073, 4234, 4538. He does not represent spiritual goodness, because that is represented by Israel. For the representation of Jacob as the outer part of the church and of Israel as the inner part, see §§4286, 4570. (It does not matter whether you say earthly goodness or the outer part of the church, whether you say spiritual goodness or the inner part of the church, because earthly goodness constitutes the outer part of the church and spiritual goodness the inner part.)

[2] *Spiritual* is the term for what exists in heaven's light, because anything existing in that light contains within it a desire for what is good and a perception of what is true. This desire and perception exist in that light because it comes from the Lord. People with spiritual goodness and truth are consequently in the inner part of the church, because they have their heads in heaven.

Earthly, on the other hand, is the term for what exists in the world's light, and nothing existing in that light contains a desire for what is good or perception of what is true *inside itself,* only *outside itself.* Heaven's light flows into the earthly dimension and illuminates everything around it, so the light comes from the outside, not the inside. This light enables people to see that goodness is good and truth is true because they have been told so, but not because they perceive it. People with earthly goodness, then, are in the outer part of the church, because they do not have their heads in heaven; no, their heads are illuminated by heaven from outside.

Jacob is called Jacob rather than Israel at this point because [the people spoken of] currently live in what is external, as the discussion above makes plain.

5966   *And they told him, saying,* symbolizes an inflow and awareness, as the following shows: *Telling* symbolizes being communicated and united, as discussed at §§4856, 5596, so it symbolizes an inflow too, since what is told flows into the listener's thoughts. And *saying* in scriptural narrative symbolizes perception, as mentioned frequently, so it also symbolizes awareness.

5967   *Joseph is still alive* means that the inner dimension had not been rejected. This can be seen from the representation of *Joseph* as inner goodness (noted at §§5805, 5826, 5827, 5869, 5877) and from the symbolism of *being alive* as still existing and therefore as not having been rejected.

Being alive means not having been rejected because the inner dimension represented by Joseph had at first been rejected by Jacob's sons and at the time was believed by their father to have been destroyed by evil and falsity (§5828). Here, then, being alive means that this is not the case.

And that he was ruling in all the land of Egypt means that the earthly mind is under its authority. This can be seen from the symbolism of his *ruling* as being under his authority and from that of the *land of Egypt* as the earthly mind, discussed at §§5276, 5278, 5280, 5301.

5968

And his heart failed, because he did not believe them symbolizes faintness of earthly life and consequently of the intellect, as the following shows: *His heart failed* symbolizes faintness of life, and since it refers to Jacob, who represents earthly goodness (§5965), it symbolizes faintness of earthly life. And *not believing* symbolizes faintness of the intellect.

5969

I use the word "consequently" because the life of the will always comes first and the life of the intellect second. This is because life is present only in the will, not in the intellect except from the will. Proof is provided by goodness belonging to the will and truth belonging to the intellect: life is present in goodness but not in truth except from goodness. Clearly what lives is always primary and what borrows life is secondary. This is the reason for speaking about faintness of earthly life and consequently of the intellect, as symbolized by *his heart failed, because he did not believe them.*

And they spoke to him all Joseph's words that he had spoken to them symbolizes an inflow of spiritual heavenliness. This can be seen from the symbolism of *speaking* as an inflow (discussed in §§2951, 5481, 5797) and from the representation of *Joseph* as spiritual heavenliness (discussed in §§4286, 4592, 4963, 5307, 5331, 5332, 5417).

5970

And he saw the wagons that Joseph had sent to bear him symbolizes teachings from that source, which were persuasive. This can be seen from the symbolism of *wagons* as teachings (discussed in §§5945, 5952), *that Joseph had sent* as what came from inner heavenliness, and to *bear him* as what was persuasive. Bearing Jacob to Joseph to see him means persuading Jacob. The sight of the wagons also persuaded him, as demonstrated by the next phrases, "The spirit of Jacob their father revived, and Israel said, 'A great thing! Joseph my son is still alive.'"

5971

And the spirit of Jacob their father revived symbolizes fresh life. This can be seen from the symbolism of *his spirit revived* as fresh life and from the representation of *Jacob* as earthly goodness, mentioned at §5965. *The spirit of Jacob revived,* then, symbolizes fresh life for earthly goodness.

5972

Life is renewed when a spiritual inflow from the inner dimension acts on the contents of the earthly plane from within. Earthly goodness then becomes spiritual, connected with the spiritual goodness represented by

Israel. That is why the text now calls Jacob Israel, saying, "the spirit of Jacob revived, and Israel said."

5973   *And Israel said,* symbolizes spiritual goodness at this point. This can be seen from the representation of *Israel* as spiritual goodness, as at §§5801, 5803, 5807, 5812, 5817, 5819, 5826, 5833. For a definition of the spiritual goodness that is Israel and the earthly goodness that is Jacob, see above at §5965.

People who do not know the Word's inner meaning cannot possibly see why Jacob should be called sometimes Jacob and sometimes Israel. A single chapter and even a single verse now uses one name and now the other. This shows plainly that the Word has an inner meaning. Here, for instance, it says, "The spirit of *Jacob* their father revived, and *Israel* said." Likewise in other places, such as these:

> Benjamin, Joseph's brother, *Jacob* did not send with his brothers, and *Israel's* sons came in the midst of those coming. (Genesis 42:4, 5)

> And *Israel* set out. God said to *Israel* in visions at night, *"Jacob! Jacob!"* and he said, "Here I am." (Genesis 46:1, 2)

> *Jacob* rose from Beer-sheba, and the sons of *Israel* bore *Jacob* their father. (Genesis 46:5)

> All the souls of the house of *Jacob* coming to Egypt: seventy. Joseph hitched his chariot and went up to meet *Israel.* And *Israel* said to Joseph, . . . (Genesis 46:27, 29, 30)

> *Israel* settled in the land of Egypt, in the land of Goshen. *Jacob* lived in the land of Egypt seventeen years. And *Israel's* days for dying came near. (Genesis 47:27, 28, 29)

> And they told *Jacob* and said, "Look: your son Joseph has come to you." And *Israel* braced himself and sat up on the bed, and *Jacob* said to Joseph, . . . (Genesis 48:2, 3)

> *Jacob* called his sons and said, "Assemble and listen, sons of *Jacob;* listen to *Israel* your father." (Genesis 49:1, 2)

And in the same chapter:

> A curse on their anger because it is fierce and on their wrath because it is hard! I will divide them in *Jacob* and scatter them in *Israel.* (Genesis 49:7)

And:

> His arms and hands will be strengthened by the hands of *strong Jacob*, from whom comes the Shepherd, the *Stone of Israel*. (Genesis 49:24)

Not to mention frequent occurrences in the Prophets.

A great thing! Joseph my son is still alive symbolizes joy that the inner dimension had not been destroyed. This is indicated by the representation of Joseph as inner heavenliness and by the symbolism of *living* as not having been destroyed or rejected, as above at §5967. The joy is obvious. **5974**

I will go and see him before I die symbolizes a longing for union before a new state begins, as the following shows: *Going and seeing* symbolizes being united. *Seeing* means this because inner sight in the spiritual world unites. Inner sight is thought, and when many people act as one in the other world, in their communities and also in choruses, one individual's thoughts are the same as another's. So thought unites them. In addition, when someone thinks of anyone else, that other becomes present, which also forms a bond. This is why *going and seeing* symbolizes union. The fact that a *longing* for union is meant flows from the joy mentioned directly above at §5974. And *before I die* means before a new state begins—before a new representation. In the Word, representational roles evolve, so that when one person dies another takes up the same role or a similar one. Either that or the role itself changes. As a result there is a new state, as detailed in §§3253, 3259, 3276. Isaac, for instance, took up Abraham's representation when Abraham died, Jacob took up Isaac's when Isaac died, and Jacob's descendants took up his when he died. This is the new state meant. **5975**

The Angels and Spirits with Us (Continued)

AT the end of the previous chapter, I showed that we each have with us two spirits from hell and two angels from heaven, who provide us with communication from both realms and give us freedom [§§5848, 5849, 5854]. **5976**

5977   The reason we have two is that there are two kinds of spirits in hell and two kinds of angels in heaven, corresponding to the two human capacities of will and intellect.

The first type of spirit is simply called a *spirit,* and spirits act on the contents of our intellect. The second type is called a *demon,* and demons act on the contents of our will. They are quite easy to tell apart. The ones simply called spirits pour falsity into us by reasoning against truth. They find their highest pleasure in making truth appear false and falsity appear true. The ones called demons, however, pour evil into us, acting on our desires and cravings. They instantly sniff out what we long for. If we want what is good, they cleverly turn it in a bad direction. They find their highest pleasure in making us sense goodness as bad and evil as good.

The demons were given permission to act on my desires, so that I could see what their character is like and how they operate. I can confess that had the Lord not protected me with angels, they would have twisted my yearnings into a desire for evil, and done it so secretly and silently that I would barely have noticed.

The ones called demons have nothing in common with the ones called spirits. The former, the demons, do not care what we are thinking, only what we love. The latter, the spirits, do not care what we love, only what we are thinking. The demons enjoy staying quiet. The spirits enjoy talking. The two groups are also completely separate from each other. The demons are in the hells deep down at the back, where they are invisible to spirits. If anyone looks in on them, they appear as flitting shadows. The spirits are in the hells at the sides and in front.

This now is why we have two spirits from hell with us.

5978   The reason we have two angels with each of us is that they are also of two kinds, one acting on the contents of our will and the other on the contents of our intellect. The angels who act on the contents of our will act on the different kinds of love we have and on our purposes, so they act on what is good in us. The angels who act on the contents of our intellect act on our faith and our basic assumptions, so they act on the truth we know.

These two groups are also quite easy to tell apart. The ones who act on our will are called *heavenly angels,* while the ones who act on our intellect are called *spiritual angels.*

Heavenly angels are the opposite of demons, and spiritual angels are the opposite of spirits.

I have been able to gather this information from much experience, since I am in company and conversation with both kinds all the time.

People who possess faith think that they have nothing but angels from heaven with them, that devilish spirits have been totally removed from them. I can assure you, though, that any who are immersed in the cravings and pleasures of self-love and materialism and who hold these as their goals have devilish spirits so close as to be right inside them. These spirits control both the thoughts and feelings of such a person. Angels from heaven cannot be within the environment of such spirits, only outside it. In consequence they actually draw back as the hellish spirits draw close. **5979**

Still, angels from heaven never abandon us completely, because it would then be all over with us. If we were to lose communication with heaven through angels, we could not live.

[2] To some extent the religious teachings of the Christian churches acknowledge that hellish spirits and heavenly angels keep us company. Their theology states that everything good comes from God, and everything evil from the Devil. Preachers confirm this by praying from their pulpits for God to govern their thoughts and their words. They also say the following: During the process of becoming righteous, people's every effort down to the very smallest comes from God. When people live a good life, they are letting God lead them, and God sends angels to serve them. Conversely, when people have committed an outrageous evil, they have allowed the Devil to lead them, and the evil is from hell. The preachers would also have said that spirits from hell flow into our inner evils, evils of will and thought, if only they had acknowledged such evils as significant.

Angels are always carefully watching evil spirits' and demons' attempts and efforts with us. So far as we let them, the angels turn evil into goodness or take it to the edge of goodness or at the very least turn it in the direction of goodness. **5980**

Sometimes in the neighborhood of hellish spirits and demons there appear horrid, detestable sights, which are essentially the same as what an evil person thinks and says. Angels, who might otherwise flee the scene entirely because of these sights, perceive them as being milder than they really are. **5981**

In order for me to learn how angels perceive them, I was granted an angelic viewpoint when I came across various horrors, and my sense of them was such that I did not shudder at all. They were mitigated in a way that cannot be described. I can compare them only to sharp, pointy objects that have had their sharp edges and points removed.

That is how the horrid, detestable reality among hell's spirits and demons is blunted for angels.

5982   The Lord places us in balance between evil and goodness, between falsity and truth, through the presence of evil spirits on one side and of angels on the other. This provides us with freedom. In order to be saved, we have to experience freedom and be led freely away from evil toward goodness. Whatever does not happen in freedom does not remain, because we do not make it our own.

The freedom results from the balance in which we are kept.

5983   As noted [§5976], the two spirits and two angels put us in contact with hell and heaven. This can be seen from the fact that one community in the next world cannot communicate with another, or with any individual, except through spirits sent out by members of the community. These emissary spirits are called delegates, because the community speaks through them as its representatives.

It is quite common in the next life to send delegates to other communities to procure contact with them for one's own community. I gained sure knowledge of the practice myself from the delegates sent to me a thousand times. Without them, a community's members had no way of knowing what was happening with me or of letting me know what was happening with them.

This shows that the spirits and demons with us are delegates who enable communication with hell and that heavenly and spiritual angels are delegates who enable communication with the heavens.

5984   When spirits in the world of spirits want to make contact with a number of communities, they usually send one delegate to each. But I observed that evil spirits send a large number of spirits out all around and set them up the way a spider sets up its web, with themselves at the center. To my surprise, they know how to do this from a kind of instinct, because people who knew nothing about the tactic during bodily life engage in it without hesitation in the other life.

This evidence too shows that emissary spirits facilitate communication.

5985   A delegate is someone in whom the thoughts and words of others are concentrated and in whom many are therefore presented as one. Delegates do not think or say anything at all on their own, only on behalf of others, and others' thoughts and words find living expression in them. As a result, the spirits who are flowing into a delegate suppose that the delegate is almost nothing, scarcely animate, a mere container for their thoughts and speech. Delegates in turn suppose that they think and speak on their own behalf alone, not on behalf of others. Illusion fools both parties.

I have often been allowed to tell delegates that they do not think or say anything on their own, only on behalf of others. I have also said that those others imagine the delegates to be incapable of thinking or speaking on their own, so that they see the delegates as lacking any intrinsic life. One delegate grew highly incensed on hearing it, but to convince him of the truth, I was allowed to speak with the spirits flowing into him. These spirits said that a delegate absolutely does not think or speak on his or her own, and they then confessed that in consequence delegates hardly seem to them like animate objects.

On one occasion a spirit who said delegates were nothing was made into one himself, and the others then said of him that *he* was nothing, which enraged him. Even so, the experience taught him how matters really stand.

It is worth mentioning how often I was shown by practical experiment that no one in either heaven or hell thinks, speaks, wishes, or acts autonomously. I was shown that we do so only because of others and so, in the end, because of the general inflow of the life force originating in the Lord.

5986

I have heard spirits saying that their delegate was thinking and saying nothing independently and that the delegate nonetheless fancied she or he was operating with complete independence. Many of those times I have had the chance to talk with the spirits flowing into the delegate. They have asserted that they were thinking and speaking on their own and that the delegate was not. Since they too imagined they were thinking and speaking on their own, I was allowed to tell them that this is an illusion, that like the delegate they were actually thinking and speaking on behalf of others. In order to prove it, I was allowed to talk with the spirits flowing into *them*. When these made the same claim, I was allowed to talk with the spirits flowing into them in turn, and so on in a constant chain. This evidence clarified that each of them thought and spoke under the influence of others.

The experience roused tremendous indignation in the spirits, who each want to think and speak on their own; but it taught them what the true situation is. So I told them that every bit of thought and will flows into them. After all, there is only one life force, and it is the source of the capacities that life entails. Life flows from the Lord in an amazing form—the form of heaven—not only into all of them generally but also into each one individually. In every case the inflow varies with the form of the recipient, depending on its harmony or lack of harmony with the heavenly form. All this I told the spirits.

The same discussion also shows how the case stands with people on earth, which will be dealt with later, where the subject of spiritual inflow is addressed [§§6053–6058, 6189–6215, 6307–6327, 6466–6496, 6598–6626].

5987 The more spirits there are who focus on a single delegate, the stronger the delegate's power of thinking and speaking becomes. The power increases with the number of compatible spirits focusing on the delegate. This was once demonstrated to me by the removal of several spirits who were flowing in, which left the delegate with less power to think and speak.

5988 There were once some delegates near my head who talked as if they were asleep, though they still spoke properly, like people who are not in a state of sleep. I observed evil spirits flowing into the delegates and inspiring malicious lies, but their inflow into the delegates dissolved as soon as it arrived. The spirits flowing in knew that the delegates had previously been subject to them, so they complained that this was no longer so. The reason for the change was that good spirits could act on them now that they were asleep, and the good spirits' inflow dispelled the harmful intentions of the evil spirits.

The evil spirits were nevertheless restricted to flowing into these spirits, not others.

This made it clear that delegates come in a range of types and kinds and that the Lord oversees the variations.

5989 Some terribly deceitful spirits above my head once selected some delegates and sent them to me in order to flow into me with their lies but found themselves greatly disappointed. One spirit on being made a delegate recoiled, closed up, and curled into a ball in order to cast off the other spirits' inflow. That is how this spirit escaped their entanglements.

They then selected another, but this one too they could not force into speaking. The spirit was cleverer than they and revealed the fact by rolling up in a spiral shape, by which they were fooled.

Moreover, it is not always their companions that evil spirits send as delegates. Instead they watch to see which spirits are near others and where they might find spirits who are naive and compliant. These spirits they turn into delegates. They do so by directing their thoughts at the spirit and pouring their feelings and distorted convictions into him or her. The spirit loses any independence and instead serves the inflowing spirits as their agent. Sometimes the dominated spirit is not even aware this is happening.

There are many spirits today who want to flow into not only the thoughts and feelings of people on earth but also our words and deeds, which is to say our bodily level. However, our bodily level is immune to a narrowly targeted inflow from spirits and angels, being governed instead by general inflow. When we express our thoughts in speech and our intentions in action, the process of expressing them or carrying them over into the body follows a set protocol rather than being regulated in a specific way by any spirits. To flow into people's bodily level is to possess them.

Spirits who wish and intend this are those who had been adulterers during bodily life—that is, who took pleasure in adultery and persuaded themselves it was acceptable. People who had been cruel fall into the same category. The reason it is these two classes is that they are more body-centered and sense-oriented than the rest. So they have rejected any thought of heaven, attributing everything to nature and nothing to the Divine. In doing so they have closed off their inner reaches and opened up their outer level. Because everything they loved in the world was external, in the other world they long to return to it through us, by possessing us.

[2] However, the Lord in his providence makes sure spirits like this do not come into the world of spirits; they are kept firmly shut up in their hells. As a result there is no outward possession today. Inward possession does exist, though, and it too is practiced by the crew of hellish spirits and devils. After all, evil people on earth think despicable thoughts, contemplate savagery against others, and entertain ideas that are hostile and hateful to what is divine. These thoughts are restrained by fear of lost position, wealth, and consequent reputation, fear of punishment by the law, and fear for one's life, but if they were not, they would break out into the open. The people who hold the thoughts would then plunge as if possessed, or worse than possessed, into the destruction of others and into blasphemies against religion. The superficial restraints mentioned keep these people from appearing possessed, but although

they are not outwardly possessed, they are inwardly so. Their possession becomes obvious in the other life, where superficial restraints are taken away. There they are devils, endlessly experiencing the thrill and desire of destroying others and demolishing any remnant of religion.

5991   Some spirits who must be described as physical once appeared to me, rising up from deep down at the side of my right foot. To the eyes of my spirit they seemed to have a body made of coarse matter. When I asked who would look like this, I was told it was individuals who in the world had possessed genius and knowledge that they used to harden themselves completely against the Divine and therefore against the tenets of religion. They wholly convinced themselves that nature was responsible for everything, so they closed off their inner levels, the realm of the spirit, more than others do. That is why they appear so coarsely physical.

Among them was a man I knew when he was alive in the world. At the time he was rather famous for his intellectual gifts and his learning. These assets are a means for proper thinking on divine subjects, but he used them as a means for tearing divinity down in his thoughts and for persuading himself that it was nothing. One who excels in genius and education has more means of proof than others. He was consequently possessed inwardly, but on the outside he appeared to be a good, well-mannered citizen.

5992   The angels through whom the Lord leads and protects us are near our head. Their job is to inspire neighborly love and faith. They also watch the direction our pleasures take, taming them and bending them toward goodness so far as our freedom allows them to. They are not permitted to act violently, breaking our cravings and our assumptions, but must proceed gently. Another function they have is to control the evil spirits from hell, and they do it in countless ways, of which I may mention only this one: When evil spirits flood us with evil and falsity, angels instill truth and goodness. Even if we do not accept the truth and goodness, they use it to at least temper the evil and falsity. Hellish spirits constantly attack us, and angels protect us. That is the way of things.

[2] Most of all, angels regulate our desires, since these constitute our life and our freedom.

Angels watch to see whether hells that were not open before open up and flow into us, which happens when we take to some new evil. So far as we allow, angels shut off these hells and remove any spirits who try to emerge from them. They also dissipate any strange new inflows that have an evil effect.

[3] Above all, angels call on the goodness and truth we have and use it to block the evil and falsity stirred up by evil spirits. We stand in the middle and do not recognize either the evil or the goodness as such. Being in the middle, we are free to turn toward one or the other.

These are the kinds of ways angels from the Lord lead and safeguard us, which they do every moment and every fraction of a moment. If they stopped for only a second, we would plunge headlong into evil from which we could never again be led away.

In doing this work, angels are motivated by love they receive from the Lord. Nothing gives them more pleasure and happiness than removing evil from us and leading us to heaven. Luke 15:7 shows that this is a joy to them.

The Lord, then, takes utmost care of us, constantly, from the first thread of our life to its end and beyond to eternity; but hardly anyone believes it.

This discussion now shows that we must have two spirits from hell and two angels from heaven connected to us if we are to be in contact with the spiritual world, and that without them we would be entirely devoid of life. We simply cannot live entirely off general inflow, as animals, which are devoid of reason, do (discussed in §5850). The reason general inflow does not suffice is that our whole life force is opposed to the code ordained for us. This being so, if we were to act on general inflow alone, we could not avoid being driven only by the hells. We would not receive motivation from the heavens, and if not, we would have no inner life and therefore no thought or will of a human sort. We would not even have the thought and will a brute animal has, because we are born completely without the use of reason and cannot be initiated into it except under an inflow from the heavens.

[2] The considerations brought in above also show that we could not live without contact with the hells through spirits from there. Every bit of life we inherit from our parents and accrue on our own is characterized by self-love and materialism, not by love for our neighbor, let alone love for God. And since every bit of our own life is marked by self-love and materialism, it is also marked by contempt for others in comparison with ourselves, and by hatred and vengefulness against anyone who does not cater to us. Consequently it is marked by cruelty,

5993

because if we hate people, we want to kill them, so we also take the greatest possible delight in their ruin. These evils must be connected with compatible spirits, and such spirits cannot come from anywhere but hell. Unless such spirits were connected with these evils, and unless they led us in keeping with the greatest pleasures of our lives, we could never be turned toward heaven. What turns us at first is these very pleasures of ours, which place us in a position of freedom and eventually in a position to choose.

Genesis 46

1. And Israel set out, with everything he owned, and he came to Beer-sheba and offered sacrifices to the God of his father Isaac.

2. And God spoke to Israel in visions at night, and he said, "Jacob! Jacob!" and he said, "Here I am."

3. And he said, "I am God, the God of your father; don't be afraid of going down to Egypt, because I will turn you into a great nation there.

4. I myself will go down with you to Egypt, and I myself will most certainly bring you up. And Joseph will put his hand on your eyes."

5. And Jacob rose from Beer-sheba, and the sons of Israel bore Jacob their father and their little children and their women on the wagons that Pharaoh had sent to bear him.

6. And they took their livestock and their gain that they had gained in the land of Canaan and came to Egypt, Jacob and all his seed with him.

7. His sons and his sons' sons with him, his daughters and his sons' daughters, and all his seed he brought with him to Egypt.

8. And these are the names of Israel's sons as they came to Egypt, of Jacob and his sons: Jacob's firstborn, Reuben.

9. And the sons of Reuben: Enoch and Pallu and Hezron and Carmi.

10. And the sons of Simeon: Jemuel and Jamin and Ohad and Jachin and Zohar and Shaul the son of a Canaanite woman.

11. And the sons of Levi: Gershon and Kohath and Merari.

12. And the sons of Judah: Er and Onan and Shelah and Perez and Zerah. And Er and Onan died in the land of Canaan, and the sons of Perez were Hezron and Hamul.

13. And the sons of Issachar: Tola and Puvah and Job and Shimron.

14. And the sons of Zebulun: Sered and Elon and Jahleel.

15. These were Leah's sons, whom she bore to Jacob in Paddan-aram, along with Dinah his daughter. All the souls of his sons and his daughters: thirty-three.

16. And the sons of Gad: Ziphion and Haggi, Shuni and Ezbon, Eri and Arodi and Areli.

17. And the sons of Asher: Imnah and Ishvah and Ishvi and Beriah and Serah their sister. And the sons of Beriah: Heber and Malchiel.

18. These were the sons of Zilpah, whom Laban gave to Leah his daughter; and she bore these to Jacob: sixteen souls.

19. The sons of Rachel, Jacob's wife: Joseph and Benjamin.

20. And there were born to Joseph in the land of Egypt those whom Asenath, daughter of Potiphera (priest of On), bore to him: Manasseh and Ephraim.

21. And the sons of Benjamin: Bela and Becher and Ashbel, Gera and Naaman, Ehi and Rosh, Muppim and Huppim and Ard.

22. These were Rachel's sons, who were born to Jacob. All the souls: fourteen.

23. And the sons of Dan: Hushim.

24. And the sons of Naphtali: Jahzeel and Guni and Jezer and Shillem.

25. These were the sons of Bilhah, whom Laban gave to Rachel his daughter; and she bore these to Jacob. All the souls: seven.

26. Every soul of Jacob's as they came to Egypt, having issued from his thigh, besides the women of Jacob's sons, all the souls: sixty-six.

27. And Joseph's sons, who were born to him in Egypt: two souls. All the souls belonging to the house of Jacob as they came to Egypt: seventy.

28. And Judah he sent before him to Joseph, to show [the way] before him to Goshen, and they came to the land of Goshen.

29. And Joseph hitched his chariot and went up to meet Israel his father, to Goshen, and was seen by him and fell on his neck and wept on his neck a long time.

30. And Israel said to Joseph, "Let me die this time, now that I have seen your face, that you are still alive."

31. And Joseph said to his brothers and to his father's household, "I will go up and tell Pharaoh and say to him, 'My brothers and my father's household, who were in the land of Canaan, have come to me.

32. And the men are shepherds of the flock, because they are men of livestock. And their flocks and their herds and everything that is theirs they have brought.'

33. And it might happen that Pharaoh calls you and says, 'What is your work?'

34. And you are to say, 'Men of livestock your servants have been from their youth right till now, both we and our fathers,' so that you can

settle in the land of Goshen. Because every shepherd of the flock is abhorrent to Egyptians."

Summary

THIS chapter in an inner sense is about the union of inner heavenliness (Joseph) with spiritual goodness on the earthly plane (Israel). Next comes a list, in order, of the different kinds of religious truth and goodness with which a bond will then be formed (the children and grandchildren of Israel who came to Egypt). **5994**

Inner Meaning

GENESIS 46:1. *And Israel set out, with everything he owned, and he came to Beer-sheba and offered sacrifices to the God of his father Isaac.* **5995**

And Israel set out, with everything he owned symbolizes the beginning of union. *And he came to Beer-sheba* symbolizes neighborly love and faith. *And offered sacrifices to the God of his father Isaac* symbolizes the resulting worship and an inflow from the divine intellect.

And Israel set out, with everything he owned symbolizes the beginning **5996** of union. This is established by the symbolism of *setting out* as developments and a continuation (discussed in §§4375, 4882, 5493). In this case setting out symbolizes a continuation of and developments in the glorification of the Lord, who in the highest meaning is Israel and Joseph. In an inward sense setting out symbolizes a continuation of and developments in a person's rebirth. In the current chapter, which continues and develops the theme of union between the earthly and spiritual selves, or the outer and inner selves, *Israel set out, with everything he owned* symbolizes the beginning of union.

And he came to Beer-sheba symbolizes neighborly love and faith. This **5997** can be seen from the symbolism of *Beer-sheba* as teachings about neighborly love and faith, discussed in §§2858, 2859, 3466. Here Beer-sheba symbolizes neighborly love and faith themselves rather than theological teachings about them, because it comes up in relation to the spiritual goodness that is Israel. Spiritual goodness is more than theology, it is the source of theology. So people who achieve spiritual goodness have no more need for others to teach them. They have reached the goal for which they were aiming and have left the means behind—and theological teachings are nothing but means toward the goal of achieving goodness. This now is the reason Beer-sheba here symbolizes neighborly love and faith.

5998   *And offered sacrifices to the God of his father Isaac* symbolizes the resulting worship and an inflow from the divine intellect. This can be seen from the symbolism of *offering sacrifices* as worship (discussed in §§922, 923, 2180) and from the representation of *Isaac* in the highest sense as the Lord's divine rationality, or divine intellect (discussed in §§1893, 2066, 2072, 2083, 2630, 3012, 3194, 3210). It follows that the divine intellect flowed into the worship, because the worship meant here is worship based on neighborly love and faith, as symbolized by Beer-sheba (§5997), where Jacob sacrificed.

The fact that Jacob sacrificed to the God of his father Isaac indicates what the ancestors of the nation of Judah and Israel were like: they each worshiped their own God. Isaac's God was different from Jacob's, which is clear from the fact that Jacob sacrificed to Isaac's God and that in visions at night he was told, "I am God, the God of your father" [Genesis 46:3]. In addition, Jacob swore by Isaac's God, as is recorded in Genesis 31: "'Let the *God of Abraham* and the *God of Nahor* judge between us—the *God of their father.*' Then Jacob swore *on the Dread of his father Isaac*" (verse 53). Jacob also failed to acknowledge Jehovah at first. This can be seen from his saying, "If God is with me and guards me on this way that I am walking and gives me bread to eat and clothing to wear, and I return in peace to the house of my father, *Jehovah will become my God*" (Genesis 28:20, 21). So he acknowledged Jehovah only on a condition.

[2] Their practice was to acknowledge their fathers' gods but to have their own personal god. This custom they inherited from their ancestors in Syria, because Terah, Abram's father, and even Abram himself when he lived there worshiped other gods than Jehovah; see §§1356, 1992, 3667. By nature, then, their descendants who were named after Jacob or Israel offered their heartfelt worship to the gods of the surrounding nations. They worshiped Jehovah with their lips only and in name only. The reason

they did so was that they focused on the external level alone, apart from any inner content. People like that cannot help believing that worship consists exclusively in saying God's name and claiming that he is their God, as long as he helps them. They do not believe at all that worship consists in a life of neighborly love and faith.

Genesis 46:2, 3, 4. *And God spoke to Israel in visions at night, and he said, "Jacob! Jacob!" and he said, "Here I am." And he said, "I am God, the God of your father; don't be afraid of going down to Egypt, because I will turn you into a great nation there. I myself will go down with you to Egypt, and I myself will [most] certainly bring you up. And Joseph will put his hand on your eyes."* **5999**

And God spoke to Israel in visions at night symbolizes a dim revelation. *And he said, "Jacob! Jacob!"* means to earthly truth. *And he said, "Here I am,"* symbolizes awareness of it. *And he said, "I am God, the God of your father,"* symbolizes divine intellect, the source of the inflow. *Don't be afraid of going down to Egypt* means that earthly truth and everything connected with it must be introduced into religious knowledge. *Because I will turn you into a great nation* means that truth will turn into goodness. *I myself will go down with you to Egypt* symbolizes the presence of the Lord in that state. *And I myself will most certainly bring you up* symbolizes being lifted up afterward. *And Joseph will put his hand on your eyes* means that inner heavenliness will bestow life.

And God spoke to Israel in visions at night symbolizes a dim revelation. **6000**
This can be seen from the symbolism of *God spoke in visions* as a revelation. Revelations were made in one of the following ways: dreams, nighttime visions, daytime visions, an inner voice, an outer message delivered by angels who could be seen, or an outer message delivered by angels who could not be seen. In the Word these events symbolize revelations of various kinds, and a nighttime vision symbolizes a dim revelation. After all, night symbolizes what is dim (§§1712, 2514), and dimness in a spiritual sense means that truth is not visible. In the Word, night also symbolizes falsity produced by evil, because anyone who clings to falsity on the basis of evil is in the dark of night. As a result, everyone in hell is said to be in the night. The inhabitants do have illumination, because they can see each other, but the light is like that produced by a flameless coal fire, and it turns to shadow and darkness when heavenly light streams in. That is why hell's inhabitants are said to be in the night and why they are called angels of night and of darkness, while the inhabitants of heaven are called angels of day and of light.

[2] The meaning of *night* as dimness and as falsity can also be seen from the following passages in the Word. In John:

> Jesus said, "Are there not twelve hours in the day? If any walk *in the day,* they do not stumble, but if any walk *in the night,* they do stumble, because there is no light in them." (John 11:9, 10)

The twelve hours stand for all states marked by truth. Walking in the day stands for living in truth, and walking in the night for living in falsity. [3] In the same author:

> I have to do the work of him who sent me while it *is still day. The night,* in which no one can work, *is coming.* (John 9:4)

The day stands for truth growing out of goodness and the night for falsity growing out of evil. Day means the first period of a church, because that is when people accept truth, since they embrace goodness. Night means the final period, because that is when people do not accept any truth, since they do not embrace goodness. When people do not possess goodness—that is, charity for their neighbor—then even if you tell them absolute truth, they do not accept it. Under those circumstances it is simply impossible to perceive what is true, because truth's light then falls on bodily and worldly rather than heavenly matters. It is only what is bodily and worldly that people like this strive for, that they love and consider real. What is heavenly seems relatively trivial and worthless to them. The light of truth therefore becomes swallowed up and smothered by murk, just as sunlight is absorbed by anything black. That is what is symbolized by "The night, in which no one can work, is coming." Today is one of those periods. [4] In Matthew:

> The groom being late, all the young women slumbered and slept. *But in the middle of the night* a shout was raised: "Look! The groom is coming!" (Matthew 25:5, 6, 7)

The middle of the night too stands for the last days of the old religion, when faith is missing because neighborly love is missing, and for the first days of the new religion. In Luke:

> I say to you, *that night* there will be two on one bed; one will be accepted, the other left. (Luke 17:34)

Here too night stands for the final period of the old church and the first period of the new. [5] In Matthew:

> Jesus said to the disciples, "You will all stumble over me on *this night.*" And to Peter, "*On this night,* before the rooster has crowed, three times you will deny [knowing] me." (Matthew 26:31, 34)

The Lord chose to be captured at night, which meant that divine truth was as dark as night to [his captors] and that falsity rising out of evil stood in its place. Peter's three-time denial that night that he knew the Lord also represented the final days of the church, when religious truth is taught but is not believed. That era is the night, because the Lord is then thoroughly denied in human hearts. The twelve apostles, like the twelve tribes of Israel, represented all aspects of faith (§§577, 2089, 2129 at the end, 2130 at the end, 3272, 3354, 3488, 3858, 3913, 3926, 3939, 4060), and Peter represented faith on the part of the church (see the prefaces to Genesis 18 and 22, and §§3750, 4738). That is why the Lord said to Peter, "On this night, three times you will deny knowing me," and to the disciples, "You will all stumble over me on this night." [6] In Isaiah:

> One is shouting to me from Seir, "Guard, *what is [left] of the night?* Guard, *what is [left] of the night?*" The guard said, "Morning comes, *and also night.*" (Isaiah 21:11, 12)

This is about the Lord's Coming, which is morning. His arrival occurred when there was no spiritual truth on the earth any longer, which is night. [7] In Zechariah:

> There will be a single day, which is known to Jehovah, *not day or night,* because *around the time of evening* there will be light. It will happen on that day that living water will go out from Jerusalem. And Jehovah will become monarch over the whole earth. On that day Jehovah will be one, and his name one. (Zechariah 14:7, 8, 9)

This too is about the Lord and about a new religion. Where it says that Jehovah will become monarch, that Jehovah will be one, and that his name will be one, the meaning is that the Lord's divine humanity will be identical with divinity itself, which is called the Father. Before the Lord's Coming, divine humanity was Jehovah's presence in the heavens, because it was by passing through the heavens that he presented himself as a divine human to many people on earth. His divine humanity at that time was not as identical with the divinity itself called the Father as it was later when the Lord made them entirely one in himself. (Earlier they were like two different things, which Genesis 19 makes plain where it says that *Jehovah* rained *sulfur* and *fire* from *Jehovah* out of the sky onto Sodom and Gomorrah; verse 24, §2447.) The day when there will be no day or night is the time of the Lord's birth, because that was the evening, or the end of mere representations of a church. Light around the time of evening is the divine truth that was then to become visible. [8] In Isaiah:

> Surely *overnight* Ar has been devastated, Moab has been cut off; surely *overnight* Kir of Moab has been devastated. (Isaiah 15:1)

Moab stands for earthly goodness and in a negative sense for adulterated goodness (§2468). In this verse it stands for the devastation of goodness. The passage says that the devastation happens overnight because night is when truth goes dim and falsity enters. In Jeremiah:

> The great city will weep hard *in the night,* and she will have tears on her cheek. (Lamentations 1:2)

This verse is about the abandonment of truth. The night stands for falsity. [9] In David:

> You will not be afraid *of the horror at night,* of the arrow that flies by day, nor of the death that ravages at midday. (Psalms 91:5, 6)

The horror at night stands for falsity based on evil, which comes from hell. The arrow that flies by day stands for falsity taught openly, which destroys goodness. The death that ravages at midday stands for evil lived openly, which destroys truth. In John:

> The gates of Jerusalem the Holy will not be shut by day *(night does not exist there).* (Revelation 21:25)

> *Night will not exist there,* and they will have no need for a lamp or sunlight, because the Lord God gives them light. (Revelation 22:5)

"Night will not exist there" means that falsity will not. In Daniel:

> Daniel said, "*I was seeing in my vision, when it was night.* Afterward *I was* again *seeing in visions at night.*" (Daniel 7:2, 7)

The visions at night again stand for dim revelation. What Daniel 7 is describing is a dim, obscure revelation involving four beasts and their horns and so on. The horses of different colors that Zechariah *saw by night* (Zechariah 1:8 and following verses) were also part of an obscure revelation.

And he said, "Jacob! Jacob!" means to earthly truth. This is clear from the representation of *Jacob* as earthly truth (discussed in §§3305, 3509, 3525, 3546, 3599, 3775, 4009, 4234, 4520, 4538). The reason the name used is Jacob, not Israel, is that earthly truth and everything connected with it must be introduced into religious knowledge, as symbolized by Jacob's going down into Egypt with his offspring; see below at §6004.

6001

And he said, "Here I am," symbolizes awareness of it, as is self-evident.

6002

And he said, "I am God, the God of your father," symbolizes divine intellect, the source of the inflow. This is clear from the representation of Isaac, *his father,* as the Lord's divine rationality, or intellect (as above at §5998), since the text says "God, the God of your father." Divine intellect is the source of the inflow because all truth, including the earthly truth represented by Jacob (§6001), is in the province of the intellect.

6003

For a definition of the divine rationality or intellect represented by Isaac, see §§1893, 2066, 2072, 2083, 2630, 3012, 3194, 3210.

In the original language, the first word for God in this verse is singular, the second plural; the first is *El,* the second is *Elohim.* This is because the symbolism in the first instance is that there is one and only one God, and in the second instance that God has many attributes. That is why the second instance is *Elohim,* or "God" in the plural form used almost everywhere in the Word. God does have many attributes, and the ancient church gave a name to each attribute, but the knowledge of this was lost to that church's descendants, who consequently believed there were many gods. Clans chose one of the gods as their own. Abram, for example, chose Shaddai (§§1992, 3667, 5628); Isaac chose a god called *Pachad,* or "Dread." Because each clan had one of the divine attributes as its god, the Lord identified himself to Abram in Genesis 17:1 as God Shaddai and to Jacob here as the God of his father.

Don't be afraid of going down to Egypt means that earthly truth and everything connected with it must be introduced into religious knowledge, as the following shows: Jacob, the one who was to go down to Egypt, represents earthly truth, as noted just above in §6001. *Going down* symbolizes being introduced, because the whole reason Jacob went down into Egypt with all his family was to represent the introduction of truth.

6004

And *Egypt* symbolizes religious knowledge (discussed in §§1462, 4749, 4964, 4966).

[2] To expand on the need for the introduction of truth into religious knowledge: Religious knowledge in those days had to do with representation and symbolism in religious ceremonies, since all ritual in the church consisted of representational and symbolic practices. Another category of religious knowledge was information that supported their teachings about neighborly love. This information told them who is meant by the poor, needy, wretched, afflicted, oppressed, widowed, orphaned, immigrant, imprisoned, naked, sick, hungry, thirsty, lame, blind, deaf, maimed, and many other classifications they had for their neighbor. This was how they taught the ways of exercising love for one's neighbor. Such was the religious knowledge of that era. Today this knowledge has been totally blotted out, as is evident from the fact that where the Word mentions these categories of people, hardly anyone knows that they mean anything besides the people so described. They take the mention of widows to mean widows, of immigrants to mean immigrants, of prisoners to mean prisoners, and so on.

Knowledge like this flourished in Egypt, so Egypt symbolizes knowledge.

The introduction of the earthly truth that is Jacob into such knowledge is represented by Jacob's going down into Egypt with everything that was his.

[3] Truth is said to be introduced into information when it is imported into it so as to exist in it. This is done so that the truth instilled into a piece of information can be recalled whenever the information itself comes to mind. For instance, since an immigrant symbolizes someone who needs instruction, the instant an immigrant comes to mind we could remember all the ways to exercise kindness toward such a person. In this way we would recall the truth. Likewise for all the other categories. When what we know is filled with truth, and when we then think from that information, our thoughts stretch out far and wide. They even reach multiple communities in the heavens simultaneously. Such information spreads out like this unbeknownst to us, because it consists of and contains so many true ideas. But for this to work, the ideas it contains do have to be true.

[4] Besides, the divine design requires that inner levels insert themselves into outer levels, or to say the same thing, that what comes earlier insert itself into what comes later. In the end, everything earlier must

insert itself into what comes last, and it must all coexist there. This happens throughout creation. If it does not happen [in us], we cannot be fully reborn. This introduction of truth into our knowledge creates harmony and unity between inner and outer qualities that would otherwise be at odds. When they are at odds, we are not focused on goodness, because we are not being genuine.

What is more, our knowledge relies on almost the same kind of illumination as our physical sight. Unless this illumination is inwardly lit with the light shed by truth, it naturally leads to falsity (especially falsity from sensory illusions) and to the evil that grows out of falsity. The testimony of experience concerning spiritual inflow will demonstrate that this is so, at the end of the [next few] chapters.

Because I will turn you into a great nation means that truth will turn into goodness. This can be seen from the representation of Jacob, of whom the words are said, as earthly truth (mentioned above at §6001), and from the symbolism of a *nation* as goodness (discussed in §§1259, 1260, 1416, 1849).

6005

The Word often mentions nations and peoples, but always with the distinction that nations symbolize what is good or else what is evil, and peoples what is true or else what is false.

I myself will go down with you to Egypt symbolizes the presence of the Lord in that state. This can be seen from the symbolism of *going down with you* as the Lord's presence. After all, the God who spoke with Jacob in visions at night means the Lord.

6006

And I myself will most certainly bring you up symbolizes being lifted up afterward. This is indicated by the symbolism of being *brought up* as being lifted (dealt with in §§3084, 4539, 5406, 5817). The upward movement symbolized here is from knowledge to something more inward. After the knowledge in our minds has been filled with truth in the manner described in §6004, we are lifted from it toward something farther within. Then what we know serves us as an underlying platform for insight.

6007

Rising toward something more inward means thinking in an inner way—eventually in the way of a spirit and an angel. The farther inward our thinking penetrates, the fuller it is, because the closer it is to the inflow of truth and goodness from the Lord.

On the point that there is inner and outer thought, see §§5127, 5141.

And Joseph will put his hand on your eyes means that inner heavenliness will bestow life. This is indicated by the representation of *Joseph* as inner heavenliness (dealt with at §§5869, 5877) and by the symbolism of *putting a hand on someone's eyes* as bestowing life. Putting a hand on someone's eyes

6008

means that the outer, physical senses will shut down and the inner senses will open up, so that the person is lifted up and therefore brought to life.

The gesture was made when people died, because death symbolized being restored to life (§§3498, 3505, 4618, 4621). When we die, we do not die but only put off the body that served our purposes in the world, passing over to the other life in a body that serves our purposes there.

6009   Genesis 46:5, 6, 7. *And Jacob rose from Beer-sheba, and the sons of Israel bore Jacob their father and their little children and their women on the wagons that Pharaoh had sent to bear him. And they took their livestock and their gain that they had gained in the land of Canaan and came to Egypt, Jacob and all his seed with him. His sons and his sons' sons with him, his daughters and his sons' daughters, and all his seed he brought with him to Egypt.*

And Jacob rose symbolizes the clarification of earthly truth. *From Beer-sheba* means by teachings about neighborly love and faith. *And the sons of Israel bore Jacob their father* means that spiritual truth caused earthly truth to advance. *And their little children* means along with the urgings of innocence. *And their women* means and with the urgings of neighborly love. *On the wagons that Pharaoh had sent to bear him* symbolizes teachings drawn from religious knowledge. *And they took their livestock* symbolizes truth-based goodness. *And their gain that they had gained in the land of Canaan* symbolizes truth amassed from the church's earlier truth. *And came to Egypt* symbolizes the introduction into religious knowledge. *Jacob and all his seed with him* means of earthly truth and of everything involved in the faith connected with that truth. *His sons and his sons' sons with him* symbolizes true concepts in their order. *His daughters and his sons' daughters* symbolizes good desires in their order. *And all his seed* symbolizes everything involved in faith and neighborly love. *He brought with him to Egypt* means that it was all inserted into religious knowledge.

6010   *And Jacob rose* symbolizes the clarification of earthly truth. This can be seen from the symbolism of *rising* as being lifted into a state of light and so as clarification (treated of in §4881), and from the representation of *Jacob* as earthly truth (noted above in §6001).

6011   *From Beer-sheba* means by teachings about faith and neighborly love. This can be seen from the discussion in §§2858, 2859, 3466 of the symbolism of *Beer-sheba* as teachings about faith and neighborly love.

6012   *And the sons of Israel bore Jacob their father* means that spiritual truth caused earthly truth to advance. This can be seen from the representation of the *sons of Israel* as spiritual truth (mentioned in §§5414, 5879) and from the representation of *Jacob* as earthly truth (discussed in §§3305,

3509, 3525, 3546, 3599, 3775, 4009, 4234, 4520, 4538). *They bore him* means that it caused it to advance because the subject is the relationship of spiritual truth to earthly truth. Earthly truth cannot move forward without spiritual truth behind it, because spiritual truth supplies earthly truth with life and the power to do things.

This is the reason, then, that Jacob's sons are spoken of here as Israel's and yet Jacob himself is called Jacob.

And their little children means along with the urgings of innocence. **6013** This can be seen from the symbolism of *little children* as innocence (discussed in §§3183, 5608). I say along with the urgings of innocence and of neighborly love because without innocence and neighborly love, spiritual truth cannot move earthly truth forward. For truth to be genuine, it has to take its essence and life from neighborly love, which has to take its essence and life from innocence. The inner attributes that bring truth alive come in the following order: The inmost is innocence, below that is neighborly love, and below that is acts of neighborly love inspired by or based on truth. The reason they come in this order is that they follow the same order in the heavens: The third or inmost heaven is the heaven of innocence. The second or middle heaven is the heaven of neighborly love, which contains innocence from the inmost heaven. The first or outermost heaven is the heaven of truth, which contains neighborly love from the second heaven, which in turn contains innocence from the third heaven. The three qualities have to maintain the same arrangement in a human being, because a person's inner depths are formed in the image of the three heavens. As a result, a person who has been reborn is an individual heaven, or heaven in miniature. A person's outer level, however, and especially a person's body, is formed in the image of the world, which is why the ancients called a human being a microcosm. The ear is formed to match entirely the nature of air and sound, the eye to match the nature of the ether and light, the tongue to sense particles dissolved and suspended in liquid, the nostrils to sense particles floating in the atmosphere, and the touch to sense cold and heat, the weight of solid objects, and so on. Just as our outer senses are formed in a complete image of the physical world, our inner senses—the senses of our intellect and will—are formed in a complete image of heaven. The purpose is for us to be an individual container of divine goodness from the Lord, just as heaven is a general container of that goodness.

And their women means and with the urgings of neighborly love. This **6014** can be seen from the symbolism of *women* as goodness, when the men they are attached to symbolize truth (discussed at §4823), and therefore as the urgings of neighborly love. All spiritual goodness has to do with charity toward one's neighbor, and all heavenly goodness with love for the Lord.

6015   *On the wagons that Pharaoh had sent to bear him* symbolizes teachings drawn from religious knowledge. This can be seen from the symbolism of *wagons* as teachings (treated of in §5945) and from the representation of *Pharaoh* as religious knowledge in general. Egypt symbolizes religious knowledge (§§1462, 4749, 4964, 4966), so its monarch symbolizes such knowledge in general, as it does in other scriptural passages. However, in many places Pharaoh, like Egypt, symbolizes knowledge that has been corrupted.

It is plain in Isaiah that Pharaoh means knowledge in general:

> Stupid are the chieftains of Zoan, the *sages among Pharaoh's advisors;* their advice has turned brutish. How will you say *to Pharaoh,* "I am the offspring of sages, the offspring of the monarchs of old"? (Isaiah 19:11)

Pharaoh stands here for religious knowledge in general. That is why he is called the offspring of sages and the offspring of the monarchs of old. Sages and monarchs of old stand for the truth known to the ancient church. In this case, though, the knowledge is understood to be nonsense, since it says, "Stupid have the chieftains of Zoan become; their advice has turned brutish." [2] In the same author:

> They leave to go down to *Egypt* (but have not asked of my mouth), to strengthen themselves *with Pharaoh's strength,* and to trust *in Egypt's shadow.* So for you *Pharaoh's strength* will turn to shame, and trust *in Egypt's shadow* to disgrace. (Isaiah 30:2, 3)

Strengthening oneself with Pharaoh's strength and trusting in Egypt's shadow stands for relying on accepted knowledge in matters of faith and not believing any spiritual truth unless what is generally known and the evidence of the senses decree it. This is backward. First place has to be given to the truth that leads to faith and second place to supportive information, because if accepted knowledge is in first place, no truth is ever believed. [3] In Jeremiah:

> Jehovah Sabaoth, God of Israel, has said, "Here, now, I am bringing punishment on Amon in No, and *on Pharaoh* and *on Egypt* and on its gods and on its monarchs, especially *on Pharaoh* and those trusting in him." (Jeremiah 46:25)

Here too Pharaoh stands for knowledge in general. Those trusting in him stand for people who rely on accepted knowledge and not on the Word, that is, not on the Lord in his Word. This is the origin of every corruption in the church's teachings, and of falsity, and of the denial that what is divine or heavenly is anything. People like this are the first to claim, "Make me see it with my own eyes, or demonstrate scientifically that it is true, and then I will believe." Nonetheless, if they saw or had it demonstrated, they still would not believe, because negativity reigns supreme in them. [4] In the same author:

> Against *Pharaoh:* Look! Water climbing from the north, which will become a flooding river and flood the earth and its abundance, the city and those living in it, so that people cry out and every resident of the land wails over the sound of the thud of hooves of his mighty horses and the commotion of his chariot, the din of its wheels. (Jeremiah 47:1, 2, 3)

Every detail of these statements about Pharaoh makes it clear that Pharaoh means knowledge in general. In this case the knowledge has been twisted out of its proper hierarchy, which destroys religious truth. The flooding river means accepted knowledge destroying any understanding of truth and therefore causing spiritual devastation. Flooding the earth and its abundance means destroying the whole church. Flooding the city and those living in it means destroying truth known to the church and consequently goodness. The thud of horses' hooves means knowledge on the lowest level, which rises directly out of sense impressions. The commotion of his chariot means the false teaching that results. The din of its wheels means sense impressions and the illusions they give rise to, on the move. [5] In Ezekiel:

> The Lord Jehovih has said: "Here, now, I am *against you, Pharaoh, king of Egypt,* you great whale, who is lying in the middle of his rivers, who says, 'The river is mine, and I have made myself.' Therefore I will put a hook into your jaws and make the fish of your rivers stick to your scales." (Ezekiel 29:2, 3, 4)

Again Pharaoh stands for knowledge in general, and once more the details of what is said about him make this plain. [6] In the same author:

> Raise a lamentation *over Pharaoh, king of Egypt.* "You are like whales in the seas, and you have emerged with your rivers and roiled the waters with your feet; you have churned their rivers. When I blot you out I

will cover the heavens. And I will blacken their stars, the sun I will cover with a cloud, and the moon will not make its light shine. All the lamps of light I will blacken above you, and I will bring darkness over your land." (Ezekiel 32:2, 3, 7, 8)

Obviously these statements, like many others in the Prophets, can be understood by no one without the inner meaning. I am talking about the statements that Pharaoh was like whales in the seas, had emerged from his rivers, and had roiled the waters with his feet, that above him the heavens would be covered, the stars and all the lamps of light would be blackened, the sun would be covered with a cloud, the moon would not shine, and darkness would be brought over his land. The inner meaning teaches the symbolism, however. The symbolism is that accepted knowledge corrupts the church's true ideas if people use it to pry into the mysteries of faith and believe nothing unless they can see it from what is generally known or, worse yet, from sensory information. An explanation of each statement shows that this is the inner meaning.

[7] Pharaoh's title *king of Egypt* refers to truth in the form of knowledge. After all, knowledge is truth on the earthly plane. (A monarch means truth; see §§1672, 1728, 2015, 2069, 3009, 3670, 4575, 4581, 4966, 5044. And the monarch of a given people has the same symbolism as that people; 4789. Pharaoh accordingly symbolizes the same thing as Egypt, but in a general way, and Egypt means knowledge, as has been demonstrated many times.) Pharaoh is said to be like *whales in the seas* because a whale, or sea monster, symbolizes general categories of knowledge (42), and seas symbolize bodies of such knowledge (28). The text also says that he *emerged with his rivers,* because rivers symbolize thoughts that exhibit intelligence (108, 109, 2702, 3051), although here it symbolizes thoughts that exhibit insanity, since they grow out of sensory information and accepted knowledge (5196). Next the passage says that he *roiled the waters with his feet* and *churned their rivers,* because waters symbolize spiritual truth (680, 739, 2702, 3058, 3424, 4976, 5668) and feet symbolize earthly elements (2162, 3147, 3761, 3986, 4280, 4938–4952). So roiling the waters with one's feet means soiling and corrupting religious truth through earthly-level knowledge, and churning their rivers means doing the same to the power of understanding.

[8] Finally the passage says that *when he is blotted out, the heavens will be covered,* because the heavens symbolize our inner reaches, these being our heavens. Our inner reaches close up when accepted knowledge

exercises power over religious truth, or the earthly level exercises power over the spiritual. When that happens, the inner knowledge of what is true and good perishes, and this is symbolized by *I will blacken the stars of the heavens and all the lamps of light.* (For the meaning of stars as this kind of knowledge, see §§2495, 2849, 4697, and for the meaning of lamps, [or lights,] as goodness and truth, 30–38.) Goodness inspired by love can no longer flow into us then, as symbolized by *the sun I will cover with a cloud.* Neither can goodness inspired by faith, as symbolized by *the moon will not make its light shine.* (For the meaning of the sun as goodness inspired by love and of the moon as goodness inspired by faith, see §§1529, 1530, 2120, 2495, 3636, 3643, 4060, 4696.) This means that falsity will take sole possession of the earthly mind, as symbolized by *I will bring darkness over your land.* (Darkness, [or shadow,] means falsity, 1839, 1860, 4418, 4531, and the land of Pharaoh—the land of Egypt—means the earthly mind, 5276, 5278, 5280, 5288, 5301.) This whole discussion now shows the meaning that lies inside those prophetic sentences.

Because Pharaoh symbolizes knowledge in general, he also symbolizes the earthly plane in general (§5799).

And they took their livestock symbolizes truth-based goodness. This can be seen from the symbolism of *livestock* as truth-based goodness. "Livestock" means both flocks and herds, as well as horses, camels, mules, and donkeys. Flocks in an inner sense mean inner goodness, and herds mean outer goodness, but horses, camels, mules, and donkeys mean different facets of the intellect, which all relate to truth. Livestock accordingly means truth-based goodness.

6016

And their gain that they had gained in the land of Canaan symbolizes truth amassed from the church's earlier truth, as the following shows: *Gain,* [or property,] symbolizes truth that has been amassed (treated of at §4105) and also goodness that has been amassed (§§4391, 4487). And the *land of Canaan* symbolizes the church (treated of in §§3686, 3705, 4447, 4517, 5136). The idea that these were amassed from the church's earlier truth follows logically, because when truth multiplies with goodness, it is multiplied by earlier truth.

6017

And came to Egypt symbolizes the introduction into religious knowledge. This can be seen from the symbolism of *coming into Egypt,* or going down there, as the introduction of truth into religious knowledge (discussed at §6004).

6018

Jacob and all his seed with him means (the introduction into religious knowledge) of earthly truth and of everything involved in the faith

6019

connected with that truth. This can be seen from the representation of *Jacob* as earthly truth (discussed in §§3305, 3509, 3525, 3546, 3599, 3775, 4009, 4234, 4520, 4538) and from the symbolism of *seed* as faith that springs from neighborly love (discussed in §§255, 1025, 1447, 1610, 1940, 2848, 3310). So *all his seed with him* means everything involved in the faith connected with earthly truth.

6020   *His sons and his sons' sons with him* symbolizes true concepts in their proper order. This can be seen from the symbolism of *sons* as truth (noted in §§489, 491, 533, 1147, 2623, 3373). *Sons' sons* also symbolize true concepts, but true concepts developing from that truth in their proper order.

6021   *His daughters and his sons' daughters* symbolizes good desires in their order. This can be seen from the symbolism of *daughters* as goodness (noted in §§489, 490, 491, 2362, 3963). *Sons' daughters* also symbolize good desires, but good desires developing out of those [true concepts], and therefore in their proper order, as mentioned just above about the sons.

6022   *And all his seed* symbolizes everything involved in faith and neighborly love. This can be seen from the symbolism of *seed* as faith that rises out of neighborly love (as above at §6019) and consequently as both faith and neighborly love, because the one exists where the other does.

6023   *He brought with him to Egypt* means that it was all inserted into religious knowledge. This is established by the symbolism of coming into Egypt, or going down there, as introducing and inserting truth into religious knowledge, as discussed above at §§6004, 6018. *Bringing it with him to Egypt* has the same symbolism; see §§5373, 6004. Truth is introduced and inserted when it takes command of knowledge, and it takes command of that knowledge when we acknowledge it as true because the Lord has said so in the Word. After that, knowledge supporting the truth may properly be welcomed, and knowledge contradicting it may be put aside. Truth then governs amid support, having rid itself of nonsupport. When we think from knowledge under these circumstances, we do not wander astray to falsity, as we do when truth is absent from our knowledge. Knowledge, you see, is not inherently true. It is only the truth it contains within itself that makes it true. The nature of the truth contained in an item of information determines what kind of general truth the information is—knowledge being a mere vessel (§§1469, 1496) capable of holding either truth or falsity, with immense variety.

[2] Take for example the religious concept that everyone is our neighbor. Truth in vast quantities can be introduced and inserted into this concept. Yes, everyone is our neighbor, but each in a different way. People

with goodness are our neighbor to the greatest degree—again in different ways, depending on the kind of goodness they have. The whole origin of a neighbor starts with the Lord himself. The closer people are to him, then (which is to say, the more they commit themselves to goodness), the more they are our neighbor, whereas the farther they stand from him, the less they are. Moreover, a community is more our neighbor than an individual and a whole country more than a community, but our own country more than other countries. Nonetheless the church is more our neighbor than our country is, and the Lord's kingdom still more. In addition, the way to love our neighbor is to do our job properly, for the good of other people or of our country or of the church. And so on.

This shows how much truth can be inserted into this one religious concept. The amount is so large that it is hard to divide it into categories and to make any one category distinct and recognizable by assigning it specific truths. (That is what the ancient churches endeavored to do.)

[3] The same concept can also be filled with vast quantities of falsity, as anyone can see by turning these truths upside down. We could say that we are each neighbor to ourselves and that we must each trace the origin of the neighbor to ourselves. This would mean that others are more our neighbor the more they cater to us and make common cause with us, presenting themselves to us as an image of us. In fact, we could say that not even our country is our neighbor, except to the extent that it benefits us materially. And so on, endlessly.

Still, the concept remains the same, that everyone is our neighbor. One person fills this concept with truth, and another fills it with falsity. Likewise for all other concepts.

Genesis 46:8–27. And these are the names of Israel's sons as they came to Egypt, of Jacob and his sons: Jacob's firstborn, Reuben. And the sons of Reuben: Enoch and Pallu and Hezron and Carmi. And the sons of Simeon: Jemuel and Jamin and Ohad and Jachin and Zohar and Shaul the son of a Canaanite woman. And the sons of Levi: Gershon and Kohath and Merari. And the sons of Judah: Er and Onan and Shelah and Perez and Zerah. And Er and Onan died in the land of Canaan, and the sons of Perez were Hezron and Hamul. And the sons of Issachar: Tola and Puvah and Job and Shimron. And the sons of Zebulun: Sered and Elon and Jahleel. These were Leah's sons, whom she bore to Jacob in Paddan-aram, along with Dinah his daughter. All the souls of his sons and his daughters: thirty-three. And the sons of Gad: Ziphion and Haggi, Shuni and Ezbon, Eri and Arodi and Areli. And the sons of Asher: Imnah and Ishvah and Ishvi and Beriah and Serah their sister.

6024

And the sons of Beriah: Heber and Malchiel. These were the sons of Zilpah, whom Laban gave to Leah his daughter; and she bore these to Jacob: sixteen souls. The sons of Rachel, Jacob's wife: Joseph and Benjamin. And there were born to Joseph in the land of Egypt those whom Asenath, daughter of Potiphera (priest of On), bore to him: Manasseh and Ephraim. And the sons of Benjamin: Bela and Becher and Ashbel, Gera and Naaman, Ehi and Rosh, Muppim and Huppim and Ard. These were Rachel's sons, who were born to Jacob. All the souls: fourteen. And the sons of Dan: Hushim. And the sons of Naphtali: Jahzeel and Guni and Jezer and Shillem. These were the sons of Bilhah, whom Laban gave to Rachel his daughter; and she bore these to Jacob. All the souls: seven. Every soul of Jacob's as they came to Egypt, having issued from his thigh, besides the women of Jacob's sons, all the souls: sixty-six. And Joseph's sons, who were born to him in Egypt: two souls. All the souls belonging to the house of Jacob as they came to Egypt: seventy.

[2] *And these are the names of Israel's sons as they came to Egypt* symbolizes the nature and orderly arrangement of true concepts supplied by the spiritual dimension that are inserted into items of religious knowledge. *Of Jacob and his sons* symbolizes earthly truth in general and earthly truth in particular. *Jacob's firstborn, Reuben* symbolizes a faith that belongs to the intellect, which seems to be in first place. *And the sons of Reuben: Enoch and Pallu and Hezron and Carmi* symbolizes general teachings about faith. *And the sons of Simeon: Jemuel and Jamin and Ohad and Jachin and Zohar* symbolizes a faith that belongs to the will and general teachings about it. *And Shaul the son of a Canaanite woman* symbolizes a teaching from an origin that is not genuine. *And the sons of Levi: Gershon and Kohath and Merari* symbolizes spiritual love and general teachings about it. [3] *And the sons of Judah: Er and Onan and Shelah and Perez and Zerah* symbolizes heavenly love and teachings about it. *And Er and Onan died in the land of Canaan* means that falsity and evil were eradicated. *And the sons of Perez were Hezron and Hamul* symbolizes the truth belonging to [heavenly] goodness, this truth being the same as charitable goodness. *And the sons of Issachar: Tola and Puvah and Job and Shimron* symbolizes heavenly marriage love and teachings about it. *And the sons of Zebulun: Sered and Elon and Jahleel* symbolizes the heavenly marriage and teachings about it. *These were Leah's sons, whom she bore to Jacob in Paddan-aram,* means that a spiritual desire produced these qualities on the earthly level, using the knowledge of what is good and true as its means. *Along with Dinah his daughter* symbolizes the church. *Every soul of his sons and his daughters: thirty-three* symbolizes a state of spiritual life and the nature of that state.

[4] *And the sons of Gad: Ziphion and Haggi, Shuni and Ezbon, Eri and Arodi and Areli* symbolizes goodness inspired by faith, the good deeds it leads to, and teachings about these things. *And the sons of Asher: Imnah and Ishvah and Ishvi and Beriah and Serah their sister; and the sons of Beriah: Heber and Malchiel* symbolizes the happiness of eternal life, pleasurable feelings, and teachings about these things. *These were the sons of Zilpah* means that these qualities belonged to the outer part of the church. *Whom Laban gave to Leah his daughter* means that they were produced by a desire for outward goodness. *And she bore these to Jacob* means that they were on the earthly level. *Sixteen souls* symbolizes their state and the nature of that state. [5] *The sons of Rachel, Jacob's wife,* symbolizes what a heavenly desire produced. *Joseph and Benjamin* symbolizes the inner core of the church, *Joseph* being its goodness and *Benjamin* the resulting truth. *And there were born to Joseph in the land of Egypt* symbolizes heavenly and spiritual depths on the earthly plane. *Those whom Asenath, daughter of Potiphera (priest of On), bore to him* means from the marriage of goodness with truth and of truth with goodness. *Manasseh and Ephraim* symbolizes a new will in the church, and the intellect that accompanies it. *And the sons of Benjamin: Bela and Becher and Ashbel, Gera and Naaman, Ehi and Rosh, Muppim and Huppim and Ard* symbolizes spiritual depth and teachings about it. *These were Rachel's sons, who were born to Jacob,* means that these qualities were produced by a heavenly desire. *All the souls: fourteen* symbolizes their state and the nature of that state. [6] *And the sons of Dan: Hushim* symbolizes sacred faith, a good life, and teachings about them. *And the sons of Naphtali: Jahzeel and Guni and Jezer and Shillem* symbolizes trials in which there is victory and teachings about them. *These were the sons of Bilhah* means that these qualities belonged to the inner part of the church. *Whom Laban gave to Rachel his daughter* means that they were produced by a desire for inner goodness. *All the souls: seven* symbolizes their state and the nature of that state. [7] *Every soul of Jacob's as they came to Egypt* symbolizes all truth and goodness introduced into religious knowledge. *Having issued from his thigh* means which marriage produces. *Besides the women of Jacob's sons* means except for associated desires that do not spring from that marriage. *All the souls: sixty-six* symbolizes the state of these qualities and the nature of that state. *And Joseph's sons, who were born to him in Egypt,* symbolizes heavenly and spiritual qualities on the earthly plane. *Two souls* symbolizes the resulting content of the will and the intellect in the church. *All the souls belonging to the house of Jacob as they came to Egypt: seventy* symbolizes the whole array laid out in order.

6025   There is no need to explain this passage further, since it is nothing but names. Their symbolism can be seen from the summary explanation just above in §6024, and the symbolism of Jacob's first generation of offspring can be seen in the explanation given where their births are discussed [§§3859–3881, 3920–3939, 3953–3969, 4591–4592].

It is worth noting that Jacob's children had no children of their own born to them in Egypt, where they had moved, even though they were still relatively young. No, all their children were born in Canaan, and they themselves in Paddan-aram, except for Benjamin. This was because the Lord's divine providence took special care to have them represent characteristics of the church from the time they were born. Their birth in Paddan-aram represented the need for people in the church to be born anew, or regenerated, by what they know about goodness and truth. Paddan-aram symbolizes knowledge of goodness and truth (§§3664, 3680, 4107). Birth represented a new birth through faith and neighborly love (§§4668, 5160, 5598) and so at first through a *knowledge* of faith and neighborly love.

The birth of the whole next generation in the land of Canaan represented the fact that [rebirth] produces what is characteristic of the church, since the land of Canaan means the church (§§3686, 3705, 4447, 4454, 4517, 5136, 5757).

Joseph did have children born to him in Egypt, though, and that was in order to represent the ruling power of the inner self in the outer self. Specifically, it represented the ruling power of the spiritual heavenly self in the earthly self. Manasseh is the will and Ephraim the intellect (characteristics of the church) in the earthly self.

6026   Genesis 46:28, 29, 30. *And Judah he sent before him to Joseph, to show [the way] before him to Goshen, and they came to the land of Goshen. And Joseph hitched his chariot and went up to meet Israel his father, to Goshen, and was seen by him and fell on his neck and wept on his neck a long time. And Israel said to Joseph, "Let me die this time, now that I have seen your face, that you are still alive."*

And Judah he sent before him to Joseph symbolizes communication between goodness in the church and inner heavenliness. *To show [the way] before him to Goshen* means concerning the center of the earthly level. *And they came to the land of Goshen* symbolizes their situation in life there. *And Joseph hitched his chariot* symbolizes teachings received from within. *And went up to meet Israel his father* symbolizes an inflow. *To Goshen* means into the central part of the earthly level. *And was seen by him* symbolizes perception. *And fell on his neck* symbolizes union. *And wept on his neck a long time* symbolizes mercy. *And Israel said to Joseph* symbolizes a perception belonging to spiritual goodness. *Let me die this time* symbolizes fresh life. *Now that I have seen your face* means following a perception of mercy. *That you are still alive* symbolizes a consequent perception of life in himself.

And Judah he sent before him to Joseph symbolizes communication between goodness in the church and inner heavenliness. This is evident from the representation of *Judah* as goodness in the church (mentioned in §§5583, 5603, 5782, 5794, 5833) and from that of *Joseph* as inner heavenliness (mentioned in §§5869, 5877). *Sending before him* obviously means communicating.

6027

The purpose of sending Judah and no one but Judah was to symbolize the direct communication that exists between one kind of goodness and another—the outer goodness represented by Judah and the inner goodness represented by Joseph. Goodness, which has to do with love for the Lord and charity toward one's neighbor, flows from the Lord through the inner plane into the outer plane. The amount of goodness that exists on the outer plane determines how much is received there. If our outer part contains only faith's truth, not goodness, the stream of goodness from the Lord through our inner plane is not accepted on our outer plane. There is no direct communication with truth, only indirect communication through goodness.

This is the reason Jacob sent no one but Judah to Joseph.

To show [the way] before him to Goshen means [communication] concerning the center of the earthly level. This is clear from the symbolism of *Goshen* as the central or inmost part of the earthly level (discussed at §5910). The central, inmost part of the earthly level means the best part there, because the best is at the center, that is, in the middle, or at the inmost core. All around it in every direction lie different kinds of goodness, arranged in the pattern of heaven, nearer or farther, depending on how many degrees of goodness separate them from the best in the center. At least, that is the way good attributes are arranged in regenerate people. In evil people the worst is at the center and different kinds of goodness are banished to the farthest edges, where they are constantly being pushed out entirely. This is the pattern in individual evil people and in the hells as a whole, so it is the hellish pattern.

6028

These remarks about the best at the center and good qualities arranged in order on the sides show what is meant by communication between goodness in the church and inner heavenliness concerning the center of the earthly level.

6029   *And Joseph hitched his chariot* symbolizes teachings received from within. This can be seen from the representation of *Joseph* as the inner dimension (mentioned often) and from the symbolism of a *chariot* as teachings (dealt with at §5321).

6030   *And went up to meet Israel his father* symbolizes an inflow—an inflow of inner heavenliness into spiritual goodness on the earthly level. This can be seen from the representation of Joseph, who *went up to meet,* as inner heavenliness (noted in §§5869, 5877), and from that of *Israel* as spiritual goodness (discussed in §§5801, 5803, 5807, 5812, 5817, 5819, 5826, 5833). The idea that *going up to meet him* means an inflow follows naturally, because it means taking himself there, or coming to him.

6031   *To Goshen* symbolizes the central part of the earthly level. This is established by the discussion of *Goshen* just above at §6028.

6032   *And was seen by him* symbolizes perception. This is indicated by the symbolism of *seeing* as understanding and recognizing (noted in §§2150, 3764, 4567, 4723, 5400) and as believing (§§2325, 2807, 3863, 3869, 4403–4421, 5400).

About seeing as understanding and therefore perceiving, and as believing, it needs to be realized that our life is made up of two things: *spiritual light* and *spiritual warmth.* Spiritual light constitutes the life of our intellect, and spiritual warmth constitutes the life of our will. Spiritual light in its first origins is divine truth radiating from the Lord's divine goodness and is consequently religious truth deriving from charitable goodness. Spiritual warmth in its first origins is the divine goodness of the Lord's divine love and is consequently the goodness of heavenly love (love for the Lord) and of spiritual love (love toward our neighbor). Again, these two things constitute our whole life.

[2] Regarding spiritual light: Spiritual light does for our intellect what physical light does for our outer sight. In order to see with our eyes, we need to have light shining. Our eye can then see everything outside it all around in the light. The same holds true for our intellectual mind, which is our inner eye. In order to see with this eye, we need heaven's light to shine from the Lord. When our inner eye has the use of this light, it can see what lies outside it all around. The objects it sees are spiritual, which is to say that they are forms of knowledge and truth. But when heaven's light does not shine, then our intellectual mind, our inner eye, like the outer, physical eye, is in the dark and sees nothing. In other words, it sees

no truth from the standpoint of knowledge and no goodness from the standpoint of truth.

The light that illuminates the intellectual mind is real light, of a kind a thousand times brighter than noonday light in the world. I can testify to this, because I have seen it. By this light all the angels in the heavens see what lies outside them all around. By the same light they also see and perceive religious truth and the quality of that truth. That is why seeing, in a spiritual sense, means the intellect and whatever is connected with the intellect, such as thought, reflection, attention, prudence, and so on. It also means faith and whatever is connected with faith, such as truth, scriptural teachings, and so on.

[3] Regarding spiritual warmth: Spiritual warmth does for our will what physical warmth does for our body, which is to give it life. In its first origins, which start with the Lord, spiritual warmth is actually divine love toward the entire human race and therefore the love we give back to the Lord and to our neighbor. This spiritual warmth is real warmth, which blesses angels' bodies with warmth at the same time it blesses their inner depths with love. As a result, warmth, flame, and fire in a positive sense in the Word symbolize different facets of love, such as desires for goodness and truth, and goodness itself.

And fell on his neck symbolizes union. This can be seen from the symbolism of *falling on someone's neck* as a deep, tight bond (discussed at §5926). **6033**

Falling on someone's neck means union because the neck joins the head and the body together. The head symbolizes the inner dimension, and the body the outer dimension, so the neck is the bond between inner and outer (see §§3542, 5320, 5328). This bond provides communication between the inner and outer realms, and between the heavenly and spiritual realms (see the same sections). The current phrase also symbolizes this union and subsequent communication, because Joseph means what is inward, and Israel what is more outward.

And wept on his neck a long time symbolizes mercy. This is clear from the symbolism of *weeping* as mercy (discussed in §§5480, 5873, 5927). The text says *on his neck a long time* because mercy—the mercy of the Lord, who is Joseph in the highest sense—is what union starts with and is also what keeps it going. **6034**

And Israel said to Joseph symbolizes a perception belonging to spiritual goodness that came from inner heavenliness, as the following shows: *Saying* in the Word's narratives symbolizes perception. *Israel,* on whose neck **6035**

Joseph wept, represents spiritual goodness. And *Joseph* represents inner heavenliness. All of this has been discussed many times before.

6036   *Let me die this time* symbolizes fresh life. This can be seen from the symbolism of *dying* as rising again into life and consequently as fresh life, which is mentioned in §§3326, 3498, 3505, 4618, 4621, 6008. The same sections also show why dying symbolizes fresh life, which is that our new life starts the instant we die. After the material body that served our purposes in the world is sloughed off, we are brought back to life.

Dying symbolizes fresh life here because new life is the result of an inflow from within (symbolized by Joseph's going up to meet Israel his father, §6030) and of union (symbolized by Joseph's falling on Israel's neck, §6033).

6037   *Now that I have seen your face* means following a perception of mercy. This is established by the symbolism of *seeing* as perception (discussed above at §6032) and from that of a *face*, when mentioned in relation to the Lord, as mercy (discussed at §§222, 223, 5585, 5816).

6038   *That you are still alive* symbolizes a consequent perception of life in himself. This is established by the symbolism of *being alive*, in an inner sense, as spiritual life (§5890). Its symbolism as a perception of that life in himself follows from the explanation above that he received fresh life from an inflow from within and from union (§6036). He also received it from the joy he felt on seeing Joseph. A feeling of joy gives one a perception of life in oneself.

6039   Genesis 46:31, 32, 33, 34. *And Joseph said to his brothers and to his father's household, "I will go up and tell Pharaoh and say to him, 'My brothers and my father's household, who were in the land of Canaan, have come to me. And the men are shepherds of the flock, because they are men of livestock. And their flocks and their herds and everything that is theirs they have brought.' And it might happen that Pharaoh calls you and says, 'What is your work?' And you are to say, 'Men of livestock your servants have been from their youth right till now, both we and our fathers,' so that you can settle in the land of Goshen. Because every shepherd of the flock is abhorrent to Egyptians."*

And Joseph said to his brothers symbolizes a perception by truth on the earthly level. *And to his father's household* means by the goodness there. *I will go up and tell Pharaoh* symbolizes communication with the earthly plane, where religious knowledge resides. *And say to him, "My brothers and my father's household, who were in the land of Canaan, have come to me,"* means concerning the need to introduce the church's truth and goodness. *And the men are shepherds of the flock* means that it leads to goodness. *Because they are men of livestock* means that they have the goodness that comes of truth. *And their flocks and their herds and everything that is theirs they have brought* means that inner and outer goodness and whatever they produce are present. *And it might happen that Pharaoh calls you* means if the earthly plane with its religious knowledge wants to unite. *And says, "What is your work?"* means and to know what is good in you. *And you are to say, "Men of livestock your servants have been from their youth right till now,"* means that from the start they have possessed the truth from which goodness comes, and they still have it. *Both we and our fathers* means that it has been so ever since their earliest kind of goodness. *So that you can settle in the land of Goshen* means that this will be your situation at the center of the earthly plane, with its religious knowledge. *Because every shepherd of the flock is abhorrent to Egyptians* symbolizes a consequent separation from distorted information that opposes religious concepts.

And Joseph said to his brothers symbolizes a perception by truth on the earthly level, as the following shows: *Saying* symbolizes a perception, as frequently noted. Israel's sons represent spiritual truth on the earthly level, as discussed at §§5414, 5879. And *Joseph* represents inner heavenliness, as discussed at §§5869, 5877. This makes it plain that *Joseph said to his brothers* symbolizes a perception by earthly-level truth received from inner heavenliness.

Joseph said does not symbolize perception *by* him, because he stands for the inner dimension, and all perception flows through the inner plane into the outer, earthly plane. What is earthly never perceives anything on its own; when it perceives, it does so under the power of something prior to itself. In fact, not even this prior level perceives anything on its own, only from something still earlier, and so on, until in the end perception comes from the Lord, who is self-existent. That is how inflow works, so that is how perception works.

Spiritual inflow resembles emergence and lasting existence. Nothing emerges from itself, only from something prior to itself, and so on, until finally everything emerges from the first origin—that is, from what exists and emerges on its own. From the same origin comes the lasting existence of everything, because lasting existence is like emergence, and this is because lasting existence is the same as emergence that is constant.

[2] I speak of a perception by earthly-level truth rather than by people with such truth because that is the spiritual way of speaking. It has the effect of drawing one's thoughts away from personality and fixing them on the subject matter. What forms the subject matter—truth and goodness—is what is alive in us and causes us to live, because it comes from the Lord, the source of all life. The same way of speaking also leads the mind away from attributing truth and goodness to individuals. It allows for a comprehensive idea, which has a broader reach than when the idea of personality is added. To speak of perception by people with earthly-level truth, for instance, is to fix the mind on those people, as usually happens. It distracts the mind from what is universal, which diminishes the amount of light cast by truth.

Besides, to think in terms of personality in the other life is to rouse whoever is being thought about, because all thoughts are shared generally there.

These are the reasons for speaking abstractly, as I have spoken here of perception by truth on the earthly plane.

6041
And to his father's household means (perception) by the goodness there. This can be seen from the symbolism of a *household* as goodness (discussed in §§3128, 3652, 3720, 4982) and from that of a *father* too as goodness (discussed in §§2803, 3703, 3704, 5581, 5902).

6042
I will go up and tell Pharaoh symbolizes communication with the earthly plane, where religious knowledge resides. This can be seen from the symbolism of *telling* as communication (mentioned at §4856) and from the representation of *Pharaoh* as the earthly plane, where religious knowledge resides (discussed in §§5799, 6015).

6043
And say to him, "My brothers and my father's household, who were in the land of Canaan, have come to me," means concerning the need to introduce the church's truth and goodness, as the following shows: Israel's sons, *his brothers,* represent spiritual truth on the earthly plane (mentioned just above at §6040). His *father's household* symbolizes the goodness there (also mentioned just above, at §6041). The *land of Canaan* symbolizes the church (dealt with in §§3686, 3705, 4447, 4517, 5136). And *coming to Joseph,* or to Egypt, where Joseph was, symbolizes being introduced into religious knowledge (discussed above in §§6004, 6018). About the introduction of the church's truth into knowledge on the earthly level, see above at §6023. About union between the two, see below at §6047.

6044
And the men are shepherds of the flock means that it leads to goodness. This can be seen from the symbolism of *shepherds of the flock* as people

who lead to what is good (discussed in §§343, 3795, 5201). A *shepherd* is someone who teaches and leads, and a *flock* is someone who is taught and led, but what is meant in an inner sense is truth that leads to goodness, since Israel's sons, the "men" and "shepherds of the flock" here, represent spiritual truth (§6040). Besides, in the people doing the teaching, truth does the leading.

I have already shown that the truth that belongs to faith leads to the good done by neighborly love [§§3332, 5526, 5804, 5954]. The same thing can also be seen from the fact that everything without exception relates to and looks toward its goal and that whatever does not look to a goal cannot survive. The Lord never created anything except for a purpose, so much so that the purpose can be called the all-in-all of every created thing. Creation has been arranged in such a way that just as the original goal looks through its means to the ultimate goal, so the ultimate goal looks to the original goal. That is what connects everything.

The goal itself, in its first origin, is actually the divine goodness sought by divine love and is therefore the Lord himself. That is why the Word calls him the First and the Last, the Alpha and the Omega, in Isaiah 41:4; 44:6; 48:12; Revelation 1:8, 11, 17; 2:8; 21:6; 22:13.

This being so, every single living quality in a human being has to relate to the goal and look toward it. Anyone with any rationality can see that our knowledge looks to truth as its purpose, that truth looks to goodness, and that goodness looks to the Lord as its original and ultimate purpose. Viewed from the standpoint of truth, he is the ultimate purpose, and from the standpoint of goodness, he is the original purpose.

That is how it is with the church's truth, that it leads to goodness; and this is symbolized by the *men, shepherds of the flock,* and by "men of livestock," as discussed next.

Because they are men of livestock means that they have the goodness that comes of truth, which can be seen from the symbolism of *livestock* as truth-based goodness, or the goodness that comes of truth (discussed at §6016). **6045**

This describes Israel's sons, who stand for spiritual truth on the earthly level (§§5414, 5879), so it describes truth. The verse is saying that this truth leads to goodness, for a discussion of which, see just above in §6044.

And their flocks and their herds and everything that is theirs they have brought means that inner and outer goodness and whatever they produce are present, as the following shows: A *flock* symbolizes inner goodness, and a *herd* outer goodness, as treated of at §5913. *Everything that is* **6046** *theirs* symbolizes whatever these produce, as at §5914. And *they have brought* symbolizes being present.

6047   *And it might happen that Pharaoh calls you* means if the earthly plane with its religious knowledge wants to unite, as the following shows: *Calling to himself* symbolizes wanting to unite. To call them to himself out of a desire that they settle in his land and form a single nation with his people is to wish for union. And *Pharaoh* represents the earthly plane with its religious knowledge, as above at §6042.

Pharaoh's call symbolizes introduction and union in return—that is, a bond formed by religious knowledge with earthly-level truth and goodness. All union must be reciprocal; there must be consent on both sides.

[2] The theme here is the bond formed between the church's truth and its knowledge, but it is important to know how to form the bond. We should not start with accepted knowledge and use it to enter into religious truth. The knowledge we possess comes from sensory information and consequently from the world, which produces countless illusions. No, we should start with the truths that lead to faith, proceeding by this path: First we ought to learn what the church teaches; then we should use the Word to examine the validity of those teachings. They are not true just because church leaders have said so and their followers agree. If that were enough, the teachings of all churches and religions would have to be declared true simply because they are someone's state church or birthright religion. So not only would the teachings of papists and Quakers be true but also those of Jews and Muslims, because their leaders have said so and their followers agree. Obviously, then, we must search the Word carefully to see whether the teachings are true. When we do this out of a desire for truth, the Lord gives us the light to tell what is true without our knowing how we can tell, and we are confirmed in the truth in accordance with the goodness we have.

If this truth is at variance with the teachings, we should be careful not to agitate the church.

[3] Afterward, once evidence from the Word has proved to us that the teachings constitute religious truth and we affirm the idea, we are allowed to use knowledge to confirm it. We are allowed to use everything we know, of whatever cast or stripe. Once we have an affirmative attitude through and through, we welcome concepts that agree and reject concepts that harbor fallacies and therefore disagree. Knowledge strengthens our faith.

On this account, we are never forbidden to search the Scriptures from a desire to know whether the teachings of the church we were born into are true. Otherwise we could never be enlightened. Neither are we forbidden to use accepted knowledge for corroboration after [confirmation by Scripture], only before. This path and no other is the one to proceed by in uniting religious truth with knowledge, and not just religious knowledge but knowledge of every kind.

Very few take this path today, though. Most people who read the Word read not with a desire for truth but with a desire to use it for proving the teachings of the church they were born into, regardless of the nature of those teachings.

[4] The Word describes the Lord's kingdom and the fact that the spiritual, rational, and informational dimensions must be united there, but the description employs symbolic names: Israel, Assyria, and Egypt. Israel depicts the spiritual element, Assyria the rational element, and Egypt the informational element. Isaiah uses these words:

> On that day there will be an altar to Jehovah *in the middle of the land of Egypt,* and a pillar to Jehovah along its border, and it will serve as a sign and witness of this to Jehovah Sabaoth in the *land of Egypt,* for they will cry out to Jehovah because of their oppressors, and he will send them a deliverer and chieftain, who will rescue them. And Jehovah will become known to *Egypt,* and the *Egyptians* will recognize Jehovah on that day, and they will offer sacrifice and minha and swear an oath to Jehovah and fulfill it. On that day there will be a path from *Egypt* to *Assyria,* and *Assyria* will come into *Egypt* and *Egypt* into *Assyria;* and *Egypt* will serve *Assyria.* On that day *Israel* will be a third to *Egypt* and *Assyria,* a blessing in the middle of the earth, whom Jehovah Sabaoth will bless, saying, "A blessing on my people *Egypt* and on the work of my hands, *Assyria,* and on my inheritance, *Israel!*" (Isaiah 19:18–25)

[5] Anyone can see that neither Egypt nor Assyria nor even Israel is meant here but that each has another meaning. Israel means the spiritual dimension of the church (see §§3654, 5801, 5803, 5807, 5812, 5817, 5819, 5826, 5833), Assyria means the rational dimension (§§119, 1186), and Egypt means knowledge (§§1164, 1165, 1186, 1462, 4749, 4964, 4966, 5700, 6004, 6015). The prophet portrays the union of these three in a person belonging to the church by saying, "There will be a path from Egypt to Assyria, and Assyria will come into Egypt and Egypt into Assyria, and

Egypt will serve Assyria. On that day Israel will be a third to Egypt and Assyria, a blessing in the middle of the earth." Anyone who wants to be a religious person has to be a spiritual and rational person, whom knowledge must serve.

This discussion now shows that knowledge must not be rejected by religious truth but rather must be joined to it, and that the path to union must start at the beginning, with faith, rather than at the end, with knowledge. See also the arguments in §§128, 129, 130, 195, 196, 232, 233, 1226, 1911, 2568, 2588, 4156, 4760, 5510, 5700.

6048   *And says, "What is your work?"* means and to know what is good in you. This can be seen from the symbolism of *work* as what is good.

Work means what is good because it comes from the will, and what the will produces is either good or evil. What the intellect produces (speech, for instance) is either true or false.

The work of Jacob's children and of their ancestors was to tend livestock and therefore to do shepherds' work. A shepherd's work also symbolizes what is good—specifically, the goodness that grows out of truth.

Correspondence is the reason for the symbolism. Lambs, sheep, kids, and goats, which are members of the flock, correspond to neighborly kindness. So do young cattle and adult cattle, which are members of the herd. The evidence for this correspondence is the fact that flocks and herds appear in various places in the world of spirits and in the first or lowest heaven when angels talk to each other with heavenly passion about neighborly kindness. When they are talking about inner types of neighborly goodness, flocks appear, but when they are talking about outer types, herds appear; see §§3218, 3219, 3220. That is why flocks and herds have this symbolism in the Word.

Keep in mind generally that every symbolism in the Word traces its origin to representations in the next life, and these trace their origin to correspondence. The reason is that the physical world results from the spiritual world the way an effect results from its cause. This enables the spiritual world to flow into the physical world and pursue its goals there. It also holds everything there on course and in order. All creation is a theater representing the Lord's kingdom, or the spiritual and heavenly components of it; see §§2758, 2987–3002, 4939, 5116.

6049   *And you are to say, "Men of livestock your servants have been from their youth right till now,"* means that from the start they have possessed the truth from which goodness comes, and they still have it. This is clear from the symbolism of *men of livestock* as truth from which goodness comes (discussed in §§6016, 6045) and from the symbolism of *from their youth right till now* as from the start, and still.

In respect to the meaning of *livestock* as truth from which goodness comes, you need to know that the term includes all work animals large and small, both those of the herd and those of the flock, and camels, horses, mules, and donkeys as well. The latter animals have a symbolism that relates to truth, while the former (the herd and flock animals) have a symbolism that relates to goodness. That is why livestock—all these work animals as a group—symbolize truth from which comes goodness. In the original language [the word for] livestock comes from a word that also means gain, and gain, in a spiritual sense, also means truth from which comes goodness, because it is through truth that we gain goodness.

[2] The smaller livestock symbolize inner types of goodness, since they are members of the flock, such as lambs, ewes, kids, goats, and rams.

Livestock symbolize truth from which goodness comes in other places in the Word too, such as Isaiah:

> Then he will give rain for the seed with which you will sow the land, and bread from the produce [of the ground]. And there will be fat and richness. On that day *your livestock* will graze in a broad meadow. (Isaiah 30:23)

Grazing stands for being taught truth about goodness (§5201). The broad meadow stands for a theology marked by truth. It is described as broad because breadth means truth (§§3433, 3434, 4482). This shows that livestock means truth from which goodness grows. In Ezekiel:

> . . . to bring your hand back over the inhabited wastelands and over a people gathered from the nations, *busy with livestock* and property, residing at the navel of the earth. (Ezekiel 38:11, 12)

The livestock again stands for truth as a means to goodness. The property stands for goodness.

Both we and our fathers means that it has been so ever since their earliest kind of goodness. This is indicated by the symbolism of *fathers* as goodness, discussed in §§2803, 3703, 3704, 5581, 5902. So the statement that they had been so, and their fathers too, means ever since their earliest kind of goodness.

What is more, in the inner meaning of many scriptural passages, their fathers do not mean Abraham, Isaac, and Jacob but the people of the ancient church, who had goodness.

6050

6051   *So that you can settle in the land of Goshen* means that this will be your situation at the center of the earthly plane, where religious knowledge resides. This can be seen from the symbolism of *settling* as life and therefore as one's situation in life, discussed in §§1293, 3384, 4451, and from that of *Goshen* as the center or inmost part of the earthly plane, discussed in §§5910, 6028. Of course that was where the religious knowledge symbolized by Egypt existed, because Goshen was the best piece of land in Egypt.

6052   *Because every shepherd of the flock is abhorrent to Egyptians* symbolizes a consequent separation from distorted information that opposes religious concepts, as the following shows: Something *abhorrent to Egyptians* symbolizes the segregation of concepts. Anything abhorrent is separated, because the reason it is abhorrent to people is that it is contrary to the basic assumptions they have chosen and to the objects of their love; and being contrary, it is opposed. In this case it is opposed to the distorted information that is symbolized by Egyptians when the text says that every shepherd of the flock is abhorrent to them. And a *shepherd of the flock* symbolizes someone who leads to goodness, as discussed above at §6044. Concepts confirming what is good are those to which distorted information is opposed. Twisted information is what destroys the truth that leads to faith and the good that is done out of neighborly love. It is also what turns the proper order upside down, as the magical knowledge existing in Egypt once did. Egypt's magicians misused many orderly systems, such as correspondence and representation, the knowledge of which they cultivated more fully than others did. These systems work as designed, even when evil people use them, and when evil people use them to control others and hurt others, the systems have been corrupted, because they are magical.

As for the segregation of this knowledge—the topic in this piece of verse—rearrangement is what brings it about. When goodness along with truth holds the center or inmost part (symbolized by Goshen), then twisted information opposed to it is cast out.

[2] So far the subject has been the union of truth with knowledge. One more necessary piece of information about this is that the inner, spiritual self can never unite with the outer, earthly self unless truth is instilled into knowledge. Knowledge, together with the pleasures of earthly desires, constitutes our outer, earthly self, so unless there is a union with knowledge, there can be no union at all. Yet if we are to be

reborn, our inner and outer parts must unite. If they do not, everything good flowing in from the Lord through our inner self into our outer, earthly self is corrupted or smothered or rejected. The inner level is then shut off, too.

The method by which the union takes place is the one depicted in this chapter: the insertion of truth into knowledge.

Spiritual Inflow, and the Interaction of the Soul with the Body

KNOWING or even thinking about spiritual inflow and the interaction of the soul with the body is completely impossible without knowing what the soul is and to some extent what its nature is. If the soul is an unknown quantity, nothing can be said about its inflow or the interaction it engages in. How can you think about the communication between two parties if you have no idea what one of the parties is like?

The world, especially the scholarly world, knows nothing about the nature of the soul. Consider that some believe the soul to be an airy something; others, a bit of flame or fire; others, the pure capacity for thought; others, a share of the common vitality; others, physical energy. What testifies even more strongly to ignorance about the identity of the soul is the fact that people assign it various seats in the body: some in the heart, some in the brain or its fibers, others in the corpora striata, others in the ventricles [of the brain], and others in some tiny gland. Some say the soul is in every part of the body, but in that case they are picturing the kind of vital energy that every living thing shares. These examples show that people are not acquainted with the soul, which is why their pronouncements on it have been mere guesses.

[2] Since they have been unable to form an idea of the soul, many have been unable to believe it is anything more than a vital energy that dissipates when the body dies. That is why scholars have less belief than the uneducated in life after death; and because they do not believe in an afterlife, they also cannot believe in any of the features of it—in any of

the heavenly and spiritual qualities belonging to faith and love. This is evident from the Lord's words in Matthew: "*You have hidden this from the wise and understanding and revealed it to children*" (Matthew 11:25). And again: "*Seeing, they do not see, and hearing, they do not hear or understand*" (Matthew 13:13). Uneducated people never think that way about the soul but trust they will live on after death. Though they do not realize it, their simple faith conceals within it the belief that they will live as human beings, see and speak with angels, and feel joy.

6054   Regarding the soul, which is said to live on after death: It is nothing but the real person, who lives inside the body—in other words, the inner self, which operates in the world through the body and enables the body to live. When this self is released from the body, it is called a spirit, and it appears in an entirely human shape. It cannot possibly be seen by physical eyes, though, only by the eyes of the spirit, and to these eyes it looks just like a person in the world. The soul has senses—namely, touch, smell, hearing, and sight—which are much keener than in the world. It has the same kind of appetites, cravings, longings, desires, and loves as in the world, but at a nobler level. It also engages in thought as in the world, but fuller thought, and it engages in conversation. In short, the soul is the same there as in the world. In fact, souls who do not reflect on the fact that they are in the other life cannot help thinking they are in the world, as I have heard spirits say a number of times. Life after death is a continuation of life in the world. This then is the human soul that lives on after death.

[2] However, to keep the reader's thoughts from falling into ignorance about the meaning of the word *soul,* because of guesses or hypotheses about it, the better course would be to speak of the human spirit, or if you prefer, the inner self. After all, there [in the next life] it looks exactly like a human being, with all the limbs and organs a person has, and is the actual person, in a body. The truth of this can be seen from the appearance of the angels mentioned in the Word, who were all seen in the human form. The human form is the form of all the angels in heaven, because it is the form of the Lord, who appeared as a human so many times after his resurrection.

The reason an angel and a human spirit are in the shape of a person is that the whole of heaven takes from the Lord the tendency to emulate the human form. That is why heaven as a whole is called a universal human. (At the end of many chapters there has been a discussion of

the universal human and of the way everything in a human being corresponds with it.) The Lord is alive in every inhabitant of heaven, and
all of heaven affects every inhabitant with an inflow it receives from the
Lord. This makes every angel an image of heaven, or a completely perfect
human form. The same is true of us after death.

[3] All the spirits I have ever seen, of which there are thousands and
thousands, have looked just like people to me. Some of them have said
they are as human as they were in the world and have added that they
never would have believed such a thing during physical life. Many have
felt quite sad that the human race knows so little about its condition after
death, that people think such hollow, empty thoughts about the soul.
They have grieved that many deep thinkers have made the soul a kind of
wisp of rarefied air, which has inevitably led to the insane misconception
that it evaporates after death.

Anyone who does not know about a person's inner levels also cannot **6055**
know about spiritual inflow or the interaction of the soul with the body,
since the interaction and inflow come by way of the inner levels.

To learn about a person's inner levels, one needs to know that there is
an inner and an outer self. The inner self is in the spiritual world, and the
outer self in the physical world. So the inner self is in heaven's light and
the outer self in the world's light.

It is also necessary to know that the inner self is so distinct from
the outer self that it can survive without the outer self, because it comes
first and is inward. The outer self, though, cannot survive without the
inner, because it comes second and is outward.

Another important fact is that the inner self is the part of us that can
properly be said to have understanding or rationality, because it exists in
heaven's light, which contains reason and true intellect. The outer self,
though, is the part that can properly be called knowledgeable, because
it contains knowledge. Such knowledge draws most of its illumination
from objects seen by the world's glimmer, when this is lit and therefore
enlivened by heaven's light.

As just mentioned, the inner self, since it comes first, can survive with- **6056**
out the outer self, which comes second, but not the other way around.
It is a universal rule that nothing can remain in existence on its own,
only from and through something else. So nothing can preserve its form
except from and through something else. Everything in nature demonstrates that this is so, and it is the same in a human being. Our outer

self can survive only from and through our inner self, and our inner self can survive only from and through heaven. Heaven cannot survive on its own, only from the Lord, the only one who subsists on his own.

The nature of spiritual inflow reflects the nature of emergence and survival, because everything survives through this inflow. It is through inflow that the Lord keeps everything in existence, not only indirectly through the spiritual world but also directly, at both the intermediate and the outermost levels; but this will be demonstrated in what follows [§§6058, 6063].

6057   Before I can mention anything about the way the soul flows into and acts on the body, it needs to be thoroughly known that the inner self has been formed in the image of heaven, and the outer self in the image of the world. In fact, the inner self is heaven in miniature, and the outer self is the world in miniature, which makes it a microcosm.

The outer, physical senses demonstrate that the outer self is an image of the world. The ear is formed to match entirely the nature of the modifications that air undergoes, and the lungs are formed to match the nature of air pressure, as is the outer surface of the body, which is kept in its form by the surrounding pressure of the air. The eye is formed to match entirely the nature of the ether and of light, and the tongue to sense particles dissolved and suspended in liquid. Together with the lungs, trachea, larynx, glottis, jaws, and lips, the tongue is also formed to exercise at will the power of modifying the air to produce articulated sounds (spoken words) and musical sounds. The nostrils are formed to sense particles floating in the atmosphere. Touch, which permeates the entire body, is formed to sense changing conditions in the air—specifically, coldness and warmth—and to sense conditions in liquids and the weight of solid objects. The form and interconnection of the inner organs, which the air cannot reach, are maintained by the rarefied air known as ether. Not to mention that all of nature's deepest secrets—all the secrets of mechanics, physics, chemistry, optics—are etched on the human body and apply to it. These considerations show that the whole of nature unites to shape a person's exterior. That is why the ancients called a person a microcosm.

[2] Just as the outer self is formed in the image of the whole world, then, the inner self is formed in the image of everything in heaven—that is, in the image of heavenly and spiritual qualities radiating from the Lord, which compose and contain heaven. The heavenly properties there include everything having to do with love for the Lord and charity for

one's neighbor. The spiritual properties there include everything having to do with faith. These qualities are intrinsically so abundant and extraordinary that the tongue cannot possibly describe one millionth of them.

The formation of the inner self in the image of all these qualities is displayed manifestly in angels, who, when they appear before one's inner eye (as they have before mine), move one's inmost depths by their presence alone. Love for the Lord and charity for their neighbor pour from them with deep effect, while the ramifications of love and charity—the elements of faith—gleam from them in an impactful way.

These and other proofs have made it plain to me that the inner self was created to be an angel and is therefore a miniature heaven.

[3] This evidence now shows that the spiritual world unites with the physical world in the human being. Consequently the spiritual world flows into the physical world in such a tangible way in us that we can sense it if we simply pay attention.

The same evidence shows what the interaction of the soul with the body is. Strictly speaking, it is communication between the spiritual attributes of heaven and the physical attributes of the world. Clearly the communication relies on spiritual inflow and varies in keeping with the union [between inner and outer].

This communication, which takes place by means of spiritual inflow in keeping with the union [between inner and outer], is unknown today, because people attribute anything and everything to nature. They know nothing about the spiritual realm, which is now so remote that when they think about it, they see it as a nonentity.

Here is what spiritual inflow is like: There is an inflow from the Lord's divinity into every angel, every spirit, and every person on earth. That is how he governs everyone, not only in a comprehensive way but also in the smallest details. He flows in directly from himself and indirectly through the spiritual world too.

6058

To show that this is what spiritual inflow is, I talked at length earlier about the correspondence between the parts of the human body and the universal human, or heaven. I also discussed the way spiritual traits are represented in earthly events and objects. These subjects were addressed at the end of the chapters [on Genesis] 23–43. Then I talked about the angels and spirits with us, at the end of the chapters [on Genesis] 44, 45.

Next I will follow up with a specific treatment of spiritual inflow and soul-body interaction. The ideas presented need to be illustrated from experience, however. Otherwise a subject as unfamiliar as this one, and as shrouded in darkness by others' hypothesizing, could never be brought out into the light. The experiences required for illustration will be presented at the end of the next few chapters [§§6189–6215, 6307–6327, 6466–6496, 6598–6626]. Let my comments here serve as an introduction.

Genesis 47

1. And Joseph came and told Pharaoh and said, "My father and my brothers and their flocks and their herds and everything that is theirs have come from the land of Canaan, and indeed, they are in the land of Goshen."

2. And from a portion of his brothers he took five men and stood them before Pharaoh.

3. And Pharaoh said to his brothers, "What is your work?" And they said to Pharaoh, "A shepherd of the flock your servants are, both we and our fathers."

4. And they said to Pharaoh, "We have come to reside as immigrants in the land, because there is no pasture for the flock that your servants own, because the famine is heavy in the land of Canaan; and now please let your servants settle in the land of Goshen."

5. And Pharaoh spoke to Joseph, saying, "Your father and your brothers have come to you.

6. The land of Egypt is before you. Settle your father and your brothers in the best of the land; have them settle in the land of Goshen. And if you know that there are among them vigorous men, you are to set them as livestock chiefs over what is mine."

7. And Joseph brought Jacob his father and stood him before Pharaoh. And Jacob blessed Pharaoh.

8. And Pharaoh said to Jacob, "How many are the days of the years of your life?"

9. And Jacob said to Pharaoh, "The days of the years of my immigrant journeys are one hundred thirty years. Few and evil have been the days of the years of my life, and they have not overtaken the days of the years of the life of my forebears, in the days of their journeys."

10. And Jacob blessed Pharaoh and went out from before Pharaoh.

11. And Joseph settled his father and his brothers and gave them a possession in the land of Egypt, in the best of the land, in the land of Rameses, as Pharaoh had commanded.

12. And Joseph sustained his father and his brothers and his father's whole house with bread enough for each baby's mouth.

13. And there was no bread in all the land, because the famine was very heavy, and the land of Egypt and the land of Canaan suffered because of the famine.

14. And Joseph gathered all the silver found in the land of Egypt and in the land of Canaan [that was paid in exchange] for the grain provisions that they were buying, and Joseph brought the silver to Pharaoh's house.

15. And the silver was used up from the land of Egypt and the land of Canaan, and all Egypt came to Joseph, saying, "Give us bread, for why shall we die in front of you because the silver is running out?"

16. And Joseph said, "Give me your livestock and I will give you [bread in exchange] for your livestock, if the silver has run out."

17. And they brought their livestock to Joseph, and Joseph gave them bread for the horses and for the livestock of the flock and for the livestock of the herd and for the donkeys, and he provided them with bread for all their livestock in that year.

18. And that year ended, and they came to him in the second year and said to him, "We will not hide from my lord that the silver has been used up, as has the animal stock for my lord; nothing is left before my lord except for our body and our ground.

19. Why shall we die before your eyes, both we and our ground? Buy us and our ground with bread, and we and our ground will live as slaves to Pharaoh. And give us seed, and let us live and not die, and may the ground not be a wasteland!"

20. And Joseph bought all the ground of Egypt for Pharaoh, because the Egyptians each sold their field, since the famine strengthened over them. And the land was Pharaoh's.

21. And as for the people, he transferred them to cities from one end of Egypt's border to its other end.

22. Only the ground of the priests he did not buy, because it was the statutory portion for the priests, from Pharaoh, and they ate their statutory portion that Pharaoh had given them, so they did not sell their ground.

23. And Joseph said to the people, "Here, I have bought you today, and your ground, for Pharaoh. Look: for you, seed; and you are to sow the ground.

24. And it will happen in the [harvests of] produce that you will give a fifth to Pharaoh, and four parts will be for you as seed for the field and as your food, and for those in your houses, and as food for your little children."

25. And they said, "You have kept us alive; may we find favor in the eyes of my lord, and we will be slaves to Pharaoh."

26. And Joseph made it a statute right to this day concerning the ground of Egypt for Pharaoh, [taxed] at one fifth. Only the ground of the priests, theirs alone, was not Pharaoh's.

27. And Israel settled in the land of Egypt, in the land of Goshen, and they had a possession in it, and they became fruitful and multiplied greatly.

28. And Jacob lived in the land of Egypt seventeen years, and Jacob's days, the years of his life, were one hundred forty-seven years.

29. And Israel's days for dying came near, and he called his son Joseph and said to him, "Please, if I have found favor in your eyes, please put your hand under my thigh, and you are to keep mercy and truth with me; you are please not to bury me in Egypt.

30. And let me lie with my ancestors, and you are to bear me out of Egypt and bury me in their grave." And [Joseph] said, "I myself shall do according to your word."

31. And he said, "Swear to me," and [Joseph] swore to him. And Israel bowed over the head of his bed.

Summary

NOW that the earthly-level spiritual goodness that is Israel has united with the inner heavenliness that is Joseph (the theme of the previous chapter), the inner meaning of the current chapter deals with the incorporation of the church's earthly-level truth into knowledge. Jacob's sons are the church's earthly-level truth. Jacob is the phenomenon of earthly-level truth in general. Pharaoh is the knowledge into which that truth is incorporated.   **6059**

Next the chapter turns to knowledge and the way inner heavenliness (Joseph) reduces it to order. First comes truth in the form of knowledge, then truth-from-goodness and goodness-from-truth, and lastly knowledge throughout the earthly level, arranged under its general category.   **6060**

6061   The final subject is the rebirth of earthly-level spiritual goodness (Israel).

Inner Meaning

6062   GENESIS 47:1. *And Joseph came and told Pharaoh and said, "My father and my brothers and their flocks and their herds and everything that is theirs have come from the land of Canaan, and indeed, they are in the land of Goshen."*

And Joseph came and told Pharaoh and said, symbolizes the presence of inner heavenliness on the earthly plane, where knowledge resides, and a consequent inflow and perception. *My father and my brothers* symbolizes earthly-level spiritual goodness and earthly-level religious truth. *Their flocks and their herds* symbolizes inner and outer truth-based goodness. *And everything that is theirs* symbolizes whatever results. *Have come from the land of Canaan* means that they originate in the church. *And indeed, they are in the land of Goshen* means that they are at the center of the earthly level, where knowledge resides.

6063   *And Joseph came and told Pharaoh and said,* symbolizes the presence of inner heavenliness on the earthly plane, where knowledge resides, and a consequent inflow and perception, as the following shows: *Coming* to someone symbolizes presence (as in §5934). *Joseph* represents inner heavenliness (mentioned in §§5869, 5877). *Telling* symbolizes an inflow (discussed at §5966). *Pharaoh* represents the earthly plane, so he represents knowledge in general (discussed in §§5799, 6015). And *saying* in the Word's narratives symbolizes a perception (discussed in §§1791, 1815, 1819, 1822, 1898, 1919, 2080, 2619, 2862, 3509, 5687). Plainly, then, *Joseph came and told Pharaoh and said* symbolizes the presence of inner heavenliness on the earthly plane, where knowledge resides, and a consequent inflow and perception.

[2] There have been many earlier discussions of the inflow of the inner dimension into the outer, earthly dimension and about perception by the outer dimension. I have shown that the earthly level survives and lives off an inflow from the inner level, or rather off an inflow from

the Lord through the inner level. Without that inflow the earthly plane has no life, because it is located in physical creation, from which it takes everything it has, and physical creation is absolutely lifeless. If the earthly plane is to live in us, then, we need the inflow from the Lord. We need it not only directly from him but also indirectly through the spiritual world, so we need it to flow into our inner dimension, because our inner dimension exists in the spiritual world. And from there it must flow into our earthly plane in order for it to live. Our earthly part has been formed to receive life from within.

This is what is meant by the inflow of inner heavenliness into the earthly plane, where knowledge resides.

Perception in the outer, earthly dimension, which Pharaoh represents, takes place under an inflow from within, because inflow and perception correspond to each other (§5743).

My father and my brothers symbolizes earthly-level spiritual good-**6064** ness and earthly-level religious truth. This can be seen from the representation of Israel, the *father,* as spiritual goodness on the earthly plane (as in §§5801, 5803, 5807, 5812, 5817, 5819, 5826, 5833) and from that of his sons as religious truth on the earthly plane (discussed in §§5414, 5879, 5951). The inflow and perception discussed just above in §6063 are about these things—about spiritual goodness and religious truth on the earthly level.

Their flocks and their herds symbolizes inner and outer truth-based **6065** goodness. This is established by the symbolism of *flocks* as inner goodness and of *herds* as outer goodness (discussed in §§5913, 6048). The reason truth-based goodness is being symbolized is that the spiritual goodness Israel represents is goodness based on truth (§4598).

The goodness existing in heaven and in people on earth has two sources: the will and the intellect. Goodness originating in the will was the kind characterizing the earliest people, whose religion was heavenly. Goodness originating in the intellect was the kind characterizing the ancients, whose religion was spiritual. The inhabitants of the third or inmost heaven are devoted to the former kind of goodness, and the inhabitants of the second or middle heaven to the latter kind. The difference and the nature of the difference has been stated many times in the explanations. Goodness rising out of the will is goodness that produces truth, but goodness rising out of the intellect is goodness resulting from truth, or truth-based goodness. In reality this kind of goodness is nothing but truth in action.

6066   *And everything that is theirs* symbolizes whatever results, as above at §6046.

6067   *Have come from the land of Canaan* means that they originate in the church. This can be seen from the symbolism of *coming from* a certain land as originating there and from the symbolism of the *land of Canaan* as the Lord's kingdom in the heavens and the Lord's kingdom on the earth, which is the church (dealt with in §§1607, 3038, 3481, 3686, 3705, 4447, 4454, 5136).

6068   *And indeed, they are in the land of Goshen* means that they are at the center of the earthly level, where knowledge resides. This can be seen from the symbolism of *Goshen* as the center or inmost part of the earthly level, as treated of in §§5910, 6028, 6031.

What is involved in being at the center? When the goodness and truth that belong to the church—that is, goodness and truth that come from the Lord's Word—are acknowledged and believed in on the earthly plane, they take the center of that plane. Whatever is directly under one's gaze is at the center, and what is not directly under one's gaze lies off to the sides. So what is at the center is clearly visible, but what lies off to the sides, only dimly visible. The situation is the same as with eyesight: whatever is directly under the eye is at the center, or in the middle, and clearly visible, but what does not lie directly under it is far from the center, off to the sides, and only dimly visible.

[2] The inner eye is the intellectual side of the mind and receives its sight from heaven's light. It gazes out on the contents of the earthly level, or items of knowledge, just as the outer eye gazes out on objects, or a field of objects.

Inner sight focuses on whatever gives it the greatest pleasure and matters most to it, and fixes its direct view on that, just as outer sight focuses on what attracts it in a field of objects. Inner sight therefore focuses on the items of knowledge that best harmonize with the truth and goodness to which a person is committed. Such knowledge is then at the center for that person.

The reason inner sight gazes on items of knowledge is that it is spiritual and therefore focuses on what is spiritual. So it focuses on items of knowledge, which fall within the range of spiritual vision.

6069   Genesis 47:2, 3, 4, 5, 6. *And from a portion of his brothers he took five men and stood them before Pharaoh. And Pharaoh said to his brothers, "What is your work?" And they said to Pharaoh, "A shepherd of the flock your servants are, both we and our fathers." And they said to Pharaoh, "We*

have come to reside as immigrants in the land, because there is no pasture for
the flock that your servants own, because the famine is heavy in the land of
Canaan; and now please let your servants settle in the land of Goshen." And
Pharaoh spoke to Joseph, saying, "Your father and your brothers have come to
you. The land of Egypt is before you. Settle your father and your brothers in
the best of the land; have them settle in the land of Goshen. And if you know
that there are among them vigorous men, you are to set them as livestock chiefs
over what is mine."

    And from a portion of his brothers he took five men symbolizes several
of the church's true concepts. *And stood them before Pharaoh* symbolizes being incorporated into knowledge. *And Pharaoh said to his brothers*
symbolizes a perception about earthly-level truth known to the church.
What is your work? means about its function and usefulness. *And they*
said to Pharaoh, "A shepherd of the flock your servants are," means that it
leads to goodness. *Both we and our fathers* means that it has been so since
ancient times. *And they said to Pharaoh* symbolizes the next perception.
We have come to reside as immigrants in the land means in order to seek
for life in knowledge. *Because there is no pasture for the flock that your*
servants own means that knowledge containing truth-based goodness is
wanting. *Because the famine is heavy in the land of Canaan* means that
the church is lacking this kind of [goodness]. *And now please let your*
servants settle in the land of Goshen symbolizes an intent to live in the
midst of [knowledge]. *And Pharaoh spoke to Joseph, saying,* symbolizes a
perception on the earthly level, where knowledge resides. *Your father and*
your brothers have come to you means concerning an inflow of inner heavenliness into earthly-level spiritual goodness and earthly-level religious
truth. *The land of Egypt is before you* means that the things known to the
earthly mind are under the oversight of inner heavenliness. *Settle your*
father and your brothers in the best of the land means that they live in the
inmost part of [knowledge]. *Have them settle in the land of Goshen* means
where the center is. *And if you know that there are among them vigorous*
men symbolizes the more outstanding points of theology. *You are to set*
them as livestock chiefs over what is mine means that they are the main
items of knowledge.

    And from a portion of his brothers he took five men symbolizes several
of the church's true concepts. This can be seen from the representation
of Jacob's sons, the *brothers,* as truth known to the church (dealt with at
§§5403, 5419, 5427, 5458, 5512) and from the symbolism of *five* as several
(dealt with at §§4638, 5291).

6070

6071   *And stood them before Pharaoh* symbolizes being incorporated into knowledge. This can be seen from the representation of *Pharaoh* as knowledge in general, as discussed in §§5799, 6015. The insertion is symbolized by *standing them before him.* The reason for presenting the brothers was to incorporate them—to incorporate the church's true concepts, which are Jacob's sons.

On the point that truth needs to be incorporated into the church's knowledge, see §§6004, 6023, 6052, but the whole concept is unknown today, so further illustration is needed. The church's knowledge today consists in the literal statements of the Word. Unless truth from the inner meaning is incorporated into this knowledge, the mind can always be led astray into heresy, but when truth is incorporated into it, the mind cannot be led astray into heresies.

[2] Take, for example, the idea that God seethes with anger, punishes us, tests us, throws us into hell, and does evil. People who absorb this idea from the Word's literal meaning can be seduced into false notions concerning him. They might think that goodness itself, which is God, can actually produce what is evil and therefore what is opposed to God, although the truth is that goodness comes from what is good, and evil from what is evil.

However, this concept has a different appearance if inner truth is incorporated into it. Take the truth that the evil in us is what angers us, tests us, punishes us, throws us into hell, and constantly generates fresh evil. Take also the truth that there is a parallel with a country's laws. The laws come from the monarch, but the harms involved in punishment do not; these come instead from the people themselves who are doing evil.

[3] Another truth: The hells are the source of all evil. They are allowed to produce evil because human nature makes it unavoidable. We take to evil and base our life on it, so if we were not left in evil we would not be free and therefore could not be reformed. Even so, nothing but goodness comes from God, because so far as we allow him to, God bends evil toward goodness.

[4] Yet another truth: We have to believe in the most general concepts first; the light shed on them by detailed truth needs to come later. This applies to the general concept that every single thing that exists comes from God, including the miseries of punishment. *How* they come from God we must learn afterward. We also need to learn the nature of events the Lord tolerates and the reasons he tolerates them.

[5] Likewise this truth: All worship of God inevitably starts with holy fear, which holds within it the idea that God rewards the good and punishes the evil. Unsophisticated people and little children have to believe this idea, because they do not yet grasp what tolerance of evil is. Their belief is in keeping with the Lord's words: "Rather, fear him who can destroy both body and soul in Gehenna" (Matthew 10:28). If at first they do not dare do wrong, out of fear, love is gradually instilled, along with goodness. Then they start to see and sense that nothing but goodness comes from God, that evil comes from themselves, and eventually that all evil comes from hell.

[6] Besides, the inhabitants of heaven perceive that nothing but goodness comes from God. The inhabitants of hell say that everything evil comes from God because he allows it and does not do away with it. But the ones of them who are in the world of spirits are given this answer: If evil were taken away from them, they would have no life, and neither would people on earth who live for evil. The evil in them punishes itself in accordance with the law, and because of the negative consequences they eventually abstain from wrongdoing. What is more, the punishment of the evil is the protection of the good.

[7] Add to all this the fact that it is imperative for people immersed in evil and people who worship outwardly but not inwardly (as the Jews of old did) to be fearful of God and to believe he inflicts punishment. Fear of God can motivate them to do good; love never can.

When these truths and many others are incorporated into that concept, it presents an entirely different appearance. The concept comes to resemble a transparent container, and the truth it contains shines through, showing the container to be a single, general truth.

And Pharaoh said to his brothers symbolizes a perception about earthly-level truth known to the church, as the following shows: *Saying* symbolizes a perception, as noted above at §6063. *Pharaoh* represents the earthly level and knowledge in general, as also noted above at §6063. And Jacob's sons, the *brothers,* represent earthly-level truth known to the church, as noted above at §6064. Clearly, then, *Pharaoh said to his brothers* symbolizes a perception by the earthly level about the religious truth there.

6072

What is your work? means about its function and usefulness. This is evident from the symbolism of *work* as something good (discussed at §6048) and therefore as function and usefulness, since these are forms of goodness. All goodness that is called charitable goodness is actually usefulness,

6073

and to be useful is actually to do work benefiting one's neighbor, one's country, the church, and the Lord's kingdom. Not even neighborly love in itself is neighborly love until it is acted on and put to work. To love others and not do them good when we can is not to love them. To do them good when we can, and to do it from the heart, is to love them. When we do that, the deed or work itself contains all our love for our neighbor. Good deeds embrace all aspects of charity and faith in us, and they are called spiritual goodness. They become good through being carried out, which means through useful activity.

[2] Since angels in heaven have goodness from the Lord, they want nothing more than to serve useful purposes. Usefulness is the core pleasure of their life and the measure of the bliss and happiness they enjoy (§§454, 696, 997, 3645), as the Lord in fact teaches in Matthew:

> The Son of Humankind will come in the glory of his Father, with his angels, and then he will repay every person *according to that person's deeds.* (Matthew 16:27)

The deeds here do not refer to deeds as they appear on the outside but as they appear on the inside, which is to say, according to the neighborly love they hold. That is exactly how angels view them.

[3] As just mentioned, deeds embrace all facets of charity and faith in us, and the way we live causes charity to be charity, and faith to be faith, and therefore to be something good. For that reason the Lord loved John above all the other disciples, and John reclined on the Lord's chest at the [Last] Supper (John 21:20), because he represented the good done by charity, or good deeds (see the prefaces to Genesis 18 and 22). For the same reason, the Lord said, *"Follow me"* to John and not to Peter, who represented faith (see the same prefaces). So faith (Peter), taking offense, said, "Lord, *but what about him?"* Jesus said to him, "If I want him to stay till I come, what is that to you? *You, follow me!"* (John 21:19, 21, 22, 23). This was a prediction that faith would develop contempt for good deeds. It was also a declaration that good deeds nevertheless reside with the Lord. This is plain to see from the Lord's words to the sheep and the goats in Matthew 25:34–46, which is simply a list of good deeds.

Faith's rejection of the Lord is evident from the portrayal of it by Peter when he three times denied knowing the Lord [Matthew 26:69–75; Mark 14:66–72; Luke 22:54–62; John 18:15–18, 25–27]. The denial happened at night, which symbolizes the church's last days, when there is no more neighborly love (§6000). The three repetitions mean that things were then complete (§§1825, 2788, 4495, 5159). They took place before the rooster crowed, which means before a new religion came into existence, because the half-light and morning that follow the night symbolize the beginning of a religion (§§2405, 5962).

And they said to Pharaoh, "A shepherd of the flock your servants are," means that it leads to goodness. This can be seen from the discussion in §6044 of the symbolism of a *shepherd of the flock* as one who leads to goodness. Here it symbolizes truth that leads to goodness, because Jacob's sons stand for the church's truth.

6074

Both we and our fathers means that it has been so since ancient times. This can be seen from the symbolism of *fathers* as the people of the ancient churches, as noted in §6050.

6075

In many places where the Word talks about Jews and Israelites, it favorably mentions their fathers, [or ancestors]. Readers who stay in the literal meaning take the fathers mentioned there simply to mean Abraham, Isaac, Jacob, and Jacob's sons. In the inner meaning of those passages, though, the fathers in a positive sense mean not those men but people who were part of the very earliest church, before the Flood, and people who were part of the ancient church, after the Flood. Both sets of people are called fathers because the church descended from them and drew its religious culture from them.

[2] Fathers mean the people of the ancient churches. In Moses:

> Jehovah delighted in *your fathers,* to love them, and he chose their seed after them. (Deuteronomy 10:15)

And in the same author:

> Remember the days of old, understand the years of generation after generation, when the Highest One gave an inheritance to the nations; when he divided the children of humankind, he set the boundaries of the peoples according to the number of the children of Israel. But when Jeshurun grew fat, he deserted God; he sacrificed to demons, to gods who arrived recently and [whom] *your fathers* did not know. (Deuteronomy 32:7, 8, 15, 17)

This passage occurs in the mystical Song of Moses, which talks about the ancient church in verses 7–14 and about Jacob's descendants in verses 15–43. The days of old symbolize states of the earliest church, which came before the Flood. The years of generation after generation symbolize states of the ancient church, which came after the Flood. States of goodness in the people of those churches are symbolized by the inheritance that the Highest One gave to the nations, and states of truth in them by the Highest One's dividing the children of humankind and setting the boundaries of the peoples according to the number of the children of Israel. Their number, twelve, means all religious truth taken together; see §§577, 2089, 2129 at the end, 2130 at the end, 3272, 3858, 3913. Their fathers, then, plainly symbolize people belonging to the ancient churches.

[3] Likewise in the following passages. In Isaiah:

> Our house of holiness and our prize jewel, *where our fathers praised you,* has become a fiery blaze. (Isaiah 64:11)

In Jeremiah:

> Didn't *your father* eat and drink and yet perform judgment and justice? After that it was well with him. (Jeremiah 22:15)

In the same author:

> They have sinned against Jehovah, the dwelling place of righteousness, and the *hope of their fathers,* Jehovah. (Jeremiah 50:7)

In David:

> God, with our ears we have heard—*our fathers* have recounted to us— the work you worked in their days, in the days of old. (Psalms 44:1)

The same for the *fathers* mentioned in Daniel 11:24, 37, 38. The fact that the fathers in these passages mean the people of the ancient churches is not apparent in the literal meaning, only from the inner meaning, which is about the church and about the goodness and truth in it.

The Word also calls the church itself in respect to goodness a father and in respect to truth a mother (§§3703, 5581), because the church is a heavenly marriage, or a marriage of goodness and truth.

6076   *And they said to Pharaoh* symbolizes the next perception. This can be seen from the symbolism of *saying* as a perception (mentioned above at §6063) and from the representation of *Pharaoh* as the earthly plane in general (mentioned before). The reason it symbolizes the *next* perception by the earthly dimension is that the phrase *they said to Pharaoh* appeared just above in §6074 as well, so this is a recurrence.

6077   *We have come to reside as immigrants in the land* means in order to seek for life in knowledge, as the following shows: *Residing as immigrants* symbolizes being taught and living a life, as discussed in §§1463, 2025.

Coming to reside as immigrants, then, means in order to seek for life. And the *land*—here, the land of Egypt—means where there is knowledge, so it symbolizes knowledge itself. The symbolism of Egypt as knowledge has been demonstrated many times.

About the idea that truth finds its life in knowledge, or rather seeks to find its life there, what needs to be known is this: Everything in the spiritual world seeks something lower down in which to exist and bring its purposes to effect, so everything in the physical world does too. The goal is for it all to be constantly producing something. This lower level is like a body, and the energy that seeks to inhabit it is like a soul. The effort does not rest until it reaches the lowest, outermost level of nature, where it runs into what is inert.

This phenomenon is visible everywhere in the physical world, and in the spiritual world as well. In the spiritual world, goodness seeks to live in truth, truth in knowledge, knowledge in empirical evidence, and empirical evidence in the world itself.

[2] Specifically regarding truth within knowledge: Be aware that inner truth can indeed be incorporated into knowledge but does not find life there until goodness is present in the knowledge. Life is present in goodness, and it is present in truth as a result of goodness. Consequently it is present in knowledge through truth as a result of goodness. Under those circumstances, goodness is like a soul to truth, and through truth it is like a soul to knowledge, which is like a body. In short, love for one's neighbor brings faith to life and animates it, and through faith it does the same for knowledge in the earthly mind.

[3] Not many people today know that truth and knowledge are different things. That is because not many possess religious truth that stems from neighborly love, and religious truth devoid of neighborly love is nothing but a set of concepts. It sits in the memory just the same as any other information there. When religious truth does stem from neighborly love, though, or holds neighborly love inside, it differs noticeably from knowledge. Truth sometimes rises above knowledge, and it then sees knowledge as lying below.

Our situation after death illustrates this principle vividly. We can then think and speak rationally about religious truth and goodness, and much more insightfully than during bodily life. However, we cannot dredge any information out of our memory. The things we knew are like matters blotted out and obliterated, even though we keep them all with us. See §§2475, 2476, 2477, 2479, 2481–2486.

This evidence shows that religious truth, which is inherently spiritual, differs from knowledge, which is inherently earthly. It also shows that devotion to the goodness urged by neighborly love raises religious truth up from the level of knowledge toward heaven.

6078   *Because there is no pasture for the flock that your servants own* means that knowledge containing truth-based goodness is wanting. This can be seen from the symbolism of *pasture for the flock* as knowledge containing truth-based goodness. *No pasture* therefore means knowledge containing no truth-based goodness.

Pasture in an inner sense is what sustains spiritual life. In particular it is truth in the form of knowledge, which our soul hungers for the way our body hungers for food. Such truth provides nourishment, so grazing in a pasture means being taught (§5201). The human longing for knowledge makes it very plain that knowledge and truth sustain the human soul. So does the correspondence of food with knowledge (§§1480, 3114, 4792, 5147, 5293, 5340, 5342, 5576, 5579, 5915). This correspondence reveals itself in humankind when we consume food: If we eat while talking and listening, the vessels that absorb chyle open up and take in more nutrients than if we dine alone. Spiritual truth and instruction in spiritual truth would have the same effect on us if we had a desire for goodness.

The reality that truth feeds our spiritual life is especially obvious among good spirits and angels in heaven. They have a constant longing for knowledge and wisdom, and when this spiritual food runs out, they feel bleak, lethargic, and famished. Not until their yearnings are satisfied are they refreshed and lifted into the bliss of their life.

Nonetheless, in order for knowledge to contribute to the healthful nourishment of the soul, it must contain the life provided by truth-based goodness. If it does not, it still sustains our inner life, but only our earthly life, not our spiritual life.

[2] Other Scripture passages also demonstrate that pasture in an inner sense means what sustains our spiritual life. In Isaiah, for instance:

> I gave you as a pact with the people, to restore the earth, to say to prisoners, "Go on out!"; to those in darkness, "Show yourselves!" *On paths they will graze,* and *on all the slopes will be their pasture.* (Isaiah 49:8, 9)

Grazing on paths stands for being taught truth. For the meaning of paths as truth, see §§627, 2333, and for that of grazing as being taught, §5201. Pasture on all the slopes stands for being sustained by goodness, since slopes, like mountains, mean a loving goodness (§§795, 796, 1430, 2722, 4210). [3] In Jeremiah:

Doom to shepherds destroying and scattering the *flock of my pasture!* (Jeremiah 23:1)

The pasture stands for that which sustains spiritual life. In the same author:

Zion's chieftains have become like deer; *they have not found pasture.* (Lamentations 1:6)

"They have not found pasture" means that they have not found the truth that grows out of goodness. [4] In Ezekiel:

I, I myself will seek my flock; *in a good pasture I will pasture them,* and on the mountains of Israel's loftiness will be their fold. So they will lie in a good fold, and *on rich pasture they will graze,* on Israel's mountains. (Ezekiel 34:11, 14)

The good and rich pasture on Israel's mountains stands for the goodness that grows out of truth. In the same author:

Is it too little for you [that] *you graze the good pasture* but the *rest of your pastures* you trample with your feet? (Ezekiel 34:18)

The meaning is similar. In Hosea:

I knew you in the wilderness, in a land of drought. *When they had pasture,* they then received their fill; they received their fill and their heart lifted. (Hosea 13:5, 6)

In Joel:

The animal sighs, the herds of cattle are confused, *because there is no pasture for them;* even the flocks of sheep are left desolate. (Joel 1:18)

In David:

Jehovah is my shepherd. He will make me lie down *in a grassy pasture;* he will lead me to quiet waters. *He will revive my soul.* (Psalms 23:1, 2, 3)

In the same author:

Jehovah made us—his people and the *flock of his pasture*—and we did not. So we are his, his people and the *flock of his pasture.* (Psalms 100:3)

[5] The pasture in these passages stands for the truth a person is taught and accordingly for something focusing on spiritual life. If our spiritual life lacks this pasture, it flags and withers, so to speak, as our body does when it lacks food.

The meaning of a pasture as the goodness and truth that refresh and sustain the human soul or spirit is clear from the Lord's words in John:

> I myself am the doorway; if any come in through me, they will be saved, and go in and out, and *find pasture*. (John 10:9)

The pasture stands for goodness and truth in people who acknowledge the Lord and seek life from him alone.

6079   *Because the famine is heavy in the land of Canaan* means that the church is lacking this kind of [goodness]. This is established by the symbolism of *famine* as a lack of goodness (discussed at §5893) and from that of the *land of Canaan* as the church (referred to above at §6067).

6080   *And now please let your servants settle in the land of Goshen* symbolizes an intent to live in the midst of [knowledge]. This is established by the symbolism of *settling* as living (discussed at §§1293, 3384, 3613, 4451, 6051) and from that of the *land of Goshen* as the center or inmost part of the earthly plane (discussed at §§5910, 6028, 6031, 6068).

6081   *And Pharaoh spoke to Joseph, saying,* symbolizes a perception on the earthly level, where knowledge resides. This is established by the symbolism of *saying* as a perception (mentioned often), from the representation of *Pharaoh* as the earthly level, where knowledge resides (discussed at §§5799, 6015, 6063), and from the representation of *Joseph* as the inner dimension (discussed at §5469), from which the earthly level receives its perceptions.

6082   *Your father and your brothers have come to you* means concerning an inflow of inner heavenliness into earthly-level spiritual goodness and earthly-level religious truth, as the following shows: Israel, the *father* here, represents spiritual goodness on the earthly level, as dealt with in §§5801, 5803, 5807, 5812, 5817, 5819, 5826, 5833. And his sons, the *brothers,* represent religious truth on the earthly level, as dealt with in §§5414, 5879, 5951.

The reason it means an inflow of inner heavenliness is that the speech is addressed to Joseph, who represents inner heavenliness (§§5869, 5877), and that the inflow into the outer, earthly plane comes from within.

6083   *The land of Egypt is before you* means that the things known to the earthly mind are under the oversight of inner heavenliness. This can be seen from the symbolism of the *land of Egypt* as the earthly mind, where knowledge resides (discussed in §§5276, 5278, 5280, 5288, 5301), and from that of *before you,* meaning under the oversight of inner heavenliness, which is Joseph (§§5869, 5877).

Settle your father and your brothers in the best of the land means that they live in the inmost part of knowledge, as the following shows: The *best of the land* symbolizes the inmost part of the earthly mind, where knowledge resides (discussed below), since the land of Egypt is that mind (as just above at §6083). *Settling* symbolizes living (discussed at §§1293, 3384, 3613, 4451, 6051), and Israel and his sons, the *father* and *brothers* who were to live there, represent earthly-level spiritual goodness and earthly-level religious truth (noted above at §6082).

6084

[2] The best part means the inmost part because what we keep directly under our gaze is the best; we always train our eye on that which moves us and delights us the most. And what we keep directly under our gaze is also at the inmost point, because it is in the middle. As a result we see it in the brightest light. Everything else lies at the edges all around and is therefore less clear, finally falling into darkness, because it does not delight or move us as much. That is the case with the items of knowledge we see with our inner eye, the objects of inner sight being actually knowledge and truth. What is pleasing and good in such objects is what draws our eye to them.

Still, it is important to know that truth and the items of knowledge compatible with it lie directly in view (or at the inmost point) for people who delight in and respond to spiritual and heavenly truth, because for them, what is compatible with truth is the best. Falsity and the items of knowledge compatible with it lie directly in view (or at the inmost point) for people who respond to and delight in the evils resulting from self-love and materialism. See also the remarks at §6068.

Have them settle in the land of Goshen means where the center is. This is clear from the symbolism of *settling* as living (as just above at §6084) and from that of the *land of Goshen* as the center or inmost point of the earthly plane (discussed in §§5910, 6028, 6031, 6068).

6085

And if you know that there are among them vigorous men symbolizes the more outstanding points of theology. This can be seen from the symbolism of *vigorous men* as the more outstanding points of theology. A *man* symbolizes a person who truly understands, and it symbolizes truth (§§158, 265, 749, 1007, 3134, 4823), so it symbolizes theology, and *vigorous* means outstanding. The original language uses a word for vigorous that

6086

also refers to ability and virtue, which in an inner sense mean something robust and therefore something relatively outstanding.

6087   *You are to set them as livestock chiefs over what is mine* means that they are the main items of knowledge. This can be seen from the symbolism of *chiefs* as the main items (dealt with in §§1482, 2089, 5044) and from that of *livestock* as truth that gives rise to goodness (dealt with in §§6016, 6045, 6049). Here the livestock symbolize items of knowledge containing such truth, because it says *over the livestock that is mine,* meaning Pharaoh's, and Pharaoh represents not truth containing goodness but items of knowledge containing such truth.

6088   Genesis 47:7, 8, 9, 10. *And Joseph brought Jacob his father and stood him before Pharaoh. And Jacob blessed Pharaoh. And Pharaoh said to Jacob, "How many are the days of the years of your life?" And Jacob said to Pharaoh, "The days of the years of my immigrant journeys are one hundred thirty years. Few and evil have been the days of the years of my life, and they have not overtaken the days of the years of the life of my forebears, in the days of their journeys." And Jacob blessed Pharaoh and went out from before Pharaoh.*

And Joseph brought Jacob his father symbolizes the presence of general truth received from within. *And stood him before Pharaoh* symbolizes incorporation into the overall mass of knowledge. *And Jacob blessed Pharaoh* symbolizes good wishes for union and consequent fruitfulness. *And Pharaoh said to Jacob* symbolizes a perception on the earthly level, where knowledge resides, concerning general religious truth. *How many are the days of the years of your life?* means concerning the state of life of the earthly level in its dependence on the spiritual level. *And Jacob said to Pharaoh* symbolizes the answer. *The days of the years of my immigrant journeys* means concerning the next stage of life. *Are one hundred thirty years* symbolizes its nature and condition. *And evil have been the days of the years of my life* means that the state of earthly life is a state full of trials. *And they have not overtaken the days of the years of the life of my forebears* means that it did not rise to the same level as the state of life among the earlier people. *In the days of their journeys* means in regard to their state of life. *And Jacob blessed Pharaoh* symbolizes good wishes again for union and consequent fruitfulness. *And went out from before Pharaoh* symbolizes a separation for the time being.

6089   *And Joseph brought Jacob his father* symbolizes the presence of general truth received from within, as the following shows. *Bringing* someone, or causing someone to come, means presenting that person, and coming to someone symbolizes presence (§§5934, 6063). *Jacob* represents a theology composed of earthly truth, and earthly truth itself, as discussed in §§3305, 3509, 3525, 3546, 4538. Here he represents truth in general, because his sons represent particular truths. The concept "received from within" is symbolized because *Joseph* is the inner dimension, the source of earthly-level truth.

General truth is called the father of Joseph because that is what we absorb before anything else. Later it is filled out with a wealth of particular truths, and last comes insight into these truths, or reason and true understanding. This pattern is plain to see in a human being, because we grow in judgment from childhood on. The same happens to spiritual truth and goodness when we are being born anew, or regenerated.

After the inner dimension has emerged from general earthly-level truth, though, the situation changes. The inner dimension now ceases to acknowledge earthly-level truth as its father and treats it as a servant instead. This view of it as a servant is demonstrated by Joseph's dream about his father, in which the sun and the moon and eleven stars bowed down to him. So his father said, "What is this dream that you dreamed? Will we really come, I and your mother and your brothers, to bow down to you to the earth?" (Genesis 37:9, 10). That explains why Jacob's sons refer to Joseph's father as his servant so many times in Joseph's presence (Genesis 43:28; 44:24, 27, 30, 31). In addition, Joseph was lord throughout the land of Egypt and was therefore master over his father as well.

And stood him before Pharaoh symbolizes incorporation into the overall mass of knowledge. The explanation above at §6071 makes this evident. **6090**

And Jacob blessed Pharaoh symbolizes good wishes for union and consequent fruitfulness. This can be seen from the symbolism of *blessing* as, in this case, good wishes for union—the earthly-level union between truth and knowledge, since that is the current subject. **6091**

Blessing symbolizes many things. It includes everything good and everything that is fortunate in a spiritual sense. So it symbolizes being gifted with a loving, charitable goodness (§§3406, 4981), and it symbolizes union (3504, 3514, 3530, 3565, 3584), fruitfulness resulting from a desire for truth (2846), and wishing someone all the best (3185). In this instance, then, it symbolizes good wishes for the endeavor under discussion, which is union. It therefore symbolizes good wishes for fruitfulness too, because fruitfulness follows from union. When union is achieved, goodness increases and truth multiplies, because there is then a marriage of goodness and truth that gives rise to further goodness and truth. Until then, goodness and truth cannot come into being except from what amounts to whoredom. The goodness that grows out of this kind of liaison is counterfeit, and so is the truth. The goodness from this liaison is self-seeking, and the truth savors of that type of goodness.

6092   *And Pharaoh said to Jacob* symbolizes a perception on the earthly level, where knowledge resides, concerning general religious truth. This is established by the symbolism of *saying* as a perception (mentioned above at §6063), by the representation of *Pharaoh* as the earthly level, where knowledge resides (mentioned in §§5799, 6015), and by the representation of *Jacob* as general religious truth (discussed above at §6089).

6093   *How many are the days of the years of your life?* means concerning the state of life of the earthly level in its dependence on the spiritual level. This is established by the symbolism of *days* and of *years* as states (discussed in §§23, 487, 488, 493, 893, 2788, 3462, 3785, 4850) and by that of *life* as spiritual life (discussed at §§5407, 5890). Here life symbolizes spiritual life on the earthly plane—in other words, the earthly plane in its dependence on the spiritual.

6094   *And Jacob said to Pharaoh* symbolizes the answer, as requires no explanation.

6095   *The days of the years of my immigrant journeys* means concerning the next stage of life, as the following shows: *Days* and *years* symbolize states, as mentioned just above at §6093. And *immigrant journeys* symbolize life and instruction, as discussed in §§1463, 2025, 3672, so they symbolize the next stage of life.

6096   *Are one hundred thirty years* symbolizes its nature and condition. This is evident from the consideration that all numbers in the Word have symbolic meaning; see §§575, 647, 648, 755, 813, 1963, 2075, 2252, 3252, 4264, 4495, 4670, 5265. So they symbolize the nature and condition of the thing being counted. The number here, then, specifically symbolizes the nature and condition of the life Jacob had lived so far—that is, the nature and condition of the spiritual life the earthly level now received from the spiritual level.

6097   *And evil have been the days of the years of my life* means that the state of earthly life is a state full of trials. This can be seen from the symbolism of *days* and *years* as states, as above at §§6093, 6095, and from that of Jacob's *life* as spiritual life on the earthly level, as also above at §6093. Trials in that state are symbolized by the fact that the days had been *evil*. All trials appear evil, because they are times of deep anguish and pain and seemingly of damnation. During trials we are thrust into a state of being conscious of our evil, which means we are thrust into the company of evil spirits, who torture our conscience by making accusations against us. We are defended, however, by angels, or rather through angels by the Lord, who keeps hope and trust alive in us. These are the fighting forces from within that enable us to resist.

It is especially when the earthly dimension accepts the spiritual that it undergoes trial, because the earthly level is where the evils in our life and the falsities in our theology reside. That is why Jacob says these words of himself, because in this verse he represents truth on the earthly level.

And they have not overtaken the days of the years of the life of my fore- 6098 *bears* means that it did not rise to the same level as the state of life among those people. This can be seen from the symbolism of *overtaking* here as rising (discussed below) and from that of the *days* and *years of life* as states of spiritual life (as above in §§6093, 6095, 6097).

Overtaking means rising here because Jacob's *forebears,* Isaac and Abraham, represented something loftier, or more inward, than Jacob. Abraham in the highest sense represented the Lord's divinity itself, Isaac the Lord's divine rationality, and Jacob his earthly divinity. For the representation of Abraham as the Lord's divinity itself, see §§1965, 1989, 2010, 3245, 3251, 3305 at the end, 3439, 3703, 4615. For that of Isaac as his divine rationality, 1893, 2066, 2072, 2083, 2630, 2774, 3012, 3194, 3210, 4615. For that of Jacob as his earthly divinity in regard to truth and goodness, 3305, 3509, 3525, 3546, 3576, 3599, 4286, 4538, 4570, 4615. As a consequence, Abraham also represents what is heavenly in us, Isaac what is spiritual, and Jacob what is earthly. This is because our rebirth is an image of the Lord's glorification (3138, 3212, 3296, 3490, 4402, 5688).

This evidence now makes it plain that *they have not overtaken the days of the years of the life of my forebears* means that [the next state of earthly life] did not rise to the same level as the state of life among those [earlier] people.

And Jacob blessed Pharaoh symbolizes good wishes for union and con-   6099 sequent fruitfulness as above at §6091.

And went out from before Pharaoh symbolizes a separation for the time   6100 being. This is indicated by the symbolism of *going out* as separating—here, separating for the time being from the earthly plane, where knowledge resides, represented by *Pharaoh.*

Here is why going out symbolizes separation for the time being: The preceding verses have dealt with the way earthly-level spiritual goodness (Israel) and earthly-level religious truth (his sons) united with inner heavenliness (Joseph). However, they have not treated yet of union with the earthly plane, only of incorporation into that plane. Upcoming verses 13–26 of this chapter do deal with that union. See the summary in §§6059, 6060. That is why *Jacob went out from before Pharaoh* symbolizes separation for the time being.

6101   Genesis 47:11, 12. *And Joseph settled [his] father and his brothers and gave them a possession in the land of Egypt, in the best of the land, in the land of Rameses, as Pharaoh had commanded. And Joseph sustained his father and his brothers and his father's whole house with bread enough for each baby's mouth.*

And Joseph settled his father and his brothers symbolizes life received by spiritual goodness and religious truth from inner heavenliness. *And gave them a possession in the land of Egypt, in the best of the land* means in the inmost part of the earthly mind, where knowledge resides. *In the land of Rameses* symbolizes the inmost part of the mind, and the nature of that part. *As Pharaoh had commanded* means with the consent of the earthly plane, where knowledge resides. *And Joseph sustained his father and his brothers and his father's whole house with bread* means that there was a constant inflow of goodness from inner heavenliness into earthly-level spiritual goodness and religious truths, which gave them life. *Enough for each baby's mouth* means into each of these according to the nature of its innocent goodness.

6102   *And Joseph settled his father and his brothers* symbolizes life received by spiritual goodness and religious truth from inner heavenliness, as the following shows: *Settling* symbolizes life, as discussed in §§1293, 3384, 3613, 4451, 6051. Israel, the *father,* represents spiritual goodness on the earthly level, as discussed in §§5801, 5803, 5807, 5812, 5817, 5819, 5826, 5833. His sons, the *brothers,* represent religious truth on the earthly level, as discussed in §§5414, 5879, 5951. And *Joseph* represents inner heavenliness, as discussed in §§5869, 5877. All this goes to show that *Joseph settled his father and his brothers* symbolizes life received by spiritual goodness and religious truth from inner heavenliness.

6103   *And gave them a possession in the land of Egypt, in the best of the land* means in the inmost part of the earthly mind, where knowledge resides, as the following shows: A *possession* symbolizes the status of one's spiritual life, as discussed at §2658. The *land of Egypt* symbolizes the earthly mind, where knowledge resides, as dealt with in §§5276, 5278, 5280, 5288, 5301. And the *best of the land* symbolizes the inmost part, as discussed above at §6084. From this it is clear that *he gave them a possession in the land of Egypt, in the best of the land* symbolizes the status of one's spiritual life in the inmost part of one's earthly mind, where knowledge resides.

In the land of Rameses symbolizes the inmost part of the mind and **6104**
the nature of that part. This can be seen from the fact that all names of
people and places in the Word have symbolic meaning (§§1888, 3422,
4298, 4442, 5095, 5225). Since the land of Goshen means the inmost
part of the earthly mind (§§5910, 6028, 6031, 6068), *Rameses,* which
was the best piece of land in the land of Goshen, means the inmost part
of the spiritual mind within the earthly mind.

The nature of this inmost core is something we can barely comprehend, because its contents are beyond counting and beyond description.
They can be seen only in heaven's light and therefore only by angels. In
this the nature of the name Rameses is no different from the nature of
any other place-names or personal names in the Word.

As Pharaoh had commanded means with the consent of the earthly **6105**
plane, where knowledge resides. This can be seen from the symbolism
of *commanding* as an inflow, as discussed in §§5486, 5732. Here, though,
it symbolizes consent, because the earthly dimension, represented by
Pharaoh, takes everything it has from an inflow from within. What the
earthly plane commands does seem to be its own demand but is really a
demand from within, so it is a matter of consent.

Our earthly level relates to our inner part almost the same way our
words relate to our thoughts. Our words seem to command or order, but
in actuality our thoughts do.

And Joseph sustained his father and his brothers and his father's whole **6106**
house with bread means that there was a constant inflow of goodness
from inner heavenliness into earthly-level spiritual goodness and religious truths, which gave them life. This can be seen from the following:
Sustaining with bread symbolizes an inflow of goodness. That is because
in this instance *sustaining* symbolizes a constant inflow, which supplies a
human being with spiritual life, and *bread* symbolizes a loving goodness
(§§276, 680, 2165, 2177, 3464, 3478, 3735, 3813, 4211, 4217, 4735, 4976,
5915). *Joseph* represents inner heavenliness, as discussed in §§5869, 5877.
Israel, the *father,* represents spiritual goodness on the earthly level, and
his sons, the *brothers,* represent religious truth on the earthly level, as
noted above at §6102. And *his father's whole house* symbolizes everything
marked by spiritual goodness and resulting from it, taken together.

This explanation shows what *Joseph sustained his father and his broth-*
ers and his father's whole house with bread symbolizes. It symbolizes a constant inflow of loving goodness from inner heavenliness into earthly-level

spiritual goodness and religious truth and into everything marked by or resulting from spiritual goodness.

6107 *Enough for each baby's mouth* means into each of these according to the nature of its innocent goodness. This can be seen from the symbolism of *enough for each mouth* as each according to its nature and from that of a *baby* as innocent goodness, as discussed in §§430, 2126, 3183, 5608.

Here is how the case stands with the idea that there is an inflow from inner heavenliness into earthly-level spiritual goodness and religious truth that accords with the nature of their innocent goodness: It is innocence coming from one's inmost core that lends its quality to all charitable, loving goodness. The Lord flows into neighborly love by means of innocence, you see, and the more innocence there is, the more neighborly love is received, because innocence is the essence itself of that love (§§2780, 3111, 3183, 3994, 4797, 6013).

Little children are a kind of mirror in which we can see what innocence is. They love their parents, whom they trust exclusively, and pleasing their parents is their only concern. In exchange they receive all the food and clothing they need or even want. Because they love their parents, young children oblige them every way they can, with sincere pleasure, doing not only what their parents command but also what they think their parents *intend* to command. What is more, they are unselfconscious. Many other illustrations are possible as well.

Still, it is important to realize that children's innocence is not real innocence but merely a semblance of it. Real innocence dwells only in wisdom; see §§2305, 2306, 3494, 4797. Wisdom means relating to the Lord in the manner in which I have just said children relate to their parents, out of a goodness inspired by love and faith.

6108 *Genesis 47:13–26. And there was no bread in all the land, because the famine was very heavy, and the land of Egypt and the land of Canaan suffered because of the famine. And Joseph gathered all the silver found in the land of Egypt and in the land of Canaan [that was paid in exchange] for the grain provisions that they were buying, and Joseph brought the silver to Pharaoh's house. And the silver was used up from the land of Egypt and the land of Canaan, and all Egypt came to Joseph, saying, "Give us bread, for why shall we die in front of you because the silver is running out?" And Joseph said, "Give me your livestock and I will give you [bread in exchange] for your livestock, if the silver has run out." And they brought their livestock to Joseph, and Joseph gave them bread for the horses and for the livestock of the flock and for the livestock of the herd and for the donkeys, and he provided* *them with bread for all their livestock in that year. And that year ended, and they came to him in the second year and said to him, "We will not hide from my lord that the silver has been used up, as has the animal stock for my lord; nothing is left before my lord except for our body and our ground. Why shall we die before your eyes, both we and our ground? Buy us and our ground with bread, and we and our ground will live as slaves to Pharaoh. And give us seed, and let us live and not die, and may the ground not be a wasteland!" And Joseph bought all the ground of Egypt for Pharaoh, because the Egyptians each sold their field, since the famine strengthened over them. And the land was Pharaoh's. And as for the people, he transferred them to cities from one end of Egypt's border to its other end. Only the ground of the priests he did not buy, because it was the statutory portion for the priests, from Pharaoh, and they ate their statutory portion that Pharaoh had given them, so they did not sell their ground. And Joseph said to the people, "Here, I have bought you today, and your ground, for Pharaoh. Look: for you, seed; and you are to sow the ground. And it will happen in the [harvests of] produce that you will give a fifth to Pharaoh, and four parts will be for you as seed for the field and as your food, and for those in your houses, and as food for your little children." And they said, "You have kept us alive; may we find favor in the eyes of my lord, and we will be slaves to Pharaoh." And Joseph made it a statute right to this day concerning the ground of Egypt for Pharaoh, [taxed] at one fifth. Only the ground of the priests, theirs alone, was not Pharaoh's.*

And there was no bread in all the land means that goodness was no longer visible. *Because the famine was very heavy* symbolizes desolation. *And the land of Egypt and the land of Canaan suffered because of the famine* means that this happened on the earthly level and within the church. *And Joseph gathered all the silver* means that he gathered all the items of knowledge that were a suitable form of truth. *Found in the land of Egypt and in the land of Canaan* means [found] on the earthly level and in the church. *For the grain provisions that they were buying* means that it sustained them. *And Joseph brought the silver to Pharaoh's house* means that it was all grouped under a general category on the earthly level. *And the silver was used up from the land of Egypt and the land of Canaan* means that suitable truth in the form of knowledge was no longer apparent on the earthly level or in the church, because of the desolation. *And all Egypt came to Joseph* symbolizes adaptation to the inner level. *Saying, "Give us bread,"* symbolizes a plea for spiritual life to be sustained. *For why shall we die in front of you because the silver is running out?* means that otherwise spiritual death would result from the lack of truth. *And Joseph said,* symbolizes the inner dimension, which answered. *Give me your livestock and I will give you [bread in exchange] for your livestock* means that they would offer truth-based goodness and be sustained. *If the silver has run out* means if truth was no longer apparent to them. *And they brought their livestock to Joseph* means that they offered truth-based goodness. *And Joseph gave them bread* symbolizes having their spiritual life sustained. *For the horses* symbolizes items of knowledge brought forward by the workings of the intellect. *And for the livestock of the flock and for the livestock of the herd* symbolizes inner and outer truth-based goodness. *And for the donkeys* symbolizes subservient information. *And he provided them with bread for all their livestock* symbolizes being sustained by an inflow of goodness from within. *In that year* symbolizes the period covered by that state. *And that year ended* symbolizes desolation after the period covered by that state. *And they came to him in the second year* symbolizes the beginning of the next state. *And said to him, "We will not hide from my lord,"* symbolizes a perception that it was known to the inner dimension. *That the silver has been used up* symbolizes truth that is not apparent, because of the desolation. *As has the animal stock for my lord* means the same for truth-based goodness. *Nothing is left before my lord except for our body and our ground* means that any containers for goodness and truth have been abandoned. *Why shall we die before your eyes, both we and our ground?* means that if they were abandoned, there would no longer be any spiritual life under the inner level. *Buy us and our ground with bread* symbolizes adoption of both in order to sustain them with what is good. *And we and our ground will live as slaves to Pharaoh* symbolizes total surrender. *And give us seed* symbolizes the consequent inflow of charity's goodness and faith's truth. *And let us live and not die* symbolizes the resulting spiritual life and an end to fear of damnation. *And may the ground not be a wasteland!* means that the mind will be cultivated with religious knowledge. *And Joseph bought all the ground of Egypt for Pharaoh* means that the inner dimension adopted the whole earthly mind (where knowledge resides) as its own and put it under general supervision. *And the Egyptians each sold their field* means that everything that serves the church was given up and made subordinate. *Since the famine strengthened over them* means because desolation reached the point of despair. *And the land was Pharaoh's* means that everything became subordinate to the earthly plane, which is within the oversight of the inner plane. *And as for the people, he transferred them to cities* means that truth in the form of knowledge was grouped under doctrinal teachings. *From one end of Egypt's border to its other end* means throughout the range of the entire earthly plane, where knowledge resides. *Only the ground of the priests he did not buy* means that the inner plane acquired its own earthly-level ability to receive goodness, because that ability comes from the inner plane itself. *Because it was the statutory portion for the priests, from Pharaoh* means that this was ordained by the earthly dimension, which is within the oversight of the inner dimension. *And they ate their statutory portion that Pharaoh had given them* means that they did not adopt any more goodness as their own than was ordained. *So they did not sell their ground* means that as a result they had no need to give up the goodness they had or surrender it. *And Joseph said to the people* symbolizes an inflow from the inner dimension into truth in the form of knowledge. *Here, I have bought you today, and your ground, for Pharaoh* means that the [inner plane] amassed this truth for itself and placed it under a general category on the earthly plane, which is under the oversight of the inner plane. *Look: for you, seed; and you are to sow the ground* symbolizes the goodness associated with neighborly love and the truth associated with faith, which need to be implanted. *And it will happen in the [harvests of] produce* symbolizes the resulting fruit. *That you will give a fifth to Pharaoh* symbolizes a remnant and the assignment of it to a general category within the oversight of the inner plane. *And four parts for you* symbolizes what is not yet part of the remnant. *As seed for the field* means for the nourishment of the mind. *And as your food, and for those in your houses* means so that it can provide truth-based goodness in the whole and in every part. *And as food for your little children* means in what is innocent. *And they said, "You have kept us alive,"* symbolizes spiritual life by no other means, from no other source. *May we find favor in the eyes of my lord* symbolizes a willingness to be made subordinate in this way, and humility. *And we will be slaves to Pharaoh* means that they are giving up their autonomy and surrendering it to the earthly dimension, which is within the oversight of the inner dimension. *And Joseph made it a statute* means what was decided on by agreement. *Right to this day* means forever. *Concerning the ground of Egypt for Pharaoh, [taxed] at one fifth* symbolizes a remnant, as before. *Only the ground of the priests, theirs alone, was not Pharaoh's* means that the ability to receive goodness comes directly from the inner dimension.

And there was no bread in all the land means that goodness was no longer visible. This can be seen from the symbolism of *bread* as a loving,

6109

charitable goodness (mentioned above at §6106), and from the symbolism of *there was none in all the land,* which means that it was no longer visible.

The next verses are about inner heavenliness and the way it reduced everything on the earthly level to order within the general whole. The goal of this rearrangement was to unite knowledge with religious truth, and through religious truth with spiritual goodness, and through spiritual goodness with inner heavenliness. However, knowledge cannot be reduced to order under its general whole unless a person is stripped of goodness, bereaved of truth, and then sustained. So these are the subjects dealt with in the inner meaning of the next verses.

For many reasons, this reorganization rarely happens in people while they are living in the world, but in the other life it happens in everyone being reborn. Since it does not happen to people in the world, it is no surprise if the information seems unfamiliar or strikes anyone as an unheard-of secret.

6110   *Because the famine was very heavy* symbolizes desolation. This is established by the symbolism of *famine* as a lack of goodness and of knowledge, as discussed in §§1460, 3364, 5277, 5279, 5281, 5300, 5579, 5893. Because of this symbolism, a *very heavy* famine symbolizes desolation (§§5360, 5376, 5415, 5576).

Regarding desolation, bear in mind that truth and goodness, and knowledge of truth and goodness, constitute the spiritual life of heaven's inhabitants. These are the heavenly and spiritual foods that nourish them. Such food is given to them daily by the Lord. When it is morning for them, they are supplied with goodness; when it is afternoon, they are supplied with truth; but when it is evening, they lack both, until the return of the half-light and then morning. All the while they have an appetite so strong that they long for goodness and truth more than the starving on earth long for food. This is the condition symbolized by famine, and it is a kind of desolation, though not the kind suffered by people in the underground realm (§§698, 699, 1106–1113).

[2] Hardly anyone in the world will be able to believe that heaven with its angels hungers for truth, goodness, and a knowledge of them to this extent. People who strive only for wealth and glory and who indulge in sensual gratification will of course be skeptical that anything of the kind keeps angels alive. They are bound to say, "What do I care about a knowledge of goodness and truth? How can that keep me alive? It is riches, honors, and creature comforts that bring me life and all its pleasures."

They need to know, however, that the life these things lend is bodily life, not the life of the soul. Bodily life perishes when the body does; the soul's life remains forever. People who never think about spiritual life while they are in the world are doing themselves a disservice.

[3] To say a little more about desolation, it is a consequence of appetite, since we receive goodness and truth in proportion to our hunger for them. The hunger gives rise to desires, and obtaining those desires brings feelings of happiness and success. So people in the other world who find themselves desolate are soon afterward refreshed and gain what they desire. These are the cycles by which everyone is perfected.

It is worth noting that the daily cycles of morning, afternoon, evening, night, and morning again in the physical world are a perfect representation of cycles in the spiritual world. The only difference is that spiritual-world cycles act on the intellect and the will and present them with opportunities for life. Physical-world cycles act on the parts of the body and sustain them.

[4] Even more worthy of note, the shadows of evening and the dark of night do not come from the Lord but from the selfhood of angels, spirits, and people. The Lord as the sun is always shining and streaming in, but evil and falsity from self-interest in people, spirits, and angels turn them around and away from the Lord, bringing the shadows of evening over them, and the dark of night over evil beings. It is like the sun of our own world, which shines and streams in constantly, while the planet turns away as it rotates, bringing shadow and darkness over itself.

[5] The reason these phenomena come into existence in the physical world is that the physical world comes into existence from the spiritual world and depends on it to remain in existence. That is why the whole of creation is a theater representing the Lord's kingdom (§§3483, 4939).

The reason these cycles occur in the spiritual world is to perfect everyone in heaven constantly. So cycles of the same kind occur in the physical world. Otherwise everything there would dry up and die.

[6] It is important to know, though, that night never falls in heaven, only evening, followed by the half-light that ushers in the morning. In hell, night does fall. Hell also has its cycles, but they are the opposite of the cycles in heaven. Morning there is the fever of cravings, afternoon is the itch of falsity, evening is anxiety, and night is torment. Yet night dominates the entire cycle. The different stages are entirely due to variations in the shadow and darkness of night.

[7] Keep in mind too that no individual in the spiritual world experiences the same cycles as another. In addition, the cycles there do not divide into set lengths of time. Rather, they are due to variations in state, because states in the spiritual world take the place of periods of time in the physical world (§§1274, 1382, 2625, 2788, 2837, 3254, 3356, 4814, 4882, 4901, 4916).

6111 *And the land of Egypt and the land of Canaan suffered because of the famine* means that this happened on the earthly level (where knowledge resides) and within the church, as the following shows: The *land of Egypt* symbolizes the earthly mind, where knowledge resides (treated of in §§5276, 5278, 5280, 5288, 5301), and the *land of Canaan* symbolizes the church (treated of above at §6067). And *famine* symbolizes desolation (as directly above at §6110). Plainly, then, *the land of Egypt and the land of Canaan suffered because of the famine* means that there was desolation on the earthly plane, where knowledge resides, and within the church.

6112 *And Joseph gathered all the silver* means that he gathered all the items of knowledge that were a suitable form of truth, as the following shows: *Gathering* means bringing together into one. *Joseph* represents inner heavenliness, as mentioned many times already. And *silver* symbolizes truth, as discussed in §§1551, 2954, 5658. Here it symbolizes items of knowledge that were a suitable form of truth, because the verse is talking about silver in the lands of Egypt and Canaan, as the next part of it says. That is why *Joseph gathered all the silver* means that inner heavenliness brought all the items of knowledge that were a suitable form of truth together into one.

Knowledge is described as a suitable form of truth if it is unclouded by illusions (which render knowledge unsuitable as long as we are unable to disperse them). It is also knowledge that has not been perverted by being connected to falsity and evil, either by others or by oneself. Once falsities or evils have been imprinted on a piece of knowledge, they stick. Items of knowledge that do not suffer from these flaws, then, are suitable and are a form of truth.

6113 *Found in the land of Egypt and in the land of Canaan* means [found] on the earthly level and in the church. This can be seen from the symbolism of the *land of Egypt* as the earthly level, where knowledge resides (mentioned above at §6111), and from that of the *land of Canaan* as the church (also mentioned above, at §6067).

By the church in this case I mean that which belongs to the church in a person. A person is a church when in possession of goodness and truth, and a group of such people constitutes a church on a larger scale.

For the grain provisions that they were buying means that it sustained them, as the following shows: *Grain provisions* symbolize religious truth (noted in §5402). And *buying* means adopting for one's own (discussed in §§4397, 5374, 5406, 5410, 5426) and therefore being sustained. What is being talked about is the spiritual food symbolized by grain provisions, and when we assimilate this food, it sustains our spiritual life.

And Joseph brought the silver to Pharaoh's house means that it was all grouped under a general category on the earthly level, as the following shows: *Bringing* something means putting it into a category and introducing it. *Silver* symbolizes suitable truth in the form of knowledge, as explained in §6112. And *Pharaoh* represents the earthly level in general, as dealt with in §§5160, 5799, 6015, so *Pharaoh's house* means a general category on the earthly level, because it means everything there as a whole.

[2] Turning now to the idea that all suitable truth in the form of knowledge is grouped under a general category: Be aware that if items of knowledge and truths are to be anything, then all of them, no matter what they are, must relate to the general whole. They have to be assigned to and contained within their general category. Otherwise they instantly dissolve. For if items of knowledge and truth are to be anything, they must become part of a structure that has them all keeping each other in view. This is not possible if they are not grouped together under their general category. So the general category is what contains them within that structure and ensures that each part of the structure has its own identity.

The general category, along with other general categories, also has to be brought into relationship with an even more general category, and the more general categories likewise into relationship with the most general. Otherwise the general and more general categories would also dissolve.

[3] The broadest universal whole, which provides for everything to be contained within it, is the Lord himself, and divine truth issuing from him is what does the containing. Collective communities in the spiritual world are the next broadest, and divine truth flows into them, distinguishing them from each other in a general way. The least broad are the more individual communities grouped under each collective community.

Collective communities are what the limbs and the major and minor organs of a person correspond to. They are connected together in such a marvelous structure that they all look toward each other mutually, contain each other mutually, and present themselves as a single whole.

In a human being, the broadest universal whole—the entity that contains all the particular elements—is the soul. Divine truth issuing from the Lord is therefore a universal entity as well, because it is constantly flowing in and making the soul a general container.

[4] Divine truth issuing from the Lord is what is called the Word through which everything was created (John 1:1, 2, 3), that is, through which everything has come into existence and consequently through which everything remains in existence.

Anyone who cares to pay attention to the phenomena of nature will discover plainly that everything throughout the physical world comes under a broad category, that every element there comes under its own category, and that otherwise none of it could survive.

6116   *And the silver was used up from the land of Egypt and the land of Canaan* means that suitable truth in the form of knowledge was no longer apparent on the earthly level or in the church, because of the desolation, as the following shows: *Being used up* symbolizes being no longer apparent. *Silver* symbolizes items of knowledge that are a suitable form of truth, as discussed above at §6112. The *land of Egypt* symbolizes the earthly level, where knowledge resides, as mentioned above at §6111. And the *land of Canaan* symbolizes the church, as also mentioned above, at §6067. Earlier discussion shows that the disappearance was on account of desolation; see §6110.

6117   *And all Egypt came to Joseph* symbolizes adaptation to the inner level. This can be seen from the symbolism of *coming to him* as adapting, from that of *Egypt* as knowledge (dealt with before), and from the representation of *Joseph* as the inner level (also dealt with before).

All knowledge on the earthly level had come within the oversight of the inner dimension, and this is symbolized by Joseph's being ruler over the whole land of Egypt. What the inner meaning is describing now, though, is union between the truth known to the church and knowledge on the earthly level.

6118   *Saying, "Give us bread,"* means for spiritual life to be sustained. This can be seen from the symbolism of *giving*, when mentioned in connection with bread, as sustaining, and from that of *bread* as spiritual life. Narrowly speaking, bread symbolizes a loving, charitable goodness, but broadly speaking, it symbolizes spiritual life, because bread as a general term means all food, as was shown at §2165. When bread means all food in general, it means spiritual life, because in a spiritual sense, food as a whole means all the goodness urged by love, and all the truth that leads to faith as well. These are the two components of spiritual life.

For why shall we die in front of you because the silver is running out? means that otherwise spiritual death would result from the lack of truth. This is established by the symbolism of *dying* as spiritual death (discussed below) and by that of *the silver is running out* as a lack of truth. For the meaning of silver as items of knowledge that are a suitable form of truth, see §6112.

6119

Why does spiritual death result when truth is lacking? Spiritual life consists in activity that follows the lead of truth and consequently in being useful. People dedicated to spiritual life hunger and long for truth for the sake of their life—that is, for the sake of living by it and so of being useful. The more they can absorb of the truth they need as a guide to usefulness, the more spiritual life they have, because the light of understanding and wisdom they enjoy increases with it. When truth runs out, then—and it runs out with the arrival of the murky state symbolized in the Word by evening (§6110)—their spiritual life suffers. They encounter times of shadow, which are times of spiritual death, because they do not then remain in the light, as they did before, but partly regress into self-absorption. Out of the shadow arises the specter of spiritual death, or damnation.

[2] The symbolism of *death* as spiritual death, or damnation, is clear from many Scripture passages. Let me quote just the following. In Isaiah:

> He will judge the poor with justice and chide the wretched of the earth with uprightness. Conversely, he will strike the earth with the rod of his mouth, and with the spirit of his lips he will *make the ungodly person die.* (Isaiah 11:4)

This is about the Lord. The rod of his mouth and the spirit of his lips stand for divine truth, which renders judgment. Dying stands for damnation. In the same author:

> He will swallow death up forever, and the Lord Jehovih will wipe away the tear from all faces. (Isaiah 25:8)

In the same author:

> The dead will not live, the Rephaim will not rise again, because you inflicted punishment on them, *you obliterated them.* (Isaiah 26:14)

In the same author:

> Your dead will live, my corpse; they will rise again. (Isaiah 26:19)

In the same author:

> You have said, "We cut a *pact with death,* and with hell we fabricated a vision. *Your pact with death* will be done away with, and your vision with hell will not stand." (Isaiah 28:15, 18)

[3] In Jeremiah:

> You wait for light, but he will turn it into the *shadow of death,* he will turn it into blackness. (Jeremiah 13:16)

In Ezekiel:

> You profaned me among my people for handfuls of barleycorns and for crumbs of bread, to *kill souls that should not die* and to keep souls alive that should not live. (Ezekiel 13:19, 22)

In Hosea:

> From the hand of hell I will redeem them; *from death I will deliver them.* I will be your plague, *death;* I will be your ruin, hell! (Hosea 13:14)

In David:

> You lift me up *out of the gates of death.* (Psalms 9:13)

In the same author:

> Give light to my eyes *to prevent me from sleeping the sleep of death.* (Psalms 13:3)

In the same author:

> The *ropes of death* and the ropes of hell encircled me. (Psalms 18:4, 5)

In the same author:

> They will be put in hell like sheep; *death will pasture them.* (Psalms 49:14)

In John:

> I have the keys of hell and of *death.* (Revelation 1:18)

In the same author:

> Those who conquer will not be hurt *in the second death.* (Revelation 2:11)

[4] In the same author:

> I know your works, that you have a reputation as being alive *but are dead.* Be watchful and strengthen what is left, *which is close to death.* (Revelation 3:1, 2)

In Matthew:

> The people sitting in darkness have seen a great light. *And on those sitting in the vicinity and gloom of death,* light has risen. (Matthew 4:16)

In John:

> Anyone who listens to my word and believes in him who sent me will have eternal life and will not come under judgment but *has passed over from death to life.* (John 5:24)

In the same author:

> I am going away, and you will seek me, but *you will die in your sin.* I told you that *you will die in your sins.* For unless you believe that I am, *you will die in your sins.* If any keep my word, *they will never see death to eternity.* (John 8:21, 24, 51, 52)

Since death symbolized damnation, the people of the representative religion were forbidden to touch the dead, and if they touched the dead, they would be unclean and would have to undergo cleansing (Ezekiel 44:25; Leviticus 15:31; 21: [1,] 2, 3; 22:8; Numbers 6:6–12; 19:11–end).

And Joseph said, symbolizes the inner dimension, which answered. This can be seen from the representation of *Joseph* as the inner dimension, as explained before. Obviously it is an answer.   **6120**

Give me your livestock and I will give you [bread in exchange] for your livestock means that they would offer truth-based goodness and be sustained. This can be seen from the symbolism of *livestock* as truth-based goodness (discussed in §§6016, 6045) and from that of *giving [bread in exchange] for it* as sustaining someone's spiritual life (discussed above at §6118).   **6121**

If the silver has run out means if truth was no longer apparent to them. This can be seen from the symbolism of *the silver has run out* as a lack of truth and therefore as the disappearance of truth, as noted above in §§6116, 6119.   **6122**

I am describing truth as not apparent because in a desolate state it appears to have fled. It is still present, because all the truth and goodness the Lord has ever given a person, spirit, or angel remain; not a bit of them is taken away. In a desolate state, though, self-interest obscures them, making them not apparent. When a state of light returns, truth and goodness stand present and visible. This clarifies what is meant by truth that is not apparent.

6123   *And they brought their livestock to Joseph* means that they offered truth-based goodness. This can be seen from the symbolism of *bringing* as offering, and from that of *livestock* as truth-based goodness (discussed in §§6016, 6045).

6124   *And Joseph gave them bread* symbolizes having their spiritual life sustained. This can be seen from the symbolism of *giving bread* as the sustaining of spiritual life, as discussed above at §6118.

6125   *For the horses* symbolizes items of knowledge brought forward by the workings of the intellect. This can be seen from the symbolism of *horses* as aspects of the intellect (discussed in §§2760, 2761, 2762, 3217, 5321). Since these particular horses are associated with Egypt, which symbolizes knowledge, they stand for items of knowledge brought forward by the workings of the intellect.

I should say what knowledge of this kind is. The intellect and the will each have a role to play in us, not only in our inner self but also in our outer self. The role of the intellect grows and increases from childhood to adulthood and consists in the development of insights on the basis of experience and learning. It also consists in tracing causes from effects, and consequences from a chain of causes. So intellectual activity consists in grasping and perceiving issues of public and private life.

It is the inflow of light from heaven that brings about activity in the intellect, so we can each develop real intellectual ability. The ability we receive individually depends on the way we apply it, the way we live, and our native character. No one of sound mind lacks intellectual capacity. It is given to us in order to provide us with freedom and choice—that is, with the freedom to choose either good or evil. If we could not use our intellect as described above, we could not choose on our own and therefore could not make anything our own.

[2] Another thing to know is that a person's intellect receives whatever is spiritual, meaning that it is a container for spiritual truth and goodness. Nothing good (no neighborly love) and nothing true (no faith) can be instilled in anyone whose intellect is not at work; no, these qualities are instilled in proportion to the workings of one's intellect. Consequently the Lord does not regenerate us until adulthood, when we have the use of our intellect. Until then, the goodness that characterizes love and the truth

that characterizes faith fall like seed into totally infertile ground. Once we have been reborn, our intellect serves us by enabling us to see and perceive what is good and accordingly what is true. It brings ideas lit by heaven's light down into ideas lit by nature's light, so that the former appear within the latter the same way deep-seated human emotion appears in a candid face.

Because the intellect serves this purpose, many passages in the Word that treat of the spiritual church also treat of the intellect in that church. This subject will be discussed elsewhere, by the Lord's divine mercy.

[3] These considerations now show how to understand the term "items of knowledge brought forward by the workings of the intellect." They are items of knowledge that confirm what we grasp and perceive with our intellect, whether bad or good. These are the items of knowledge symbolized in the Word by horses from Egypt. In Isaiah, for instance:

Doom to those going down into Egypt for help! And *on horses they rely*, and they trust in chariots (that they are numerous) *and in riders* (that they are very strong), and they do not look to the Holy One of Israel, and Jehovah they do not seek. Because Egypt is a human and not God, and *its horses* are flesh and not spirit. (Isaiah 31:1, 3)

The horses from Egypt stand for items of knowledge produced by twisted workings of the intellect. [4] In Ezekiel:

[Israel's prince] rebelled against [Babylon's monarch], sending his ambassadors to Egypt [demanding] *that it give him horses* and a large populace. Will he succeed? Will the one who does this be rescued? (Ezekiel 17:15)

Once again the horses from Egypt stand for items of knowledge produced by twisted workings of the intellect. Some people consult this accepted knowledge in matters of faith and refuse to believe in the Word, that is, in the Lord, except on the basis of such knowledge. As a result they cannot possibly believe, because denial reigns supreme in a twisted intellect.

[5] The destruction of knowledge like this is represented by the sinking of Pharaoh's horses and chariots in the Suph Sea. The horses symbolize such knowledge, and the chariots symbolize false doctrinal teachings, which is why the story mentions horses and chariots so many times; see Exodus 14:17, 18, 23, 26, 28. It is also why the Song of Moses and Miriam says:

Pharaoh's horse—and his chariots and *his riders*—went into the sea. But Jehovah brought back over them the waters of the sea. Sing to Jehovah, because he has risen very high; the *horse* and *its rider* he has cast into the sea. (Exodus 15:19, 21)

[6] The same kind of knowledge is also symbolized by Moses' guidelines for a king over Israel:

If they should want a king, a king from the midst of their kin shall be put over them. *Only he must not multiply horses for himself* or take the people back to Egypt to *multiply horses.* (Deuteronomy 17:15, 16)

A king represented the Lord's divine truth (§§1672, 1728, 2015, 2069, 3009, 3670, 4575, 4581, 4789, 4966, 5044, 5068). So a king also represented the Lord's power of understanding, because when understanding is real, it comes from divine truth. We are to acquire this power through the Word, which is divine truth, and not through knowledge produced by the workings of our own intellect. This necessity is symbolized by the order that the king not multiply horses and not take the people back to Egypt to multiply horses.

6126 *And for the livestock of the flock and for the livestock of the herd* symbolizes inner and outer truth-based goodness. This can be seen from the symbolism of a *flock* as inner goodness and from that of a *herd* as outer goodness (discussed at §5913). Since truth-based goodness is being symbolized, the text talks about *livestock of the flock* and *livestock of the herd*— *livestock* being truth-based goodness (§§6016, 6045, 6049).

6127 *And for the donkeys* symbolizes subservient information. This is established by the explanation in §§5958, 5959 of the symbolism of *donkeys* as subservient information.

6128 *And he provided them with bread for [all] their livestock* symbolizes being sustained by an inflow of goodness from within, as the following shows: *Providing with bread,* or giving them bread, means sustaining their spiritual life, as explained above at §6118. *Livestock* symbolizes truth-based goodness, as noted just above at §6126. And *Joseph,* who provided the bread, represents the inner level, as discussed before. It follows that an inflow of goodness from within was the means, because when spiritual life is sustained on the earthly level, it is always accomplished by an inflow from the inner plane. Or rather it is accomplished by the Lord working through the inner plane.

Since I use the term *inflow* so often, and since there may not be many who understand what is meant by it, I should explain. What spiritual inflow is can be seen by comparison with the kinds of inflow that exist in nature. Warmth from the sun, for instance, flows into everything on the planet, bringing life to plants; and light flows into everything too, creating the support system for life in plants, and a resulting color and beauty as well. Then there is the inflow of warmth into the surface of our own body, and of light into our eye. Likewise the inflow of sound into our ear, and so on. These examples make it possible to grasp what the inflow of life from the Lord is. He is the sun of heaven, the source of warmth (love) and spiritual light (faith). This inflow is clearly sensed, too: heavenly warmth, or love, generates the vital heat in us, and heavenly light, or faith, generates the light of understanding in us. These vary, though, depending on how we receive them.

In that year symbolizes the period covered by that state. This is clear from the symbolism of a *year* as a whole period of time from beginning to end, as discussed at §2906.

6129

And that year ended symbolizes desolation after the period covered by that state. This is clear from the symbolism of *that year ended,* which means after the period covered by that state. For the meaning of a year as the period filled by one whole state, see just above at §6129. What follows next makes it clear that desolation came after that period.

6130

And they came to him in the second year symbolizes the beginning of the next state. This can be seen from what precedes without further explanation.

6131

And said to him, "We will not hide from my lord," symbolizes a perception that it was known to the inner dimension. This can be seen from the symbolism of *saying* as a perception (mentioned above at §6063), from the representation of Joseph, the *lord* here, as the inner dimension (discussed before), and from the symbolism of *not hiding from him* as being known. In an inner sense, not hiding means being known because everything that exists and happens on the earthly level is known to the inner dimension. After all, the earthly plane takes everything it has from the inner plane and can therefore hide nothing from it. Still, that is how the idea is expressed in the outer sense, especially of the narratives. It is like the times when the Lord talks to a person [in the Word]: first he asks the person about the matter at hand, even though he is intimately familiar with it. That is how the angel of Jehovah speaks to Hagar in Genesis 16:7, 8, to Abraham in Genesis 18:9, and to Moses in Exodus 4:2. Besides, nothing else satisfies the outer self; if it does not speak a thing out loud, it believes no one knows about it.

6132

6133   *That the silver has been used up* symbolizes truth that is not apparent, because of the desolation, as can be seen from the remarks above at §6116, where similar words occur.

6134   *As has the animal stock for my lord* means the same for truth-based goodness. This can be seen from the symbolism of *animal stock,* or livestock of the flock and herd, as inner and outer truth-based goodness, as mentioned above at §6126. This too was no longer apparent, on account of the desolation, as the comments on the silver just above at §6133 show.

6135   *Nothing is left before my lord except for our body and our ground* means that any containers for goodness and truth have been abandoned. This can be seen from the symbolism of a *body* as a container for goodness, as discussed below, and from that of the *ground* as a container for truth. The ground is a container for truth because it receives seed. The seed sown in it specifically symbolizes instances of the faith that rises out of neighborly love and therefore of the truth that rises out of goodness (§§1025, 1447, 1610, 1940, 2848, 3038, 3310, 3373). This makes the ground a container for truth. See also previous statements and evidence concerning the ground, in §§566, 1068, 3671. The abandonment of these containers is symbolized by *nothing is left before my lord except for* [these things].

[2] In a genuine sense, a body symbolizes goodness prompted by love, and the ground symbolizes truth born of faith. When the truth and truth-based goodness symbolized by silver and livestock are no longer apparent because of desolation, a body symbolizes a mere container for goodness, and the ground a container for truth.

A body in its genuine sense symbolizes goodness prompted by love because the body (or the whole person, which is what *body* means) is a container for life from the Lord. So the body is a container for goodness, since the goodness we love makes the actual life in us. Vital heat, which is love, is the warmth itself of life, and unless we have this warmth in us, we are just a dead thing. That is why a body in an inner sense means a loving goodness.

Even if we harbor hellish rather than heavenly love, the inmost core of our life still comes from heavenly love. This love constantly flows in from the Lord, generating in us a warmth that starts as vital heat. As it moves through us we corrupt it, which gives rise to hellish love, and this gives off impure heat.

[3] From angels I have been able to see quite plainly that a body in its genuine sense is a loving goodness. When angels are presented

in person, so much love pours forth from them that you would think they are nothing but love, and it pours from their whole body. Their body also appears bright and shining with the light from that love. A loving goodness is like a flame that radiates the light of the resulting faith and its truth.

If this is what angels in heaven are like, then, imagine what that implies about the Lord! He is the source of all the love in angels, and his divine love appears as a sun. This sun supplies the whole of heaven with its light and all the inhabitants with their heavenly warmth, or love, and consequently life. It is the Lord's divine humanity that appears this way and supplies all those elements. These considerations show what the Lord's body means: it means his divine love, just as his flesh does (as explained at §3813). In addition, love is exactly what the Lord's actual body is, now that it has been glorified, that is, made divine. What other way is there to think of divinity, which is infinite?

[4] From this discussion you can see that the Lord's divine love for the entire human race is precisely what is meant by the body in the Holy Supper, spoken of in the Gospels this way:

> Jesus, taking the bread and blessing it, broke it and gave it to the disciples and said, "Take it, eat; *this is my body.*" (Matthew 26:26; Mark 14:22; Luke 22:19)

When Jesus said, "This is my body," he was talking about the bread, because bread too symbolizes divine love (§§276, 680, 2165, 2177, 3464, 3478, 3735, 4735, 5915).

[5] The Lord's body also symbolizes divine love in John:

> Jesus said, "Take apart the temple, yet in three days I will raise it up." But he was speaking *about the temple of his body.* (John 2:19, 21)

The temple of his body means divine truth stemming from divine goodness. (For the meaning of the Temple as the Lord and his divine truth, see §3720.) Because a body in the highest sense means the divine goodness belonging to the Lord's divine love, everyone in heaven is said to be in the Lord's body.

[6] The meaning of the Lord's body as divine goodness is also clear from these words in Daniel:

> I raised my eyes and looked: here, now, a lone man clothed in linen, whose hips were girded with the gold of Uphaz, and his body was like tarshish, and his face, like the appearance of lightning, and his eyes,

like fiery torches, and his arms and his feet, like the radiance of burnished bronze, and the sound of his words, like the sound of a throng. (Daniel 10:5, 6)

The gold of Uphaz girding his hips, the appearance of lightning in his face, the fiery torches of his eyes, and the radiant bronze of his arms and feet symbolize the goodness that comes of love. (For the meaning of gold as a loving goodness, see §§113, 1551, 1552, 5658. For that of fire as the same, §§934, 4906, 5215. Since fire has this meaning, so does lightning. For the meaning of bronze as the earthly-level goodness associated with love and charity, see §§425, 1551.) The tarshish that the rest of his body resembled—the part of his body between the head and the hips—symbolizes the goodness associated with charity and faith, because a tarshish is a precious stone that flashes like lightning.

6136   *Why shall we die before your eyes, both we and our ground?* means that if they were abandoned, there would no longer be any spiritual life under the inner level, as the following shows: *Before your eyes* means under the inner level, since these words are addressed to Joseph, and he represents the inner level. *Both we and our ground* symbolizes containers for goodness and truth, as just above at §6135, so it symbolizes containers for spiritual life. These containers are said to *die* when they have no spiritual life inside. After all, dying symbolizes desolation, or deprivation of goodness and truth, which constitute our spiritual life.

6137   *Buy us and our ground with bread* symbolizes adoption of both in order to sustain them with what is good, as the following shows: *Buying* symbolizes adoption, as discussed in §§4397, 5374, 5406, 5410, 5426. *Us and our ground* symbolizes containers for goodness and truth, as above at §§6135, 6136, so it symbolizes both [goodness and truth]. And *with bread* symbolizes being sustained by what is good. The reason bread symbolizes the goodness sought by both love and faith is that it can mean all food in general (§6118).

6138   *And we and our ground will live as slaves to Pharaoh* symbolizes total surrender, as the following shows: *We and our ground* symbolizes containers for goodness and truth, as just above in §§6135, 6136, 6137. And *as slaves* symbolizes being without the freedom of self-guidance, as mentioned in §§5760, 5763, so it symbolizes total surrender.

By containers I mean the actual forms that compose a human being, because we are nothing but forms designed to receive life from the Lord. By heredity and practice, these forms are such that we refuse spiritual life from the Lord. Once we have renounced such containers so thoroughly that we no longer have any self-directed freedom, we are in total surrender. If we are being reborn, our repeatedly being desolated and then sustained eventually reduces us all the way to the point where we no longer want to be our own but the Lord's. When we have become the Lord's, we enter a state in which we grieve and worry if left to our own devices, and once released from that state, return to our joy and bliss. This is the state of all angels.

[2] The Lord wants our total surrender so he can make us blessed and happy. That is, he does not want us to be partly our own and partly his, because then there are two masters, and we cannot serve two masters at once (Matthew 6:24). Total surrender is also meant by the Lord's words in Matthew:

> Whoever loves father and mother above me is not worthy of me. And whoever loves son and daughter above me is not worthy of me. (Matthew 10:37)

Father and mother in general symbolize aspects of our selfhood that we have acquired by heredity, and son and daughter, aspects that we have acquired by practice. Human selfhood is also symbolized in John by the soul:

> Those who love their soul will lose it, but those who hate their soul in this world will keep it into eternal life. If any attend to me, let them follow me, and where I will be, there my attendant will be too. (John 12:25, 26)

Entire surrender is also symbolized by the Lord's words in Matthew:

> Another disciple said, "Lord, let me first go and bury my father." But Jesus said to him, "Follow me, and let the dead bury their dead." (Matthew 8:21, 22)

[3] Submission has to be total, as the first commandment for the church makes obvious:

> You shall love the Lord your God with all your heart and with all your soul and with all your mind and with all your powers. This is the first commandment. (Mark 12:30)

Since love for the Lord comes not from us but from the Lord himself, then, all our heart, soul, mind, and powers—which are containers [for love]—must be the Lord's. So our submission has to be total.

This kind of surrender is what is symbolized by *we and our ground will live as slaves to Pharaoh*. *Pharaoh* represents the earthly plane in general, which is under the oversight of inner heavenliness, or in the highest sense, under the oversight of the Lord, who in that sense is Joseph.

6139   *And give us seed* symbolizes the consequent inflow of charity's goodness and faith's truth. This can be seen from the symbolism of *seed* as charity's goodness and faith's truth, as dealt with in §§1025, 1447, 1610, 1940, 2848, 3038, 3310, 3373. *Giving* these two things obviously means an inflow, since they enter us through an inflow from the Lord.

6140   *And let us live and not die* symbolizes the resulting spiritual life and an end to fear of damnation. This can be seen from the symbolism of *living* as spiritual life (discussed at §5890) and from that of *dying* as damnation (discussed at §6119). Here dying symbolizes fear of damnation, because when a person is being reborn, there is no damnation during a desolate state, only fear of damnation.

6141   *And may the ground not be a wasteland!* means that the mind will be cultivated with religious knowledge, as the following shows: The *ground* symbolizes a container for truth, as above in §§6135, 6136, 6137. The actual container is the mind, in this case the earthly mind, since the ground is in Egypt. And *being a wasteland* means being without visible truth. In this case it means being without religious knowledge, because Egyptians symbolize that knowledge (§§4749, 4964, 4966, 6004), which is also earthly-level truth.

The land of Egypt is the earthly mind, where knowledge resides (see §§5276, 5278, 5280, 5288, 5301), so the ground of Egypt symbolizes that specific level of the mind. As a consequence, *may the ground not be a wasteland!* means that the mind will be cultivated with knowledge.

6142   *And Joseph bought all the ground of Egypt for Pharaoh* means that the inner dimension adopted the whole earthly mind (where knowledge resides) as its own and put it under general supervision, as the following indicates: *Joseph* represents the inner dimension, as frequently noted. *Buying* means adopting as one's own, as discussed in §§4397, 5374, 5406, 5410, 5426. The *ground of Egypt* symbolizes the earthly mind, where knowledge resides, as noted just above at §6141. And *Pharaoh* represents the earthly level in general, as discussed in §§5160, 5799, 6015. So the statement that the ground was Pharaoh's means putting it under general oversight on the earthly level.

6143   *And the Egyptians each sold their field* means that everything that serves the church was given up and made subordinate, as the following shows: *Selling* something symbolizes disowning it so completely as to end all connection with it, as discussed in §§4098, 4752, 4758, 5886, so it means giving it up and making it subordinate. And a *field* symbolizes the church's theology, and in a broad sense the church itself, as discussed in §§368, 2971, 3310, 3766. Clearly, then, *the Egyptians each sold their field* means that everything that serves the church was given up and made subordinate.

Because the famine strengthened over them means because desolation reached the point of despair. This can be seen from the symbolism of *famine* as desolation concerning that which the church has to offer, as discussed in §§5415, 5576. When the famine is said to *strengthen*, it symbolizes despair, as in §5279, because the final phase of desolation is despair.

6144

Desolation and spiritual crisis ultimately lead to despair (§§5279, 5280) for many reasons. Let me cite only the following:

Despair leads us to acknowledge in a practical and conscious way that nothing true or good comes from ourselves, that on our own we are damned, that the Lord delivers us from damnation, and that salvation comes by way of truth and goodness.

Another purpose of despair is to allow us to feel that the Lord has made us fortunate in life. When we emerge from a despairing state, we are like death row inmates freed from prison.

Desolation and crisis also allow us to perceive states contrary to heavenly life, which instills a feeling and sense for the blessings and happiness a heavenly life offers. Nothing yields this feeling and sense of blessing and happiness except a contrast with its opposite. In order for us to weigh the opposites against each other fully, then, our desolations and trials are taken to their peak, which is the point of despair.

And the land was Pharaoh's means that everything became subordinate to the earthly plane, which is within the oversight of the inner plane, as the following shows: *The land was his* means that everything symbolized by that land was adopted and made subordinate. And *Pharaoh* represents the earthly plane in general (treated of in §§5160, 5799, 6015), to which all the knowledge symbolized by Egypt was referred (§6115). The reason for adding that it is within the oversight of the inner plane is this: The fact that the whole earthly plane, in whole and in part, is within the oversight of the inner plane is symbolized by Joseph's role as ruler over all the land of Egypt and as the officer over Pharaoh's household. See Genesis 41:40, 41, 42, 43, and Genesis 45:8: "Joseph said to his brothers, 'God has made me like a father to Pharaoh and like a master to all his household,

6145

and I rule in all the land of Egypt.'" This now is why the earthly dimension is said to be within the oversight of the inner dimension.

6146   *And as for the people, he transferred them to cities* means that truth in the form of knowledge was grouped under doctrinal teachings, as the following shows: A *people* symbolizes truth, as discussed in §§1259, 1260, 3295, 3581—in this case, truth in the form of knowledge, since it is associated with the people of Egypt. And *cities* symbolize doctrinal teachings, as discussed in §§402, 2449, 3216, 4492, 4493. *Transferring the people to cities,* then, means grouping truth that is in the form of knowledge under doctrinal teachings.

This concept follows from the earlier statement that truth was being grouped under the general category of the earthly level (§6115). Doctrinal teachings are the general categories to which truths belong, because the church's theology is divided into headings, and each heading is a general religious category. Moreover, that is why Joseph transferred the people to cities, so that this action could represent the assignment of truth to general categories and therefore to various doctrinal teachings.

6147   *From one end of Egypt's border to its other end* means throughout the range of the entire earthly plane, where knowledge resides. This can be seen from the symbolism of *from one end of the border to its other end,* which means throughout the entire range, and from that of *Egypt* as knowledge on the earthly plane (discussed many times before) and therefore as the earthly level, where knowledge resides. The earthly level is a container, and items of knowledge are its contents. So Egypt symbolizes both the container and the contents—that is, both the earthly plane and knowledge. Accordingly, Pharaoh, king of Egypt, also symbolizes both the earthly dimension in general (§§5160, 5799) and knowledge in general (§6015); and the land of Egypt also symbolizes the earthly mind (§§5276, 5278, 5280, 5288, 5301).

6148   *Only the ground of the priests he did not buy* means that the inner plane acquired its own earthly-level ability to receive goodness, because that ability comes from the inner plane itself, as the following shows: Joseph, the subject of this sentence, represents the inner plane, as noted before. The *ground* symbolizes a container for truth, as discussed above in §§6135, 6136, 6137. Here it symbolizes the ability to receive goodness. This ability is a receptiveness that has to be present for a container to be a container. The ability comes from goodness, or rather from the Lord through goodness. Unless the Lord flowed into us with a loving goodness, none of us would have any ability to receive either truth or goodness. The inflow of a loving goodness from the Lord makes everything inside us open to reception. The fact that this ability to receive goodness is on the earthly level is symbolized by the ground's being in Egypt, since Egypt symbolizes the earthly dimension in regard to knowledge (§6142). *Priests* symbolize goodness, as discussed below. And *not buying* means not adopting those abilities as its own in the same way it adopted truth and truth-based goodness, along with their containers—by repeatedly being desolated and sustained. The reason the inner plane did not adopt those abilities is that it was the *source* of them. That is why *only the ground of the priests he did not buy* means that the inner plane acquired its own earthly-level ability to receive goodness, because that ability comes from the inner plane itself.

[2] Here is the situation: Our ability to receive truth and goodness comes directly from the Lord; we do not help acquire it for ourselves at all. The ability to receive goodness and truth is always maintained in us, and it supplies us with intellect and will. The times we do not receive them are when we turn toward evil. Under those circumstances we still keep the ability, but access to such thoughts and feelings is blocked. The capacity to see truth and sense goodness consequently dies out to the extent that we turn toward evil and harden ourselves in it by our life and beliefs.

People realize that we contribute nothing whatever to our ability to accept truth and goodness, because of the teaching in the church that none of faith's truth and none of charity's goodness comes from us, only from the Lord. We can, however, destroy the ability in ourselves.

This now shows how to understand the assertion that the inner plane acquired its own earthly-level ability to receive goodness, because that ability comes from the inner plane itself.

I assign the ability to the earthly level because the inflow of goodness from the Lord comes through the inner level into the earthly level, which is the Lord's doing. When an ability to receive it is acquired on the earthly level, the inflow takes place, because it is then received; see §5828.

[3] Regarding the symbolism of *priests* as goodness, it needs to be known that two things come from the Lord: goodness and truth. Divine goodness was once represented by priests, and divine truth by monarchs. That is why priests symbolize goodness, and monarchs, truth. On the priestliness and kingliness attributed to the Lord, see §§1728, 2015 at the end, 3670.

In the ancient representative church, the two functions of priesthood and monarchy were united in one person, because goodness and truth are united as they issue from the Lord, and they are united in heaven among the angels.

[4] A figure in the ancient church in whom the two functions were united was the person named Melchizedek, or "king of righteousness." This can be seen from his coming to Abraham, as told in these words: "Melchizedek, king of Salem, brought out bread and wine; and he was a priest to God the Highest. And he blessed Abraham" (Genesis 14:18, 19). That he represented the Lord in both functions is evident from the fact that he was both a king and a priest and was allowed to bless Abraham and offer him bread and wine, which even in those days symbolized love's goodness and faith's truth. Further evidence that he represented the Lord in both roles appears in David:

> Jehovah has sworn and will not go back on it: "You are a priest forever after the manner of Melchizedek." (Psalms 110:4)

These words are about the Lord. "After the manner of Melchizedek" means that he is both a monarch and a priest, which in the highest sense means that from him come divine goodness and divine truth together.

[5] Since a representative religion should also have been established among Jacob's descendants, a single figure should have simultaneously represented both divine goodness and divine truth, which are united as they emanate from the Lord. But on account of wars and of that people's idolatry, the two functions were divided at first. The individuals who reigned over the people were termed leaders, and later, judges, while the individuals who performed religious ceremonies were called priests. The latter were from the seed of Aaron and were Levites. Later the two functions were combined in a single person, as in Eli and in Samuel. The nature of the people, though, prevented a representative religion from being established among them. Because of the idolatry that reigned among them, only a representation of a religion could be established. So the two roles were allowed to be separated. Monarchs represented the Lord's divine truth, and priests represented his divine goodness.

The word of Jehovah to Samuel shows that the separation took place to satisfy the people, not to please the Lord:

> Obey the people's voice in all that they have said to you, because they have not rejected you but have rejected me from ruling over them. And you must tell them the rights of a monarch. (1 Samuel 8:7–end; 12:19, 20)

[6] The reason the two roles were not to be separate was that divine truth that has been separated from divine goodness condemns everyone, whereas divine truth united with divine goodness saves everyone. Divine truth has condemned us to hell, but divine goodness releases us from hell and lifts us into heaven. Salvation is a matter of mercy and as such results from divine goodness. Damnation occurs when we refuse mercy and therefore cast away divine goodness, leaving ourselves under a judgment by truth.

On the point that monarchs represented divine truth, see §§1672, 1728, 2015, 2069, 3009, 3670, 4575, 4581, 4966, 5044, 5068.

[7] The idea that priests represented the Lord in regard to divine goodness and therefore symbolize goodness is clear from the inner meaning of all the regulations established for the priesthood when Aaron and later the Levites were chosen for the role. For instance, only the high priest was to enter the Holiest Place and minister there. What was holy to Jehovah was for the priest (Leviticus 23:20; 27:21). Priests were not to have a lot or inheritance in the land, but instead Jehovah was to be their lot and inheritance (Numbers 18:20; Deuteronomy 10:9; 18:1). The Levites were given to Jehovah in place of the firstborn, and Jehovah gave them to Aaron (Numbers 3:9, 12, 13, 40–end; 8:16–19). The high priest and the Levites were in the middle of the camp when the Israelites pitched it and when they moved out (Numbers 1:50–54; 2:17; 3:23–38; 4:1–end). No one of Aaron's seed in whom there was any blemish was to approach to offer burnt offerings or sacrifices (Leviticus 21:17–20). Not to mention other rules, such as those in Leviticus 21:9, 10, 11, 12, 13, and elsewhere. [8] In the highest sense all these regulations represented the Lord's divine goodness, so in a secondary sense they represented a loving, charitable goodness. On the other hand, Aaron's garments, called garments of holiness, represented divine truth rising out of divine goodness, as will be discussed where the relevant parts of Exodus are explained, in the Lord's divine mercy.

[9] Since monarchs symbolize truth and priests goodness, they are often mentioned together in the Word, as in John:

Jesus Christ has made us *monarchs and priests* to his God and Father. (Revelation 1:6; 5:10)

Religious truth makes us into what are called monarchs and charitable goodness makes us into what are called priests. So truth and goodness join together in people who live in the Lord, as they join together in heaven (this was said above). That is what is meant by becoming monarchs and priests. [10] In Jeremiah:

> It will happen on that day that the heart of the *monarch* and of the chieftains will perish, and the *priests* will be stupefied, and the prophets will be dazed. (Jeremiah 4:9)

In the same author:

> [Those of] the house of Israel have been shamed—they, *their monarchs,* their chieftains, and *their priests* and their prophets. (Jeremiah 2:26)

In the same author:

> . . . the *monarchs of Judah,* chieftains, *priests,* and prophets, and residents of Jerusalem. (Jeremiah 8:1)

In these passages the monarchs stand for truth, the chieftains for the most important truths (§§1482, 2089, 5044), the priests for goodness, and the prophets for people who teach [theology] (§2534).

[11] It is also important to know that Joseph's not buying the ground of the priests was a gesture representing the fact that all ability to receive truth and goodness comes from the Lord. This can be seen from a similar law concerning the Levites' fields in Moses:

> *No field in the area surrounding the Levites' cities shall be sold, because it is an eternal possession for them.* (Leviticus 25:34)

In an inner sense this means that we should never claim for ourselves any of the goodness that goes with religion—goodness marked by love and charity—because it belongs to the Lord alone.

6149   *Because it was the statutory portion for the priests, from Pharaoh* means that this was consequently ordained by the earthly dimension, which is within the oversight of the inner dimension. This can be seen from the symbolism of a *statutory portion* as something ordained and from the representation of *Pharaoh* as the earthly dimension in general (discussed in §§5160, 5799, 6015). What was ordained on the earthly level came from the inner level, which is the reason for adding "within the oversight of the inner dimension." Besides, this oversight was represented by Joseph's being lord over the whole of Egypt and also over Pharaoh's household (see §6145).

6150   *And they ate their statutory portion that Pharaoh had given them* means that they did not adopt any more goodness as their own than was ordained.

This is established by the symbolism of *eating* as adopting as one's own (dealt with in §§3168, 3513 at the end, 3596, 3832, 4745) and by that of a *statutory portion* as something ordained (as just above at §6149). *Eating their statutory portion,* then, means that they did not adopt any more goodness as their own than was ordained.

The amount was ordained by the earthly level represented by *Pharaoh,* or rather was ordained on the earthly level under the oversight of the inner level; again, see just above in §6149.

So they did not sell their ground means that as a result they had no need to give up the goodness they had or surrender it, as the following shows: *Selling* something symbolizes giving it up, as mentioned above at §6143, and therefore surrendering it, since what is given up is surrendered to someone or something else. And this *ground* belonging to Egypt's priests symbolizes an ability to receive goodness on the earthly plane, as also discussed above, at §6148. The idea that "as a result they had no need"—no need to give it up or surrender it—is symbolized by *so they did not.*   **6151**

And Joseph said to the people symbolizes an inflow from the inner dimension into truth in the form of knowledge, as the following shows: *Saying* symbolizes a perception, as noted at §6063, and since the inner plane (Joseph) is the one saying, it symbolizes an inflow, because what is perceived on an outer level flows in from an inner level. *Joseph* represents the inner dimension, as noted many times. And a *people* symbolizes truth in the form of knowledge, as explained at §6146.   **6152**

Here, I have bought you today, and your ground, for Pharaoh means that the [inner plane] amassed this truth for itself and placed it under a general category on the earthly plane, which is under the oversight of the inner plane, as the following shows: *Buying* symbolizes adopting and acquiring, as discussed in §§4397, 5374, 5406, 5410, 5426. The *ground* symbolizes containers for truth, as discussed in §§6135, 6136, 6137. The placement of truth under the general category of the earthly plane is symbolized by his buying it *for Pharaoh,* who represents the earthly plane in general, as discussed in §§5160, 5799, 6015. To say that it is under the oversight of the inner plane accords with the explanation above at §6145.   **6153**

Look: for you, seed; and you are to sow the ground symbolizes the goodness associated with neighborly love and the truth associated with faith, which need to be implanted, as the following shows: *Seed* symbolizes truth born of goodness, or faith born of neighborly love, so it symbolizes both, as discussed in §§1025, 1447, 1610, 1940, 2848, 3038, 3310, 3373, 3671. *Sowing* symbolizes implanting. And the *ground* symbolizes containers, as discussed   **6154** in §§6135, 6136, 6137. When truth and goodness have been implanted, though, the ground no longer symbolizes a container but some aspect of the church, as a field does (§566).

6155   *And it will happen in the [harvests of] produce* symbolizes the resulting fruit. This can be seen from the symbolism of *produce* as fruit, because the harvest produced by a field is its fruit.

6156   *That you will give a fifth to Pharaoh* symbolizes a remnant and the assignment of it to a general category within the oversight of the inner plane. This can be seen from the symbolism of five and a *fifth* as a remnant (discussed in §§5291, 5894) and from the representation of *Pharaoh* as a general category on the earthly plane, as above at §6153. The earthly plane is described as within the oversight of the inner plane for the reason given above at §6145.

For the definition of a remnant, see §§1050, 1738, 1906, 2284, 5135, 5897, 5898. A remnant is the goodness and truth the Lord has stored away in our inner self. It returns into our outer, earthly self when we are in a positive state, but as soon we enter a negative state, it draws back and hides. The reason it draws back and hides is to avoid mixing with evil and being destroyed in the process.

At times when people cannot be reborn, their remnant is preserved intact deep within them; but when a person is being reborn, then to the extent of that rebirth, the remnant reemerges from the inside to the outside. This is because rebirth unites inner and outer levels to form a single unit. At first the remnant is placed back in its general categories, but eventually it moves by stages into particular details. Since the current topic of the inner meaning is the rebirth of the earthly level, this discussion shows what is meant by the assignment of this remnant to a general category on the earthly level.

6157   *And four parts for you* symbolizes what is not yet part of the remnant. This is evident from the symbolism of *four parts*—when it describes what is left over from a fifth part that symbolizes a remnant (§6156)—as what is not yet part of the remnant.

Four, like two, symbolizes attributes that are paired and united (§1686), as goodness and truth are. A situation in which they have not yet become part of a remnant is symbolized here by four parts. Goodness and truth do not become part of our remnant until we make them our own, and we first make them our own when we accept them freely and sincerely.

6158   *As seed for the field* means for the nourishment of the mind. This is established by the symbolism of *seed* as truth and goodness and therefore as faith and neighborly love (mentioned above at §6154) and from that of a *field* in a broad sense as the church (discussed in §§2971, 3766). In a narrower sense it symbolizes the church in a person and therefore a person who has the church inside—in other words, a person who receives truth and goodness. When such a person is called a field, it is the person's mind that is meant. What makes us human is not our outer form but our mind, or the intellect and will that compose our mind, as well as the religious truth and charitable goodness that make up a still deeper layer of the mind. Since the mind is the real person, it is nourished and sustained by truth and goodness, and as seed symbolizes truth and goodness, it symbolizes nourishment too. The same thing is plain from the next few phrases: "as your food, and for those in your houses, and as food for your little children."

This now is why *seed for the field* means nourishment for the mind.

And as your food, and for those in your houses means so that it can provide truth-based goodness in the whole and in every part. This can be seen from the symbolism of *food* as truth-based goodness (mentioned in §§5410, 5426, 5487, 5582, 5588, 5655) and from the symbolism of *those in your houses* as the whole and every part of truth-based goodness. So *as food for those in your houses* means truth-based goodness in the whole and in every part.

6159

To say more about truth-based goodness in the whole and in every part: As we are being reborn, goodness is working its way into every single aspect of us. A desire for goodness comes to reign supreme throughout our being, and what reigns supreme throughout reigns supreme in the smallest details; that is, it reigns in the whole and in every part.

This can be seen from the desire that dominates in each of us. Whatever that desire may be, it is present in every impulse of our will and in every inkling of our thought. Although it does not always *appear* to be present in our thoughts, it is. If the ruling desire disappears, that is because in those moments happenstance superimposes its own desires. As the extraneous desires are shed, the ruling desire makes itself visible.

Nothing provides a better illustration of the situation than spirits and angels. Spirits who are evil, or spirits in whom evil predominates, are evil in whole and in part, even when they say what is true and do what is good. Their only intent in doing so is to fool others, make people believe they are good, and so deceive them under the guise of virtue. When they do so, it can be heard clearly in the mere sound of their words, and it is perceived from the atmosphere surrounding them. Angels in heaven, in whom goodness predominates, or reigns supreme throughout, are good in whole and in part. In other words, with them goodness from the Lord beams from the whole and from every part. Even if they do something that looks bad outwardly, their goal or intent is still for good to come out of it.

This demonstrates that where goodness reigns throughout something, it reigns in the whole and in every part; and that the same is true where evil reigns. A quality first comes to reign universally when the whole and every part reflects it, and the nature and amount of the whole and every part determines the nature of the quality. Anything described as universal is universal because it exists in every part individually.

6160   *And as food for your little children* means in what is innocent. This is established by the symbolism of *food* as truth-based goodness (as just above at §6159) and from that of *little children* as innocence (dealt with in §§430, 3183, 5608).

6161   *And they said, "You have kept us alive,"* symbolizes spiritual life by no other means, from no other source. This can be seen from the symbolism of *keeping someone alive* as spiritual life, as discussed at §5890. The preceding verses have been talking about preservation of the earthly plane's life, or its rebirth, and have depicted the whole process, which happens in the way described and no other. That is the reason for adding "by no other means, from no other source."

6162   *May we find favor in the eyes of my lord* symbolizes a willingness to be made subordinate in this way, and humility. This can be seen from the fact that these words, coming after the people have given up everything they own, are words of acknowledgment and therefore of willingness to be made subordinate in this way. So they are words of humility.

The presence of this attitude within the words is evident from the state the people were then in. What that state was can also be seen from the story line before and after.

6163   *And we will be slaves to Pharaoh* means that they are giving up their autonomy and surrendering it to the earthly dimension, which is within the oversight of the inner dimension, as the following indicates: *Slaves* symbolize being without the freedom of self-rule, as discussed at §§5760, 5763, so they symbolize being made to give up self-rule. And *being Pharaoh's* symbolizes surrender to the earthly dimension, which is within the oversight of the inner dimension, as explained in §6145.

6164   *And Joseph made it a statute* means what was decided on by agreement. This can be seen from the symbolism of *making it a statute* as deciding by agreement. A policy made into a statute is so made by agreement between two parties and is therefore counted as a contractual duty.

Right to this day means forever, as can be seen from the discussion in §§2838, 4304 of the symbolism of *right to this day* as forever.

6165

Concerning the ground of Egypt for Pharaoh, [taxed] at one fifth symbolizes a remnant, as before, in §6156.

6166

Only the ground of the priests, theirs alone, was not Pharaoh's means that the ability to receive goodness comes directly from the inner dimension, also as before, in §6148.

6167

These remarks just now—about the union of the earthly and inner dimensions and consequently about the rebirth of the earthly plane by means of repeated desolation and preservation—cannot help striking the modern religious reader as unheard of. Nonetheless the situation is as I have described it and is quite familiar even to unsophisticated spirits in the other world. When we read the Word, then, the inhabitants of that world, who are attuned to the Word's inner meaning, not only take it all in but also see countless secrets within it—secrets that by their very nature are impossible to express in any human language. The ideas I have brought forward are by comparison only a few.

Genesis 47:27, 28, 29, 30, 31. *And Israel settled in the land of Egypt, in the land of Goshen, and they had a possession in it, and they became fruitful and multiplied greatly. And Jacob lived in the land of Egypt seventeen years, and Jacob's days, the years of his life, were one hundred forty-seven years. And Israel's days for dying came near, and he called his son Joseph and said to him, "Please, if I have found favor in your eyes, please put your hand under my thigh, and you are to keep mercy and truth with me; you are please not to bury me in Egypt. And let me lie with my ancestors, and you are to bear me out of Egypt and bury me in their grave." And [Joseph] said, "I myself shall do according to your word." And he said, "Swear to me," and [Joseph] swore to him. And Israel bowed over the head of his bed.*

6168

And Israel settled in the land of Egypt means that spiritual goodness lived among religious knowledge. *In the land of Goshen* means at the center of it. *And they had a possession in it* means that this is what the inner plane gave and ordained. *And they became fruitful and multiplied greatly* means that neighborly kindness and religious truth resulted. *And Jacob lived in the land of Egypt* means that earthly-level truth lived in knowledge. *Seventeen years* symbolizes his state there. *And Jacob's days, the years of his life, were one hundred forty-seven years* symbolizes his overall state and its quality. *And Israel's days for dying came near* symbolizes a state just before rebirth. *And he called his son Joseph* symbolizes the presence of the inner level. *And said to him, "Please, if I have found favor in your eyes,"* symbolizes a longing. *Please put your hand under my thigh* symbolizes a sacred obligation. *And you are to keep mercy and truth with me* symbolizes humility. *You are please not to bury me in Egypt* symbolizes rebirth, but not in knowledge. *And let me lie with my ancestors* symbolizes a life like that of the ancients. *And you are to bear me out of Egypt* means so as to rise above knowledge. *And bury me in their grave* symbolizes this kind of rebirth. *And he said, "I myself shall do according to your word,"* means that it will happen so, as provided for by the Divine. *And he said, "Swear to me,"* symbolizes an intent to make it irreversible. *And [Joseph] swore to him* means that it was irreversible. *And Israel bowed over the head of his bed* means that he turned toward the concerns of the inner earthly level.

6169   *And Israel settled in the land of Egypt* means that spiritual goodness lived among religious knowledge. This is established by the symbolism of *settling* as living (discussed in §§1293, 3384, 3613, 4451), by the representation of *Israel* as spiritual goodness (discussed in §§5801, 5803, 5807, 5812, 5817, 5819, 5826, 5833), and by the symbolism of the *land of Egypt* as the earthly mind, where knowledge resides (discussed in §§5276, 5278, 5280, 5288, 5301; for the symbolism of Egypt as *religious* knowledge, see §§4749, 4964, 4966, 6004).

6170   *In the land of Goshen* means at the center of it. This is clear from the symbolism of the *land of Goshen* as the center or inmost part of the earthly level, as discussed in §§5910, 6028, 6031, 6068. It therefore means at the center of the knowledge, because Goshen was the best piece of land in Egypt.

6171   *And they had a possession in it* means that this is what the inner plane gave and ordained. This is clear from the symbolism of a *possession* as the status of one's spiritual life, as mentioned in §6103. Since Joseph gave them this possession (verse 11), the symbolism is that their status was given and ordained by the inner plane. The symbolism follows from the thread of the story.

6172   *And they became fruitful and multiplied greatly* means that neighborly kindness and religious truth resulted. This can be seen from the symbolism of *becoming fruitful* as bringing forth neighborly kindness and from that of *multiplying* as bringing forth religious truth. Both are discussed at §§43, 55, 913, 983, 2846, 2847. After all, the word *fruitful* has to do with fruit, and fruit in an inner sense means deeds of neighborly love. The word *multiply* has to do with manyness, which in an inner sense applies to religious truth, because Scripture uses the word *many* where truth is dealt with and the word *great* where goodness is.

And Jacob lived in the land of Egypt means that earthly-level truth lived in knowledge. This can be seen from the symbolism of *living* as spiritual life (discussed in §5890), from the representation of *Jacob* as truth on the earthly level (discussed in §§3305, 3509, 3525, 3546, 3599, 3775, 4009, 4234, 4520, 4538), and from the symbolism of the *land of Egypt* as religious knowledge (as just above in §6169).

6173

Seventeen years symbolizes his state there, as the following shows: *Seventeen* means from beginning to end, or from the beginning to a new stage, as discussed in §§755, 4670 at the end. And *years* symbolize states, as discussed in §§487, 488, 493, 893. In this case, then, the seventeen years Jacob lived in Egypt symbolize the beginning of a state of spiritual life within knowledge on the earthly level, all the way to the end of that state. All numbers in the Word have symbolic meaning; see §§575, 647, 648, 755, 813, 1963, 1988, 2075, 2252, 3252, 4264, 4495, 4670, 5265.

6174

And Jacob's days, the years of his life, were one hundred forty-seven years symbolizes his overall state and its quality. This can be seen if the meaning of the numbers seven, forty, and one hundred is unfolded. For the meaning of seven, see §§395, 433, 716, 728, 881, 5265, 5268; for that of forty, §§730, 862, 2272, 2273; and for that of one hundred, §§1988, 2636, 4400. However, numbers that are combined this way cannot easily be explained, because they contain too much to summarize or to express intelligibly. These numbers taken together contain the whole state of what Jacob represented and the nature of that state, which angels see in its entirety from the number alone. Among angels, you see, all numbers in the Word translate into the idea of real things, as I was able to see from an experience I had many times. I would see a long series of numbers, and angels would then say that the numbers held inside them a series of subjects they were discussing. From this the earliest people (whose religion was heavenly) had numerical calculations expressing such heavenly matters as were not very accessible to the thinking of the earthly mind.

6175

After their time, though, this knowledge died out, along with the perception of heavenly ideas. All that remained was a concept of the general meaning of the most basic numbers, like three, six, seven, and twelve, and not as much the meaning of combined numbers.

Today nobody even knows that the numbers in the Word mean anything but a number, so this claim might seem rather unbelievable.

6176 *And Israel's days for dying came near* symbolizes a state just before rebirth, as the following shows: *Coming near* means being at hand and therefore being just before. *Days* symbolize states, as discussed in §§23, 487, 488, 493, 893, 2788, 3462, 3785, 4850. *Israel* represents spiritual goodness, as noted above in §6169. And *dying* symbolizes rising again and being stirred to life—spiritual life specifically—as discussed in §§3326, 3498, 3505, 4618, 4621, 6036. So it symbolizes being reborn, because one who is reborn rises again from spiritual death and is stirred to life anew.

6177 *And he called his son Joseph* symbolizes the presence of the inner level. This can be seen from the symbolism of *calling* someone to oneself as bringing that person into one's presence and therefore as presence itself, and from the representation of *Joseph* as the inner level (as before, many times: §§6089, 6117, 6120, 6128, 6132, 6136, 6145, 6149, 6152, 6153, 6156, 6163, 6167).

6178 *And said to him, "Please, if I have found favor in your eyes,"* symbolizes a longing. This is evident from the emotion Jacob felt when he said these words to Joseph; the emotion is present in the turn of speech. After all, *please, if I have found favor in your eyes* is simply an idiom expressing a feeling and therefore a longing of the will, as above in §6162 as well.

6179 *Please put your hand under my thigh* symbolizes a sacred obligation. This can be seen from the symbolism of *placing a hand under the thigh* as an obligation laid with full power on someone through reference to the marriage relationship and its love. A *hand* symbolizes power (§§878, 3091, 4931–4937, 5328, 5544), and a *thigh* symbolizes the marriage relationship and its love (discussed at §§3021, 4277, 4280, 4575, 5050–5062).

The highest form of marriage relationship is the union of divinity and divine humanity in the Lord. From this comes the union of divine goodness and divine truth in heaven, because what emanates from the Lord is divine truth rising out of divine goodness. This causes heaven to be heaven and to be called a marriage, because combined goodness and truth there, coming from the Lord, are what bring it about. Since the Lord is the goodness in heaven, and heaven is the truth rising out of that goodness, the Word calls the Lord a bridegroom and calls heaven and the church a bride. Goodness and truth make a marriage, and their union is what is meant by the marriage relationship. This shows how sacred an obligation that had reference to the marriage relationship was, as symbolized by putting a hand under the thigh.

True marriage love descends from this marriage, the marriage of goodness and truth. For a discussion of marriage love and its holiness, see §§2727–2759.

And you are to keep mercy and truth with me symbolizes humility. This **6180** can be seen from the symbolism of *keeping mercy* as the goodness that comes of love and from that of *keeping truth* as the truth that composes faith, both of which are discussed below. When these words are spoken, they are words of entreaty and therefore of humility.

Keeping mercy symbolizes the goodness that comes of love because all mercy comes of love. People with love or charity also have mercy. Love and charity turn into mercy in us when our neighbor is needy or miserable and we help her or him in that state. That is why mercy symbolizes the goodness that comes of love.

Keeping truth symbolizes the truth that composes faith because all truth is part of faith; and for that reason the same word in the original language means faith.

[2] The close union between the goodness that comes of love and the truth that composes faith, and the impossibility of either without the other, gave rise to this stock phrase among the ancients. They knew that love's goodness was inseparable from faith's truth. Because they are inseparable, the two terms are often linked in the Word, as in Exodus:

Jehovah, great in *mercy* and *truth*. (Exodus 34:6)

In 2 Samuel:

David said to the men of Jabesh, "May Jehovah keep *mercy* and *truth* with you." (2 Samuel 2:5, 6)

And in the same book:

David to Ittai the Gittite: "Return and take your brothers back with you in *mercy* and *truth*." (2 Samuel 15:20)

In Hosea:

Jehovah has a dispute with the residents of the land, because there is *no truth*, and *no mercy*, and no knowledge of Jehovah in the land. (Hosea 4:1)

In David:

All the ways of Jehovah are *mercy* and *truth*, for those who keep his pact. (Psalms 25:10)

In the same author:

> Jehovah, you will not withhold your mercies from me; *your mercy* and *your truth* will constantly guard me. (Psalms 40:11)

In the same author:

> *Jehovah's* eternal *mercies* I will sing; for generation after generation [I will sing] *your truth* with my mouth. For I said, "*Mercy* will be built up forever; in the very heavens you will make your *truth* firm. Justice and judgment are the underpinning of your throne; *mercy* and *truth* stand before your face." (Psalms 89:1, 2, 14)

Other instances in David: Psalms 26:3; 36:5; 57:3, 10; 61:7; 85:10; 86:15; 89:24, 33; 92:2.

6181   *You are please not to bury me in Egypt* symbolizes rebirth, but not in knowledge. This is clear from the symbolism of being *buried* as resurrection and rebirth (discussed at §§2916, 2917, 4621, 5551) and from that of *Egypt* as knowledge (discussed many times before).

For a definition of rebirth outside of knowledge, see just below, at §6183.

6182   *And let me lie with my ancestors* symbolizes a life like that of the ancients, as the following shows: *Lying* symbolizes life, because in this case it means being buried among them. Since being buried means resurrection and rebirth, lying among them means life, because it is into life that one is resurrected and reborn. And *ancestors,* [or fathers,] symbolize the people of the ancient and earliest churches, as discussed at §6075, so they symbolize the ancients.

6183   *And you are to bear me out of Egypt* means so as to rise above knowledge, as the following shows: *Bearing me* symbolizes a lifting up, because in traveling from Egypt to the land of Canaan one is said to go up, which symbolizes a lifting (§§3084, 4539, 4969, 5406, 5817, 6007). The same thing is consequently meant by bearing someone to Canaan from Egypt. And *Egypt* symbolizes knowledge, as noted before.

What it is to be lifted out of knowledge needs to be defined briefly. The earthly level is reborn by an infusion of spiritual life from the Lord into the knowledge on that level by way of the inner self. This infusion is the subject of the current chapter. When we have been reborn to this extent, though, if our nature allows us to regenerate further, we are raised up from there to an inner earthly level that is under the direct supervision of the inner dimension. If our nature does not allow, our spiritual life stays on the outer earthly plane.

The way we are lifted is by being drawn out of sensory information and knowledge and therefore raised above them. We then reach a state of inner thought and feeling, which means that we go deeper into heaven.

People in this state are in the inner part of the church, but people who are in the previous state are in the outer part of the church. The latter are represented by Jacob, the former by Israel. These words were said in order to allow Jacob to be Israel and as Israel to represent spiritual goodness on the inner earthly level and accordingly to represent the inner, spiritual part of the church.

And bury me in their grave symbolizes this kind of rebirth. This can be seen from the symbolism of being *buried* as rebirth, a topic addressed above at §6181. Being buried *in their grave,* then, or in the same grave [as the ancients], means their kind of rebirth. **6184**

And he said, "I myself shall do according to your word," means that it will happen so, as provided for by the Divine. This can be seen from the symbolism of *doing according to someone's word* as its happening so. The reason for adding "as provided for by the Divine" is that Abraham, Isaac, and Jacob represented three things, but three things that become one. In the highest sense—in the Lord—Abraham represented divinity itself, Isaac represented divine rationality, and Jacob represented earthly divinity (§§3305 at the end, 4615, 6098). In a secondary sense—in humankind—they represent the inmost core, or heavenly goodness; the inner level, or spiritual goodness; and the outer level, or earthly goodness. These levels are symbolized by the three men in one grave, because a grave symbolizes rebirth and resurrection into life (§§2916, 2917, 4621, 5551). **6185**

And he said, "Swear to me," is an intent to make it irreversible. This is indicated by the symbolism of *swearing* as irreversible confirmation (discussed at §2842). **6186**

And [Joseph] swore to him means that it was irreversible. This is indicated by the symbolism of *swearing* as something irreversible, as just above at §6186. **6187**

And Israel bowed over the head of his bed means that he turned toward the concerns of the inner earthly level. This can be seen from the symbolism of *bowing* here as turning and from that of a *bed* as the earthly level (discussed below). The *head* of the bed, then, is the higher part of the **6188** earthly level, that is, the inner part. Where the Word speaks of a head, it symbolizes what is inward, relative to the body, which is outward.

"He turned toward the concerns of the inner earthly level" means that earthly truth (Jacob) rose up toward spiritual goodness (Israel), as described and explained above in §§6183.

[2] A *bed* is the earthly level because the earthly level lies below the rational level and serves it like a bed. Rationality more or less lies down on the earthly level, and the earthly level, since it is laid out underneath this way, is therefore called a bed. There is an example in Amos:

> As the shepherd has rescued from the mouth of the lion two legs or a piece of an ear, so will the children of Israel living in Samaria be rescued, *on the corner of a bed* and *on the end of a couch.* (Amos 3:12)

"On the corner of a bed" means on the lowest part of the earthly plane, and "on the end of a couch" means on the sensory plane. The people Israel, whose capital was Samaria, represented the Lord's spiritual kingdom, and they are said to be at the head of the bed, as here [in Genesis 47:31] their father Israel is said to be. Spiritual goodness, represented by their father Israel, is the head of the bed. When they turn from there to matters on the lowest part of the earthly level and on the sensory level, they are said to be on the corner of the bed and on the end of the couch.

[3] In the same author:

> . . . who lie *on beds of ivory* and sprawl *on their couches* but do not grieve over the wreckage of Joseph. (Amos 6:4, 6)

Beds of ivory are the base pleasures of haughty people, on the lowest part of the earthly plane. Not grieving over the wreckage of Joseph stands for not being at all concerned that goodness has disappeared from the inner plane. In David:

> If I enter within the tent of my house, if I *climb onto the couch of my bed,* . . . (Psalms 132:3)

The "tent of my house" stands for holy love (§§414, 1102, 2145, 2152, 3312, 4128, 4391, 4599). "Climbing onto the couch of my bed" stands for climbing over the earthly level toward truth that comes of love's goodness. Anyone can see that entering within the tent of one's house and climbing onto the couch of one's bed is enigmatic language that cannot be understood without the inner meaning.

Spiritual Inflow, and the Interaction of the Soul and Body (Continued)

A T the end of the chapters on [Genesis] 44 and 45, I showed that we **6189** each have two angels from heaven and two spirits from hell with us, that this provides us communication with both heaven and hell, and that it also provides us the freedom to turn to one or the other. But what humankind does not know, and so may hardly believe, is that everything in us comes from elsewhere, in keeping with our freedom. Evil flows in from hell, and goodness from heaven, or from the Lord through heaven.

Since this inflow is the current focus, and since I use the term so **6190** often, I should start by explaining what it is.

There is no better way to see what is meant by spiritual inflow than by considering earthly inflows that exist visibly in the world. Warmth from the sun, for instance, flows into everything on the planet, in all the variety determined by time of year and climatic region of the earth. Light flows into everything too, again in all the variety determined by time of day and year and in different ways depending on the climatic region.

These are examples, then—that warmth from the sun flows into everything on the planet, bringing life to plants; and that light flows into everything too, creating the support system for that life, and also colors and beauty of different kinds. Then there is the inflow of the same warmth into the surface of our own body, and of light into our eye. Likewise the inflow of sound into the ear, and other similar illustrations. These examples make it possible to grasp what the inflow of life from the Lord is. He is the sun of heaven, the source of heavenly warmth (the goodness sought by love) and heavenly light (the truth taught by faith). The inflow of these forces is clearly sensed, too: Heavenly warmth, or love, generates the vital heat in us, and heavenly light, or faith, generates our ability to understand, since faith's truth, coming from the Lord, enlightens our intellect. Both inflows vary greatly, though, because their nature depends on the way we receive them.

The fact that the Lord governs us through angels and spirits is some- **6191** thing I have been given to see through such plain experience that I have not even a hint of remaining doubt about it. For many years now, all my thoughts and all my feelings in their very smallest points have flowed in by means of spirits and angels, and I have been allowed to perceive it so plainly that nothing is plainer. I have sensed, seen, and heard who they are, what they are like, and where they are. When anything untoward has dropped into my thought or will, I have talked with them and lodged a vehement complaint. I have also noticed that angels rein in those spirits' power to pour such things into me and have seen how they do it. Often the spirits are driven away, and when that happens, I have noted, their place is taken by new spirits, who also flow in. I have been able to tell where these spirits were from—in other words, which communities they were delegates for—and many times I have been given the opportunity to talk with the communities themselves.

Yet although all the smallest possible elements of my thoughts and feelings were flowing in through spirits and angels, I still used my mind as before, exercised my will as before, and interacted with people in this world as before. No one observed any difference from my previous life.

I know that hardly anyone will believe such a thing, but it is an eternal truth.

6192   I was given a personal demonstration of the way spirits flow into a person on earth. When they come to us, they take on our entire memory—everything we have learned and absorbed since infancy. The spirits imagine the information is theirs, so they play our part inside us. However, they are not allowed to enter any further than our inner levels, the levels of thought and will; they are not allowed to reach our outer levels, the levels of deed and word. These come into play through a general inflow from the Lord, without the mediation of individual spirits and angels.

Nonetheless, although spirits play our part inside us, so far as the activity of our thought and will is concerned, they are still unaware they are with us, because they possess everything in our memory and believe it all to be theirs, not someone else's. Another reason for them not to know they are with us is so that they will not hurt us. If the spirits from hell with us did not think our memory was theirs, they would make every effort to destroy us, body and soul. This is the essence of hellish pleasure.

6193   So spirits possess everything in our thought and will, and angels possess what is even deeper, which means that we are bound tightly to them. As a result we cannot help sensing and feeling that we ourselves are the ones thinking and intending.

Communication in the other world works the same way. In a single community, where everyone is similar, each member believes that what belongs to another is his or her own. When good [spirits] go to a heavenly community, then, they immediately enter into all the understanding and wisdom of that community, so thoroughly that they are completely convinced it exists inside themselves. The same is true for a person on earth, and for a spirit with that person.

What flows in from spirits from hell is evil and falsity, but what flows in from angels from heaven is goodness and truth. The opposing inflows keep us in the middle and therefore in freedom.

[2] Because more of the angels' inflow comes by an inward way, it is not as perceptible outwardly as the evil spirits' inflow.

Furthermore, angels by their very nature are completely unwilling to hear that goodness or truth flows in from them, only from the Lord. It upsets them if anyone thinks otherwise, because they have a clear perception that this is so. They love nothing more than willing and thinking under the Lord's power rather than their own.

Evil spirits, conversely, grow angry if told they do not think or will on their own, because this goes against the kinds of pleasure they love. It makes them even angrier to be told that life does not exist in them but comes from elsewhere. When the fact is demonstrated to them by personal experience (as it often is), they concede its truth, since they cannot argue with experience. However, a little while later they deny it and want never to have it confirmed by experience again.

It has sometimes happened that I was thinking to myself, or even speaking with others, without reflecting that I had spirits with me rousing the thoughts. The spirits have addressed me right afterward, though, and described the state they were in at the time, which was that they had no idea they were not the ones thinking. In fact, the impression that they were doing my thinking was so strong that the ones closest to me were totally convinced. The more distant were less convinced, and the even more distant even less convinced. **6194**

I was also shown which communities were flowing into these spirits as their delegates.

Some spirits who were neither very good nor very evil were with me for a long time, slightly above my head. They were able to flow deeply into my feelings, and since that was what they wanted, they came in for a while. They tied themselves to me so firmly that it seemed as if they could hardly be removed. I talked with them about the situation, saying **6195** they ought to detach, but they could not. When they tried it, and pulled away a little bit, they made my mind so dull that I could think only in a confused and disjointed way. I also had the kind of headache people have when they faint.

This showed me how varieties of love bind people together and that love is what unites everyone in the other world. Consequently, spirits who enter directly into another's feelings possess that other. The same thing happens in the world when one person caters to what another person loves. Truth does not bind people together, however; only a desire for truth does.

[2] From this I was able to see how we are united with either heaven or hell: through different kinds of love. Love for ourselves and love for worldly advantages unite us with hell, but love for our neighbor and love for God unite us with heaven.

It was also evident that a person tied to hell can never be released except by the Lord and by divine means. This was demonstrated by the spirits who were tied to me just by mild feelings. I was freed from them only through intermediate kinds of love that gradually united them to others. As they were being detached, they appeared to move away from me, out in front and to the left. I observed the process through changes in the state of my feelings, because as my feelings changed, the spirits withdrew.

This experience also makes it clear what causes appearances of distance in the other life.

6196 Abundant experience has taught me that what we love determines which spirits associate with us. Whenever I began to feel an intense love for something, spirits with the same love would immediately appear, and they would not be removed until my feeling of love for it stopped.

6197 Sometimes something would occur to my thoughts and to the desires of my will whose source I would not know. Whenever I wanted to know, I was shown where it came from—specifically, from which communities, and occasionally through which spirits as their delegates. They would talk with me then and admit they had thought it up and knew it would flow into me and seem to me to be inside me.

Deceitful spirits who appear directly above my head sometimes flowed into me so subtly that I did not know where the inflow came from. I could scarcely perceive what flowed in as being anywhere but inside me and from me, the way others usually perceive such things. But I always knew for certain that it came from somewhere else, so the Lord would give me an awareness keen enough to make out every stream of the spirits' inflow as well as their whereabouts and identity. When the spirits noticed this, they would become extremely resentful, especially of my reflection on the fact that it came from them. The reflection was flowing in through angels.

[2] These dishonest spirits mainly instilled thoughts and feelings denigrating the Lord. When they did, I was inspired to reflect on the fact that no one in hell acknowledges the Lord. No, they insult him as much as they are allowed, although they are not unwilling to hear him called the Father, the creator of the universe. This is an unmistakable sign showing that the Lord is the one who rules all of heaven, as he teaches in Matthew:

> All power in heaven and on earth has been given to me. (Matthew 28:18)

The same sign also shows that [hell's inhabitants] are opposed to the Lord, because they are opposed to heaven, where the Lord is the all in all.

I once had spirits with me who thought they were the ones who were alive and that my life came only from them, so that they were me. When I told them that they were separate spirits and that I too was a spirit inside, they could not believe it. In order for them to see it was so, they were separated from me and in this way shown that they were their own spirits. They still kept refusing to believe, though, and stubbornly persisted. They were gone awhile, and when they came back they still had the same conviction.   **6198**

This incident too shows that spirits have no idea that what is ours is not theirs.

However, spirits whose belief is as tenacious as this are not readily given entrance to us, because it is difficult to detach them. The other spirits have a similar trait embedded in them to make them useful to us, but the trait is different in them.

Another spirit also thought he was me. In fact, when he spoke with me in my native tongue, he believed he was talking in his own tongue, saying it was his language. But I showed him that the language proper to spirits is entirely different. It is the universal language of all spirits, and ideas in that language flow into my language. So spirits do not speak in their own terms, they speak in me. This is an indication, I said, that they not only take over what is ours but also imagine it is theirs.   **6199**

Having been in constant company with spirits and angels for nine years now, I have carefully observed how spiritual inflow works.   **6200**

When I engaged in thought, the matter-based ideas in my thinking appeared in the middle of a kind of wave. I have noticed that the wave actually consisted of those contents of my memory that were linked with the central topic. Spirits see the entire thought, then, but all that comes to the thinker's consciousness at the time is the part in the middle, the part that appeared to be made of physical matter. To me the surrounding wave was like spiritual wings carrying the topic that was under consideration up out of the memory. That is how the thinker comes to conceive the idea.

The fact that the wave of surrounding material held countless ideas conforming with the central one was apparent to me from this: that to spirits in a more rarified dimension, the wave revealed everything I had ever known about the subject. So spirits fully absorb and adopt everything in us. Demons, who pay attention only to cravings and desires, absorb and adopt what we love.

[2] For an illustrative example, when I thought about someone I knew, a mental image of that person as he appears when mentioned to others was presented at the center. Around it, like an airborne wave, lay everything I had ever known or thought about the person since childhood. So the entire person, as he had existed in my thoughts and feelings, appeared instantaneously to spirits.

Again, when I thought about a given city, from the wavelike environment around the thought, spirits could then instantly tell everything I had seen or known of that city.

The situation was the same with scholarly matters.

6201   This is how my thinking appeared to spirits when I was lifted a little above my physical senses, but when my thinking was mired in my senses, no such wave appeared. Instead the thought was entirely matter-based and was not very different from the visual experience of the outer eye. This kind of thinking is described as sensory-level. When one thinks more deeply, that is described as being drawn up out of the physical senses. The ancients knew that we are capable of this, so some of them wrote about the state.

People who engage in sensory-level thinking are called sense-oriented, and sense-oriented spirits attach to them. These spirits pick up on hardly anything in us that does not come to our own awareness. They function on a coarser level than the others.

When people operate on the level of the senses without rising above it, I have noticed, they have no thoughts but those connected with the body and the world. They do not want to know about anything involving eternal life. In fact, they object to hearing about such things.

[2] I have been let down into the sensory level a number of times in order to learn that this is how the matter stands, and thoughts like these have always arisen immediately. At the same time, spirits in that coarser dimension have poured in ugly, offensive notions. As soon as I have been drawn up out of the sensory plane, though, such thoughts have disappeared.

People who lead a sensory life include most of those who indulge in bodily pleasures. They also include people who have utterly refused to extend their thoughts beyond what they can see and hear, and especially those who have refused to think about eternal life. As a result they scorn both kinds of higher thinking, and listening to such talk makes them sick.

Spirits like this abound in the other life today. They come from the world in droves, and influence people on earth to indulge in luxury and to live for themselves and the world rather than for others—except to the extent that others coddle them and their base pleasures.

To be elevated above all this, one must think about eternal life.

I observed another inflow, too, not through the spirits accompanying a person but through other spirits sent from a certain hellish community into the aura given off by a person's life. These spirits talk to each other in ways that are inimical to the person, producing a general inflow that is uncomfortable, unpleasant, sad, or anxious, with a great deal of variety. I have often had spirits like this with me, and I have sensed some in the area of my stomach who flooded me with worries. Not that I could tell where the worries came from, but the spirits were exposed every time, and then I heard that they had been making remarks to each other of a kind hostile to my desires. Greedy spirits have sometimes appeared in the same area but a little higher up, and they flooded me with an anxious concern for the future. I was allowed to scold them, telling them that they correlate with stomach contents that are undigested, bad smelling, and therefore nauseating. I also saw them driven away, and when they were gone, the worrying stopped completely. The experience occurred a number of times so that I could know for sure they were the source.

6202

[2] This is the nature of the inflow into people who are depressed and anxious for no reason. It is also the nature of the inflow into people undergoing spiritual trials, but then it is not just a general inflow from such spirits. No, hellish spirits also dredge up the particular evils the

person has done, and they twist and misinterpret the person's good qualities through which angels are fighting back.

People who are being reborn come into this state by being let down into their own self-centeredness. It happens when they immerse themselves too much in worldly and bodily interests and when they need to be elevated to spiritual considerations.

6203   About the origin in hell of the inflow of evil: When we plunge into evil, first by consent, then with set purpose, and finally as our heart's delight, the hell that revels in the same sort of evil opens up. (Different kinds of evil, in all their variety, distinguish the hells from each other.) When we come into evil this way, then if that hell also flows into us, the evil clings. The hell whose sphere of influence we are then in is at the peak of its pleasure, because it is indulging in its evil, so it does not let up but presses on relentlessly. It makes us think about the evil, intermittently at first but then whenever anything related comes up. In the end it comes to dominate our entire mind. When that happens, we then round up arguments confirming that the thing is not bad, until eventually we fully persuade even ourselves. After that we work as hard as we can to remove any external restraints. We make the activity out to be allowable and clever, and at last to be decent and honorable. This includes adultery, theft by fraud and deception, different kinds of arrogance and boastfulness, contempt, verbal abuse, persecution dressed up as justice, and so on.

Evil of this type resembles open theft, in that once we have deliberately committed it two or three times, we cannot stop anymore. It clings incessantly to our thoughts.

6204   It is important to know, though, that the evil that enters our *thoughts* does not hurt us at all. Spirits from hell are constantly pouring evil in, and angels constantly repel it. But when evil enters our *will,* it does harm us, because it then issues in action, whenever outward restraints do not hold us back.

Evil enters our will when we keep it in our thoughts, when we agree to it, and especially when we commit it and then enjoy it.

6205   I have often noticed that evil spirits mainly adopt our persuasions and cravings and that when they adopt these, they have us at their command. After all, those who insert themselves into our cravings and our persuasions subject us to their power and make us their slaves. In contrast, any inflow through angels adapts to our desires, which angels guide in a gentle way, bend in a good direction, and do not break. Their actual inflow is silent and barely perceptible (since it acts on our inner depths), and freedom is always its means.

It also needs to be recognized that all evil flows in from hell, and all goodness from the Lord through heaven. The only reason evil is ever attributed to us as ours is that we believe and convince ourselves that we think it up and do it on our own. So we make it ours. If we believed the fact of the matter, goodness from the Lord would be attributed to us, not evil. That is because the moment evil flowed in we would think, "This is from the evil spirits with us," and when we did, angels would turn it away and cast it aside. Angelic inflow acts on what we know and believe, not on what we do not know or believe. It attaches only when there is something in us to attach to.

6206

[2] When we adopt evil this way, we attract to ourselves the atmosphere, [or aura,] of that evil, which is the point of contact with spirits from hell who live in the same kind of evil atmosphere. Like bonds with like.

The spiritual aura around a person or spirit is a breath given off by the life force of that individual's passions. It allows the character of the person or spirit to be recognized at a distance. Auras determine how bonds form among all the inhabitants of the other world and among the communities. They also determine how bonds break, because contrary auras clash and repel each other. As a result, any atmosphere belonging to a love for what is evil is found in hell, and any atmosphere belonging to a love for what is good is found in heaven. That is, the individuals with those atmospheres are found there.

Angelic inflow acts mainly on a person's conscience; that is the plane on which it works. This plane lies deep inside a person.

6207

There are two levels of conscience: inner and outer. Inner conscience concerns itself with spiritual goodness and truth. Outer conscience concerns itself with justice and fairness. This latter conscience currently exists in many people, but inner conscience in few. Still, people who possess an [outer] conscience are saved in the other life. Their nature is such that if they go against goodness and truth or justice and fairness, they suffer and agonize inside. This is not because it costs them prestige or prosperity or reputation but simply because they have gone against goodness and truth or justice and fairness.

In people without these kinds of conscience, however, there is sometimes something very base that mimics conscience. It consists in their doing what is true and good, fair and just, not from any love for those qualities but for the sake of themselves and their prestige and financial benefit. These people also suffer and agonize when things go against them, but such a conscience is no conscience. It consists in self-love and materialism and contains no love for God or for their neighbor, so it is not visible in the other life.

[2] People like this are also able to serve in high-ranking office, just like people with the use of a genuine conscience. Outwardly they act the same, but for the sake of their own status and reputation. The more they fear the loss of these advantages, then, the better they carry out public duties benefiting their neighbor and their country. Any who do not fear such loss are totally discardable limbs in the body of the republic.

People with this counterfeit type of conscience do not even know what conscience is. When they hear others describe it, they sneer, considering it a mark of ignorance or mental illness.

These remarks have been made to reveal how matters stand with spiritual inflow. The discussion was intended to show that conscience is the plane into which angels flow; that this is where they act specifically on desires for goodness and truth, for justice and fairness; and that in this way they keep us bound, though still free.

6208   There are many who inherit an earthly goodness that gives them pleasure in helping others but who [during earthly life] were not trained to do good on the basis of principles drawn from the Word, the church's theology, or their own religious tradition. As a result they were unable to receive any gift of conscience. Conscience grows not out of earthly, inherited goodness but out of teachings about truth and goodness, and a life lived in accordance with those teachings.

When people like this go to the other world, they express surprise that they are not welcomed into heaven, claiming they lived a good life. They are told, though, that a good life based on earthly heredity is not a good life. Rather, a good life is based on what theology teaches about goodness and truth and on living by that. It is through these principles that we develop convictions about truth and goodness and receive a conscience—the plane into which heaven flows.

To teach them that this is the case, they are sent to various communities, where they allow themselves to be led astray into all sorts of evil, simply through arguments persuading them that evil is good and goodness evil. Everywhere they go, they fall prey to this persuasion and blow

around like straw in the wind. They lack principles, you see, and have no
plane in them on which angels can operate to lead them away from evil.

An inflow from angels is not perceived the same way by us as an inflow **6209**
from spirits. What flows in from angels is not matter-based but spiritual,
and it all appears as a stream of air. What comes from inner angels seems
to be made of light, and what comes from angels even farther within
appears fiery. More about this at the end of the following chapters, by the
Lord's divine mercy [§§6307–6327, 6466–6496, 6598–6626].

On several occasions it happened that I was thinking intently about **6210**
worldly matters and about concerns most people harbor—about pos-
sessions, acquisition of wealth, physical pleasures, and so on. At those
times I noticed that I was falling back to the sensory plane. The more
my thoughts were immersed in these subjects, the farther I was removed
from company with angels.

The experience showed me that people deeply immersed in these concerns cannot interact with inhabitants of the other world. When thoughts
like those completely take over our psyche, they drag the more irrational
parts of it down, like weights that make it sink. When we make such concerns our ultimate goal, they remove us from heaven. We can be raised to
heaven only through a goodness inspired by love and faith.

The same point was further clarified for me by the following experience:
Once, when I was led through some neighborhoods in heaven while pon-
dering a spiritual idea, I happened to drop suddenly into worldly thinking. When I did, the whole spiritual idea evaporated and disappeared.

Sometimes I wondered why speech and actions are not governed by **6211**
specific spirits, as thought and will are, but I was taught that speech follows from thought, and action from will, in a natural flow. So it comes
about through a general inflow. Nonetheless there are spirits dedicated to
each organ of speech and each organ of motion, although the spirits do
not know it.

General inflow is a constant force the Lord exerts by means of heaven
as a whole on the individual details of a person's life.

It is known from the Word that the world of spirits and heaven **6212**
flowed into the prophets, partly through dreams, partly through visions,
and partly through speech. With some prophets the inflow came directly
into their words and actions and therefore into something bodily. Under
that inflow they did not speak or act on their own but under the power
of the spirits who then occupied their body. All this is known. Some of

the prophets acted insane as a result of that inflow: Saul lay naked, others hurt themselves, others put horns on, and so on.

Since I wanted to know how spirits acted on the prophets, I was shown by personal experience.

[2] For my instruction, I was possessed by spirits for a whole night. They took over my physical self so completely that I could not sense it as my own body except in the vaguest way.

As the spirits arrived, they looked like little clouds heaped together into various shapes, usually pointed ones. The cloudlets were black.

In the morning I saw a chariot with a pair of horses, and a man riding in it. Next I saw a horse with someone sitting on it who was then tossed off behind it and lay there while the horse kicked back at him. Then I saw another person sitting on the horse. The horses were noble steeds.

[3] Angels afterward described these sights as having symbolic meaning. The chariot with the man in it symbolized the spiritual meaning within the prophetic things that the prophets said and that were represented [by their actions]. The horse that tossed and kicked back at its rider symbolized the people of Judah and Israel—the recipients of the prophecies—who focused solely on the outermost level, which caused the power of intellect to reject them and "kick" them away. The other person sitting on the horse symbolized the intellect in people awake to the inner meaning of the Word's prophetic part.

[4] This state, which I experienced through the night all the way till morning, taught me how the prophets were possessed by spirits who spoke and acted through them. What I learned was that spirits took over their body so thoroughly that little was left, although the prophets did not realize it.

There were certain spirits active in this work who did not want to possess people, only to gain access to a person's physical responses—which gave them access to everything in a person's body.

The spirits who usually accompany me said that I was gone from them while I remained in that state.

[5] The spirits who possessed my body the way they once possessed the prophets' bodies talked with me afterward. Among much else, they said that at the time they had no idea whatever they were not living a bodily type of life.

I also heard that the prophets received other kinds of inflow as well. Specifically, they would have command of themselves and their thoughts except that the spirits would talk to them, mostly inside them. This inflow did not act on their thought and will. Instead, it was merely speech that came to their ear.

So hell, through its spirits, is constantly pouring evil and falsity into us and corrupting and obliterating truth and goodness, while the Lord through angels is constantly turning those efforts aside, negating them, softening them, and moderating them. Many years of almost continuous experience have made me so familiar with this idea that I cannot even consider doubting it.

6213

However, if angels are to turn aside hell's inflow, we must possess truth in our faith united to goodness in our life for angels to flow into. They need this as a plane on which to act.

If we do not possess these attributes, hell carries us off, and the Lord through angels then governs us by external means called outward restraints. These grow out of a self-interested shrewdness that aims to keep us superficially looking as if we loved our neighbor and our country. Our real motivation, though, is high position, wealth, and consequent reputation, or a fear of legal penalties, including death. These are the outer restraints through which we are governed when we have no inner restraints, which are the restraints of conscience.

In the other life, though, these external restraints make no difference. They are taken from us, and when they have been removed, we appear as we had truly been inside.

The following experience revealed to me how hard it is for people to believe that spirits know their thoughts: Once, before I had regular conversation with spirits, a spirit happened to say a few words to me about some thoughts I was thinking. I was dumbfounded that the spirit knew what I was thinking, because I imagined that such things were hidden and were known to God alone.

6214

Later, when I started speaking with spirits, I was upset that I could think nothing without their knowing about it, and I was afraid it would prove disturbing to me; but then after numerous days of exposure I grew used to it.

Eventually I realized that spirits perceive not only everything we think and will but also much more than we ourselves are aware of. Angels perceive still more, since they discern our intentions and ultimate goals, from original aims through means to results. And the Lord knows not only what we are like through and through but also what we will be like forever.

From this you can see that absolutely nothing is hidden, that what we think and plot inside stands out to view in the other life as clear as day.

6215   The subject of spiritual inflow and of the interaction of soul and body continues at the end of the next chapter [§§6307–6327].

Genesis 48

1. And it happened after these words that they said to Joseph, "Here now, your father is sick." And he took his two sons with him, Manasseh and Ephraim.

2. And they told Jacob and said, "Look: your son Joseph has come to you." And Israel braced himself and sat up on the bed.

3. And Jacob said to Joseph, "God Shaddai appeared to me in Luz in the land of Canaan and blessed me

4. and said to me, 'Here now, I am making you fruitful and will cause you to multiply, and I will turn you into an assemblage of peoples and give this land to your seed after you as an eternal possession.'

5. And now your two sons born to you in the land of Egypt—before my coming to you, to Egypt—are mine, Ephraim and Manasseh; like Reuben and Simeon they will be to me.

6. And the generation that you generate after them will be yours. They will be called by the name of their brothers in their inheritance.

7. And as for me, as I was coming from Paddan, Rachel died beside me in the land of Canaan, on the way, when there was still a stretch of land to go to Ephrata, and I buried her there on the way to Ephrath, that is, Bethlehem."

8. And Israel saw Joseph's sons and said, "Whose are these?"

9. And Joseph said to his father, "They are my sons, whom God gave to me here." And he said, "Bring them to me, please, and I will bless them."

10. And Israel's eyes were heavy with age; he could not see. And he made them approach him and kissed them and hugged them.

11. And Israel said to Joseph, "I didn't think I would see your face, and here, God has caused me to see your seed too."

12. And Joseph brought them from [Israel's] thighs and bowed his face to the earth.

13. And Joseph took them both, Ephraim in his right hand on Israel's left, and Manasseh in his left on Israel's right, and made them approach him.

14. And Israel put out his right hand and placed it on the head of Ephraim (and he was the younger) and his left on the head of Manasseh; he crossed his hands, as Manasseh was the firstborn.

15. And he blessed Joseph and said, "May the God before whom my fathers, Abraham and Isaac, walked—the God shepherding me from then to this day,

16. the angel redeeming me from every evil—bless the boys. And my name will be given to them, and the name of my fathers, Abraham and Isaac; and may they grow into a throng in the middle of the land."

17. And Joseph saw that his father put his right hand on Ephraim's head, and it was wrong in his eyes, and he took his father's hand to remove it from Ephraim's head onto Manasseh's head.

18. And Joseph said to his father, "Not that way, my father, because this one is the firstborn; put your right hand on his head."

19. And his father refused and said, "I know, my son, I know; this one too will become a people, and he too will become great. And nevertheless his younger brother will become greater than he, and his seed will be a fullness of nations."

20. And he blessed them on this day, saying, "By you Israel will pronounce a blessing, saying, 'May God make you like Ephraim and like Manasseh!'" And he put Ephraim before Manasseh.

21. And Israel said to Joseph, "Here now, I am dying, and God will be with you and take you back to the land of your ancestors.

22. And I am giving you one portion more than your brothers, which I took from the hand of the Amorite with my sword and with my bow."

Summary

6216 THE inner meaning of this chapter is about the church's intellect, consisting of truth, and its will, consisting of goodness. The church's intellect is Ephraim, and the church's will is Manasseh.

6217 In the church, the truth that leads to faith, which belongs to the intellect, seems to stand in first place, while the goodness that comes of neighborly love, which belongs to the will, seems to come second. This is symbolized by Israel's putting his right hand on Ephraim's head and his left on Manasseh's.

Inner Meaning

GENESIS 48:1, 2. *And it happened after these words that they said to Joseph, "Here now, your father is sick." And he took his two sons with him, Manasseh and Ephraim. And they told Jacob and said, "Look: your son Joseph has come to you." And Israel braced himself and sat up on the bed.* **6218**

And it happened after these words symbolizes what follows from before. *That they said to Joseph* symbolizes a noteworthy perception. *Here now, your father is sick* symbolizes the next stage of rebirth. *And he took his two sons with him, Manasseh and Ephraim,* symbolizes the church's will and the church's intellect, born of the inner dimension. *And they told Jacob* symbolizes a perception by earthly-level truth. *And said, "Look: your son Joseph has come to you,"* means concerning the presence of the inner dimension. *And Israel braced himself* symbolizes new strength through spiritual goodness. *And sat up on the bed* means that it turned toward what was earthly.

And it happened after these words symbolizes what follows from before. **6219** This can be seen from the symbolism of *words* as the themes in the previous parts of the text. *After these words,* then, means what follows from before.

That they said to Joseph symbolizes a noteworthy perception. This can **6220** be seen from the symbolism of *saying* as a perception (discussed in §§1791, 1815, 1819, 1822, 1898, 1919, 2080, 2619, 2862, 3509, 5687). The perception was noteworthy because the focus in what follows is the church's intellect and will and therefore its truth and goodness, received under an inflow of inner heavenliness, which is *Joseph.*

Here now, your father is sick symbolizes the next stage of rebirth. This **6221** can be seen from the symbolism of *dying* as resurrection into life, and rebirth (discussed in §§3326, 3498, 3505, 4618, 4621, 6036). *Being sick,* then, which precedes dying, is taking another step toward rebirth and is therefore the next stage of it.

The idea that dying means rebirth and that being sick means the next stage of rebirth cannot help seeming beyond belief, but anyone who knows anything about angels' thought and speech will acknowledge it. Angels know nothing about death or sickness, so they do not have a mental image of it. Consequently when we read about it [in the Word], they instead picture continuing with life and rising again. Why? Because when we die, we shed only what was useful to us in the world and enter the life we had lived in our spirit. This is the image that occurs to angels when we read about dying or falling sick. The thought of rebirth occurs, too, because rebirth is resurrection into life. Prior to rebirth we are spiritually dead, but when we have been reborn we come alive and become children of the resurrection.

[2] Even people living in the body can think this way. If they long for heaven, they too do not think of death or of the sickness before it as anything but resurrection into life. When they think about heaven, they withdraw their minds from ideas of the body, especially when they are sick and approaching death. Clearly, then, the spiritual concept of bodily death is a concept of new life.

That is why resurrection and rebirth end up being portrayed by these kinds of images whenever a discussion of either subject in heaven filters down and is expressed in worldly terms.

The situation with the Word is that everything in it came down from the Lord, passing through heaven into the world. As it came down, it clothed itself in forms suited to the comprehension of heaven on its three levels and eventually of people on earth, this last form being the literal meaning.

6222   *And he took his two sons with him, Manasseh and Ephraim,* symbolizes the church's will and the church's intellect, born of the inner dimension. This can be seen from the representation of *Manasseh* as a new will on the earthly level, and its quality (discussed at the end of §5354), and from that of *Ephraim* as a new intellect on the earthly level, and its quality (discussed in §5354). Their being born of the inner dimension is symbolized by the fact that the two were *sons* of Joseph, who represents inner heavenliness (§§5869, 5877).

[2] I should define the church's intellect and the church's will. The intellect of the church, [or its true power of understanding,] is to perceive from the Word what the truth belonging to faith and the goodness belonging to neighborly love are. The Word's literal meaning, as everyone knows, is such that people use it to prove absolutely any creed they adopt. This is because the literal statements of the Word are general containers for truth. Not until truth has been put into these containers, which are transparent, so to speak, does their true nature become visible. They are therefore mere generalizations, which we have to absorb first in order to be ready and able to accept specific ideas and details.

It is quite plain that the Word's literal meaning by its very nature enables people to use it for proving absolutely any creed they adopt. The evidence is the number of heresies that have existed and still exist in the church. Each of them has adherents that prove its validity from the Word's literal meaning, and prove it so thoroughly as to create implicit belief in it. With these convictions, even if the adherents could hear the truth straight from heaven they would not accept it at all. The reason is that they do not have the true power of understanding characteristic of the church.

[3] The church's intellect consists in reading the Word, carefully comparing one passage with another, and from this seeing what we ought to believe and what we ought to do. This practice is possible only for people whom the Lord enlightens and whom the Christian world calls enlightened. And this enlightenment is possible only for people who long to know truth, not for the sake of reputation and glory but for the sake of living by it and putting it to use. The illumination itself is received in a person's intellect, because the intellect is what is enlightened, and this is plain from the consideration that people with little power of understanding cannot see from the Word what it is that they ought to believe and do. Instead they put their trust in those whom they consider enlightened.

It is also important to know that people who have been reborn receive from the Lord an intellect that can be enlightened. The light of heaven from the Lord is what flows into the intellect and enlightens it. That is the only source from which the intellect receives its light, its power of vision, and therefore its capacity to perceive.

[4] However, this power of understanding, which I am calling the church's intellect, is deeper than an intellect that consists solely of knowledge. It is an awareness that a thing is true not because philosophy and accepted knowledge say so but because the Word in its spiritual meaning does. For example, people who possess the church's intellect can perceive clearly that the Word at every single point teaches that love for the Lord and charity for one's neighbor are the essential ingredients of religion, that our life awaits us after death, and that our life is made up of what we love. They can tell that faith detached from charity is not faith and that faith makes no difference to our eternal life except to the extent that we connect it with good done out love for the Lord and good done out of charity for our neighbor. Faith and goodness must therefore unite if there is to be spiritual life. The truth of these concepts is something that can

be perceived plainly by people with an enlightened intellect, but people without such an intellect cannot possibly see it.

[5] There is a belief that people who know how to prove the dogmas or doctrines of their religion with an abundance of evidence, to the point of imparting conviction, are the ones with an intellect for religious matters. People who are skillful at refuting all kinds of heresies are put in the same category. But the church's intellect does not consist in this kind of activity, because confirmation of dogma is not the province of the intellect. No, it is the province of a sensory-level cleverness and sometimes lies within the reach of even the worst people. Utter nonbelievers and even advocates of outright falsity can come up with proofs. For both types of people, nothing is easier than corroborating whatever they please, so well that they persuade the uneducated. On the contrary, the church's intellect consists in perceiving and seeing the truth (or not) of a dogma *before* it has been confirmed, and only then confirming it.

[6] This is the intellect that Ephraim represents, but the church's goodness, as represented by Manasseh, is the goodness that constitutes charity. The Lord instills this kind of goodness in the people of the church by means of the truth that constitutes faith. This truth, and charitable goodness along with it, are what flow into the intellect and enlighten it. They also cause the intellect and the will to form a single mind.

The fact that both the intellect and the will are born of the inner dimension is clear from many previous remarks and explanations: Enlightenment comes by way of a desire for goodness and truth, and this desire never flows in from anywhere but the inner dimension. So it is never born of anything but the inner dimension—that is, of the Lord *through* the inner dimension.

6223   *And they told Jacob* symbolizes a perception by earthly-level truth. This can be seen from the symbolism of *telling* as a perception (dealt with in §§3608, 5601) and from the representation of *Jacob* as earthly-level truth (dealt with in §§3305, 3509, 3525, 3546, 3599, 3775, 4009, 4234, 4520, 4538, 6001).

6224   *And said, "Look: your son Joseph has come to you,"* symbolizes the presence of the inner dimension. This is clear from the representation of *Joseph* as the inner dimension (§6177) and from the symbolism of *coming to* someone as presence (mentioned in §§5934, 5941, 5947, 6063, 6089).

Joseph stands for the inner dimension in some places and inner heavenliness in others, depending on what lies below it on the earthly plane. When the relationship is with the lower parts of the earthly plane, represented by

Jacob, Joseph is said to stand for the inner dimension, and likewise when the relationship is with Pharaoh. When the relationship is rather with the inner parts of the earthly plane, represented by Israel or his ten sons, Joseph is said to stand for inner heavenliness or inner goodness, because of its inflow into them.

And Israel braced himself symbolizes new strength through spiritual goodness. This is indicated by the symbolism of *bracing oneself* as receiving new strength and by the representation of *Israel* as spiritual goodness on the earthly plane (discussed in §§4286, 4598, 5801, 5803, 5807, 5812, 5817, 5819, 5826, 5833). The reason it means *through* spiritual goodness is that Jacob is called Jacob just above but Israel here. As the text says, "They told *Jacob* and said, 'Look: your son Joseph has come to you,'" and *Israel* braced himself." Israel stands for spiritual goodness on the earthly plane, but Jacob for earthly-level truth, and earthly-level truth (which belongs to earthly-level faith) is strengthened by spiritual goodness (which is the goodness belonging to neighborly love). Israel also stands for the inner part of the church, and Jacob for its outer part (§§4286, 4292, 4570), and the outer part has no other source of strength or support than the inner part. The people in the inner part of the church are those intent on charitable goodness, which is the goodness belonging to faith, or the goodness belonging to truth, or spiritual goodness. These are all Israel. The people in the outer part, on the other hand, are those intent on religious truth but not yet on goodness, in any obvious way, although the truth they know does contain goodness. This is Jacob.

And sat up on the bed means that it turned toward what was earthly. This can be seen from the symbolism of a *bed* as the earthly plane, as treated of at §6188.

The reason *Israel sat up on the bed* means that spiritual goodness turned toward what was earthly is this: The final verse of the previous chapter, Genesis 47, said that Israel bowed over the head of the bed, which meant that spiritual goodness turned toward the concerns of the inner earthly level; see §6188. The fact that he moved away from there and sat up on the bed, then, means that spiritual goodness turned toward what was [outwardly] earthly.

What it means to turn toward the inner earthly level or the outer earthly level cannot be explained in a comprehensible way, because very few realize that inner and outer earthly levels exist. Very few realize that our thoughts move back and forth between the two. People who do not realize this do not reflect on it, so they could never gain any knowledge of

6225

6226

the subject from experience. Everyone's thinking shifts levels all the time, though, in individual ways. After all, our thoughts now soar high, now sink low, so that our minds look now upward, now downward.

[2] Besides, anyone can see that Israel's bowing over the head of the bed and then sitting up on it would be too trivial for mention in something as sacred as the Word if it did not hide a secret. The secret can be revealed only by the inner meaning and consequently only by a knowledge of the symbolism of each word in its spiritual sense—the sense of which angels are aware. Unlike people on earth, angels base their thinking on objects in heaven rather than objects belonging to our world, the body, or the earth. (The difference between the two kinds of objects is especially plain to see from the correspondences discussed at the ends of many chapters.)

6227   Genesis 48:3, 4, 5, 6, 7. *And Jacob said to Joseph, "God Shaddai appeared to me in Luz in the land of Canaan and blessed me and said to me, 'Here now, I am making you fruitful and will cause you to multiply, and I will turn you into an assemblage of peoples and give this land to your seed after you as an eternal possession.' And now your two sons born to you in the land of Egypt— before my coming to you, to Egypt—are mine, Ephraim and Manasseh; like Reuben and Simeon they will be to me. And the generation that you generate after them will be yours. They will be called by the name of their brothers in their inheritance. And as for me, as I was coming from Paddan, Rachel died beside me in the land of Canaan, on the way, when there was still a stretch of land to go to Ephrata, and I buried her there on the way to Ephrath, that is, Bethlehem."*

And Jacob said to Joseph symbolizes a communication from earthly-level truth to the inner dimension. *God Shaddai appeared to me in Luz in the land of Canaan* symbolizes the Divine visible on the earthly plane in an earlier state. *And blessed me* symbolizes a prediction of life bestowed. *And said to me, "Here now, I am making you fruitful and will cause you to multiply,"* symbolizes life bestowed through charitable goodness and religious truth. *And I will turn you into an assemblage of peoples* symbolizes unending growth. *And give the land to your seed after you as an eternal possession* symbolizes the Lord's kingdom belonging to people with that goodness and truth. *And now your two sons born to you in the land of Egypt* symbolizes goodness and truth on the earthly plane, produced by the inner dimension. *Before my coming to you, to Egypt,* means before earthly-level truth was present within knowledge on that level. *Are mine* means that they are *in me. Ephraim and Manasseh* symbolizes the church's intellect and will. *Like Reuben and Simeon they will be to me* means that these will consist in truth and truth-based goodness. *And the generation that you generate after them* symbolizes the inner truth and goodness that will come later. *Will be yours* means in the rational mind, which lies within. *They will be called by the name of their brothers in their inheritance* means that they will have the same nature as the church's truth and goodness and will be counted as part of it. *And as for me, as I was coming from Paddan* means from a state of religious knowledge. *Rachel died beside me in the land of Canaan* symbolizes the end of the previous desire for inner truth. *On the way, when there was still a stretch of land* symbolizes a midpoint. *To go to Ephrata* symbolizes heavenly spirituality in an earlier state. *And I buried her on the way to Ephrath* symbolizes a rejection of that state. *That is, Bethlehem* symbolizes its replacement with a new state of desire for truth and goodness.

And Jacob said to Joseph symbolizes a communication from earthly-level truth to the inner dimension, as the following shows: *Saying* symbolizes perception (noted above at §6220) and also communication (noted in §§3060, 4131), because what is perceived by another is communicated to that person. *Jacob* represents earthly-level truth (mentioned just above at §6223). And *Joseph* represents the inner dimension (also mentioned above, at §6224). **6228**

God Shaddai appeared to me in Luz in the land of Canaan symbolizes the Divine visible on the earthly plane in an earlier state, as the following shows: *God Shaddai* symbolizes the Divine, since Shaddai was the name for the God of Abraham, Isaac, and Jacob (§§3667, 5628). He was Jehovah himself, or the Lord, so he was the Divine, and this can be seen from Genesis 28:13, [16,] 19. *Appeared to me* means that it was visible. *Luz* symbolizes the earthly level in an earlier state (discussed at §4556). And the *land of Canaan* symbolizes the church (discussed before). **6229**

This shows that *God Shaddai appeared to me in Luz in the land of Canaan* symbolizes the Divine visible on the earthly plane, where the truth known to the spiritual church resides.

And blessed me symbolizes a prediction of life bestowed, as can be seen from the symbolism of *blessing.* In this case it is a prediction of life bestowed, because the blessing was that God would make Jacob fruitful, multiply him, turn him into an assemblage of peoples, and give the land to his seed after him as an eternal possession. All of these are a prediction that life would be bestowed. It was not that Jacob's offspring would **6230** receive life but that people dedicated to religious truth and charitable goodness would, since they are Jacob and Israel in an inner sense.

6231   *And said to me, "Here now, I am making you fruitful and will cause you to multiply,"* symbolizes life bestowed through charitable goodness and religious truth. This can be seen from the symbolism of being *fruitful,* which relates to charitable goodness, and of *multiplying,* which relates to religious truth, as discussed in §§43, 55, 913, 983, 2846, 2847. These are what bring a person to life, which is why I speak of life bestowed through them.

6232   *And I will turn you into an assemblage of peoples* symbolizes unending growth. This can be seen from the symbolism of an *assemblage of peoples* as truth springing endlessly from goodness. *Peoples* symbolize truth (§§1259, 1260, 3295), and an *assemblage* symbolizes a large amount, so *turning someone into an assemblage of peoples* means making truth grow abundantly. The reason the growth is unending is that everything in the spiritual world—where infinity is the source of it all, including truth and goodness—can multiply and grow without end.

"Without end" describes anything that cannot be limited or defined by a number. Nonetheless, what is endless is still finite compared to infinity, so much so that there is no ratio between them.

[2] The ability of truth and goodness to grow without limit comes from their origin in the Lord, who is infinite. The fact that they *can* grow without limit is evident from this: First, the whole of heaven is devoted to truth and goodness, but no individual has the same kind as another. This would be true even if heaven were thousands and thousands of times larger. Second, angels go on improving forever—they constantly grow in goodness and truth—and yet they can never reach any point of perfection. There is always endless room left. After all, true ideas are boundless in number, and each one holds boundless truth, and so on.

[3] The principle is still easier to see from what occurs in nature. Even if the human population grew indefinitely, no one would have the same face as another. No one would have the same inner face, that is, the same personality as another, or even the same voice. Plainly, then, everything comes in endless variety, and nothing can exist that is the same as something else. This variation is even more unbounded when it comes to truth and goodness, which belong to the spiritual world, because any one thing in the physical world corresponds to thousands upon thousands in the spiritual world. The farther within something lies, then, the less limited it is.

[4] This boundlessness of everything in the spiritual world and in the physical world as well is due to the fact that it all emerges from what is infinite, as mentioned above. If it did not, it could never be free of limits. The endlessness that exists in both worlds therefore shows plainly that the Divine is infinite.

And give the land to your seed after you as an eternal possession symbolizes the Lord's kingdom belonging to people with that goodness and truth, as the following shows: *Land,* and in this case the land of Canaan, symbolizes the Lord's kingdom, as treated of in §§1607, 3038, 3481, 3705, 4240, 4447. *Seed* symbolizes the truth that leads to faith and the goodness embraced by neighborly love, as treated of in §§1025, 1447, 1610, 1940, 2848, 3038, 3310. The seed of Abraham, Isaac, and Jacob symbolizes people with goodness and truth, who are called the children of the kingdom (§3373). And an *eternal possession* symbolizes reception of the Lord's life. People with that life are the children of the kingdom. **6233**

And now your two sons born to you in the land of Egypt symbolizes goodness and truth on the earthly plane, produced by the inner dimension, as the following shows: Manasseh and Ephraim, the *two sons* here, represent the church's will and the church's intellect on the earthly plane, born of the inner dimension, as explained above at §6222. Since the will contains goodness and the intellect contains truth, the same boys symbolize goodness and truth in the church. *Born to you* (to Joseph) means produced by the inner dimension. And the *land of Egypt* symbolizes the earthly mind, where religious knowledge resides, as noted in §§5276, 5278, 5280, 5288, 5301. It also symbolizes the earthly plane (§6147). **6234**

Before my coming to you, to Egypt, means before earthly-level truth was present within knowledge. This can be seen from the meaning of *before my coming to you* as before it was present; from the representation of Jacob, who says this of himself, as earthly level truth (mentioned above at §6223); and from the symbolism of *Egypt* as knowledge on the earthly level (discussed in §§1164, 1165, 1186, 1462, 4749, 4964, 4966, 5700, 6004). As shown in the last two chapters, the arrival of Jacob and his sons in Egypt represented the incorporation of truth into religious knowledge (see §6004). **6235**

Are mine means in me. This can be seen from the representation of Jacob, who says this about himself, as earthly-level truth (discussed below), and from that of Manasseh and Ephraim, about whom he is speaking, as the church's will and the church's intellect on the earthly level (discussed **6236** in §§5354, 6222). The reason *are mine* means *in me* is that Jacob, representing earthly-level truth, also represents the earthly level itself in regard to truth, and the earthly level is where the intellect and will represented by Ephraim and Manasseh are situated. Because they are in the earthly dimension, then, *are mine* means *in me*.

Jacob stands for the earthly dimension. In the highest sense he stands for the Lord's earthly divinity; see §§3305, 3509, 3525, 3576, 4009, 4538, 4570, 6098. In a secondary sense he stands for truth on the earthly plane and therefore also for the earthly plane in regard to truth (§§3509, 3525, 3546). And because Jacob in general means truth on the earthly plane, his ten sons mean the church's earthly-level truths in particular (§§5403, 5419, 5427, 5458, 5512). Joseph's sons therefore have the same meaning at this point in the text.

Pharaoh too represents the earthly level, but in regard to knowledge rather than truth. Knowledge is lowlier and can have truth introduced and instilled into it, as represented by the arrival in Egypt of Jacob and his sons.

6237   *Ephraim and Manasseh* symbolizes the church's intellect and will; see §§5354, 6222.

6238   *Like Reuben and Simeon they will be to me* means that these will consist in truth and truth-based goodness, as the following shows: *Reuben* represents faith that belongs to the intellect and doctrinal truth through which goodness can be attained in one's life (discussed in §§3861, [3863,] 3866). So more broadly he represents truth belonging to the intellect. And *Simeon* represents faith that belongs to the will and consequently truth in action, which is goodness that comes of faith, or truth-based goodness (discussed in §§3869, 3870, 3871, 3872, 4497, 4502, 4503, 5626, 5630). So more broadly he represents goodness belonging to the new will. The representation of Ephraim and Manasseh is similar to this, of course. However, Reuben profaned his representative role (4601), and Simeon befouled his (4497, 4502, 4503), and a curse was therefore pronounced on them (Genesis 49:3, 4, 5, 6, 7). For this reason they lost their rights as firstborn, and Joseph's sons Ephraim and Manasseh were acknowledged as firstborn in their place (1 Chronicles 5:1).

Nonetheless, Reuben and Simeon kept their representative meaning, because it makes no difference what kind of personality represents something (§§665, 1097 at the end, 4281). In other words, Reuben continued to represent faith that belongs to the intellect, and Simeon faith that belongs to the will, but Ephraim took on a role representing the church's intellect itself, and Manasseh, the church's will.

And the generation that you generate after them symbolizes the inner truth and goodness that will come later, as the following shows: A *generation* symbolizes attributes of faith and neighborly love (discussed in §§613, 2020, 2584) and therefore truth and goodness. And *after them* symbolizes something inward that comes later.

The reason something inward is being symbolized is that anything the inner dimension generates later is farther within. Earlier generations serve as a means by which the inner plane leads subsequent generations farther within, gradually raising what is earthly to its own level.

This is evident from the way everything belonging to the intellect is generated in us. We start out operating on a sensory level but then move farther and farther within until we gain the use of the intellect. It is the same when we are generated anew through faith and neighborly love. That is how we are gradually perfected. (See the remarks at §6183 on our progressive rise to inner levels when we are being reborn.)

[2] A generation in the Word symbolizes attributes of faith and neighborly love because no other kind of generation than spiritual generation can be meant in an inner sense. That is the kind of generation meant in David:

> They will fear greatly, because God is among the *generation of the righteous*. (Psalms 14:5)

The generation of the righteous stands for truth that stems from goodness, because righteousness relates to goodness. In Isaiah:

> They will not labor in vain and will *not father a generation* destined for terror. They are the seed of those blessed by Jehovah. (Isaiah 65:23)

In the same author:

> Who that *calls the generations from the beginning* has managed and done this? I, Jehovah, who am first; and with those coming last I am the same. (Isaiah 41:4)

In Ezekiel:

> Your trading and *your generations* are from the land of the Canaanite; your father is an Amorite and your mother a Hittite. As for *your generations*,

on the day when you were born your umbilical cord was not cut, and you
were not washed with water in my sight. (Ezekiel 16:3, 4)

This is about abominations in Jerusalem. Obviously the generations are
generations in a spiritual sense. [3] In Isaiah:

Wake up, as in the days of eternity, [as in] the *generations of eternal ages!*
(Isaiah 51:9)

The days of eternity stand for the state and times of the earliest church.
Eternity is mentioned in connection with that church because it possessed
the goodness that goes with love for the Lord. This kind of goodness
comes directly from the Lord, so it is described as eternal. The generations of eternal ages stand for different types of goodness resulting from
this kind of goodness. [4] Similarly in Moses:

Remember the days of eternity, understand the *years of generation after*
generation. (Deuteronomy 32:7)

The days of eternity stand for the state and times of the earliest church,
a heavenly religion that came before the Flood. The years of generation
after generation stand for the state and times of the ancient church, a spiritual religion that came after the Flood. This passage in Moses is about
those churches. [5] In Joel:

Judah will abide to eternity and Jerusalem *for generation after generation.*
(Joel 3:20)

Eternity is associated with Judah because he represents a heavenly religion
(§3881). Generation after generation is associated with Jerusalem because
it symbolizes a spiritual religion (§402). [6] In Isaiah:

My justice will last to eternity, and my salvation *to generation after gen-*
eration. (Isaiah 51:8)

This passage speaks of eternity in relation to a loving goodness, since this
is associated with justice (§§612, 2235), and of generations in relation to a
goodness based on faith. [7] In David:

Your kingship is a kingship to all eternity, and your dominion is *for all*
generations. (Psalms 145:13)

Likewise here. If eternity did not have to do with heavenliness, and generations with spirituality, only one of the two words would be used. To
use both would be empty repetition.

[8] The following rules also symbolize something involving the state of a person's faith: No one born illegitimate was to come into Jehovah's assembly *to the tenth generation* (Deuteronomy 23:2). No Ammonite or Moabite was to do so, not even *to the tenth generation* (Deuteronomy 23:3). And an Edomite or an Egyptian was indeed to come into Jehovah's assembly *to the third generation* (Deuteronomy 23:8). The same symbolism applies to the commandment in the Decalogue that Jehovah God would bring the consequence of the parents' wickedness on their children, *on the third and fourth generation,* so far as they hated him (Exodus 20:5).

The reason generations stand for attributes of faith and neighborly love is that no other generations are meant in a spiritual sense than those of rebirth or of a person reborn. It is like scriptural mention of birth, delivery, and conception, which have to do with faith and neighborly love; see §§1145, 1255, 3860, 3868, 4668, 5160, 5598.

Will be yours means in the rational mind, which lies within. This can be seen by considering that the inner heavenliness represented by Joseph exists in the rational mind (§§4286, 4963). *Will be yours* therefore means in the rational mind, just as the earlier phrase "are mine" means in the earthly realm, which contains the earthly-level truth represented by Jacob (§6236).

6240

I should offer a brief definition of rationality. The intellectual capacity of the inner self is called rational, but that of the outer self is called earthly. So that which is rational lies within, while that which is earthly lies without, and they are very different.

A truly rational person is actually the kind called a heavenly person, the kind who perceives what is good and, from goodness, what is true. People who do not have this sort of perception but only knowledge (the knowledge that something is true because that is what they have been taught) and therefore conscience are not truly rational. Instead they are relatively deep, earthly-minded people. People in the Lord's spiritual church are like this.

The two types are as different as moonlight and sunlight. For this reason the Lord looks like a moon to the spiritual and like a sun to the heavenly (§§1521, 1529, 1530, 1531, 4060, 4696).

[2] Many in the world think that rational people are those who can reason brilliantly on many subjects and string arguments together so well that their conclusions seem true. But this skill occurs even in the worst people, who can deduce through clever rationalization that evil is good, that falsity is true, and the reverse. Such reasoning is depraved delusion, not rationality, as anyone who reflects on it can see.

Rationality is inwardly seeing and perceiving that goodness is good and therefore that truth is true. Such sight and perception comes from heaven.

The reason people who belong to the Lord's spiritual church are relatively deep earthly-minded people is that all they acknowledge as true is what they have imbibed from their parents and teachers and then confirmed for themselves. They do not see inwardly or perceive whether truth is to be found anywhere other than in what they have proved to themselves. It is different with the heavenly. That is why the latter operate on a rational level but the former on a deep earthly level.

Inner heavenliness, represented by Joseph, lies on the rational plane, but spiritual goodness, represented by Israel, on an inner earthly plane (§4286). Spiritual individuals are the ones represented by Israel, and heavenly individuals by Joseph.

6241   *They will be called by the name of their brothers in their inheritance* means that they will have the same nature as the church's truth and goodness and will be counted as part of it, as the following shows: A *name* and being *called* by a name symbolize the quality of something, as discussed in §§144, 145, 1754, 1896, 2009, 2724, 3006, 3421. Ephraim and Manasseh, the *brothers* here, represent the church's intellect and will (§§3969, 5354, 6222) and therefore its truth and goodness (§6234). And *in their inheritance* means being counted among that truth and goodness.

6242   *And as for me, as I was coming from Paddan* means from a state of religious knowledge. This is established by the symbolism of Paddan-aram as knowledge of truth and goodness, as dealt with at §§3664, 3680, 4107. *Paddan* therefore symbolizes a state of religious knowledge.

6243   *Rachel died beside me in the land of Canaan* symbolizes the end of the previous desire for inner truth. This can be seen from the symbolism of *dying* as something's ceasing to be what it was (discussed at §494) and as the end of an earlier representation (§§3253, 3259, 3276, 5975), and from the representation of *Rachel* as a desire for inner truth (discussed at §§3758, 3782, 3793, 3819).

6244   *On the way, when there was still a stretch of land* symbolizes a midpoint, as is self-evident.

6245   *To go to Ephrata* symbolizes heavenly spirituality in an earlier state. This is evident from the discussion in §§4585, 4594 of the symbolism of *Ephrata* as heavenly spirituality in an earlier state.

6246   *And I buried her on the way to Ephrath* symbolizes a rejection of that state. This can be seen from the symbolism of *burying* as rejection (discussed

in §4564) and from that of Ephrata as heavenly spirituality in an earlier
state (§6245).

That is, Bethlehem symbolizes its replacement with a new state of desire
for truth and goodness. This is evident from the symbolism of *Bethlehem*
as heavenly spirituality in a new state (discussed at §4594) and therefore a
new state of desire for truth and goodness. Heavenly spirituality is truth
from goodness and therefore a desire for this truth.

I should expand on the contents of this verse's inner meaning. The
subject is the rejection of an earlier desire for truth and the acceptance
of a new desire. The earlier desire for truth is one we feel when we are
being reborn, and the later (or new) desire, when we have been reborn.
In the earlier state we want to learn truth in order to become intelligent,
but in the later state, in order to become wise. To put the same thing
another way, in the earlier state we desire truth for the sake of theology,
but in the later state, for the sake of living by it. When theology is the
goal, we view goodness from the standpoint of truth, but when life is
the goal, we view truth from the standpoint of goodness. The later state
is consequently the reverse of the earlier. So when we are being reborn
we reject the earlier state and welcome the later state, which is new. The
earlier state compared to the new, later state is impure, because when we
desire truth for the sake of theology in order to become intelligent, we
also desire recognition and glory. This desire cannot help being present at
that stage, and it is permitted as a way of getting started, because such is
human nature. When we desire truth for the sake of living by it, though,
we reject glory and recognition as goals and embrace goodness in our life,
or love for our neighbor.

Genesis 48:8, 9. *And Israel saw Joseph's sons and said, "Whose are these?"
And Joseph said to his father, "They are my sons, whom God gave to me
here." And he said, "Bring them to me, please, and I will bless them."*

And Israel saw Joseph's sons symbolizes a perception about the church's
intellect and will. *And said, "Whose are these?"* means and about their origin. *And Joseph said to his father* symbolizes a reply from within. *They are
my sons, whom God gave to me here,* means that they come from the inner
dimension and exist on the earthly level. *And he said, "Bring them to me,
please,"* means so that they can approach spiritual goodness. *And I will
bless them* symbolizes a prediction about goodness and truth.

And Israel saw Joseph's sons symbolizes a perception about the church's
intellect and will, as the following shows: *Seeing* symbolizes perception,
as treated of in §§2150, 3764, 4403–4421, 4567, 4723, 5400. And Ephraim

6247

6248

6249

and Manasseh represent the church's intellect and will, born of the inner dimension, which is *Joseph,* as treated of in §§5354, 6222.

6250   *And said, "Whose are these?"* means and about their origin—that is, a perception [about the church's intellect and will and about their origin]—as the following shows: *Saying* symbolizes a perception, as noted above at §6220, and *whose are these?* means about their origin. In the inner meaning, a question denotes something known by perception; see §§2693, 6132.

6251   *And Joseph said to his father* symbolizes a reply from within. This needs no explanation, since *Joseph* means the inner plane (§6177). After all, when perceptive people ask themselves a question, they answer themselves from within. What is more, I have observed that when spirits ask me a question, they receive their answer only by looking into my thoughts.

6252   *They are my sons, whom God gave to me here,* means that they come from the inner dimension and exist on the earthly level. This can be seen from the representation of Joseph, whose *sons* they were, as the inner dimension (mentioned in §§6177, 6224) and from the symbolism of the land of Egypt, to which *here* refers, as the earthly mind (mentioned in §§5276, 5278, 5280, 5288, 5301) and therefore the earthly level.

6253   *And he said, "Bring them to me, please,"* means so that they can approach spiritual goodness, as the following shows: *Bringing them to him* means so that they can approach, and Israel, whom they were to approach, represents spiritual goodness (dealt with in §§5801, 5803, 5807, 5812, 5817, 5819, 5826, 5833).

6254   *And I will bless them* symbolizes a prediction about goodness and truth. This can be seen from the symbolism of *blessing* as prediction (as above at §6230). The blessing here concerns the goodness and truth represented by Manasseh and Ephraim.

Blessing is such a common word that its symbolism varies. One thing it symbolizes is a prediction of events both good and bad, as becomes plain in the next chapter, where Israel predicts to his sons what will happen to them. For some, such as Reuben, Simeon, and Levi, he predicts a bad future, and for others, such as Judah and Joseph, a good future. In verse 28 of that chapter his prediction is called a blessing: "This is what their father spoke to them, and he *blessed them; each* according to *his blessing he blessed them.*" The fact that the blessing is a prediction is clear from the words of the first verse there: "Jacob called his sons and said, 'Gather, and *I will tell you what will happen to you* at the end of days.'"

6255   Genesis 48:10, 11, 12, 13, 14. *And Israel's eyes were heavy with age; he could not see. And he made them approach him and kissed them and hugged* *them. And Israel said to Joseph, "I didn't think I would see your face, and here, God has caused me to see your seed too." And Joseph brought them from [Israel's] thighs and bowed his face to the earth. And Joseph took them both, Ephraim in his right hand on Israel's left, and Manasseh in his left on Israel's right, and made them approach him. And Israel put out his right hand and placed it on the head of Ephraim (and he was the younger) and his left on the head of Manasseh; he crossed his hands, as Manasseh was the firstborn.*

And Israel's eyes were heavy symbolizes his dim power of perception. *With age* means because he was at the end of his representative role. *He could not see* means not noticing. *And he made them approach him* symbolizes presence. *And kissed them* symbolizes union out of a desire for truth. *And hugged them* symbolizes union out of a desire for goodness. *And Israel said to Joseph* symbolizes being lifted to the inner dimension. *I didn't think I would see your face* means never having expected to feel his love flowing in. *And here, God has caused me to see your seed too* symbolizes a perception not only of love flowing in but also of the resulting goodness and truth. *And Joseph brought them from [Israel's] thighs* symbolizes goodness in the will, and truth in the intellect, on the earthly plane, separated from the love and affection felt by spiritual goodness. *And bowed his face to the earth* symbolizes their humility. *And Joseph took them both, Ephraim in his right hand on Israel's left* symbolizes second place, so to speak, for truth in the intellect. *And Manasseh in his left on Israel's right* symbolizes first place for goodness in the will. *And made them approach him* symbolizes a connection. *And Israel put out his right hand and placed it on the head of Ephraim* means that he considered truth to be in first place. *And he was the younger* means even though it is in second place. *And his left on the head of Manasseh* means that he considered goodness to be in second place. *He crossed his hands* means that it was therefore backward. *As Manasseh was the firstborn* means since goodness is actually in first place.

And Israel's eyes were heavy symbolizes his dim power of perception, as the following shows: *Eyes* symbolize the intellect's ability to see, as discussed in §§2701, 4403–4421, [4523–4534]; [therefore they symbolize perception,] §§4083, 4339; and seeing also has this symbolism (above at §6249). *Israel* represents spiritual goodness on the earthly level, as noted above at §6253. And when the eyes are said to *be heavy,* it symbolizes dimness, so the phrase symbolizes a dim power of perception.

Israel's perceptiveness was dim when he blessed Joseph's sons because he was at the end of his representative role, but also more generally because

6256

the spiritual goodness he represents has dim perception. That goodness partakes of the earthly plane, where the main illumination is an earthly glimmer rather than heavenly light, which contains spiritual and heavenly goodness partaking of the rational plane. That is what the outer self, also called the earthly self, is like.

When spiritual goodness on the earthly plane is mentioned, it means people with that goodness—that is, people who are part of the Lord's spiritual church. So Israel also represents the spiritual church (§4286). Spiritual people—the people of that church—live in relative darkness (see §§2708, 2715, 2716, 2718, 2831, 2849, 2935, 2937, 3246, 3833, 4402), and because they do, they put faith and its truth in first place, as Israel does here in setting Ephraim ahead of Manasseh.

[2] The reason spiritual people consider truth more important is that truth introduces them to goodness (§2954), and even after they have been introduced, they are not consciously aware of goodness. This is because goodness enters into their desire for truth from fairly deep within, so it does not come to their awareness until they have been reborn.

That is why they refer to any good done out of neighborly love as the fruits of faith. Yet little concern for these fruits is exhibited by people who decide that faith alone saves us, without good deeds, and saves us in the final hour of death, no matter how we had previously lived. It is not hard to recognize that this constitutes a dim perception of goodness and truth.

Nonetheless, the fact of the matter is that people who put faith ahead of neighborly love on theological principles but still live a charitable life are the people who belong to the Lord's spiritual church. They are saved, because they put neighborly love and its good actions first in their lives, even if they put faith and its true concepts first in their theology.

6257   *With age* means because he was at the end of his representative role. This is evident from the symbolism of *age* as a new representative role (discussed at §3254) and therefore as the end of a previous role.

6258   *He could not see* means not noticing. This is established by the symbolism of *seeing* as perception (mentioned above at §6249) and therefore as noticing.

6259   *And he made them approach him* symbolizes presence. This can be seen from the symbolism of *making them approach* as causing them to be present.

6260   *And kissed them* symbolizes union out of a desire for truth. This can be seen from the symbolism of *kissing* as union out of desire, as discussed in §§3573, 3574, 4215, 4353, 5929. The desire is for truth because the next clause says he hugged them, which symbolizes union out of a desire for goodness. Hugging stands for a deeper and therefore closer union than kissing, just as a desire for goodness is deeper than a desire for truth.

And hugged them symbolizes union out of a desire for goodness. This **6261** can be seen from the symbolism of *hugging* as a bond of love (discussed at §4351) and so as union out of a desire for goodness (see just above at §6260). The fact that people use hugs to show love makes it obvious that hugging means a desire for something good; a hug is an action stemming from that emotion. Every spiritual feeling has a human physical gesture corresponding to it. The gesture represents the feeling. Everyone knows this is true of a kiss (discussed just above).

And Israel said to Joseph symbolizes being lifted to the inner dimen- **6262** sion. This is established by the symbolism of *saying* as a perception and an inflow, as discussed before [§§5966, 6063, 6152]. The clause symbolizes being lifted up because the current verse is talking about an inflow of love from the inner dimension and therefore of goodness and truth, and this inflow is an elevation to the inner dimension. You see, the outer dimension cannot love the inner dimension except by an inflow from and a lifting up by the inner dimension. The very love felt on the outer level belongs to the inner level. Every active force has something that reacts or responds to it, which enables an effect to result. The active force is the cause, and the reactive element is the thing caused. So even the reaction belongs to the active force, just as that which is caused belongs to that which causes it, because all power in the thing caused comes from the cause. That is how matters stand with all reactions throughout nature.

I didn't think I would see your face means never having expected to feel **6263** his love flowing in, as the following shows: A *face* symbolizes inner depths (discussed in §§358, 2434, 3527, 3573, 4066, 4796, 4798, 5695), so it symbolizes feelings, which beam from the face especially (§§4796, 5102). The face of God, then, is divine love and consequently mercy (§5585). And *I didn't think* means never having expected.

Seeing his face symbolizes love flowing *in,* as the words just before and just after this make plain.

And here, God has caused me to see your seed too symbolizes a perception **6264** not only of love flowing in but also of the resulting goodness and truth. This can be seen from the representation of Manasseh and Ephraim, the *seed* here, as goodness in the will and truth in the intellect (discussed in §§5354, 6222), and also from the symbolism of "seed" itself as goodness and truth (§§1610, 2848, 3310, 3373, 3671). The symbolism is a perception not only of love flowing in but also [of the resulting goodness and truth] because the text says, "I didn't think I would see your face, and here, God has caused me to see [your seed too]." (For the idea that seeing his face symbolizes an inflow of love, see §6263 just above.)

6265   *And Joseph brought them from [Israel's] thighs* symbolizes goodness in the will, and truth in the intellect, separated from the love and affection felt by spiritual goodness, as the following shows: *Joseph* represents inward heavenliness, as described in §§5869, 5877. Manasseh and Ephraim, the ones Joseph *brought,* represent goodness in the will and truth in the intellect, as discussed in §§5354, 6222. *Thighs* symbolize love and affection, as discussed in §§3021, 4277, 4280, 4575, 5050–5062. The fact that the love and affection were felt by spiritual goodness comes from Israel, who stands for spiritual goodness (§6253).

The symbolism is that inward heavenliness took goodness belonging to the will and truth belonging to the intellect and removed them from spiritual goodness, that is, from its affectionate love. This was because this goodness and truth had been brought to Israel by Israel himself (who represents spiritual goodness) rather than being led to him by Joseph (who represents inner heavenliness). So they were taken away and then brought to him by Joseph, as the next verse says. The reason is that this is the direction love flows: from inner heavenliness through spiritual goodness into goodness and truth. This sequence is orderly. That is why this outward ritual had to be strictly observed when the boys were being blessed, because in it they were being presented to the Lord for a prediction from him (symbolized here by the blessing, §6254).

This now is why Joseph took his sons from his father's thighs and then brought them there himself.

6266   *And bowed his face to the earth* symbolizes their humility. This can be seen from the symbolism of *bowing his face to the earth* as inward humility, as discussed at §5682. Prostration is an act of the body that corresponds to humility of the mind, so people who worship God from the heart bow down to him this way.

The text says "he bowed" [in the singular] because Joseph was bowing down on behalf of [his sons]—not to Israel but to the Lord, who gave the benediction through Israel.

Joseph bowed down for [his sons] because that is what happens in spiritual affairs. Goodness in the will, and truth in the intellect, on the earthly level cannot humble themselves before the Lord on their own, only under an inflow from the inner level. In fact, without an inflow through the inner dimension into the earthly plane, no will or intellect exists on that plane. There is not even any life, because the inner plane is the conduit that carries life from the Lord to the earthly plane.

And Joseph took them both, Ephraim in his right hand on Israel's left symbolizes second place, so to speak, for truth in the intellect. *And Manasseh in his left on Israel's right* symbolizes first place for goodness in the will. This can be seen from the following: *Ephraim* represents truth in the intellect, and *Manasseh* goodness in the will (discussed at §§5354, 6222). And the *right* symbolizes first place, while the *left* symbolizes second, as all custom shows.

6267

Further explanation will be given just below [§6269].

And made them approach him symbolizes a connection, as can be seen without explanation.

6268

And Israel put out his right hand and placed it on the head of Ephraim means that he considered truth to be in first place, as the following shows: *Putting out his right hand* means considering it to be in first place. (Plainly the right hand is first place.) And *Ephraim* represents the intellect and therefore the truth taught by faith, since this resides in the intellectual part of a person's mind, which has the power to see by heaven's light and consequently the power of spiritual sight (see §6222).

6269

Israel's putting his right hand on Ephraim's head and his left on Manasseh's is the subject of this verse and of verses 17, 18, 19 below. It means that he considered faith with its truth to be in first place and neighborly love with its goodness in second. The reason was that spiritual people, represented by Israel (§§4286, 6256), cannot evaluate the situation any other way until they have been reborn. They consciously notice faith's truth but not charity's goodness, because the latter arrives by an inner route but the former by an outer route (such as knowledge).

[2] People who are not being reborn, though, say flatly that faith is in first place. That is, they call it the crucial element of religion, because this allows them to live however they wish but still say they expect to be saved. That is why neighborly love has made itself so scarce today that hardly anyone knows what it is. Faith has consequently disappeared as well, because neither can exist without the other.

If neighborly love were in first place and faith in second, the church would have a different face, because no one would be called Christian except those who live a life in keeping with faith's truth, or a life of neighborly love. People would know what neighborly love is, too. They would not multiply denominations, distinguishing them by their opinions on faith and its truth. Rather they would speak of one church containing everyone who lives a good life. And in that number they would include not only people within the world of the Christian denominations but also outside it. The church would thus receive enlightenment in matters having to do with the Lord's kingdom, because charity sheds light in a way that faith without charity never does. The errors that a detached faith imposes would be seen clearly.

[3] This shows what other face the church would have if the goodness sought by neighborly love took first place (as the essential ingredient) and the truth comprising faith took second (as the form of that essence). The face of the church would then be like the face of the ancient church. This church equated religion with neighborly love and had no religious doctrines except those teaching charity, so its people had wisdom from the Lord.

The nature of the ancient church is depicted in these words from Moses:

> Jehovah enveloped them, instructed them, guarded them as the pupil of his eye. As an eagle stirs its nest, moves constantly over its chicks, spreads its wings, he took them, carried them on his wing. Jehovah alone led them, nor was there a foreign god with them. He made them ride on the heights of the earth and fed them with the produce of the fields. He made them suck honey from a crag and oil from a boulder of rock; the butter of the herd and the milk of the flock, together with the fat of lambs and of rams—the sons of Bashan—and of goats, together with the fat of the kidneys of wheat; and you drink the blood of the grape as unmixed wine. (Deuteronomy 32:10–14)

The people of that church are consequently in heaven and enjoy all the happiness and glory there.

6270   *And he was the younger* means even though it is in second place. This can be seen from the symbolism of *younger* as second-place.

6271   *And his left on the head of Manasseh* means that he considered goodness to be in second place. This can be seen from the symbolism of "putting out his left" as considering it to be in second place and from the representation of *Manasseh* as the will and therefore as the goodness urged by neighborly love. For more on the topic, see just above at §6269.

6272   *He crossed his hands* means that it was therefore backward. This can be seen from the symbolism of *crossing hands* as a backward arrangement, because the gesture makes the younger the firstborn and the reverse. It consequently assigns a higher, more important position to the truth composing faith and a lower, less important position to the good done by charity, because the birthright consists in supremacy and priority (§3325).

The extent of the evil this viewpoint introduces into the church stands out plainly, because it causes the people of the church to thrust themselves into darkness—such great darkness that they cannot tell what is good or therefore what is true. Goodness is like a flame, and truth like light from that flame. If you take away the flame, the light dies too. Any light still visible is like illusory light that is not produced by flame. That is why churches clash with each other and quarrel over the truth, one group saying that something is true and another that it is false.

[2] What is worse, once the members of a church have awarded faith first place, they start to detach faith from neighborly love, which they disparage as comparatively worthless. They accordingly lose all interest in the question of how to live, as humans naturally tend to do. This destroys religion. It is the way we live that makes the church in us, not our theology apart from our life. So there is also an absence of serene trust, which is consummate faith, because real trust is possible only in people with love for their neighbor. That is the source of serenity in life.

Besides, goodness and charity are really the firstborn, or really in first place, but truth and faith appear to be. See §§3324, 3539, 3548, 3556, 3563, 3570, 3576, 3603, 3701, 4243, 4244, 4247, 4337, 4925, 4926, 4928, 4930, 4977.

As Manasseh was the firstborn means since goodness is actually in first place. This can be seen from the representation of *Manasseh* as goodness in the will, as discussed before [§§5354, 6222], and from the symbolism of *being firstborn* as being first and uppermost, as dealt with at §3325. The firstborn is therefore the one in first place.

6273

Who cannot see by earthly illumination alone (with only a little enlightenment added) that goodness comes first, as does the human will, while truth comes after, as does human thought? That our intentions are what make us think one way and not another? That what we hold as good consequently makes this or that idea true? Truth clearly stands in second place, then, and goodness in first. Ponder and consider whether the truth that constitutes faith can be rooted in anything but goodness, and whether faith not so rooted *is* faith. From this you can conclude what the essential or most important element is for the church, or for a person who has the church inside.

6274   Genesis 48:15, 16. *And he blessed Joseph and said, "May the God before whom my fathers, Abraham and Isaac, walked—the God shepherding me from then to this day, the angel redeeming me from every evil—bless the boys. And my name will be given to them, and the name of my fathers, Abraham and Isaac; and may they grow into a throng in the middle of the land."*

And he blessed Joseph symbolizes a prediction about truth in the intellect and goodness in the will, which receive life from the inner dimension. *And said, "May the God before whom my fathers, Abraham and Isaac, walked,"* symbolizes the divinity from which inner goodness and inner truth received life. *The God shepherding me* symbolizes this divinity as giver of life to earthly-level goodness that grows out of spiritual truth. *From then to this day* means without stop. *The angel redeeming me from every evil* symbolizes the Lord's divine humanity, which delivers people from hell. *Bless the boys* means may it grant that they receive truth and goodness. *And my name will be given to them* means that they will display the nature of the earthly-level goodness that grows out of spiritual truth. *And the name of my fathers, Abraham and Isaac,* means and the nature of inner goodness and truth. *And may they grow into a throng in the middle of the land* symbolizes an expansion from the inmost core.

6275   *And he blessed Joseph* symbolizes a prediction about truth in the intellect and goodness in the will, which receive life from the inner dimension, as the following shows: *Blessing* symbolizes prediction, as dealt with in §§6230, 6254. And Ephraim and Manasseh, who are *Joseph* here, represent truth in the intellect and goodness in the will, on the earthly level, born of the inner dimension, as explained in §§6234, 6267.

By "Joseph" are meant his sons, as is clear from the actual blessing, which says, "May the angel redeeming me from every evil *bless the boys; and my name will be given to them.*" The reason his sons are meant is that the earthly-level goodness and truth represented by Manasseh and Ephraim are the inner dimension itself as it exists on the earthly level. The inner and outer planes are admittedly distinct from each other, but on the earthly plane, where they coexist, the inner dimension is more or less in an outward form suited to it. This outward form never acts on its own, only under the power of the inner element within, so it is only acted *on*.

The situation resembles that of a specific cause within its given effect. The cause and the effect are distinct from each other, but the cause lies within the effect, which serves as an outward form suited to it. Through this embodiment, the cause pursues its purpose in the realm where the effect appears.

The case is the same with earthly-level goodness and truth in us. They are born of the inner dimension, because it clothes itself with the kind of material that belongs to the earthly plane so that it can exist on that plane and live a life there. The material with which it clothes itself, though, is a mere covering, which does absolutely nothing on its own.

And said, "May the God before whom my fathers, Abraham and Isaac, walked," symbolizes the divinity from which inner goodness and inner truth received life, as the following shows: *God* symbolizes divinity. *Walking* symbolizes living, or receiving life, as discussed in §§519, 1794. And *Abraham* in the highest sense represents the Lord's divinity itself, while *Isaac* represents his divine rationality and therefore his inner human nature. Jacob represents the Lord's earthly divinity, or his outer human nature. These matters are discussed in §§2010, 3245, 3305 at the end, 3439, 4615. In a representative sense, though, Abraham is inner goodness and Isaac inner truth (§§3703, 6098, 6185). The reason this is what Abraham and Isaac mean in a representative sense is that inner goodness itself and truth itself in the Lord's kingdom emanate from his divinity and divine humanity and cause the Lord himself to be present there, so that he himself is his kingdom. **6276**

The God shepherding me symbolizes this divinity as giver of life to earthly-level goodness that grows out of spiritual truth, as the following shows: *Shepherding* means giving life. See §6044 for the idea that shepherding means instructing and §6078 for the idea that pasture means that which sustains humanity's spiritual life. The shepherding and pasture mentioned there, however, relate to a flock, whereas the shepherding here relates to Jacob. It refers to his being sustained with food and the necessities of life, and this has approximately the same meaning in an inner sense [as in the literal sense]. What sustains and enlivens bodily life has as its inner-level symbolism that which sustains spiritual life and enlivens it. And Israel represents spiritual goodness on the earthly level, as dealt with in §§5801, 5803, 5807, 5812, 5817, 5819, 5826, 5833. Spiritual goodness, represented by Israel, grows out of truth, so it is described here as goodness that grows out of spiritual truth. **6277**

What Israel really stands for is the spiritual church, and the goodness in that church is truth-based goodness. The people in it are instructed by truth about goodness, and when they act on the truth in which they have been instructed, that truth is called goodness. Such goodness is the type that is called truth-based and is represented by Israel.

From then to this day means without stop. This can be seen from the symbolism of today and *to this day* as that which is never-ending and **6278** eternal (discussed at §§2838, 4304, 6165). Because that is the symbolism, *from then to this day* here means without stop—that is, giving life (shepherding, §6277) without stop.

6279   *The angel redeeming me from every evil* symbolizes the Lord's divine humanity, which delivers people from hell. This is clear from the symbolism of an *angel* as the Lord's divine humanity, discussed below; from that of *redeeming* as delivering, also discussed below; and from that of *evil* as hell.

Evil means hell because hell itself is nothing but evil. For it is all the same whether you say that everyone in hell is evil or that hell is evil. When evil is mentioned [in the Word], in a spiritual sense it means hell, because people awake to the spiritual meaning, as angels in heaven are, think and speak very broadly and therefore without reference to individuals. To them evil is therefore hell. So is sin, when "sin" means a ruling evil, as in Genesis 4:6, 7: "Jehovah said to Cain, 'If you do not do well, *sin* lies at your door. [Abel] longs for you, but you rule him.'" The sin here stands for hell, which is at hand when we do wrong.

Furthermore, the evil in us truly is nothing but hell, because it comes to us from hell. Then, [when we are under the sway of evil,] we are a hell in miniature, like everyone there. By the same token, the goodness in us truly is nothing but heaven in us, because goodness comes to us from the Lord through heaven. If we are under the sway of goodness, we are a heaven in miniature, like everyone in heaven.

6280   You can see that the *redeeming angel* is the Lord in his divine humanity from the consideration that he redeemed humankind (or delivered us from hell) by taking on a human nature and making it divine. Because he did, the Lord in his divine humanity is called the Redeemer.

The divine humanity is called an angel because *angel* means "one sent," and the Lord in his divine humanity is described as having been sent, as is clear from many places in the Gospels of the Word.

Before the Lord's coming into the world, moreover, the divine humanity was Jehovah himself, flowing in [to people] through heaven when his word was being spoken. Jehovah was above the heavens, but what passed from him through the heavens was the divine humanity of those times. It presented the image of a human, as a result of Jehovah's inflow into heaven, and the divinity itself coming from it was a divine human. This now is the divine humanity that existed from eternity. It is what is described as having been sent (which means going forth) and is the same as the angel here.

[2] However, Jehovah could no longer flow into people through this divine humanity of his, because they had distanced themselves too much from it. So he took on a human nature and made it divine. Through the inflow he had into heaven as a result, he was able to reach all the way to the human race. The people he reached were those who accepted neighborly love with its goodness, and faith with its truth, from the divine humanity, which had become visible in the process. As a consequence, he was able to deliver such people from hell, which never could have happened otherwise. This liberation is what is called redemption, and the divine humanity that freed or redeemed them is what is called the redeeming angel.

[3] Still, it is important to know that the Lord's divine humanity is above the heavens, just as his divinity itself is. After all, he is the sun that shines down on heaven. So heaven is far below him. The divine humanity that is present in heaven is divine truth that emanates from him, or the light radiating from him as the sun. The Lord in his essence is not divine truth; it merely comes from him as light comes from the sun. No, he is divine goodness itself, which is identical with Jehovah.

[4] The Lord's divine humanity is called an angel in other passages in the Word too. For instance, there is the time when the divine humanity appeared to Moses in the bramble, as reported in Exodus:

> When Moses came to the mountain of God, to Horeb, *the angel of Jehovah appeared to him* in a fiery flame from the middle of the bramble. *Jehovah* saw that Moses turned aside to see, so God cried out to him from the middle of the bramble. And he said further, *"I am the God of your father: the God of Abraham, the God of Isaac, and the God of Jacob."* (Exodus 3:1, 2, 4, 6)

The Lord's divine humanity is what is being called the angel of Jehovah here, and the passage says clearly that the angel was Jehovah himself. Jehovah was there in his divine humanity, as can be seen from the fact that his divinity itself was not visible except through his divine humanity, in keeping with the Lord's words in John:

> God has never been seen by anyone; the only-born Son, who is in the Father's embrace, is the one who has revealed him. (John 1:18)

And in another place:

> You have never heard the Father's voice or seen his form. (John 5:37)

[5] Further, the Lord in his divine humanity is called an angel in a passage about the people's being led into the land of Canaan. Here is what Exodus says:

> *Watch: I am sending an angel before you* to guard you on the way and to lead you to the place that I have prepared. Be careful before him, because he will not tolerate your transgressing, *since my name is within him.* (Exodus 23:20, 21, 23)

The angel here is plainly the divine humanity, because it says, "Since my name (that is, Jehovah himself) is within him." "My name" symbolizes the nature of Jehovah, which is within his divine humanity. To see that the Lord in his divine humanity is the name of Jehovah, consult §2628; to see that the name of God means his nature and, collectively, every means of worshiping him, consult §§2724, 3006. [6] In Isaiah:

> In all their anguish, he had anguish, and the *angel of his presence* delivered them. In his love and his forbearance *he redeemed them* and picked them up and carried them all the days of old. (Isaiah 63:9)

The angel of Jehovah's presence is of course the Lord in his divine humanity, because it says that he redeemed them. [7] In Malachi:

> "Watch: suddenly to his temple will come the Lord, whom you seek, and the *Angel of the Covenant,* whom you desire. Watch: He is coming!" states Jehovah Sabaoth. But who will be able to endure the day of his coming, and who will stay standing when he appears? Then the minha of Judah and Jerusalem will be sweet to Jehovah, as in the days of old and as in former years. (Malachi 3:1, 2, 4)

Obviously the Angel of the Covenant is the Lord in his divine humanity, since the subject is his Coming. "Then the minha of Judah and Jerusalem will be sweet to Jehovah" means that worship filled with love for him and faith in him will then be sweet. Judah clearly does not mean Judah here, nor does Jerusalem mean Jerusalem, since neither then nor later was the minha of Judah or Jerusalem sweet. The days of old mean states of the earliest church, which was heavenly, and the former years mean states of the ancient church, which was spiritual; see §6239.

In the Word's inner sense, an angel does not mean an angel anyway, but something divine in the Lord (§§1925, 2319, 2821, 3039, 4085).

6281   In regard to *redeeming,* properly speaking it means reclaiming one's property. The word can be used in connection with servitude, death, or evil. When mentioned in connection with servitude, ["the redeemed"] means people who were once enslaved, and in a spiritual sense, people who have been emancipated from hell. When mentioned in connection with death, it means people who have experienced damnation. When mentioned in connection with evil, as it is here, it means people in hell, because the evil from which the angel redeemed Jacob stands for hell (§6279).

Since the Lord delivered humankind from these miseries by making his human nature divine, it is his divine humanity that the Word calls the Redeemer, as in Isaiah:

"I myself am aiding you," says Jehovah, "and *your Redeemer, the Holy One of Israel.*" (Isaiah 41:14)

In the same author:

This is what Jehovah has said—*Israel's Redeemer, his Holy One.* (Isaiah 49:7, 26)

In the same author:

Jehovah Sabaoth is his name, and *your Redeemer, the Holy One of Israel,* will be called God of the whole earth. (Isaiah 54:5)

These passages distinguish between the divinity itself, named Jehovah, and the divine humanity, called the *Redeemer, the Holy One of Israel.*

[2] But the Redeemer is Jehovah himself in his divine humanity, as the following passages show. In Isaiah:

This is what Jehovah, Israel's King, has said, and *its Redeemer, Jehovah Sabaoth:* "I am the First and I am the Last, and besides me there is no God." (Isaiah 44:6)

In the same author:

This is what *Jehovah your Redeemer* has said: "I am Jehovah your God, teaching you." (Isaiah 48:17)

In the same author:

You are our Father, for Abraham does not know us and Israel does not acknowledge us. *You are Jehovah our Father, our Redeemer;* your name is age-old. (Isaiah 63:16)

In David:

> *Jehovah, who redeemed* my life from the pit, . . . (Psalms 103:4)

[3] These passages also show that in the Word, "Jehovah" means no other than the Lord (§§1343, 1736, 2921, 3035, 5663), and that Jehovah the Redeemer means his divine humanity. For that reason, Isaiah refers to people who have been redeemed as Jehovah's ransomed hostages:

> Say to the daughter of Zion, "Watch: your salvation is coming! Watch: his reward comes with him and his wage stands before him." They will call them a holy people, *Jehovah's ransomed hostages.* (Isaiah 62:11, 12)

It is perfectly clear that the Lord is the one who is described as ransoming Jehovah's hostages, because in regard to his Coming the passage says, "Watch: your salvation is coming! Watch: his reward comes with him."

See also Isaiah 43:1; 52:2, 3; 63:4, 9; Hosea 13:14; Exodus 6:6; 15:13; Job 19:25, where redemption is plainly a rescue from servitude, death, or evil.

6282   *Bless the boys* means may it grant that they receive truth and goodness, as the following shows: *Blessing* means endowing with truth and goodness, as that is exactly what a blessing in a spiritual sense involves (§§1420, 1422, 4981). And Ephraim and Manasseh, the *boys,* represent the church's intellect and the church's will, which were to receive truth and goodness. The intellect was to receive truth, and the will goodness.

6283   *And my name will be given to them* means that they will display the nature of the earthly-level goodness that grows out of spiritual truth. This can be seen from the symbolism of *giving one's name to someone* as putting one's character in that person (discussed in §§1754, 1896, 2009, 3421) and from the representation of Israel as earthly-level goodness that grows out of spiritual truth (discussed above at §6277). Because the boys displayed Israel's nature, they were included among Jacob's sons and became tribes—the tribe of Manasseh and the tribe of Ephraim. They were two of the twelve tribes that received an inheritance (as described in Joshua and in Ezekiel 48), once the tribe of Levi was transformed into a body of priests and therefore ceased to be part of the count.

6284   *And the name of my fathers, Abraham and Isaac,* means and the nature of inner goodness and truth. This is evident from the symbolism of a *name* as the nature of something (as just above in §6283) and from the representation of *Abraham* and *Isaac* as inner goodness and truth (discussed above in §6276).

Inner goodness and truth must lie within outer goodness and truth if the latter are to be good and true. As noted above at §6275, the outer dimension is essentially just a form designed to house the inner dimension and provide it with a setting for its life, which it lives in response to the Lord's inflow into it. The same can be said of the inner dimension in relation to the highest entity, which is the Lord, the source of all life. Anything below that highest level is merely a form that receives life, and these forms receive life one after another in order down to the lowliest, which is the body.

And may they grow into a throng in the middle of the land symbolizes an expansion from the inmost core. This is established by the symbolism of the *middle* as the inmost core (discussed in §§2940, 2973, 6068, 6084, 6103). *Growing into a throng,* then, symbolizes an expansion. You see, truth (symbolized by the *throng*) reaches out all around from the inmost depths, which are its center. The further out it spreads, and the more its expansion harmonizes with the heavenly pattern, the more complete the state of the truth. This state is what is symbolized by this part of the blessing: *may they grow into a throng in the middle of the land.* **6285**

Genesis 48:17, 18, 19, 20. And Joseph saw that his father put his right hand on Ephraim's head, and it was wrong in his eyes, and he took his father's hand to remove it from Ephraim's head onto Manasseh's head. And Joseph said to his father, "Not that way, my father, because this one is the firstborn; put your right hand on his head." And his father refused and said, "I know, my son, I know; this one too will become a people, and he too will become great. And nevertheless his younger brother will become greater than he, and his seed will be a fullness of nations." And he blessed them on this day, saying, "By you Israel will pronounce a blessing, saying, 'May God make you like Ephraim and like Manasseh!'" And he put Ephraim before Manasseh. **6286**

And Joseph saw that his father put his right hand on Ephraim's head symbolizes an awareness that he considered truth to be in first place. *And it was wrong in his eyes* symbolizes displeasure. *And he took his father's hand* symbolizes an inflow into his dim power of perception. *To remove it from Ephraim's head onto Manasseh's head* means in order to steer him away from making a mistake. *And Joseph said to his father, "Not that way, my father, because this one is the firstborn,"* symbolizes a perceptible inflow attributing priority to goodness. *Put your right hand on his head* means that doing so would assign it first place. *And his father refused* symbolizes disagreement. *And said, "I know, my son, I know,"* means that this is how things are but not how they look. *This one too will become a people, and he too will become great* means that truth-from-goodness (and therefore heavenly people) will also increase. *And nevertheless his younger brother will become greater than he* means that goodness-from-truth (and therefore spiritual people) will grow by a larger amount. *And his seed will be a fullness of nations* means that faith and its truth will reign supreme. *And he blessed them on this day* symbolizes eternal foresight and providence. *Saying, "By you Israel will pronounce a blessing, saying, 'May God make you like Ephraim and like Manasseh!'"* means ensuring that his spiritual aspect would reside in truth belonging to the intellect and in goodness belonging to the will. *And he put Ephraim before Manasseh* means that he considered truth to be in first place, because he was spiritual.

6287   *And Joseph saw that his father put his right hand on Ephraim's head* symbolizes an awareness that he considered truth to be in first place, as the following shows: *Seeing* means understanding and perceiving (discussed at §§2150, 2807, 3764, 4567, 4723, 5400). *Joseph* represents inner heavenliness (discussed at §§5869, 5877, 6224). Israel, the *father,* represents spiritual goodness on the earthly plane. *Putting his right hand on someone's head* means considering something to be in first place (noted above at §6269). And *Ephraim* represents truth in the intellect, on the earthly plane (noted above in §§6234, 6238, 6267). This shows that *Joseph saw that his father put his right hand on Ephraim's head* symbolizes an awareness by inner heavenliness that spiritual goodness on the earthly level considered truth to be in first place; see the comments and explanations above at §§6256, 6269, 6272, 6273.

6288   *And it was wrong in his eyes* symbolizes displeasure, as is self-evident.

Joseph was displeased because he represents inner heavenliness, which lies above the spiritual goodness represented by Israel. Something higher can evaluate what happens lower down, so it can tell whether the thinking down there is valid or not. A higher entity can see what is lower because it sees by heaven's light. Inner heavenliness (Joseph) therefore saw the mistake being made by spiritual goodness on the earthly level (Israel) and was accordingly displeased.

6289   *And he took his father's hand* symbolizes an inflow into his dim power of perception. This can be seen from the symbolism of *taking a hand* as an inflow into the power of perception. When the inner dimension wants to use its inflow to make the outer level form certain thoughts or intentions, it "takes" that level. In this case it takes hold of the power of perception symbolized by the hand. For the symbolism of a hand as power, see §§878, 3387, 4931–4937.

The perception is described as dim because spiritual people (represented by Israel) live in dimmer light than heavenly people (represented by Joseph). For the idea that spiritual people live in dimmer light, see §§2708, 2715, 2716, 2718, 2831, 2849, 2935, 2937, 3833, 4402.

[2] It is plain to see that conditions are dim for spiritual people, since they are totally in the dark about truth and goodness until they have been reborn. While they are being reborn, moreover, the truth they acknowledge is the kind embodied in their church's theology, and they believe it whether it is true or not. Yet this truth is what becomes goodness in them when it becomes part of their will and consequently part of their life. It is then the kind of goodness called truth-based goodness or the goodness urged by faith or spiritual goodness or the goodness of a spiritual religion. The nature of goodness from such a source can be recognized by anyone who ponders it.

Nonetheless the Lord embraces the goodness that grows out of such truth, even in people outside the church, as long as it adopts charity for one's neighbor as its principle, and as long as this charity contains innocence.

To remove it from Ephraim's head onto Manasseh's head means in order to steer him away from making a mistake. This can be seen from the symbolism of *removing,* which means steering (someone) away, and from that of *from Ephraim's head onto Manasseh's head,* which means from making a mistake. The mistake was that he considered truth to be in first place and goodness in second, as shown above.

6290

And Joseph said to his father, "Not that way, my father, because this one is the firstborn," symbolizes a perceptible inflow attributing priority to goodness. This is established by the symbolism of *saying,* when applied to inner heavenliness *(Joseph),* as an inflow (explained at §6152). In this case it symbolizes a perceptible inflow, because Joseph not only took his father's hand, he also said, *"Not that way, my father, because this one is the firstborn."*

6291

Put your right hand on his head means that doing so would assign it first place. This can be seen from the symbolism of *putting one's right hand on someone's head* as considering it to be in first place, as above at §§6269, 6287.

6292

The gesture of putting his hand on the head of the person he was blessing came from a ritual taken from the ancients. With our head we understand and intend; with our body we act on and obey our intellect and intent. Placing a hand on a head, then, represented the bestowal of a blessing on someone's intellect and will and therefore on the whole person.

The same ritual from those ancient times still lasts today, used as it is for inducting people into office and blessing them.

6293   *And his father refused* symbolizes disagreement, as can be seen without explanation.

6294   *And said, "I know, my son, I know,"* means that this is how things are but not how they look. This can be seen from the symbolism of *knowing*, which in this case means knowing that this is how things are but not how they look.

It was due to an inflow of inner heavenliness (Joseph) that spiritual goodness (Israel) now perceived this fact. That inflow is treated of above at §§6289, 6291.

When spiritual goodness is enlightened by this inflow, it perceives that this is how things *are*—that goodness is in first place and truth in second—though not how they *look*. But then, just below [§6296], it assigns priority to truth because truth is going to reign over goodness. As a result, Israel keeps his right hand on the head of the younger and his left on the head of the firstborn.

6295   *This one too will become a people, and he too will become great* means that truth-from-goodness (and therefore heavenly people) will also increase. This can be seen from the symbolism of a *people* as truth (discussed in §§1259, 1260, 3581, 4619), from that of *becoming great* as increasing, and from the representation of Manasseh, the person these words refer to, as goodness belonging to the will, on the earthly level, born of the inner dimension (discussed in §§6234, 6238, 6267). The fact that truth-from-goodness is the province of a heavenly person can be seen from what I have said and shown about heavenly people many times before: Heavenly people are those for whom the workings of the will lead to goodness and from there to truth; and they are different from spiritual people, for whom the workings of the intellect lead to truth and from there to goodness. As Manasseh stands for goodness in the will, he represents a heavenly person, but a shallow heavenly person, or a person belonging to the outer part of a heavenly religion. After all, Manasseh is goodness in the will on the earthly level and therefore in the outer self. Joseph, though, is a person belonging to the inner part of a heavenly religion, because he stands for goodness in the will on the rational level and therefore in the inner self.

[2] I should also say a few words about the truth-from-goodness that is the province of a heavenly person. This truth is called truth but is actually goodness.

Heavenly people have in them a goodness that comes of love for the Lord and a goodness that comes of love for their neighbor. The goodness that comes of love for the Lord is their inner level, but the goodness that comes of love for their neighbor is their outer level. People in a heavenly religion, then, are on the inner level of that religion if they focus on love for the Lord, and are on the outer level if they focus on love for their neighbor. The goodness that comes of this love—the love the heavenly have for their neighbor—is what is being called truth-from-goodness here. That is what is represented by Manasseh.

Heavenly people by their very nature do not reason from or about truth, because goodness (or rather the Lord working through goodness) gives them a perception that a thing is either so or not (§§202, 337, 2715, 3246, 4448). Nonetheless the goodness that comes of charity in them is called truth, or at least heavenly truth.

And nevertheless his younger brother will become greater than he means that goodness-from-truth (and therefore spiritual people) will grow by a larger amount, as the following shows: Ephraim, the *younger brother,* represents truth belonging to the intellect, on the earthly level, born of the inner dimension (discussed in §§6234, 6238, 6267). In this case, though, Ephraim represents goodness-from-truth (discussed below). And *becoming greater than the other* means growing by a larger amount.

6296

Ephraim stands for goodness-from-truth here because he represents a person in a spiritual religion—the outer part of a spiritual religion, anyway, just as Manasseh represents a person belonging to the outer part of a heavenly religion (§6295).

Goodness based on truth is what constitutes this person—a person in a spiritual religion. The inner part of such a religion is what Israel represents, but the outer part is what Ephraim represents.

People in a spiritual religion differ from those in a heavenly religion in that the goodness of the former is planted in the intellectual side of their mind, while the goodness of the latter is planted in the will-related part; see §§863, 875, 895, 927, 928, 1023, 1043, 1044, 2256, 4328, 4493, 5113. Ephraim therefore represents a spiritual person and Manasseh a heavenly one.

[2] Goodness based on truth (or the spiritual individual) was to grow by a larger amount than goodness that leads to truth (or the heavenly

individual) because the human will was constantly being debased. It was finally debased so far that evil took it over completely, until no soundness remained to it. To keep humankind from perishing, then, the Lord saw to it that the intellectual side of people's minds would be able to be reborn and they could be saved in the process. That is why few people have any soundness in the will side of their mind. So there are few who can become heavenly people, but many who can become spiritual. The spiritual will therefore grow by a larger amount than the heavenly. This now is what is meant by *his younger brother will become greater than he.*

6297   *And his seed will be a fullness of nations* means that faith and its truth will reign supreme, as the following shows: *Seed* symbolizes faith and neighborly love, as discussed in §§1025, 1447, 1610, 1940, 2848, 3187, 3310, 3373, 3671. Here it symbolizes faith, since it is described as Ephraim's. And a *fullness of nations* symbolizes an abundance and therefore something that will reign supreme.

In the Word, fullness means "all," and where it does not mean "all," it means "abundant." What is more, it applies to both truth and goodness. Large numbers apply to truth, and large size to goodness, but fullness applies to both. In Jeremiah, for instance:

> Look! Water climbing from the north, which will become a flooding river and flood the earth *and its fullness,* the city and those living in it. (Jeremiah 47:2)

The earth and its fullness stands for everything belonging to the church—both truth and goodness. That is why the passage adds "the city and those living in it," because a city symbolizes truth, and its residents, good qualities (§§2268, 2451, 2712). [2] In Ezekiel:

> They will eat their bread with anxiety and drink their water in shock, so that the *land of [Jerusalem]* may be stripped *of its fullness.* (Ezekiel 12:19)

The land stands for the church, and its fullness for goodness and truth in the church. The words just before this ("they will eat bread with anxiety and drink water in shock") show that both are symbolized, because bread symbolizes the goodness urged by love, and water, the truth that leads to faith. These are referred to as the fullness of the land. [3] The meaning is similar in Amos:

> Jacob's pride and his palaces I hate, so I will shut up the city *and its fullness.* (Amos 6:8)

In David:

> Yours are the heavens; yours also the earth. The city *and its fullness* you founded. (Psalms 89:11)

And in another place in the same book:

> Jehovah's is the earth *and its fullness,* the world and those living in it. He himself founded it on seas and established it on rivers. (Psalms 24:1, 2)

Here too the fullness stands for truth and goodness. The earth stands for the church narrowly defined, and the world for the church in a larger sense. Jehovah's founding the world on seas means on the use of knowledge (§28). His establishing it on rivers means on the use of intelligence (§3051). Surely anyone can see that it does not mean Jehovah founded the world on seas and established it on rivers, because those are not what the world was founded or established on. A reader who takes the time to think, then, can see that the seas and rivers have some other meaning and that this other meaning is the Word's inward, spiritual plane.

And he blessed them on this day symbolizes eternal foresight and providence, as the following shows: *Blessing* symbolizes a prediction, as mentioned in §§6230, 6254. In the highest sense, though, it symbolizes the Lord's foresight, and as it symbolizes foresight it also symbolizes providence, since one is not possible without the other. Evil is foreseen, and goodness is provided. Moreover, when evil is foreseen, providence channels it into something good. The reason blessing means foresight and providence here is that in the highest sense, Israel—the one pronouncing the blessing—is the Lord (§4286). And *on this day,* or "today," symbolizes eternity, as discussed in §§2838, 3998, 4304, 6165.   **6298**

Saying, "By you Israel will pronounce a blessing, saying, 'May God make you like Ephraim and like Manasseh!'" means ensuring that his spiritual aspect would reside in truth belonging to the intellect and in goodness belonging to the will. This is established by the representation of *Israel* as spiritual goodness (dealt with at §§5801, 5803, 5807, 5812, 5817, 5819, 5826, 5833), and by that of *Ephraim* as truth in the intellect and of *Manasseh* as goodness in the will (dealt with above). Ensuring that what was spiritual (Israel) would reside in this truth and goodness is symbolized by the words *by you he will pronounce a blessing* and *may God make you.*   **6299**

[2] To expand on the idea that the spiritual element represented by Israel would reside in truth belonging to the intellect and in goodness

belonging to the will, as represented by Ephraim and Manasseh: Spiritual goodness, represented by Israel, is the spiritual aspect of the inner part of the church, but the truth and goodness represented by Ephraim and Manasseh belong to the outer part of the church; see above at §6296. If the inner part of the church is to be the inner part, it has to reside in the outer part, because the outer part functions as a foundation that the inner part must rest on, and forms a container it must flow into. That is why the earthly plane (the outer part) has to be reborn. If it is not reborn, the inner part has no foundation or container, and if it has no foundation or container, it dies out completely.

This now is what it means to say that his spiritual aspect would reside in truth belonging to the intellect and in goodness belonging to the will.

[3] Take this example as an illustration of the matter: A genuine attitude of neighborly love consists in feeling tranquil and blessed when we help our neighbor without any thought of repayment. Such a feeling is the inner dimension of the church. Another possibility, though, is wanting to help or actually helping someone on the basis of truth—that is, because the Word commands us to do so. This is the outer dimension of the church. Sometimes our earthly part (the outer dimension) does not go along; it neither helps nor wants to help, because we see no benefit in it and therefore nothing for ourselves. The outer, earthly self tends this way naturally as a result of both our inheritance and our actual behavior. If our outer dimension balks like this, then the inner dimension has no foundation or container corresponding to it. Instead it has something that rejects or corrupts or snuffs out its inflow. As a result, our inner dimension dies, which is to say that it is closed up and blocked off. Nothing seeps through from heaven into the earthly level by way of the inner plane except a bit of the commonly available light that enters through cracks scattered all around. This light makes it possible for us to think, will, and speak, but only in keeping with that which exists on the earthly plane and therefore in favor of evil and falsity and against goodness and truth. We take the modicum of commonly available spiritual light that flows in through cracks scattered all around and force it to serve these purposes for our personal benefit.

6300   *And he put Ephraim before Manasseh* means that he considered truth to be in first place, because he was spiritual. This can be seen from the explanations above at verses 13, 14, 17, 18, 19 [§§6267–6273, 6287–6297].

Genesis 48:21, 22. *And Israel said to Joseph, "Here now, I am dying, and*   **6301**
God will be with you and take you back to the land of your ancestors. And
I am giving you one portion more than your brothers, which I took from the
hand of the Amorite with my sword and with my bow."

And Israel said to Joseph, "Here now, I am dying," symbolizes a perception received by spiritual goodness from inner heavenliness about new
life and about the end of his representative role. *And God will be with you*
symbolizes the Lord's divine providence. *And take you back to the land of*
your ancestors means to the state of both early churches. *And I am giving*
you one portion more than your brothers means that truth in the intellect,
and goodness in the will, would have more there. *Which I took from the*
hand of the Amorite means as a result of victory over evil. *With my sword*
means through truth engaged in battle. *And with my bow* means on the
basis of theology.

And Israel said to Joseph, "Here now, I am dying," symbolizes a percep-   **6302**
tion received by spiritual goodness from inner heavenliness about new
life and about the end of his representative role, as the following shows:
Saying symbolizes a perception, as noted above in §6220. *Israel* represents spiritual goodness, as also noted above, in §6225. *Joseph* represents
inner heavenliness, as noted in §§5869, 5877. And *dying* symbolizes being
restored to life, as discussed in §§3498, 3505, 4618, 4621, 6036, 6221. It
also symbolizes the end of a previous representation (§§3253, 3259, 3276),
and that is another symbolism of the word "dying" here. When an individual who had represented some facet of the church dies, that person
is replaced by another, who carries on the representation in turn. After
Abraham died, then, Isaac in his turn kept up the representative function,
as Jacob did next, and his sons after him.

Likewise, when Moses died, Joshua took over his representation, as
did the judges in turn, until replaced by the kings, and so on.

And God will be with you symbolizes the Lord's divine providence.   **6303**
This is evident from the symbolism of *God will be with you* as the Lord's
divine providence, because when the Lord is with someone, he leads that
person and provides that every event, whether sad or happy, turns to
that person's benefit. That is what divine providence is.

The reason for speaking of this providence as the Lord's is that the
verse says "God will be with you," and in the Word, "God" and "Jehovah"
mean the Lord, because there is no other God besides him. He is the
Father himself, and he is the Son himself, because they are one. The Father

is in him and he is in the Father, as he teaches in John 14:9, 10, 11. See §§1343, 1736, 2921, 3035, 5663.

6304   *And take you back to the land of your ancestors* means to the state of both early churches. This can be seen from the symbolism of the *land* as the church (discussed in §§566, 662, 1066, 1068, 1733, 1850, 2117, 2118, 3355, 4447, 4535, 5577) and from that of *ancestors* as the people of the ancient and earliest churches (discussed at §6075).

I speak of a return to the state of both early churches because like the people of the early churches, the children of Israel and their descendants represented the Lord's heavenly and spiritual kingdoms in every detail. What is more, a very real role was assigned to them—to the Jewish nation, a role representing the heavenly kingdom, and to the Israelite people, a role representing the spiritual kingdom. Yet it was merely representation that could be established among the people of that generation, not any quality belonging to the church or to the Lord's kingdom. They absolutely refused to see or acknowledge anything but the outer surface of their representative objects and rituals, not any inward content.

[2] Nonetheless, in order for a representation to come into being that would enable some kind of communication with heaven and through heaven with the Lord, the people were kept to external things. The Lord also provided for communication at that time to exist through an outward representation alone, without any inward counterpart.

This was the state to which Jacob's descendants were able to be brought.

The external representations existing with them still held a divine message hidden within, though. In the highest sense this message focused on the Lord's divine humanity, and in a secondary sense on the Lord's kingdom in the heavens and in the church.

This is the state of the two early churches symbolized by "God will take you back to the land of your ancestors."

6305   *And I am giving you one portion more than your brothers* means that truth in the intellect and goodness in the will would have more there, as the following shows. Joseph in this case (as above in §6275) stands for Ephraim and Manasseh, who represent truth in the intellect and goodness in the will, as explained many times before. And *giving them one portion more than their brothers* means having more there—in the church symbolized by the land (§6304). Goodness in the will and truth in the intellect were to have more because the two of them are the essential components of the church.

That is also why the birthright passed to Joseph's sons (1 Chronicles 5:1).

Which I took from the hand of the Amorite means as a result of victory over evil. This can be seen from the representation of an *Amorite* as evil (discussed at §1857) and from the symbolism of *taking from the hand* as gaining something through victory.

As far as Amorites go, it is important to realize that they symbolize evil, just as Canaanites and the other nations of that land that are mentioned in the Word symbolize different types of evil and of falsity too. That was the representation of the nations there when the children of Israel came into possession of Canaan. The purpose of the representation was for those nations to represent hellish qualities while the children of Israel were representing heavenly qualities. In this way the land of Canaan would represent every condition encountered in the other life. Since the nations represented something hellish, they were given to destruction and the Israelites were forbidden to enter into a pact with any that might remain.

[2] The fact that the children of Israel seized and settled a land belonging to people who represented hell had its own representation, which was this: Around the time of the Lord's Coming, hellish spirits occupied much of heaven. By coming into the world and making the human nature in himself divine, the Lord drove them out and cast them down into the hells. In this way he liberated heaven from them and gave it as an inheritance to people belonging to his spiritual kingdom.

[3] Passages mentioning the Amorite nation show that it represented evil in general. In Ezekiel, for example:

> Jerusalem, your trading and your generations are from the land of the Canaanite; *your father is an Amorite* and your mother a Hittite. (Ezekiel 16:3, 45)

In an inner sense, a father symbolizes the goodness in the church, but in a negative sense, the evil, while a mother symbolizes the truth accepted by the church, but in a negative sense, the falsity. That is why it says, "Your father is an Amorite and your mother a Hittite." [4] In Amos:

> As for me, before their faces I have destroyed the *Amorites,* whose height was like the height of cedars; and they were strong, like an oak. I led them in the wilderness, to take possession of the land of the *Amorite.* (Amos 2:9, 10)

Here too Amorites stand for evil, because the passage uses the height of cedars and the strength of an oak to depict the evil that grows out of

self-love. The reason an Amorite means evil in general is that the whole
Canaanite land was called the land of the Amorite. After all, it says, "I led
them in the wilderness, to take possession of the land of the Amorite."
Besides, the Book of Kings says:

> Manasseh, king of Judah, *did more evil than all the evil that the Amorites
> before him did.* (2 Kings 21:11)

[5] *With my sword* means through truth engaged in battle. This can be
seen from the discussion in §§2799, 4499 of the symbolism of a *sword* as
truth engaged in battle.

And with my bow means on the basis of theology. This can be seen
from the symbolism of a *bow* as theology, as discussed in §§2686, 2709.

[6] Obviously it was on account of the inner meaning that Israel said
these words, "the portion that I took from the hand of the Amorite with
my sword and with my bow," because Jacob did not take that portion
from the Amorites with a sword or a bow. He bought it from the children
of Hamor, as is plain in Genesis 33, where these words occur:

> Jacob came to Salem (the city of Shechem, which is in the land of Canaan)
> in coming from Paddan-aram. And he camped before the face of the city.
> And *he bought the portion of the field* where he had spread his tent, from
> the hand of the children of Hamor, Shechem's father, for a hundred kesi-
> tahs. (Genesis 33:18, 19)

This field was the portion he gave Joseph, as the Book of Joshua makes
evident:

> Joseph's bones, which the children of Israel brought up from Egypt,
> they buried in Shechem, in the part of the field *that Jacob had bought
> from the children of Hamor,* Shechem's father, for a hundred kesitahs.
> And [the bones] became an inheritance of Joseph's children. (Joshua
> 24:32)

It is clear, then, that this portion had been bought and that it was the
portion given to Joseph. Plainly the reference is not to the nearby city of
Shechem, in which Simeon and Levi killed every male and which they
took with the sword (Genesis 34). After all, Jacob loathed what Simeon
and Levi had done, cursed them for it, and in the chapter after this completely dissociated himself from the crime, saying:

> *Into their conspiracy my soul is not to come; with their band my glory is
> not to unite,* because in their anger they killed a man, and in their good

pleasure they hamstrung an ox. A curse on their anger because it is
fierce and on their wrath because it is hard! I will divide them in Jacob
and scatter them in Israel. (Genesis 49:5, 6, 7)

From all this you can now see that Israel said these words, "the portion that I took from the hand of the Amorite with my sword and with
my bow," when the spirit of prophecy was on him, for the sake of the
inner meaning.

Spiritual Inflow, and the Interaction
of the Soul and Body (Continued)

B Y now, many years of experience have taught me that the spiritual   **6307**
world flows into people's feelings and thoughts through angels and
through spirits. I see it so clearly that nothing is clearer. I have sensed the
inflow not only into my thoughts but also into my feelings. When evil
and falsity have flowed in, I could tell which hells they came from, and
when goodness and truth have flowed in, I could tell which angels they
came from.

The sensation has consequently become so familiar to me that I can
finally recognize the source of every single thought and feeling. Yet the
thoughts have still been my thoughts, just as they were before.

The inflow occurs through spirits and angels.   **6308**

The pattern of inflow is that evil spirits flow in first and angels dispel
their effect.

People on earth are not aware that spiritual inflow is like this, because
they are kept in freedom of thought by a balance maintained between
the two inflows, and because they do not pay attention to any of this.
Evil people could not see it even if they did pay attention, because evil
and goodness are not balanced in them, but people with goodness *can*
see. They also know from the Word that we have something inside that
combats evil and falsity in us. They know that our spiritual self fights our
earthly self, so that angels, who occupy our spiritual depths, fight evil
spirits, who occupy our earthly level. That is why the church is described
as militant.

However, evil that flows from evil spirits into our thinking does not hurt us at all if we do not accept it. If we do accept it and transfer it from our thoughts into our will, we make it our own. We then move closer toward alliance with hellish spirits and farther from the angels of heaven.

This is what the Lord teaches in Mark:

> What comes into people does not defile them, but what comes out of them does, because this comes from the heart, [that is, the will]. (Mark 7:14–23)

6309

I have spoken with good spirits about the inner and outer self, and what I have said is this: Although people in the church know from the Word that there is an inner self, distinct from the outer self, surprisingly few of them believe it. Yet they can see it from a mere glance at their daily thoughts and intentions. That is to say, they often think differently on the inside than they do on the outside. What they think on the outside they publish in word, look, and deed, but not what they think on the inside. This they hide deep down, as every imposter, hypocrite, and swindler knows.

People intent on what is good can recognize the same thing by considering that they reprimand themselves, thinking, "I should not do this"—from which they can see that they have an inner self, separate from their outer self.

[2] They do not pay attention to this, though, and even if they do pay attention to it, they do not perceive it. One reason is that they think life belongs to the body. Another is that when they occupy all their thoughts with bodily and worldly concerns, any insight into the inner self—and in fact any belief that it exists—dies. This too I have been allowed to learn from experience. When I was contemplating some heavenly idea but then fell into thoughts on worldly and earthly subjects, the heavenly concepts were erased so completely that I hardly acknowledged them. This happened because anything that heaven's light shines on goes dark when it falls within reach of the world's glimmer, since the two realms are opposed.

To do away with opposition between the two, we are reborn and are raised from preoccupation with our senses to something farther within; and the farther within we rise, the more we relinquish evil and falsity. We cannot rise, though, unless in both our faith and our life we focus on goodness.

Our inner depths are distinguished into different levels by deriva-
tion. There are also different kinds of light on the different levels.

6310

The inner sensory level, which is closest to the physical senses themselves, has the harshest light. Through much experience I have learned to
recognize this light. I have also observed that whenever I sink into such
light, I meet with falsity and evil of many kinds. I even encounter slander
against what is heavenly and divine, and filth and vileness as well. The
reason is that this light pervades the hells and is the main conduit by
which the hells flow into us.

[2] When we use this light, our thoughts are lit by almost the same
light that our physical eyes use, and we are almost in our body.

People who avail themselves of this light should be called *sense-oriented,*
because their thoughts are unable to transcend the physical senses. What
lies beyond the senses they neither perceive nor believe in. All they believe
in is what they can see and touch.

Such light is used by people who have never developed any depth,
living a life that ignores and despises everything rational and spiritual. In
particular it is used by the greedy and adulterous, and by people who
have filled their lives with nothing but sensual pleasure and shameful idleness. As a result these people think thoughts that are unclean and often
sacrilegious.

As I said, the hells live in this light, but so do some individuals who
are not as wicked. These are people who at one time were not grasping,
adulterous, or hedonistic but became so because they did not cultivate
their rational mind.

6311

I was allowed to see these spirits in a kind of half-light. They appeared
in clusters in a public area, carrying bags filled with raw materials, hefting
them, and carting them off.

At the same time there were some sirens not far away, and I heard
them saying they wanted to be there because they can see people on earth
with their own eyes. Since sirens are women who had been particularly
adulterous and had opposed everything heavenly and spiritual, the only
spirits visible to them are the ones who see by the light of the senses. After
all, that is how they themselves are.

Because the hells dwell in this sensory-level light, we cannot help being
destroyed if we are not lifted out of hell. The goodness that faith teaches
is what lifts us.

6312

There are also hells that occupy a subtler realm, though. These hells
contain deeply malicious spirits who had devised numerous schemes for

depriving others of their property and hatched numerous plots for taking power.

However, I noticed that this realm flows into the superficial, sensory-level realm, and does so through the back part [of the head], where our involuntary processes are. This is what makes the sensory realm as powerful as it is.

6313   When we rise toward inner levels, we go from the harsh light of the senses to a gentler light. At the same time, we move beyond the reach of inflows that are religiously offensive or sordid, closer to all that is just and fair, because we move closer to the angels with us and therefore closer to heaven's light.

The ancients, even outside the church, knew about this elevation out of the sensory realm. As a result their philosophers said that when the mind withdraws from sense impressions, it comes into inner light, and a state of calm, and a kind of heavenly bliss. Even they therefore concluded that the mind was immortal.

We are capable of rising still farther within than that, and the farther within we go, the brighter the light we encounter, until we reach heavenly light, which is actually wisdom and understanding granted by the Lord.

The three heavens are distinguished from each other only by the degree to which they rise toward what is within and therefore by levels of light as well. The third heaven is the inmost, so it has the greatest light and therefore a wisdom that far exceeds the wisdom of the lower heavens.

6314   With regard to a person's vital heat, the case is the same as that with light. By no means does this vital heat originate in the warmth from the sun of the world but in spiritual warmth, which is love and which radiates from the Lord. That is the warmth angels enjoy. The more love we have, then, the more vital heat we have.

Our body makes use of worldly warmth, as does our inner sensory plane; but vital heat flows into this warmth and enlivens it.

There are purer and coarser types of heat, as there are of light.

This heat is what holy fire refers to when mentioned in the Word, so holy fire there symbolizes heavenly love. In a negative sense this heat is what hellfire refers to, so the hellfire mentioned in the Word symbolizes hellish love and the cravings that accompany it.

6315   People who are lifted above their senses by faith-inspired goodness in their lives alternate between the light of the senses and inner light.

When they focus on worldly cares, when they interact with others on a thoroughly shallow plane, when they indulge in luxury, they are living the life of the senses. Under those circumstances they avoid and even resist speaking or thinking about God or religious matters. If they did speak or think about those subjects at that time, they would discount them as worthless, unless the Lord suddenly lifted them up to an inner level.

When the same people are not wrapped up in worldly endeavors but benefit from inner light, they base their thinking on justice and fairness. If they enjoy light that is still farther within, they base their thinking on spiritual truth and goodness.

People who live good lives are lifted from one kind of light to another, and they are quickly raised into inner light when they start to think wrongly, because angels are near them.

I was able to learn these things from experience, because I often sensed I was being lifted up, and when I did, I perceived the state of my feelings and thoughts changing.

You will be surprised to hear that most scholars are sense-oriented. **6316** They are sense-oriented because they have gathered knowledge just to gain a reputation so that they can advance to high position and accumulate wealth. Their purpose was not to gain wisdom. All knowledge available in the scholarly world is a means of becoming wise and also a means of becoming insane.

When scholars attain high office, they pursue the life of the senses more than the uneducated do. By then they consider it naive to attribute anything to the Divine rather than to human prudence and nature or (as a last resort) to luck.

There were once some spirits with me who had been called highly **6317** educated when they lived as people in the world. They were sent back into the state of thought that had been customary for them when they lived in their bodies, and this thinking of theirs—specifically about spirits—was communicated to me. What was their thinking like? They could never be led to believe that spirits have the use of any of the senses. Beyond that their former thoughts about spirits, or souls after death, were completely indefinable.

The reason they thought this way was that they located life in the body. They also hardened their minds against the life of their spirit or soul after death, by scientific and philosophical arguments. As a consequence, they closed their inner dimension off to themselves and therefore could not possibly be raised up into it.

If they had been told the very truth itself after hardening their minds against life after death and all that goes with it, they would have reacted to it like the blind who cannot see and the deaf who cannot hear. Some of them even sneer; and the wiser they consider themselves to be in relation to others, the more they sneer.

The uneducated who have devoted themselves to the goodness urged by faith, though, are not like this, because they have never used science or philosophy to harden their minds against religious matters. Their perceptiveness is therefore farther-reaching and clearer. Because they have not closed off their inner reaches, they are able to accept goodness and truth.

6318   There are other people who are more than sense-oriented; they are body-centered. These are the ones who have hardened their minds entirely against the Divine and ascribed everything to nature. So they have lived without taking justice and fairness into account at all, except when they do so just for show. Because they are like unreasoning animals inside, despite looking human outside, they are more oriented toward their senses and appear to themselves and others in the next life as if they had physical bodies.

I saw them out in front near my right foot, rising up from a great depth. They were extremely hairy and what you might call solid. When they had finished rising, a kind of sword appeared to hang over their head.

I talked with them, and they said it seemed to them exactly as though they were in their body.

6319   In regard to angels' inflow into us, it is not what people think it is; it relies on correspondence. Angels think spiritually, but people perceive it in an earthly way. So spiritual concepts drop down into the ideas we have that correspond to and therefore represent them. For example, when a person talks about bread, sowing seed, harvest, fatness, and similar things, angels think about goodness that springs from love and charity, and so on.

I once had a common type of dream. When I woke up, I told some angels all about it from start to finish. They said my story perfectly matched a conversation they had been having. It was not the same things they were discussing that I dreamed about but something corresponding to and representing their ideas, down to the smallest details. Then I talked with them about spiritual inflow.

The angels with us do not see objects the same way we see them with our eyes. They also do not take in words the same way we hear them with our ears, but the way we think a thought. You can see that thought works in an entirely different way than speech by considering that we can think more in a minute than we can verbalize in half an hour, because thought is dissociated from spoken words.

This shows to some extent what the interaction of the soul with the body is like: it resembles the inflow of the spiritual world into the physical world. Our soul, or spirit, lives in the spiritual world, while our body lives in the physical world. So the interaction relies on correspondence.

When angels flow in, they attach feelings to the inflow, and the feelings themselves contain too many elements to count. But we accept only a few of these countless elements—only the ones that relate to what we already have in our memory. The rest of the angelic inflow surrounds these core items and holds them in its embrace, so to speak. **6320**

I was given the opportunity to learn by experience that there is an inflow from angels and that we cannot live without it. **6321**

There are malicious spirits who have thought up schemes for blocking the angels' inflow, though they block it only partially. They were allowed to do this to me so that I could learn from experience that it was true. As they obstructed the inflow, the liveliness of my thoughts fluctuated, until eventually it became like the mental activity of someone who is fainting. I was quickly restored, though, and the spirits were thrown down into their hell.

They appeared to the left on a level with the top of my head, which is where they secretly positioned themselves at first.

It looks exactly as though our outer senses—such as sight and hearing—act on our thoughts and stir up ideas there. It seems that objects stimulate our senses (first our outer and then our inner senses) and that speech does too. But although this appearance is strong, it is misleading. What is outside is coarse and made of matter, so it cannot act on or stimulate what is inside, which is pure and spiritual. This is contrary to nature. **6322**

It is the inner senses, or the senses of the spirit itself, that do the sensing through the outer senses. The inner senses also see to it that the outer sense organs take in the objects of the senses at the will of the inner senses. The sense organs, such as the organ of sight (the eye), therefore adjust to all those objects instantly, in keeping with the individual nature of the object. The organs would not do this if there were no inflow into them from within. All the fibers and small appendages that crowd around each sense organ instantly adapt to suit the nature of the object, and in fact the state of the organ itself immediately conforms as well.

[2] Spirits have often discussed among themselves the appearance [that sensation affects thinking]. Whenever they have, angels have answered that inflow cannot possibly go from what is external to what is internal, only from internal to external, and that this accords with a pattern that inflow cannot violate.

Two or three times I have seen spirits removed from an angelic community because they believed on the basis of appearance that the outer dimension acts on the inner. So they believed in a physical rather than a spiritual inflow. The reason they were removed was that their belief could have led to the conclusion that the hells, which are superficial, could act on the heavens, which have depth. It could also have led to the conclusion that life did not flow in from the Lord, when in reality all life flows from him, because he is at the inmost core, and in relation to him, *everything* is external.

6323 The goodness that comes from love, which flows in from the Lord through angels, contains all truth, and this truth would spontaneously reveal itself if we lived a life of love for the Lord and love for our neighbor. This fact is clear not only from phenomena in heaven but also from phenomena on the lower rungs of nature. The lower physical phenomena are in plain sight, so let me select examples from them to cite as illustrations.

[2] Brute animals can act only as directed by the passions and accompanying drives with which their species was created and they were then born. All animals are carried wherever their drive and passion draw them. This being so, they possess all possible knowledge relating to those passions. From a love resembling the love in marriage they know how to mate, beasts in one way and birds in another. Birds know how to make nests, lay eggs and sit on them, hatch chicks, and feed them, all without instruction—simply from the love that mimics marriage love and from love for their young. All this knowledge is inherent in those two passions. Similarly, they know which foods to eat for nourishment and how to find the food. Again, bees know how to find their nourishment in various types of blossoms and how to gather wax for the cells in which they first deposit their larvae and then store food. They also know how to prepare for the winter. Not to mention many other behaviors. All this knowledge is included in their loves and dwells there from the start. Animals are

born with the knowledge because they follow the code of the nature they were created for, and from birth on they are driven by a general inflow from the spiritual world.

[3] If we followed the code we were created to live by, we would possess love for our neighbor and love for the Lord, these being the loves proper to us. Under those circumstances, we would excel all animals by being born not just with all knowledge but even with all spiritual truth and heavenly goodness. So we would be born with all wisdom and understanding. After all, we can think about the Lord, unite with him in love, and in this way rise to what is divine and eternal, which brute animals cannot. We would then be ruled solely by the general inflow from the Lord through the spiritual world.

We are not born into our proper code, though, but rather into opposition to it. As a result we are born with ignorance on every score. This being the case, it was provided that we could afterward be reborn and in this way enter into understanding and wisdom, to the extent that we freely accept goodness and, through goodness, truth.

Spirits in the other world who spend a lot of time reasoning do not often perceive what is true and good. Consequently they cannot be let into the inner angelic communities, because no measure of understanding can be communicated to them there.

6324

In fact, they argued with each other about the idea that all thoughts and feelings flow to us from elsewhere. They kept saying that if this were true, no one could be held accountable or pay a penalty for any failing. I always answered, though, that everything good and true comes from the Lord and everything evil and false from hell. If people believed in this, the true situation, they could not be held accountable for any failing or have evil imputed to them. People believe that it all comes from themselves, though, so they adopt evil as their own. That is what this belief does. The evil therefore clings to them and cannot be detached. In fact, people would naturally be offended if anyone told them their thoughts and intentions come from others, not from themselves.

It is an eternal truth that the Lord rules heaven and earth, that no one but the Lord has independent life, and that all life consequently flows in; life that contains goodness flows in from the Lord, and life that contains evil flows in from hell. This is the faith of the heavens. When we have the same faith—which we can have when we have goodness—evil cannot attach to us or be assigned to us as ours, because we know it comes from

6325

hell, not from ourselves. In this state we can receive the gift of peace, because only then do we trust in the Lord. Furthermore, peace can be given only to people who adopt that faith as a result of love for their neighbor. All others subject themselves to constant worries and cravings, which leave them agitated.

Spirits who wish to be their own masters imagine that [to allow the Lord mastery] would be to lose the exercise of their own will. This would be to lose their freedom and therefore all pleasure and consequently all life and all sweetness in life.

They talk and think this way because they do not know how the matter really stands. You see, people who are led by the Lord have real freedom and therefore real pleasure and blessedness. What is good and true is given to them as their own. They receive a desire and longing to do good, and nothing is then more pleasant for them than to be useful. They are given the ability to see and also to perceive what is good, and they are given understanding and wisdom. All this they receive as their own, because they are then containers for the Lord's life.

The scholarly world knows that a principal cause and an instrumental cause form a single cause together. As a form designed to receive the Lord's life, a human being is an instrumental cause, and life from the Lord is the principal cause. The instrument senses this life in itself as its own even though it is not.

6326 There was a philosopher I once spoke with about the different planes of life in a person. This philosopher was one of the sane and fairly famous ones and had died a few years earlier. "A person consists of nothing but forms created to receive life," I said to him. "These forms are nested one within the other, and each came into existence and remains in existence from the other. When the lower or outer form is discarded, the higher, inner form still lives on.

"All operations of the mind are variations in form," I continued. "The variations in the purer substances are so perfect they cannot be described, and the thoughts we think are nothing but such variations. They occur in response to changes in the state of our emotions.

"The great perfection found in variations of the purer forms can be deduced from the lungs, which bend and change shape in various ways for every spoken word, every sung note, every physical motion, and every state of thought or feeling. What must the variation be like on inner levels, which are in a far more perfect state than even so marvelous an organ as the lungs?"

The philosopher agreed and strongly asserted that he had known all this when he lived in the world. "The world should apply philosophy to these kinds of purposes," he said. "It should not concentrate on bare terminology and controversies over wording, sweating away in the dust."

This subject continues at the end of the next chapter [§§6466–6496]. **6327**

Genesis 49

1. And Jacob called his sons and said, "Gather, and I will tell you what will happen to you at the end of days.

2. Assemble and listen, sons of Jacob, and listen to Israel your father.

3. Reuben, my firstborn, you are my strength and the beginning of my vigor, excelling in prominence and excelling in worth.

4. Light as water, do not excel! For you climbed onto your father's beds, then you profaned them; my pallet he climbed onto.

5. Simeon and Levi are brothers; tools of violence are their blades.

6. Into their conspiracy my soul is not to come; with their band my glory is not to unite, because in their anger they killed a man, and in their good pleasure they hamstrung an ox.

7. A curse on their anger because it is fierce and on their wrath because it is hard! I will divide them in Jacob and scatter them in Israel.

8. You are Judah; your brothers will celebrate you. Your hand is on your enemies' neck; your father's sons will bow down to you.

9. A lion's cub is Judah; fed with prey, my son, you have risen. He crouched; he lay like a lion and like an aging lion. Who will arouse him?

10. The scepter will not be taken from Judah, or a lawgiver from between his feet, until Shiloh comes; and to him will be the obedience of the peoples.

11. He ties his young donkey to the grapevine and his jenny's foal to the rare vine. He washes his clothing in wine, and his garment in the blood of grapes.

12. He is red of eye from wine and white of teeth from milk.

13. Zebulun will reside at a harbor on the seas, and at a harbor for ships, and his flank will be toward Sidon.

14. Issachar is a bony donkey lying down between its burdens.

15. And he will see his resting place, that it is good, and the land, that it is delightful, and he will bend his shoulder to take on heavy loads and will serve as tribute, working like a slave.

16. Dan will judge his people as one of Israel's tribes.

17. Dan will be a snake on the path, a darting serpent on the track, biting the horse's heels, and its rider will fall off behind it.

18. Your salvation I await, Jehovah!

19. Gad: a troop will ravage him, and he will ravage their heel.

20. From Asher: rich with fat is his bread, and he will offer royal delicacies.

21. Naphtali is a doe let loose, delivering elegant words.

22. The son of a fertile woman is Joseph, the son of a fertile woman above the spring; daughters [each] stepped onto the wall.

23. And he is vexed and shot at and hated by the archers.

24. And he will sit in the sturdiness of his bow. And his arms and hands are strengthened by the hands of powerful Jacob, from whom comes the Shepherd, the Stone of Israel;

25. by the God of your father, who will help you; and with Shaddai, who will bless you with the blessings of the sky from above, with the blessings of the abyss lying below, with the blessings of breasts and womb.

26. The blessings of your father will prevail over the blessings of my forebears, even to the desire of the age-old hills. They will be on the head of Joseph and on the crown of the head of the Nazirite among his brothers.

27. Benjamin, a wolf, will seize [game] in the morning, eat the spoils, and at evening divide the prey."

28. All these are the twelve tribes of Israel, and this is what their father spoke to them, and he blessed them; each according to his blessing he blessed them.

29. And he commanded them and said to them, "I am being gathered to my people. Bury me near my forebears at the cave that is in the field of Ephron the Hittite,

30. in the cave that is in the field of Machpelah, which is before Mamre in the land of Canaan, [the cave] that Abraham bought along with the field from Ephron the Hittite, for the possession of a grave,

31. where they buried Abraham and Sarah his wife, where they buried Isaac and Rebekah his wife, and where I buried Leah—

32. the purchase of the field and of the cave that is in it, from the children of Heth."

33. And Jacob finished commanding his sons and gathered his feet onto the bed and breathed his last and was gathered to his peoples.

Summary

THIS chapter in its inner meaning is not about the future of Jacob's off-spring but about the true concepts that lead to faith and the kinds of goodness that come from love, represented and symbolized by the twelve tribes named for Jacob's sons.

6329   The first topic is faith detached from neighborly love, which is categorically rejected. This is Reuben, Simeon, and Levi.

6330   The next topic is a heavenly religion, which is the tribe of Judah. The highest meaning here has to do with the Lord's divine humanity.

6331   The text also deals with the rest of the tribes according to the state of the goodness and truth they represent.

6332   The final topic is a heavenly church of a spiritual type, which is Joseph. Here too the highest sense has to do with the Lord's divine humanity.

Inner Meaning

6333   WHAT Jacob says in this chapter makes it quite plain that the Word contains some other meaning than the one that appears in the literal text. After all, Jacob, who by now is Israel, says he will tell what will happen to his sons at the end of days (verse 1), but none of the events he tells about and predicts happened to them. An example is the prediction that the descendants of Reuben, Simeon, and Levi would be cursed more than the others, and that Simeon and Levi would be divided in Jacob and scattered in Israel (foretold in verses 3, 4, 5, 6, 7). The opposite happened to Levi, though; he was blessed, because the priesthood fell to him.

[2] What is said about Judah did not happen to him, either, except for the fact that a representation of a religion remained longer with him than with the others. Besides, no one can know what the kinds of statements made about him mean, except from another meaning buried within. Examples are the statements that he crouched and lay like a lion, tied his young donkey to the grapevine and his jenny's foal to the rare vine, washed his clothing in wine and his garment in the blood of grapes, and was red of eye from wine and white of teeth from milk (verses 9, 11, 12). Considering the nature of all these details, anyone can grasp that something lies hidden inside them, something known in heaven that can be disclosed to us only from there.

[3] The same is true for Israel's statements about the rest of his sons: that Zebulun would reside at a harbor on the seas, a harbor for ships, with his flank toward Sidon; that Issachar, a bony donkey lying down between its burdens, would bend a shoulder to take on heavy loads; that Dan would be a snake on the path, a darting serpent on the track, biting the heels of a horse whose rider would fall off behind it; and so on for the other sons. To repeat, these details make it obvious that there is an inner meaning.

The Word was given to us in order to unite heaven and earth, or to unite angels with people. It was therefore written in such a way as to be understood by angels in a spiritual way while being understood by people in an earthly way. Something holy would then flow in from angels and bring about the union.

That is the nature of both the narrative and the prophetic parts of the Word, but the inner meaning is less visible in the narrative than in the prophetic parts. The narratives were composed in a different style, though a style that still used symbolism.

[4] The narratives were provided to get younger and older children started reading the Word. The stories are appealing and capture a child's imagination, so they supply communication with the heavens. This communication is pleasing [to the Lord], because children are in a state of innocence and mutual charity. That is the reason the narrative part of the Word exists.

The prophetic part exists because when it is read, it is not comprehended except in a dim way, and when people like those of today comprehend it dimly, angels perceive it clearly. Much experience (discussed elsewhere, with the Lord's divine mercy) has shown me this.

Genesis 49:1, 2. *And Jacob called his sons and said, "Gather, and I will tell you what will happen to you at the end of days. Assemble and listen, sons of Jacob, and listen to Israel your father."*

6334

And Jacob called his sons symbolizes orderly arrangement on the earthly plane of the true ideas of faith and good attributes of love. *And said, "Gather,"* symbolizes all of them in general, placed together. *And I will tell you what will happen at the end of days* symbolizes what the state of the church would be like under the pattern in which they would then be arranged. *Assemble* means so that they would arrange themselves in order on their own. *And listen, sons of Jacob* symbolizes truth and goodness on the earthly plane. *And listen to Israel your father* symbolizes a prediction concerning them made by spiritual goodness; and in the highest sense it symbolizes the Lord's foresight.

6335 *And Jacob called his sons* symbolizes orderly arrangement on the earthly plane of the true ideas of faith and good attributes of love, as the following shows: *Calling* means arranging in order, because the reason for calling the sons together was to present religious truth and charitable goodness in that arrangement. And *Jacob* and *his sons* represent the true ideas of faith and the good attributes of love on the earthly plane. Jacob represents them generally (see §§3509, 3525, 3546, 3659, 3669, 3677, 3775, 3829, 4234, 4273, 4337, 5506, 5533, 5535, 6001, 6236), and his sons, or the tribes named for his sons, represent them individually (§§3858, 3926, 3939, 4060).

Regarding the orderly arrangement of religious truth and loving goodness that is symbolized here and presented in the chapter's inner meaning: Be aware that in general the twelve tribes of Israel represented all truth and goodness combined. So they represented all truth and goodness coming from the Lord, and consequently all truth and goodness that heaven contains and is composed of. Because they represent all these things in general, they also represent each variety in particular, since general categories contain specific items, just as a whole contains parts.

[2] Goodness and the truth that grows out of it determine how light varies in heaven, and light determines how states of understanding and wisdom vary. That is why light sparkled and flashed through the Urim and Thummim in different ways, depending on the circumstances of the matter being asked about. This happened because the twelve tribes, which symbolized all truth and goodness in general, were represented on the breastplate, or in the Urim and Thummim, since one precious stone stood for each tribe. The reason for the use of precious stones was that they symbolize spiritual and heavenly truth (§§114, 3720), and the gold in which they were set symbolizes goodness (§§113, 1551, 1552, 5658). This is the secret symbolized by the Urim and Thummim.

[3] This symbolism of the twelve tribes is clear from passages in the Word that mention them. It is especially clear from the tribes' inheritance in the land of Canaan as described in Joshua [chapters 13–19]; from their inheritance in the Lord's kingdom, as described in the final chapters of Ezekiel, which treat of the new land, new Jerusalem, and new temple [Ezekiel 40–48]; and in John in Revelation 7:4–8. It is also evident from the arrangement of the tribes when they camped in the wilderness [Numbers 2], which was such that it enabled them to represent truth and goodness in their proper pattern and led to this prophecy by Balaam:

> When Balaam raised his eyes *and saw Israel dwelling by its tribes,* the spirit of God came over him and he uttered a pronouncement and said, "How

good are your tents, Jacob; your dwellings, Israel! They are planted as val-
leys are, as gardens beside the river; like sandalwoods has Jehovah planted
them, like cedars beside the water." (Numbers 24:2, 3, 5, 6)

See also what was shown in §§2129, 3858, 3862, 3926, 3939, 4060, 4603
about the tribes and the ways they were arranged.

And said, "Gather," symbolizes all of them in general, placed together. **6336**
This can be seen from the symbolism of *gathering* as being together. In
this case what stands together is all the religious truth and loving goodness symbolized by Jacob's twelve sons; see just above at §6335.

And I will tell you what will happen at the end of days symbolizes what **6337**
the state of the church would be like under the pattern in which they
would then be arranged. This can be seen from the symbolism of *telling
what will happen* as communicating and predicting and from that of the
end of days as the conclusion of the state in which they are together. *Days*
are states (§§23, 487, 488, 493, 893, 2788, 3462, 3785, 4850), and an *end*
is a conclusion, so the *end of days* is the conclusion of a state—a state in
which truth and goodness in general, arranged in order, are together.

The state symbolized is the state of the church because the truth and
goodness represented by Jacob and his sons are those that constitute the
church. Jacob therefore represents the church (§§4286, 4439, 4514, 4520,
4680, 4772, 5536, 5540), so his sons do too (§§5403, 5419, 5427, 5458,
5512). The *nature* of the state is symbolized because the order in which
Jacob's sons or the tribes are named in the Word determines how the
church's truth and goodness are represented (see §§3862, 3939). One kind
of state is symbolized when Reuben's name comes first and another when
Judah's name does. When Reuben comes first, it is a kind of state that starts
with faith, but when Judah comes first, it is one that starts with love, and
yet another when it starts with someone else. The nature of the state also
varies according to the order in which the rest of the sons or tribes are
named after the first. This results in countless and even infinite variations. The variations multiply further when the general categories of truth
and goodness symbolized by the twelve tribes undergo individual variation, each category exhibiting countless variations. This changes the face
of each category of truth and goodness. And the variations multiply yet
again when those specific categories undergo countless detailed variation;
and so on. Infinite variations result, as can be illustrated by many natural
phenomena.

This now is why the twelve tribes have one symbolism when they
are named in one order in the Word and another symbolism when they are

named in another. So their symbolism is different in this chapter than elsewhere.

6338   *Assemble* means so that they would arrange themselves in order on their own. This can be seen from the symbolism of *assembling* as being arranged in order. That is exactly what assembling is in a spiritual sense, because truth and goodness cannot assemble unless they are also put in order. A universal force coming from the Lord arranges them, because this force contains everything individually inside itself, down to the smallest detail. All of it taken together constitutes the universal force, which reduces everything in the heavens into order. When the universal force acts, it looks as though goodness and truth organize on their own and glide into order spontaneously. The same is true for heaven as a whole: it exists in order and is constantly held in order by a universal inflow from the Lord. The same is also true for heavenly communities in general and heavenly communities in particular; as soon as angels or spirits assemble, they are immediately arranged into order as if on their own. In this form they constitute a heavenly community, which is an image of heaven. It would never happen if the universal force emanating from the Lord did not contain everything inside itself in the smallest detail and if all of it did not display the most perfect order. If God had a universal inflow lacking in specifics, as most people think he does, and if people, spirits, or angels were in charge of themselves in the details, there would be chaos rather than order. There would be no heaven, no hell, no human race, and even no physical world.

This fact can be illustrated by much human evidence. For instance, unless our thoughts were organized both as a whole and individually by the emotions of which love consists, they could never run in a rational or analytical vein. Neither could our actions. Again, if our soul did not flow into all our physical organs as a whole and into each organ individually, no part of our body would be well organized or regulated. When the soul acts on each organ and therefore on all of them, however, everything falls in line as if on its own.

This discussion is intended to show what is meant by the statement that truth and goodness arrange themselves in order on their own.

6339   *And listen, sons of Jacob* symbolizes truth and goodness on the earthly plane. This is established by the discussion above in §6335 of the representation of the *sons of Jacob* as the church's truth and goodness on the earthly plane.

And listen to Israel your father symbolizes a prediction concerning them made by spiritual goodness; and in the highest sense it symbolizes the Lord's foresight. This can be seen from the symbolism of *listening*— listening to what will happen at the end of days—as a prediction, and from the representation of *Israel* as spiritual goodness, as in §§5801, 5803, 5807, 5812, 5817, 5819, 5826, 5833. Since in an inner sense listening to what will happen at the end of days symbolizes a prediction, in the highest sense it symbolizes the Lord's foresight, because all prediction comes from the Lord's foresight.

6340

The statement that Jacob's sons were to listen to Israel means that people in the church were to listen to the Lord—that is, to the Lord in the Word. They were to hear what he teaches there about the true concepts of faith and the good attributes of love, and what he predicts about people who possess the kind of truth and goodness symbolized by one or another of Jacob's sons. For example, they should note what he teaches and predicts about people who subscribe to faith detached from neighborly love, as symbolized here by Reuben, Simeon, and Levi. They should note what he teaches and predicts about people who have heavenly goodness and are symbolized by Judah, and about people with spiritual goodness, as symbolized by Joseph. The same applies to people with the qualities symbolized by the other sons.

Genesis 49:3, 4. *"Reuben, my firstborn, you are my strength and the beginning of my vigor, excelling in prominence and excelling in worth. Light as water, do not excel! For you climbed onto your father's beds, then you profaned them; my pallet he climbed onto."*

6341

Reuben, my firstborn, symbolizes faith, apparently in first place. *You are my strength* means that through faith goodness has power. *And the beginning of my vigor* means that through faith truth has its initial power. *Excelling in prominence and excelling in worth* means that from these come renown and authority. *Light as water* means that faith alone does not have these properties. *Do not excel* means that it also possesses no renown or authority. *For you climbed onto your father's beds* means because when detached from neighborly kindness it forms a disgraceful union. *Then you profaned them* means that if it unites with evil, profanation results. *My pallet he climbed onto* means because it has polluted spiritual goodness on the earthly level.

Reuben, my firstborn, symbolizes faith, apparently in first place. This is established by the representation of *Reuben* as a faith that belongs to

6342

the intellect (discussed in §§3861, [3863,] 3866) and as a confession of the church's faith in general (§§4731, 4734, 4761), and from the symbolism of being *firstborn* as being in first place (discussed at §3325). Faith is not in first place, however, except in appearance (see §§3539, 3548, 3556, 3563, 3570, 3576, 3603, 3701, 4925, 4926, 4928, 4930, 4977, 6256, 6269, 6272, 6273).

6343   *You are my strength* means that through faith goodness has power. This can be seen from the representation of Reuben, *you,* as a faith that belongs to the intellect (mentioned just above at §6342) and from the symbolism of *strength* as the power that belongs to goodness.

Regarding power—the power to think and will, perceive, do good, believe, disperse falsity and evil—all of it comes from goodness through truth. Goodness is the main force, and truth is only a means (§§3563, 4932, 5623).

The reason the power that belongs to goodness is meant is that *strength* symbolizes that kind of power. *Vigor* symbolizes the power of truth, though, which is why "the beginning of my vigor," the next phrase, symbolizes truth's initial power. The term for vigor in the original language in the Word applies to truth, but the term for strength applies to goodness.

[2] Obviously the Word is holy, and extremely so in its inner depths, since every expression in it contains a heavenly marriage—the marriage of goodness and truth—and therefore heaven itself. Furthermore, the inmost meaning at every point contains the marriage between the Lord's divine humanity and his kingdom and church. In fact, the highest meaning contains the union in the Lord of divinity itself and divine humanity. These features, which are extremely sacred, are present in every detail of the Word—a plain sign that the Word came down from the Divine.

The fact that this is so can be seen from the consideration that where the text speaks of goodness it also speaks of truth, and where it speaks of something inward it also speaks of something outward. What is more, there are words that always symbolize goodness, words that always symbolize truth, and words that symbolize both goodness and truth. Words that do not symbolize goodness and truth at least relate to them or imply them. The implications and symbolism of these words show, as I say, that every detail holds inside it the marriage of goodness and truth, or the heavenly marriage. They also show that in the inmost, highest sense it all contains the divine marriage in the Lord and therefore the Lord himself.

[3] This kind of marriage is present throughout the text, but not very openly, except in places where a single idea is repeated and only the words change. In the current chapter, for instance, where it talks about Reuben, we read: "You are *my strength* and the *beginning of my vigor,*" and "*excelling in prominence* and *excelling in worth.*" *Strength* here relates to goodness and *vigor* to truth. *Excelling in prominence* here relates to truth, and *excelling in worth* to goodness.

The next verse about Reuben contains something similar:

> You climbed onto your father's *beds,* then you profaned them; my *pallet he climbed onto.* (verse 4)

Again later on, concerning Simeon and Levi:

> A curse on *their anger because it is fierce* and on *their wrath because it is hard!* I will *divide them in Jacob* and *scatter them in Israel.* (verse 7)

The anger here symbolizes loathing for what is good, and the wrath, loathing for what is true. Jacob is the outer level of the church and Israel its inner core. Concerning Judah:

> *Your brothers* will celebrate you. *Your father's sons* will bow down to you. (verse 8)

And also:

> He ties *his young donkey to the grapevine* and *his jenny's foal to the rare vine.* He washes *his clothing in wine,* and *his garment in the blood of grapes.* (verse 11)

Concerning Zebulun:

> He will reside at a *harbor on the seas,* and at a *harbor for ships.* (verse 13)

Concerning Dan:

> He will be a *snake on the path, a darting serpent on the track.* (verse 17)

[4] Similar pairs crop up frequently in Psalms and in the Prophets. In Isaiah, for instance:

> Babylon will *be uninhabited forever,* it will *not be lived in for generation after generation. Its time is near* and will come, *and its days will not be prolonged.* (Isaiah 13:20, 22)

In the same author:

> Inquire from above in the book of Jehovah and read. *Not one of them will be missing; they will not lack for one another.* Because *by mouth he himself commanded,* and *his spirit itself gathered them.* And he himself *cast a lot for them,* and *his hand gave shares to them by rule.* To *eternity they will possess it;* to *generation after generation they will live in it.* (Isaiah 34:16, 17)

Likewise in a thousand other passages.

Readers need to know that expressions in the Word symbolize spiritual and heavenly traits and that some words refer to goodness but others to truth. Otherwise they would inevitably believe that the pairs are redundancies, inserted only as filler, and are consequently hollow by definition. As a result, people who view the Word cynically include its repetitiveness among their reasons for contempt. In reality, though, hidden within the repetition is something truly divine: the heavenly marriage (which is heaven itself) and the divine marriage (which is the Lord himself).

This very meaning is the glory that holds the Lord within it, and the literal meaning is the cloud containing that glory (Matthew 24:30, Luke 21:27; see the preface to Genesis 18 and §5922).

6344   *And the beginning of my vigor* means that through faith truth has its initial power. This can be seen from the symbolism of the *beginning of vigor* as initial power. Since *vigor* relates to truth, truth's initial power is what is symbolized, as it also is in Isaiah:

> Jehovah gives the weary person *strength,* and to one who has no *vigor* he multiplies *power.* (Isaiah 40:29)

The strength here applies to goodness and the vigor to truth. The power applies to both.

I need to explain briefly how to understand the idea that through faith, goodness has power, and truth has its initial power, as symbolized by "Reuben, my firstborn, you are my strength and the beginning of my vigor." All power in the spiritual world comes from goodness through truth. Truth can do absolutely nothing without goodness, because truth is like a body and goodness is like that body's soul, just as for the soul to accomplish anything, it must use the body. Clearly, then, truth without goodness has no power whatever, just as the body has no power without a soul. A soulless body is a corpse, and so is truth without goodness.

[2] When goodness first gives birth to a belief in truth, the truth seems to have power. That power is what is being called the power truth initially

has through faith, symbolized by the beginning of vigor. The phrase has the same meaning in other parts of the Word that talk about the firstborn. In David, for instance:

> He struck every firstborn in Egypt, the *beginning of their vigor* in the tents of Ham. (Psalms 78:51)

And in another place:

> He struck every firstborn in their land, the *beginning of all their vigor*. (Psalms 105:36)

And in Deuteronomy:

> [A father] must acknowledge a firstborn son from the hated wife, so as to give him two shares of all that will be found with him [the father], *because [that son] is the beginning of his vigor;* [the son] has the right of the firstborn. (Deuteronomy 21:17)

[3] In its proper sense, the firstborn symbolizes the goodness that results from neighborly love, but in the sense that fits appearances, it symbolizes the truth that composes faith (§§3325, 4925, 4926, 4928, 4930). For this reason, and since these two elements are the foundations of the church, the ancients called a firstborn his father's strength and the beginning of his vigor. Plain evidence for these symbolisms of a firstborn is the fact that every firstborn belonged to Jehovah, or the Lord, and that the tribe of Levi was taken in place of all the firstborn and was given the priesthood.

[4] No one in this world is very likely to know about the power truth has from goodness. It is apt to be known only to the inhabitants of the other world and consequently only by revelation from there. People who subscribe to truth on the basis of goodness—that is, who possess faith as a result of neighborly love—have power through truth from goodness. It is a power that all angels have, which is why the Word refers to angels as powers. They have the ability to control evil spirits, even when one angel goes up against a thousand spirits at once. With people on earth they exert their power to the utmost, sometimes protecting us against a large number of hells in thousands upon thousands of different ways. This power they receive from the goodness belonging to neighborly love through the truth belonging to faith. Faith comes to them from the Lord, though, so the Lord alone is their power.

[5] This power that comes from the Lord by means of faith is meant by the Lord's words to Peter:

> On this rock I will build my church. And the gates of hell will not prevail over it. And I will give you the keys to the kingdom of the heavens; and whatever you bind on earth will be bound in the heavens, and whatever you unbind on earth will be unbound in the heavens. (Matthew 16:18, 19)

These words were addressed to Peter because he represented faith; see the preface to Genesis 22, and §§3750, 4738, 6000, 6073 at the end. In addition, faith is symbolized by "rock" (as Peter is called there) throughout the Word in its inner sense. In the highest sense Peter symbolizes the Lord in regard to faith.

6345   *Excelling in prominence and excelling in worth* means that from these come renown and authority, as the following shows: *Excelling in prominence* symbolizes renown, because anyone who is prominent is renowned, and *excelling in worth* symbolizes authority, because a person of worth carries authority.

The renown here, [or glory,] relates to faith and its truth (§5922). The authority relates to neighborly love and its goodness. That is why I say that renown and authority come *from these*—from the truth taught by faith and the goodness sought by neighborly love, as identified just above.

6346   *Light as water* means that faith alone does not have these properties (prominence and worth). This is clear from the symbolism of being *light as water* as carrying no weight, or worth. The fact that the subject is faith alone, or faith detached from neighborly love, is evident from statements to follow concerning Reuben [§6348] and concerning Simeon and Levi [§6352]. In this chapter, under the figures of Reuben, Simeon, and Levi the text deals with a detached faith, or faith alone.

6347   *Do not excel* means that it also possesses no renown or authority. This can be seen from the symbolism of *not excelling*—not excelling in prominence or worth, as in the phrase just above [§6345], to which this one refers—which means that faith alone possesses no renown or authority.

6348   *For you climbed onto your father's beds* means because when detached from neighborly kindness it forms a disgraceful union. This can be seen from the symbolism of *climbing onto his father's beds* as forming a disgraceful union. It is faith detached from neighborly kindness that forms the union. If a doctrinal, intellectual faith (which is what Reuben represents here) is not introduced into and united with goodness, it either evaporates and disappears or is introduced into and united with evil and falsity. The latter is the disgraceful union symbolized, because it is an act of profanation.

You can see that this is so by considering that faith can have no other dwelling place than goodness. If it has no dwelling place there, inevitably it either disappears or unites with evil.

This is quite plain in the other life. In people who had been committed to faith alone and lacked love for their neighbor, faith evaporates there, but if they had combined that faith with evil, they find their lot with the profane.

[2] In the Word's inner meaning, adultery symbolizes adulteration of what is good, and whoredom symbolizes falsification of what is true (§§2466, 3399). However, the disgraceful unions that are called degrees of forbidden relations (dealt with in Leviticus 18:6–24) symbolize various types of profanation. Profanation is involved here [in Genesis 49:4] as well, of course, because the text says, "You climbed onto your father's beds, *then you profaned them; my pallet he climbed onto." What is being referred to is the profanation of goodness through detached faith, as may be seen in §4601, where this unspeakable deed of Reuben's is discussed.

[3] Here is the situation with faith alone, or faith detached from charity: If we start out believing in religious truth, and especially if we start out living by it, but then deny and live contrary to it, we combine faith alone with evil. When we do, profanation occurs. At that first stage, you see, religious truth and charitable goodness become rooted in our inner depths through the teachings we accept and the life we live. Then we call them forth from there and bind them to evil. People who do this suffer the worst lot of all in the other life, because goodness cannot be separated from evil in them, in spite of the fact that they *are* separated in the other life. Such people also have no remnant of goodness stored up in their inner reaches, because all remaining traces of it have perished in wickedness. Their hell is out in front and off to the left a long way away. To angelic eyes the inhabitants look like skeletons, almost devoid of life.

To prevent the profanation of goodness and truth, then, people who by nature will not allow themselves to be reborn (and the Lord foresees this) are withheld from faith and neighborly love and are permitted to remain in evil and therefore in falsity. Then they cannot profane anything. (See what has been said and demonstrated before concerning profanation, §§301, 302, 303, 571, 582, 593, 1001, 1008, 1010, 1059, 1327, 1328, 2051, 2426, 3398, 3399, 3402, 3479, 3898, 4289, 4601.)

6349   *Then you profaned them* means that if [faith alone] unites with evil, profanation results. This is evident from the remarks just above at §6348.

6350   *My pallet he climbed onto* means that it has polluted spiritual goodness on the earthly level. This is established by the symbolism of *climbing onto the pallet* as polluting something by profaning it (discussed just above at §6348) and from the representation of Israel, whose pallet it was that Reuben climbed onto, as spiritual goodness on the earthly level (mentioned at §6340).

6351   Genesis 49:5, 6, 7. *"Simeon and Levi are brothers; tools of violence are their blades. Into their conspiracy my soul is not to come; with their band my glory is not to unite, because in their anger they killed a man, and in their good pleasure they hamstrung an ox. A curse on their anger because it is fierce and on their wrath because it is hard! I will divide them in Jacob and scatter them in Israel."*

Simeon and Levi are brothers symbolizes a faith that belongs to the will, and neighborly love, but the opposite here, because what is being symbolized is faith detached from neighborly love. *Tools of violence are their blades* means that doctrinal teachings serve to destroy works of neighborly love and therefore neighborly love itself. *Into their conspiracy my soul is not to come* means that spiritual goodness does not want to know about the evil in their will. *With their band my glory is not to unite* means that neither does the truth belonging to spiritual goodness want to know about the resulting falsity in their thinking. *Because in their anger they killed a man* means that they turned their backs completely and in doing so extinguished faith. *And in their good pleasure they hamstrung an ox* means that with base intent they utterly crippled the outer goodness that comes of charity. *A curse on their anger because it is fierce* symbolizes a strong aversion to goodness, and consequent damnation. *And on their wrath because it is hard* symbolizes an aversion to the consequent truth—a confirmed aversion. *I will divide them in Jacob* means that such things have to be eliminated from the earthly self. *And scatter them in Israel* means that they have to be eliminated from the spiritual self.

6352   *Simeon and Levi are brothers* symbolizes a faith that belongs to the will, and neighborly love, but the opposite here, because what is being symbolized is faith detached from neighborly love, as the following shows: *Simeon* represents a faith that belongs to the will, as discussed in §§3869, 3870, 3871, 3872, 4497, 4502, 4503, 5482, 5626, 5630. And *Levi* represents charity, as discussed in §§3875, 3877. Here they symbolize the opposite, though, because they symbolize faith detached from charity. When Reuben symbolizes such faith, as the explanation at verse 4 shows he does, it follows that there is no faith belonging to the will and accordingly no neighborly love, these two qualities being represented by Simeon and Levi. That is because they follow in a series from their starting point. So Simeon represents falsity that belongs to the will, and Levi represents evil put into action, since these are the opposite of faith that belongs to the will and neighborly love. The fact that Simeon and Levi are being cursed shows that this is the meaning.

Tools of violence are their blades means that doctrinal teachings serve **6353** to destroy works of neighborly love and therefore neighborly love itself, as the following shows: *Tools of violence* symbolize something that serves to destroy neighborly love. Plainly *tools* are something that serves, and soon I will show that *violence* is the destruction of neighborly love. And *blades* symbolize doctrinal teachings. Swords mean religious truth used for battling falsity and evil (§2799), so blades mean doctrinal teachings. Here they are doctrinal teachings used for battling truth and goodness and for wiping them out, because the teachings are wielded by people committed to faith alone, or to faith separated from neighborly love, in whom the meaning is negative.

[2] The teachings by which people devoted to faith alone do away with works of neighborly kindness are mainly these: We are saved by faith alone without acts of neighborly love, and such acts are not imperative. Faith alone saves us even in the final hour of death, no matter how we lived during the entire course of our life. This means that we are saved even if we practiced nothing but cruelty, theft, adultery, or profanation. Salvation therefore is simply being let into heaven, so admission to heaven is limited to those of us who have received that favor at the end of our lives. Some of us have been mercifully chosen, then, and some have been ruthlessly damned.

The reality, though, is that the Lord denies heaven to no one. What makes it impossible for people to be in heaven is rather their life force and the communication of this life force, sensed there the way a smell is sensed on earth by people exposed to it. The evil of their own life tortures such people more in heaven than it would in the deepest hell.

[3] It is clear in John that a *blade* symbolizes falsity fighting and killing:

> There went out another horse, red, and the one sitting on it was granted
> to take peace away from the earth *so that people would kill each other;* so
> *a large blade was given to this one.* (Revelation 6:4)

In the same author:

> If anyone *kills with a blade,* that person must be *killed with a blade.*
> (Revelation 13:10, 14)

[4] The meaning of *violence* as abuse inflicted on neighborly love is clear from many scriptural passages. In Isaiah, for example:

> *The violent will cease to exist,* and the scornful will come to an end; all will be cut off who rush judgment, who with their words make people sin, and they ensnare their accuser in the gate and turn judgment aside in the morning. (Isaiah 29:20, 21)

The word for a violent person in the original language here is different but has the same meaning. The idea that the violent are those who inflict abuse on neighborly love is symbolized by the statements that with their words they make people sin and that they turn judgment aside. [5] In the same author:

> Their works are works of wickedness, and *an act of violence is in their hands.* Their feet run to evil, and they hurry *to shed innocent blood.*
> (Isaiah 59:6, 7)

The violence here stands for abuse inflicted on neighborly love, an abusiveness also symbolized by the shedding of blood (see §§374, 1005). In the same author:

> *There will no longer be violence in the land,* devastation or wreckage within your borders. (Isaiah 60:18)

The violence stands for the destruction of neighborly love, which is the cause of devastation and wreckage in the land, that is, the church. [6] In Jeremiah:

> *Violence* and devastation I proclaim, because the word of Jehovah has become a reproach and insult to me all day. (Jeremiah 20:8)

Again the violence stands for spiritual violence and consequently for the destruction of charity and of faith. In Ezekiel:

> The earth is full of *judgment on [crimes of] blood,* and the city is *full of violence.* (Ezekiel 7:23)

The judgment on [crimes of] blood stands for the destruction of faith, the violence for the destruction of charity. [7] In the same author:

> If he produces a *violent son, a shedder of blood,* who does one of any of these things—if he eats on the mountains, or defiles the wife of a companion, oppresses the wretched and needy, plunders plunder, does not

restore collateral, or lifts his eyes to idols, does something abominable, lends at a profit and charges interest—shall he live? He shall not live; he shall surely die. (Ezekiel 18:10, 11, 12, 13)

This passage describes what a violent son and shedder of blood is. The behaviors listed are all the works of neighborly love that such a person destroys. A violent son and shedder of blood is therefore a destroyer of charity and faith. [8] In David:

Deliver me, Jehovah, from the evil person; *from the man of violence preserve me,* [from those] who think evil in their heart—all day they gather for war. They sharpen their tongue like a snake; the venom of an asp is on their lips. Guard me, Jehovah, from the hands of the ungodly person; *from the man of violence preserve me.* Do not let a man with a [slandering] tongue endure on the earth! A *man of violence* hunts evil to the point of ruination. (Psalms 140:1, 2, 3, 4, 11)

The man of violence stands for people who destroy the truth taught by faith and the goodness sought by neighborly love. Their assault on these qualities is symbolized by "all day they gather for war," "they sharpen their tongue like a snake," "the venom of an asp is on their lips," and "he hunts evil to the point of ruination."

There are [instances of "violence"] elsewhere too, such as Ezekiel 12:19; Joel 3:19; Malachi 2:16, 17; Zephaniah 3:4; Psalms 18:48; 55:9, 10, 11; 58:2, 3, 4, 5; Deuteronomy 19:16.

Into their conspiracy my soul is not to come means that spiritual goodness does not want to know about the evil in their will. This can be seen from the representation of Israel, who says this about himself, as spiritual goodness (mentioned at §6340) and from the symbolism of *into their conspiracy may it not come* as not wanting to know—to know about evil in the will (the will being symbolized by Simeon and Levi, §6352). The text speaks of *my soul* because the soul here symbolizes the living type of goodness that spiritual goodness has. The living type of truth that it has is symbolized by "glory," which is discussed just below.

With their band my glory is not to unite means that neither does the truth belonging to spiritual goodness want to know about the resulting falsity in their thinking, as the following shows: Israel represents spiritual goodness, as noted in §6340. *With their band it is not to unite* symbolizes not wanting to link up with the false ideas in their thinking and therefore not wanting to know about them either. The falsity in their thinking is symbolized by the *band,* because like a throng a band is mentioned

6354

6355

in connection with truth, and in a negative sense with falsity. The symbolism of *glory* too has to do with truth (as discussed in §§4809, 5922), because to people with spiritual goodness, truth is glory.

6356   *Because in their anger they killed a man* means that they turned their backs completely and in doing so extinguished faith, as the following shows: *Anger* symbolizes a departure from neighborly love and therefore a turning away from [or aversion to] it, as discussed in §§357, 5034, 5798. *Killing* means extinguishing. And a *man* symbolizes faith and its truth (discussed in §§3134, 3309, 3459, 4823).

6357   *And in their good pleasure they hamstrung an ox* means that with base intent they utterly crippled the outer goodness that comes of charity. This can be seen from the symbolism of *good pleasure* as intent, and here as base intent; from that of *hamstringing* as crippling; and from that of an *ox* as the outer, earthly goodness that comes of charity (discussed in §§2180, 2566, 2781).

An ox is spoken of here and a man just above because a man symbolizes the truth belonging to faith and an ox the goodness belonging to neighborly love. The purpose in mentioning both is for truth to be addressed whenever goodness is, on account of the heavenly marriage in every detail of the Word (§6343).

6358   *A curse on their anger because it is fierce* symbolizes a strong aversion to goodness, and consequent damnation, as the following shows: A *curse* symbolizes damnation, since anyone who is cursed is damned. And *anger* symbolizes an aversion to goodness, as dealt with in §§357, 5034, 5798, 6356, so *fierce anger* means a strong aversion.

6359   *And on their wrath because it is hard* symbolizes an aversion to the consequent truth—a confirmed aversion, as the following shows: *Wrath* symbolizes an aversion to truth. For the relationship of wrath to truth and of anger to goodness, see §3614. And *hard* means confirmed, because falsity that is confirmed to the point of conviction is hard. Experience has taught me that it is hard, since in spirits and angels, truth born of goodness appears and presents itself as soft, but falsity born of evil as hard. The more fully such falsity has been confirmed, the harder it appears. When it has been confirmed by so many proofs that it becomes conviction, it seems as hard as bone there.

This rigidity resembles physical hardness, because rays of light bounce off a hard object. So when heavenly light from the Lord falls on the hardness of falsity-from-evil, it is turned back, but when the same light falls on the softness of truth-from-goodness, it is absorbed.

I will divide them in Jacob means that such things have to be elim- **6360**
inated from the earthly self. This can be seen from the symbolism of
dividing as separating and isolating something from truth and goodness
(discussed at §4424) and therefore as eliminating it, and from the representation of *Jacob* as the earthly, outer self (discussed in §§3305, 3576,
4286, 4292, 4570, 6236).

And scatter them in Israel means that they have to be eliminated from **6361**
the spiritual self. This can be seen from the symbolism of *scattering* too
as eliminating. The difference between scattering and dividing is that the
latter word is used for the outer self and for truth, the former for the
inner self and for goodness. Jacob represents the earthly, outer self, and
Israel the spiritual, inner self; see §§4286, 4292, 4570.

These statements of Israel's about Simeon and Levi and about Reuben
do not refer to what would happen to their descendants at the end of days,
as verse 1 says they do. Notice that in actuality Simeon's and Levi's descendants were not cursed or divided in Jacob or scattered in Israel. The tribe
of Simeon lived among the other tribes as one of them; and the tribe of
Levi became the priests, so it was blessed rather than cursed. Likewise the
tribe of Reuben, which was no lowlier than other tribes. This is plain evidence that what the chapter said would happen to the children of Jacob at
the end of days is not what was going to happen to those actual people
but to the people meant by them in an inner sense. The current set of
verses tells what was going to happen to people who possess a faith detached
from neighborly love, because they are the people meant in an inner sense
here by Reuben, Simeon, and Levi.

Obviously, then, there is an inner meaning to the Word that is invisible in the literal meaning. It is also invisible to anyone who does not
know how physical and spiritual phenomena correspond, and utterly
invisible to anyone who does not know what the spiritual and heavenly
dimension is.

Genesis 49:8, 9, 10, 11, 12. *"You are Judah; your brothers will celebrate* **6362**
you. Your hand is on your enemies' neck; your father's sons will bow down
to you. A lion's cub is Judah; fed with prey, my son, you have risen. He
crouched; he lay like a lion and like an aging lion. Who will arouse him?
The scepter will not be taken from Judah, or a lawgiver from between his
feet, until Shiloh comes; and to him will be the obedience of the peoples. He
ties his young donkey to the grapevine and his jenny's foal to the rare vine.
He washes his clothing in wine, and his garment in the blood of grapes. He
is red of eye from wine and white of teeth from milk."

You are Judah symbolizes a heavenly religion, and in the highest sense the Lord's heavenly divinity. *Your brothers will celebrate you* means that this religion is more prominent than any others. *Your hand is on your enemies' neck* means that the hellish, devilish horde will flee at its presence. *Your father's sons will bow down to you* means that truth will spontaneously subject itself. *A lion's cub is Judah* symbolizes innocence containing inborn powers. *Fed with prey, my son, you have risen* symbolizes the deliverance of many from hell by the Lord through what is heavenly. *He crouched; he lay like a lion and like an aging lion* symbolizes a loving goodness and the resulting truth, in their power. *Who will arouse him?* means that [a person with heavenly goodness] is safe among everyone in the hells. *The scepter will not be taken from Judah* means that authority will not depart from the heavenly kingdom. *Or a lawgiver from between his feet* symbolizes truth from that kingdom, on lower levels. *Until Shiloh comes* symbolizes the Lord's Coming and the peace and tranquillity then. *And to him will be the obedience of the peoples* means that his divine humanity will exude truth. *He ties his young donkey to the grapevine* symbolizes truth on the earthly plane for the outer part of the church. *And his jenny's foal to the rare vine* symbolizes truth on the rational plane for the inner part of the church. *He washes his clothing in wine* means that his earthly level consists in divine truth growing out of his divine goodness. *And his garment in the blood of grapes* means that his intellectual plane consists in divine goodness growing out of his divine love. *He is red of eye from wine* means that his intellect, or his inner human nature, is pure goodness. *And white of teeth from milk* means that his earthly divinity is pure truth-based goodness.

6363   *You are Judah* symbolizes a heavenly religion, and in the highest sense the Lord's heavenly divinity. This can be seen from the representation of *Judah* in the highest sense as the Lord's divine love, or his heavenly divinity, but in a secondary sense as the Lord's heavenly kingdom and therefore a heavenly religion, as discussed at §3881. For a definition of the heavenly kingdom or a heavenly religion and of the heavenly quality itself, see §§640, 641, 765, 895, 2048, 2088, 2669, 2708, 2715, 2718, 2896, 3235, 3246, 3374, 3886, 3887, 4448, 4493, 5113, 5922, 6295.

6364   *Your brothers will celebrate you* means that this religion is more prominent than any others, as the following shows: Being *celebrated* means being prominent. Judah, *you,* represents a heavenly religion, as noted just above at §6363. And *brothers* symbolize the truth known to that religion, so they also symbolize religions adhering to the kinds of truth represented by Judah's brothers (since a religion is made up of truth and goodness).

Your (Judah's) *brothers* symbolize the truth known to a heavenly religion, but his father's sons symbolize the truth known to a spiritual religion (below at §6366).

Your hand is on your enemies' neck means that the hellish, devilish **6365** horde will flee at its presence, as the following shows: *Enemies* symbolize the hellish, devilish horde, these being one's enemies in a spiritual sense. And a *hand on their neck* symbolizes pursuit of people who are in flight, because when enemies flee, the hand of their conqueror is on their neck. The reason for saying they will flee at the presence [of the heavenly religion] is that when any of hell's crew approach an angel from the Lord's heavenly kingdom, they flee at that angel's presence. They cannot endure it, because they cannot endure an atmosphere of heavenly love, which is an atmosphere of love for the Lord. To hellish spirits such an aura is like a scorching, tormenting fire.

Besides, heavenly angels never fight, let alone put their hand on the neck of their enemies. In fact, for their own part they do not even consider anyone an enemy. Still, the text expresses it this way because that is what happens in the world. The meaning nonetheless is that the hellish, who for their own part *are* inimical, flee at the angels' presence.

Your father's sons will bow down to you means that truth will spon- **6366** taneously subject itself. This can be seen from the symbolism of *bowing down* as subjecting oneself and from that of *your father's sons* as truth springing from spiritual goodness. After all, Israel's sons stand for spiritual truth (§§5414, 5879, 5951), and Israel stands for spiritual goodness (§§5801, 5803, 5807, 5812, 5817, 5819, 5826, 5833).

The reason this truth subjects itself spontaneously is that when heavenly love (represented by Judah) acts on spiritual truths (represented by Israel's sons), it arranges them in order and in the process makes them subject to the Lord. Something heavenly has the ability to produce this effect through its inflow into what is spiritual; that is, goodness can produce this effect through its inflow into truth. What is more, the Lord's heavenly kingdom is consequently the third or inmost heaven and is therefore closest to the Lord. His spiritual kingdom is the second or middle heaven and is therefore farther from the Lord. As a result of this arrangement, the Lord acts on the spiritual kingdom indirectly, through the heavenly kingdom, in addition to acting directly on it. The nature of the inflow is such that the spiritual kingdom is kept in order through the heavenly and in this way is made subject to the Lord.

The heavenly kingdom flows into the spiritual through love for one's neighbor. Neighborly love is the outer level of the heavenly kingdom and the inner level of the spiritual kingdom, and this circumstance unites the two; see §5922.

6367   *A lion's cub is Judah* symbolizes innocence containing inborn powers. This can be seen from the symbolism of a *lion,* which means a loving goodness and the truth it gives rise to, in all their might (discussed below). A lion's *cub,* then, means innocence with certain powers. The reason inborn powers are meant is that Judah here stands for heavenly love, and heavenly love is located in our volitional side (§§895, 927, 4493, 5113), so it has inborn powers. This is because we are born into the capacities of our volitional side. As a consequence, the people of the earliest church, which was heavenly, were born into a loving goodness, so far as they had goodness in their volitional side. This then is why the powers are described as inborn.

A lion's cub stands for innocence because a lion stands for the goodness that goes with heavenly love, and a cub is more or less the infant of that kind of goodness, so it stands for innocence.

[2] Passages in the Word that mention a lion show that it stands for the goodness that comes of heavenly love and for the truth this gives rise to, in all their might, and in a negative sense for the evil that comes of self-love, in all its might. The goodness that comes of heavenly love is meant in John:

> Look: *the lion who is from the tribe of Judah,* the root of David, *was victorious* in opening the book and undoing its seven seals. (Revelation 5:5)

The Lord is called a lion here because of the omnipotence belonging to his divine love and therefore to his divine truth. Jehovah, or the Lord, is compared to a lion in other parts of the Word as well, such as Hosea:

> They will walk after Jehovah. *Like a lion he will roar,* because *he will roar* and his children will approach respectfully from [the direction of] the sea. (Hosea 11:10)

[3] And in Isaiah:

> This is what Jehovah has said to me: "As the *lion roars*—and the *young lion*—over its prey, when an abundance of shepherds happens upon it, by whose voice [the lion] is not dismayed and by whose commotion

it is not distressed; so Jehovah Sabaoth will come down to do battle on Zion's mountain and on its hill." (Isaiah 31:4)

In this passage the omnipotence of divine goodness is compared to a lion, and the omnipotence of the divine truth stemming from it to a young lion, because it says that Jehovah Sabaoth will come down to wage war on Zion's mountain and on its hill. Zion's mountain symbolizes the goodness sought by divine love, and its hill symbolizes the divine truth stemming from it (§§795, 796, 1430, 4210).

[4] In consequence, the four living creatures in Ezekiel and in John (a living creature meaning a guardian being) had the faces of a human, lion, ox, and eagle. In Ezekiel:

> The likeness of the faces of the four living creatures: the face of a human, and the *face of a lion* on the right for the four of them, and the face of an ox for the four of them on the left, and the face of an eagle for the four of them. (Ezekiel 1:10; 10:14)

And in John:

> In front of the throne were four living creatures full of eyes in front and behind, and the *first living creature like a lion,* the second living creature like a calf, the third living creature having a face like a human, the fourth living creature like a flying eagle. (Revelation 4:6, 7)

Chapter 10 of Ezekiel shows that these living creatures were guardian beings, and the fact is clear from John's description of them as having eyes in front and behind, because guardian beings symbolize the Lord's foresight and providence (§308). They had the face of a lion because of the omnipotence of divine truth growing out of divine goodness, which is the omnipotence of providence. The same is true of the guardian beings around the new temple in Ezekiel 41:[18,] 19.

[5] Heavenly people, who have power from the goodness and consequent truth they receive from the Lord, are meant by lions, as is clear in David:

> There will be no lack for those who fear Jehovah; *young lions* will go without and starve, but those who seek Jehovah will not lack anything good. (Psalms 34:9, 10)

In the same author:

> *Lions are roaring for prey* and to seek food from God. The sun rises, they gather and recline in their dens. (Psalms 104:21, 22)

In the prophecy of Balaam:

> At that time it will be said to Jacob and Israel, "What has God done?"
> Watch: a people will rise like an *old lion* and lift itself like a *young lion;*
> it will not rest until it eats its prey. (Numbers 23:23, 24)

[6] And further on:

> When Balaam saw Israel dwelling by its tribes, he said, *"He crouches,*
> *he lies like a lion,* and like an *old lion. Who will arouse him?"* (Numbers
> 24:2, 9)

It is the heavenly dimension that is being depicted here, because it is the
heavenly pattern—represented by the tribes in their encampments—that
Balaam saw in the spirit when he saw Israel dwelling by its tribes (§6335).
The heavenly pattern comes from divine goodness by way of divine truth,
received from the Lord. It contains all power, which in this passage is the
lion that crouches and lies. [7] In Micah:

> The survivors of Jacob will live among the nations, in the middle of
> many peoples, *like a lion among the animals of the forest,* like a *young lion*
> among flocks of sheep, which, if it passes through them, will trample
> and scatter them, and none rescuing. Your hand will be lifted over your
> foes, and all your enemies will be cut off. (Micah 5:8, 9)

The lion and *young lion* here stand for heavenly goodness and heavenly
truth, which is what the survivors of Jacob are. A lion or young lion
stands for something similar in Isaiah 21:8; Jeremiah 25:38; Ezekiel 38:13;
Zechariah 11:3. The same thing was also represented by the *lions* on
Solomon's ivory throne, *two* next to the arms of the throne, and *twelve*
on the six steps (1 Kings 10:18, 19, 20), and by the *lions* on the rails of
the ten stands of bronze (1 Kings 7:29, 36).

[8] The negative symbolism of a lion as the evil that comes of self-
love, in all its might, is evident from the following passages. In Isaiah:

> *No lion will be there,* and the ravenous of the wild animals will not go
> up on it; they will not be found there. But free people will walk there;
> thus those ransomed by Jehovah will return and come to Zion with
> song. (Isaiah 35:9, 10)

In Jeremiah:

> Why has Israel become plunder? *Against him roar the young lions,* they
> utter their voice, they reduce his land to a wasteland. (Jeremiah 2:14, 15)

In the same author:

> The lion has gone up from its briar patch, and the destroyer of nations has set out, has left its place, to reduce the land to a wasteland. (Jeremiah 4:7)

In the same author:

> They did not know the way of Jehovah, the judgment of their God, so a *lion from the forest* has struck them, and a wolf of the plains will devastate them. (Jeremiah 5:4, 6)

In Nahum:

> Where is the den of *lions* and the pasture of *young lions?* Where did the *lion,* the *old lion,* the *lion cub* walk, and none frightening them? *The lion is capturing enough for the cubs,* and strangling [enough] for *his old lionesses,* and filling his holes with prey and his dens with capture. "Here, now, I am against you," says Jehovah Sabaoth, "and I will ignite their chariot with smoke, and a sword will devour *your young lions.* And I will cut off your prey from the earth." (Nahum 2:11, 12, 13)

This is about Nineveh. In these passages the lion stands for the strength that the evil growing out of self-love has when it destroys and lays waste. The meaning is the same in Jeremiah 12:8; 49:19; 50:17, 44; 51:38; Ezekiel 19:2–9; 32:2; Joel 1:6; Zephaniah 3:3; Psalms 57:4; 58:6; 91:13; Revelation 13:2.

Fed with prey, my son, you have risen symbolizes the deliverance of **6368** many from hell by the Lord through what is heavenly. This can be seen from the symbolism of *rising fed with prey* as deliverance from hell (discussed below) and from the representation of Judah, *my son,* as heavenly divinity (mentioned at §6363).

Here is why *rising fed with prey* means deliverance from hell: On our own we live in hell, because a self-centered will and self-centered thoughts are nothing but evil and the resulting falsity, which bind us so tightly to hell that we can be torn away only by force. This tearing away and deliverance is what is called prey. The Lord's divine goodness accomplishes this, and that is why I speak of deliverance of many from hell by the Lord through what is heavenly.

[2] Bear in mind, though, that no one can be torn away and delivered from hell who was not led during bodily life to spiritual goodness, that is, to neighborly love through faith. Unless a person has been led by faith to that kind of goodness, there is nothing that can hold the goodness flowing in from the Lord. It flows right through, with no place to

attach. People like this are therefore unable to be wrenched from hell, or delivered from it. In the next life we keep all the states of mind we acquired during bodily life, and they are amplified. Good people keep their good states of mind, which are amplified with more goodness and lift the people to heaven. Evil people keep their evil states of mind, which are amplified with more evil and drag the people down to hell. That is how the saying goes: as we die, so we remain. This shows who can be delivered from hell by the Lord through divine heavenliness.

6369 *He crouched; he lay like a lion and like an aging lion* symbolizes a loving goodness and the resulting truth, in their power, as the following shows: *Crouching* means putting oneself in a powerful position, because when a lion crouches, it tenses its muscles and gathers its strength; and it does this when it catches sight of prey. *Lying* means lying down in safety, free of fear. And a *lion* and an *aging lion* symbolize a loving goodness and the resulting truth, in their power, as discussed just above at §6367. A young lion is a person who has power through truth from goodness, and an aging lion is a person who has power directly through goodness. People with heavenly goodness never fight; goodness keeps them safe. Wherever such people go, the evil flee, unable to bear their presence (see §6365). These are the people symbolized by an aging lion.

6370 *Who will arouse him?* means that [a person with heavenly goodness] is safe among everyone in the hells, as can be seen from the fact that *who will arouse?* means being safe.

"Among everyone in the hells" is meant because such a person is safe in the midst of all evil, even in the middle of the hells. Love for the Lord and love for one's neighbor carry this safety with them, because people who have such love are closely united with the Lord and are in the Lord, since they are in the divine quality that emanates from him. So nothing bad can touch them.

Please be aware that there are countless hells, divided up according to all the different categories, subcategories, and individual types of evil and resulting falsity. Each hell is organized, and the Lord keeps it organized, both directly and indirectly, through heavenly angels. Sometimes angels are also sent to a hell to reduce the chaos there to order, and while they are there, they are safe. That is what is meant by the statement that a person with a heavenly quality is safe among everyone in the hells.

6371 *The scepter will not be taken from Judah* means that authority will not depart from the heavenly kingdom, as the following shows: *Being taken* means departing. A *scepter* symbolizes authority, and specifically the authority that goodness lends to truth, as discussed at the end of §4876. A scepter is an emblem of royal authority, after all, and royalty symbolizes truth (§§1672, 1728, 2015, 2069, 3009, 4575, 6148). And *Judah* represents the heavenly kingdom, as dealt with above at §6363. This demonstrates that *the scepter will not be taken from Judah* means that authority will not depart from the heavenly kingdom.

From the literal meaning it appears as though the verse is saying that the monarchy would not be taken from the Jewish people until the Lord came, and this is true, but as a piece of history (like all the rest of the history) it has an inner meaning. The idea that the monarchy would be taken from the Jewish people at the Lord's Coming is a worldly element. The spiritual element, which belongs to the inner meaning, becomes clear when the scepter is taken to mean authority, and Judah to mean the heavenly kingdom.

[2] The concept that authority would depart from the heavenly kingdom when the Lord came is a secret no one can know without revelation. Here is the situation: Before the Lord's arrival in the world, life flowing into people and into spirits from Jehovah (the Lord) came through the heavenly kingdom—that is, through angels in the heavenly kingdom. This lent the angels the power they then had. When the Lord came into the world, though, he made the humanity in himself divine and in doing so took on the role played by the angels of the heavenly kingdom. So he took on the power that had been theirs. Up till then, you see, the divine inflow coming through that heaven had been [the Lord's] human divinity and was also the divine human being that appeared when Jehovah presented himself in human form. But this human divinity came to an end when the Lord himself made the humanity in himself divine.

From this discussion you can see how matters stand with the secret here.

The angels of the heavenly kingdom do still have tremendous authority, but they have it to the extent that they are in the Lord's divine humanity because they love him.

See previous remarks and discussion on this topic in §§1990, 2803, 3061, 4180, 4687, 5110, 6280.

Or a lawgiver from between his feet symbolizes truth from that kingdom, on lower levels. This can be seen from the symbolism of a *lawgiver* as truth (discussed in what follows) and from that of *feet* as something earthly (discussed in §§2162, 3147, 3761, 3986, 4280, 4938–4952, 5328) and therefore as lower levels. Earthly attributes lie below; heavenly attributes (the previous topic of discussion) lie above.

6372

The phrase a *lawgiver from between the feet* is used to symbolize heavenly spirituality, or truth as a product of goodness. At that time there was no spiritual kingdom distinct from the heavenly kingdom, as there has been since the Lord's Coming. Rather the spiritual kingdom was one with the heavenly, except that it was the outer part. For that reason, "from between the feet" is part of the phrase, so that it can symbolize truth from goodness. This is what the inner part of the lower leg symbolizes, because of the way it communicates with the genital area.

The text is saying that when Shiloh came this kind of truth would also be taken away, or rather its authority would, just as the heavenly authority discussed just above at §6371 would. The heavenly kingdom exercised its power through truth-from-goodness at that time, and because it did so, such truth is called a lawgiver.

[2] Truth-from-goodness is meant by a lawgiver in an inner sense in Isaiah too:

> Jehovah is our judge; *Jehovah is our lawgiver;* Jehovah is our monarch. (Isaiah 33:22)

When Jehovah is called a judge, it means he acts out of goodness. When he is called a lawgiver, it means he acts out of truth-from-goodness. When he is called a monarch, it means he acts out of truth. And the three follow in that order. In David:

> I own Gilead, I own Manasseh, and Ephraim is the strength of my head; *Judah is my lawgiver.* (Psalms 60:7; 108:8)

Judah as lawgiver stands for heavenly goodness and the heavenly truth that goes with it. In Moses:

> A spring: the chieftains dug, the nobles of the people excavated, *by [the word of] the Lawgiver,* with their staffs. (Numbers 21:18)

And in the same author:

> Gad saw to some firstfruits for himself, since that is where the lot of the *hidden lawgiver* lies, for which reason the heads of the people came. He carried out Jehovah's justice and his judgments for Israel. (Deuteronomy 33:21)

Here too the lawgiver stands for truth-from-goodness.

6373   *Until Shiloh comes* symbolizes the Lord's Coming and the peace and tranquillity then. This is evident from the symbolism of *Shiloh* as the

Lord. He is called Shiloh because he brought peace and tranquillity to everything, since in the original language, "Shiloh" comes from a word that means tranquillity. The reason the Lord is called Shiloh here can be seen from the remarks just above at §§6371, 6372 about the heavenly kingdom and its authority. Intranquillity prevailed when the divine presence was manifested through that kingdom, because neither in heaven nor in hell could conditions be reduced into order through it. Divinity flowing through the heavenly kingdom could not remain pure, since heaven is not pure and the heavenly kingdom is therefore not strong enough for everything to be kept in order by means of it. As a consequence, infernal and diabolical spirits at that time climbed up out of hell and gained control over souls coming from the world. [2] The result was that none could then be saved except the heavenly. Eventually even they could barely have been saved had not the Lord taken on a human nature and made this humanity in himself divine. By these means the Lord reduced everything to order—first everything in heaven, then everything in the hells. Peace and tranquillity resulted.

On the following subjects, see the sections cited: Spiritual people—in other words, people in a spiritual religion—were saved by the Lord's Coming (§§2661, 2716, 2833, 2834). When the Lord was in the world, he reduced everything into order (§§1820, 4287). Divine truth from Jehovah (the Lord) flowed through heaven into the human race, but this was inadequate once people abandoned what was good. So the Lord came into the world and made the human nature in himself divine. His purpose was for divine truth to radiate from his own divine humanity and in this way save humankind, which would receive goodness by means of truth (§§4180, 6280).

And to him will be the obedience of the peoples means that his divine humanity would exude truth that could be accepted, as the following shows: *Obedience* symbolizes acceptance of truth that comes from the Lord. And *peoples* symbolize those who subscribe to truth, so they also symbolize truth itself (treated of in §§1259, 1260, 3581) and accordingly people in a spiritual religion (§2928).

6374

He ties his young donkey to the grapevine symbolizes truth on the earthly plane for the outer part of the church, as the following indicates: *Tying to* means uniting. A *grapevine* symbolizes a spiritual church, as discussed in §§1069, 5113. Here it symbolizes the outer part of a spiritual church, because a rare vine (spoken of next) symbolizes the inner part. And a *young donkey* symbolizes truth on the earthly plane (discussed at §2781).

6375

This shows that *he ties his young donkey to the grapevine* symbolizes union with the outer part of the church through truth on the earthly level.

6376   *And his jenny's foal to the rare vine* symbolizes truth on the rational plane for the inner part of the church, as the following shows: A grapevine symbolizes a spiritual church, as discussed in §§1069, 5113, so a *rare vine* symbolizes the inner part of a church, because the inner part is of a rarer quality than the outer. And a *jenny's foal* symbolizes rational truth, as discussed at §2781.

The distinction between the outer and inner aspects of a religion is that the outer part is on the earthly level and therefore exists in a person's outer self, but the inner aspect is on the rational level and therefore exists in the inner self. People in the outer part of a church are intent on truth, but those in the inner part are intent on what is good. The former respond less to charitable goodness than to religious truth, while the latter respond to charitable goodness and in consequence to religious truth. The latter are the ones symbolized by the rare vine, the former by the grapevine.

6377   *He washes his clothing in wine* means that his earthly level consists in divine truth growing out of his divine goodness, as the following shows: *Washing* means purifying, as discussed at §3147. *Wine* symbolizes the doing of good out of neighborly love and the doing of good out of faith, and in the highest sense it symbolizes divine truth from the Lord's divine goodness, as discussed below. And *clothing* symbolizes something outward that covers something inward, as discussed at §5248. As a result it symbolizes the earthly level, since this is outward and forms a covering for the rational level, which is within. Clothing also symbolizes truth, then, since truth is more external, and provides a covering for inner goodness (§§2576, 4545, 4763, 5319, 5954).

[2] The fact that *wine* means love for one's neighbor and the doing of good out of faith is evident from the explanation in §§2165, 2177, 3464, 4581, 5915 concerning the bread and wine of the Holy Supper. The explanation showed that bread means goodness that comes of heavenly love and wine goodness that comes of spiritual love.

The same thing can be seen from the minha and libation of the sacrifices. The sacrificial minha symbolized goodness that comes of love and the libation goodness that comes of faith. The minha consisted of ingredients that symbolized love's goodness, while the libation consisted of wine, which symbolized faith's goodness. The sacrifices themselves were even referred to as bread (§2165). For the use of a libation of wine in the sacrifices, see Exodus 29:40; Leviticus 23:12, 13, 18, 19; Numbers 15:2–15; 28:6, 7, 18–end; 29:1–7 and following verses.

[3] The symbolism of wine as love for one's neighbor and the doing of good out of faith is also clear in Isaiah:

> Everyone who is thirsty, come to the water, and whoever does not have silver, come, buy and eat, and come, without silver and without the price buy *wine* and milk! (Isaiah 55:1)

It is impossible not to see that they were not to buy wine and milk but that which wine and milk symbolize: love for their neighbor and faith. These the Lord gives without silver or price. [4] In Hosea:

> Threshing floor and *winepress* will not feed them, and the *new wine* will prove false to them. Ephraim will return to Egypt, and in Assyria they will eat what is unclean. *They will not pour a libation of wine to Jehovah,* and their sacrifices will not be pleasing to him. (Hosea 9:2, 3, 4)

Again the inner meaning deals with goodness springing from love and goodness springing from faith, saying they will come to an end. Goodness springing from love is the threshing floor, because of the grain there and the bread made from it. Goodness springing from faith is the winepress, new wine, and libation of wine. "Ephraim will return to Egypt" means that the intellect would consult accepted knowledge to evaluate the mysteries of faith; "in Assyria they will eat what is unclean" means that it would rely on skewed reasoning. (For the meaning of Ephraim as the church's intellect, see §§5354, 6222, 6238, 6267; of Egypt as knowledge, §§1164, 1165, 1186, 1462, 5702; and of Assyria as skewed reasoning, §1186.) The string of phrases itself also reveals that there is something more to these words than appears in the literal text. In the inner meaning they follow in logical order, but in the outer meaning they do not. For instance, it says that threshing floor and winepress will not feed them and the new wine will prove false to them, and then that Ephraim will return to Egypt and eat what is unclean in Assyria. Besides, if there is no inner sense, what can it mean to say that Ephraim will return to Egypt and eat what is unclean in Assyria? [5] Winepress and wine are used in Jeremiah as well to depict the end of mutual love and of goodness springing from faith:

> On *your vintage a destroyer has fallen,* so gladness and joy have disappeared from Carmel and from the land of Moab, because *wine from the*

winepresses I have put an end to; no one will tread the hedad. (Jeremiah 48:32, 33)

[6] The symbolism of wine as goodness springing from mutual love and faith is also seen in John:

I heard a voice from the midst of the four living creatures saying, "*Do not hurt the oil or the wine.*" (Revelation 6:6)

The oil stands for goodness springing from heavenly love, the wine for goodness springing from spiritual love. [7] Oil and wine have a similar meaning in the Lord's parable of the Samaritan in Luke:

A certain Samaritan was traveling, and seeing the man who had been wounded by robbers, he was moved at heart; so, approaching, he bandaged the man's wounds [and] *poured on oil and wine.* (Luke 10:33, 34)

His pouring on oil and wine symbolizes his performing acts of love and charity. For the meaning of oil as a loving goodness, see §§886, 3728. There is similar meaning to the fact that the ancients poured oil and *wine* on a pillar when they were consecrating it (Genesis 35:14; §§4581, 4582). [8] The meaning of wine as goodness springing from love and faith is clear from the Lord's words when he established the Holy Supper. What he then said about wine was this:

I say to you that from now on I will not drink *any of this product of the grapevine* until that day when I drink it new with you in my Father's kingdom. (Matthew 26:29; Luke 22:17, 18)

Anyone can see that the Lord was not planning to drink wine there [in his Father's kingdom] but that what is symbolized is a goodness based on love and faith, which he would give to citizens of his kingdom. The symbolism of wine is the same in Isaiah 24:9, 11; Lamentations 2:11, 12; Hosea 14:7; Amos 9:13, 14; Zechariah 9:15, 16; Luke 5:37, 38, 39.

[9] Since wine symbolizes a goodness born of love and faith, in the highest sense it symbolizes divine truth from the Lord's divine goodness, because it is from this that a goodness born of love and faith flows to people who accept it.

[10] Because most words in Scripture also have a negative meaning, wine does too. In a negative sense it symbolizes falsity growing out of evil, as in Isaiah:

Doom to those getting up in the morning at dawn, who pursue *strong drink,* loitering till the twilight *so that wine can inflame them. Doom to*

those heroic at drinking wine and *to men valiant at mixing strong drink.*
(Isaiah 5:11, 22)

In the same author:

> *These also err through wine* and *go astray* through *strong drink.* Priest and
> prophet *err through strong drink; they are swallowed up by wine; they go
> astray through strong drink;* they err among seers; they stagger in judg-
> ment. (Isaiah 28:7)

In the same author:

> Shepherds do not know how to understand; they all look to their own
> way. Come, *let me take wine* and *let us get drunk on strong drink.* And on
> the next day as on this, let there be great abundance. (Isaiah 56:11, 12)

Other examples are found in Jeremiah 13:12; Hosea 4:11; 7:5; Amos 2:8;
Micah 2:11; Psalms 75:8; Deuteronomy 32:33. Falsity based on evil is also
symbolized by the *goblet of the wine of [God's] anger* (Jeremiah 25:15, 16; Revelation 14:8, 10; 16:19), by the *winepress of the wine of the fury* of God's anger
(Revelation 19:15), and by the *wine of whoredom* (Revelation 17:2; 18:3).

And his garment in the blood of grapes means that his intellectual plane   **6378**
consists in divine goodness growing out of his divine love, as the following shows: The *blood of grapes* symbolizes goodness growing out of love,
and in the highest sense, the Lord's divine goodness, growing out of his
divine love, as discussed below. And a *garment* symbolizes the intellectual
plane. The intellect takes things in, and whatever takes things in is a vessel, so it is like a garment. Why does a garment symbolize the intellectual
plane, when clothing (as discussed just above at §6377) symbolizes the
earthly plane? The reason is that the previous phrase is about the outer
level, while this phrase is about the inner. Where the Word talks about
something outward it also talks about something inward, for the sake of
the heavenly marriage, and where it deals with truth it also deals with
goodness; see §6343. This feature sometimes looks like redundancy, as it
does here. In the sentence "He washes his *clothing* in *wine,* and his *garment* in the *blood of grapes,"* the wine and the blood of grapes seem the
same, as do the clothing and the garment. They are not the same, though,
because they express something external and something internal.

[2] The meaning of the *blood of grapes* as divine goodness rising out
of the Lord's divine love is plain from the discussion in §4735 of the symbolism of *blood* as divine truth rising out of the Lord's divine goodness.
Grapes in the highest sense symbolize the Lord's divine goodness in the

inhabitants of his spiritual kingdom, so in a secondary sense they symbolize good that is done out of neighborly love (§5117). The blood of the grape has the same symbolism in the Song of Moses:

> . . . the butter of the herd and the milk of the flock, together with the fat of lambs and of rams—the sons of Bashan—and of goats, together with the fat of the kidneys of wheat; and *you drink the blood of the grape as unmixed wine.* (Deuteronomy 32:14)

6379   *He is red of eye from wine* means that his intellect, or his inner human nature, is pure goodness, as the following shows: *Red* symbolizes a loving goodness, because of both fire and blood, which are red (discussed at §3300). So *red from wine* symbolizes pure goodness. *Eyes* symbolize the intellect (discussed in §§2701, 3820, 4403–4421, 4523–4534), and since the phrase describes the Lord, his inner human nature is what is meant here by his intellect. After all, the next phrase, "white of teeth from milk," symbolizes his outer human nature.

6380   *And white of teeth from milk* means that his earthly divinity is pure truth-based goodness, as the following shows: The symbolism of *white* has to do with truth, as discussed in §§3301, 3993, 4007, 5319. *Teeth* in their positive sense symbolize the earthly plane, because the hard parts of the human body—the teeth, bones, cartilage—correspond to truth and goodness on the lowest earthly level. And *milk* symbolizes what is heavenly-spiritual—in other words, truth-based goodness—as discussed at §2184.

It is in relation to people who believe in and love the Lord that his earthly divinity is called truth-based goodness. People in the outer part of the church cannot lift their thinking to anything higher than the Lord's earthly divinity, but people in the inner part of the church lift their thinking above the earthly level to an inner level. All who believe in the Lord have an idea of him that matches their ability to raise their thoughts. People who know what the inner level is can have an idea of that level, but people who do not know what the inner level is picture what is outward. That is why the Lord's earthly divinity is *called* truth-based goodness, when in reality his human nature consists entirely in the divine goodness that comes of divine love.

6381   This discussion of Judah now shows plainly that the Word has an inner meaning and that unless one knows what is wrapped up in that meaning, one cannot possibly know what the description of Judah here means. One cannot know the meaning of a lion's cub, or of the idea that he rose fed with prey, crouched, and lay like a lion and like an aging lion; the meaning of a lawgiver from between his feet; the meaning of Shiloh; the meaning of tying his young donkey to the grapevine and his jenny's foal to the rare vine; the meaning of washing clothing in wine and a garment in the blood of grapes; the meaning of being red of eye from wine and white of teeth from milk. All these details would lie completely hidden if they were not uncovered by means of a sense lying deep within.

Genesis 49:13. *"Zebulun will reside at a harbor on the seas, and at a harbor for ships, and his flank will be toward Sidon."*   6382

Zebulun symbolizes the living together of goodness and truth. *Will reside at a harbor on the seas* symbolizes a life in which knowledge is used as a basis for drawing conclusions about truth. *And at a harbor for ships* means in which teachings from the Word are present. *And his flank will be toward Sidon* means reaching on one side to a knowledge of what is good and true.

Zebulun symbolizes the living together of goodness and truth. This   6383 is established by the representation of *Zebulun* as the heavenly marriage (discussed in §§3960, 3961) and therefore as the union of goodness and truth, since this union is the heavenly marriage. It is described as the living together of goodness and truth because in the original language "Zebulun" means a living together.

Under the image of Zebulun, the text is talking about people in the church who use knowledge as a basis for drawing conclusions about spiritual truth and fixing it firmly in their minds.

It is important, though, to realize that Zebulun does not mean people who refuse to believe an idea unless knowledge and sensory information decree it and until then are disposed to deny it. Such people never believe the idea, because they are always under the sway of negativity. When a negative attitude is always in control, people are influenced by items of knowledge that contradict an idea, not those that confirm it, and these are the types of knowledge they collect. Knowledge that confirms the idea is shunted aside or else reinterpreted in favor of negative information. This reinforces their negativity.

[2] On the contrary, Zebulun here means people who believe teachings from the Word, and therefore people in whom something affirmative always prevails. Nonetheless, their faith dwells in knowledge rather than truth. They apply knowledge to these teachings, and this is how they reinforce their positive attitude.

The people who are Zebulun, then, do not rise above knowledge. When they hear or think about religious truth, they immediately drop down to knowledge. That is the case with many people in the world. The Lord also

makes sure that knowledge and sensory information will serve this purpose
for them.

6384   *Will reside at a harbor on the seas* symbolizes a life in which knowledge is used as a basis for drawing conclusions about truth, as the following shows: A *harbor* symbolizes the point at which knowledge ends and
begins. Here it symbolizes a situation in which knowledge is used as a basis
for drawing conclusions about truth, because under the image of Zebulun
the text is talking about people for whom religious truth is in that very
situation. *Seas* stand for all types of knowledge collectively, as dealt with in
§28. And *residing* symbolizes life, as dealt with in §§1293, 3384, 3613, 4451,
6051. Clearly, then, *will reside at a harbor on the seas* symbolizes a life in
which knowledge is used as a basis for drawing conclusions about truth.

Regarding such a life, see the comments just above at §6383; but here
is another important piece of information: This kind of life exists in the
outer, earthly self, and in some it exists on the lowest earthly level, which
is the level of the senses. People like this have religious truth so tightly
bound up with knowledge that it cannot be lifted above knowledge. So
they are more in the dark than anyone else in the spiritual church. Their
intellect does not lend them much light, because it is immersed in knowledge and sensory evidence.

The situation is different for people who have adopted an affirmative
attitude and used knowledge to back up religious truth but in such a way
that the truth can be lifted above the knowledge, or above the earthly level
where the knowledge resides. People like this have an enlightened intellect,
so they have some perception of spiritual truth. Lower-lying knowledge
serves their perceptive powers as a mirror in which the truth taught by faith
and charity is reflected and acknowledged, like emotions in a person's face.

6385   *And at a harbor for ships* means in which teachings from the Word are
present. This can be seen from the symbolism of a *harbor* as a situation
(as directly above at §6384) and therefore a situation in which they are
present, and from the symbolism of *ships* as teachings from the Word.

Ships symbolize these teachings because they cross seas and rivers and
carry the necessities of life. Seas and rivers symbolize different types of
knowledge, and the necessities of life that the ships carry are doctrinal
teachings and even truth itself from the Word. The following passages
show that this is what ships symbolize. In Isaiah:

> In me the islands will trust, as will the *ships of Tarshish,* from the start,
> to bring your sons from far away, their silver and their gold with them.
> (Isaiah 60:9)

The ships of Tarshish stand for religious teachings and truth that are taken from the Word, which is why the verse says that they will bring the sons, with their silver and gold. Sons symbolize people with truth. Silver symbolizes truth itself, and gold symbolizes what is good. Anyone can see that the passage is not talking about ships of Tarshish or about sons or silver and gold. [2] In Ezekiel:

> In the heart of the sea are your borders; *your builders* perfected your beauty. Of pines from Senir they built you *all your boards;* cedar from Lebanon they took *to make a mast for you.* Of oaks from Bashan *they made oars. Your planking* they made of ivory—the *daughter of a step* from the islands of Kittim. Fine linen with embroidery from Egypt was *what you spread out* to serve you as a banner. Blue-violet and red-violet fabric from the islands of Elishah was *your covering.* The inhabitants of Sidon and Arvad *were rowers for you.* Your sages who were within you, Tyre, *were your captains.* The elders of Gebal and its sages were in you *strengthening your seam. All the ships of the sea* and *their sailors* were in you to deal in your business dealings. (Ezekiel 27:4–9)

This is about Tyre, which symbolizes knowledge of goodness and truth (§1201). The knowledge is depicted in the kinds of items that belong to a ship: boards, mast, oars, planking, spread-out [sail], covering, oars, captains, sailors. Who can fail to see that none of these is to be taken literally? But when the ships are taken to mean a knowledge of what is true and good (this being Tyre) together with teachings from the Word, everything applies beautifully. [3] In David:

> How numerous are your works, Jehovah! You have made them all in wisdom. This sea is large, and wide in its extent. *In it will be ships,* [and] the great sea creature that you formed to play in it. (Psalms 104:24, 25, 26)

In the same author:

> Let those people sacrifice the sacrifices of acclamation and proclaim Jehovah's deeds with a glad shout *who go down to the sea with ships,* doing their work in many waters. These have seen Jehovah's deeds and his marvels in the deep. (Psalms 107:22, 23, 24)

Again the ships stand for religious knowledge and religious teachings. The great sea creature stands for general categories of knowledge (§42). And because ships mean religious knowledge and teachings, the passage says that those who go down to the sea with ships are the ones who have seen

Jehovah's deeds and his marvels in the deep. Jehovah's deeds and marvels
are seen by people who possess knowledge and teachings from the Word.
[4] In John:

> The second angel trumpeted, and what seemed to be a large moun-
> tain burning with fire was thrown into the sea. And a third of the sea
> became blood. For which reason a third of the creatures that were in the
> sea, having souls, died. And *a third of the ships were ruined.* (Revelation
> 8:8, 9)

A large mountain burning with fire stands for self-love (§1691). The sea
stands for the earthly level, where knowledge resides (28). Blood stands
for violence inflicted on neighborly love (374, 1005). Creatures in the sea
having souls stand for truth in the form of knowledge, together with good
qualities. A third stands for something that is not yet complete (2788 at
the end). "They died" means that they had no spiritual life (6119). So "a
third of the ships were ruined" means that the truth and goodness found
in teachings from the Word were distorted. This information shows what
this prophecy means.

[5] In a negative sense, ships symbolize knowledge and teachings consisting of falsity and evil, as in Daniel:

> At the time of the end, the king of the south will clash with [the king
> of the north]; therefore the king of the north will storm onto him
> with chariot and with riders and *with many ships* and will come into
> various lands and flood them and invade. (Daniel 11:40)

The king of the south stands for truth-from-goodness, the king of the
north for falsity-from-evil, and the chariot with riders and ships for distorted teachings. The various lands stand for various religions, of which
it says that falsity-from-evil would flood and invade them at the time of
the end. [6] In John:

> Every *pilot,* and everyone among the company *on ships,* and *sailors,* and
> all who *engage in commerce on the sea* stood far off and were shouting,
> seeing the smoke of Babylon's conflagration, saying, "What else is like
> the great city? Alas, alas, you great city, in which all *who have ships on
> the sea* became rich off its costly merchandise." (Revelation 18:17, 18, 19)

These ships are plainly religious knowledge and teachings consisting of
falsity and evil, because Babylon stands for worship that looks holy on

the outside but is profane on the inside. No one can help seeing that the ships too mean something besides ships. In Isaiah:

> This is what Jehovah, our Redeemer, the Holy One of Israel, says: "Because of you I have sent to Babylon, so that I may throw down all the bars of the gates and the Chaldeans, *in whose ships there is shouting.*" (Isaiah 43:14)

Likewise here. Falsity growing out of evil is also symbolized by ships in Isaiah 2:16; 23:1, 14; Psalms 48:7.

And his flank will be toward Sidon means reaching on one side to a knowledge of what is good and true. This can be seen from the symbolism of a *flank* as a reach on one side and from that of *Sidon* as superficial concepts of what is good and true (discussed at §1201).

6386

In talking about Zebulun here I have mentioned concepts, teachings, and knowledge. I have said that Zebulun reaches on one side to a concept of what is good and true and that conclusions about truth on the basis of knowledge coexist with teachings from the Word. So I need to say how the three differ from each other. Teachings are what come from the Word. Concepts are what partake of those teachings on one side and of knowledge on the other. Knowledge is what develops out of experience—both personal experience and the experience of others.

Genesis 49:14, 15. *"Issachar is a bony donkey lying down between its burdens. And he will see his resting place, that it is good, and the land, that it is delightful, and he will bend his shoulder to take on heavy loads and will serve as tribute, working like a slave."*

6387

Issachar symbolizes repayment for one's efforts. *Is a bony donkey* symbolizes the lowliest kind of slave. *Lying down between its burdens* symbolizes a life saddled with effort. *And he will see his resting place, that it is good,* means that doing good without being repaid is full of happiness. *And the land, that it is delightful,* means that it is enjoyed by the inhabitants of the Lord's kingdom. *And he will bend a shoulder to take on heavy loads* means that they still work with maximum effort. *And will serve as tribute, working like a slave* means in order to earn credit.

Issachar symbolizes repayment for one's efforts. This can be seen from the representation of *Issachar* as mutual love, which is a reward or repayment (discussed at §§3956, 3957). Here he represents repayment for one's efforts, as is evident from the inner meaning of every word in this prophetic utterance concerning Issachar. Besides, "Issachar" in the original language means a reward.

6388

Issachar symbolizes repayment for one's efforts here even though he symbolized mutual love before [§§3956, 3957]. This is because Issachar now means people who put on a show or appearance of mutual love, or of charity for their neighbor, and want recompense for the good they do. As a result they not only taint but also pervert real mutual love, or charity. People with the genuine form of that love are in their true pleasure and bliss when they are helping their neighbor, because there is nothing they would prefer. This pleasure, this bliss, is what a reward means in the Word, because it is itself the reward. In the next life it turns into the joy and happiness of heaven, so it actually becomes heaven for such people. When people with mutual love there act usefully and do good to others, they feel such joy and happiness that they then seem to themselves for the first time to be in heaven. This is their gift from the Lord, given in accord with the particular use they serve.

[2] This happiness vanishes as soon as they think about repayment, though, because to look for repayment while they are already being repaid is to sully that love and pervert it. The reason is that they are then thinking about themselves rather than their neighbor; they are figuring out how to make themselves happy, not others, except so far as others make *them* happy. Consequently they turn love for their neighbor into love for themselves, and the more they do so, the less joy and happiness from heaven can be communicated to them. They center the happiness flowing in from heaven on themselves and pass none along to others. They resemble objects that do not reflect rays of light but absorb them. Objects that reflect light appear lit up and glow, but objects that absorb light appear dark and do not glow at all. Anyone seeking repayment, then, is removed from the company of angels as a being who has nothing in common with heaven.

These are the people depicted here as Issachar.

6389 *Is a bony donkey* symbolizes the lowliest kind of slave. This can be seen from the symbolism of a *donkey* as something subservient (discussed in §§5958, 5959) and from that of *bone* as something with little spiritual life (discussed in §§5560, 5561). So a *bony donkey* is the lowliest kind of slave. People who do good for the sake of reward are useful and do serve others, but they live among the bottom-tier inhabitants of the Lord's kingdom. This is because they do not distribute the goodness communicated to them, except to those who can compensate them. Anyone else in dire need of help they ignore. If they do benefit the needy, they do it in order to be repaid by the Lord. They then regard their actions as deserving, so

they regard the Lord's mercy as their due. This means that they abandon humility, and the further they travel from humility, the further they
travel from a state in which they can accept bliss and happiness through
heaven from the Lord.

This discussion shows that they are indeed put to use in the other life
but as the lowliest slaves.

Lying down between its burdens symbolizes a life saddled with effort.   **6390**
This can be seen from the symbolism of *lying down* as life, but a dim sort
of life, and from that of *burdens* as efforts. Burdens symbolize efforts of
this kind because what moves such people to do good is not love for their
neighbor but love for themselves. Tasks that flow from motives of self-
love are like burdens that menial donkeys carry, because they are among
the most menial kinds of service.

All slavery results from being moved by love for oneself and for worldly
advantages, while all freedom results from being moved by love for the
Lord and for one's neighbor. The reason for this association is that motivation by the former kind of love flows in from hell, which exercises violent
control, but motivation by the latter love flows in from the Lord, who
leads rather than controls.

This shows once again that people who do good for the sake of a
reward are the lowliest kind of slaves and that their efforts are burdens.

[2] Burdens have a similar symbolism in Judges:

> *Chieftains in Issachar* are with Deborah, *and Issachar* is thus with Barak.
> In the valley [Issachar] will be sent at [Barak's] feet, in the divisions
> of Reuben, who is great in statutes of the heart. *Why would you sit
> between burdens* to listen to the hissings of the flocks? (Judges 5:15, 16)

Here too Issachar stands for people who want to be repaid for their deeds.
Being sent in the valley at [Barak's] feet stands for serving others in the lowliest duties. The divisions of Reuben stand for people who have a knowledge of religious truth, and [the people represented by Issachar] are in with
them but in a place below them. Listening to the hissings of the flocks
stands for being viewed poorly by people who do good out of neighborly
love, who are the flocks. Sitting between burdens stands for sitting among
efforts for which one seeks credit.

And he will see his resting place, that it is good, means that doing   **6391**
good without being repaid is full of happiness, as the following shows:
Rest symbolizes qualities of heaven and therefore qualities found in good
done out of neighborly love, or in good deeds done without repayment,

as discussed below. And *that it is good* means that such deeds are full of happiness.

The reason *rest* means good deeds done without repayment is that in the highest sense, rest, or peace, symbolizes the Lord. In a secondary sense it symbolizes heaven and therefore goodness that is from the Lord (see §§3780, 4681, 5662). The only people who enjoy the benefits symbolized by rest, or peace, are those with the goodness that comes of neighborly love, or those who do good deeds without the intention of being repaid, so these things are what rest symbolizes. This meaning follows from the series of ideas in the inner meaning.

[2] To focus on the subject at hand: People who do good for the sole purpose of being repaid cannot see that doing good without reward contains happiness so great as to be heavenly happiness. The reason they cannot see it is that they find happiness in the pleasure of self-love, and the more pleasure we take in self-love, the less pleasure we take in heavenly love, since they are opposites. That pleasure—the kind that flows from self-love—snuffs out every bit of the pleasure that comes from heavenly love. It snuffs it out so completely in us that it leaves us with no idea what heavenly pleasure is, and if anyone describes such pleasure to us, we disbelieve and even deny it.

[3] This I was able to learn from evil spirits in the other world, who when they were still alive did nothing good for others or for their country that was not for their own sake. They do not believe it is possible to find any pleasure in doing good without aiming for remuneration, because if the goal of remuneration is absent, they imagine, then all pleasure ceases. You can tell them further that where this kind of pleasure ends, heavenly pleasure begins, but they are dumbstruck to hear it. Their astonishment increases when they hear that this heavenly pleasure flows in through a person's inmost core and brings inexpressible happiness to the person's inner reaches. This idea astounds them even more, and they say they cannot understand it. In fact, they say they do not even want to understand. They believe that if they give up the pleasure of self-love they will be wretchedly unhappy, because they will then be without any joy in life. They also apply the term *naive* to anyone with a different attitude.

People who do what they do in order to be repaid are not too different from these evil spirits, because they do good deeds for their own sake, not for the sake of others. It is themselves they look to in their work, not their neighbor or their country or heaven or the Lord, except as debtors who owe them a favor.

That is what the contents of this verse about Issachar describe in the inner meaning.

And the land, that it is delightful, means that it—happiness—is enjoyed by the inhabitants of the Lord's kingdom, as the following shows: The *land* symbolizes the church and therefore the Lord's kingdom as well, as stated in §§662, 1066, 1068, 1413, 1607, 1733, 1850, 2117, 2118, 4447. The reason the land has this meaning is that the land of Canaan, which is the land meant in the Word, represented the Lord's kingdom, because the church had been there since the earliest times (§§3038, 3481, 3686, 3705, 4447, 4454, 4516, 4517, 5136). And *that it is delightful* symbolizes the happiness found in doing good deeds without recompense.

There is a reason why the text says, "He will see his *resting place,* that it is *good,* and the *land,* that it is *delightful,*" and why both symbolize the happiness in the Lord's kingdom. The reason is that seeing a *resting place,* that it is *good,* relates to what is heavenly, or good, and seeing the *land,* that it is *delightful,* relates to what is spiritual, or true. This is because of the marriage of goodness and truth, which is described in §6343.

[2] There is something else that needs to be known about the happiness in good deeds done without the intention of being repaid: Very few today realize that doing good deeds without seeking repayment contains heavenly happiness. They do not know there is any other kind of happiness than rising to high position, being waited on by others, abounding in riches, and living a life of sensual pleasure. That there is a higher happiness than those, a happiness that touches a person's inner depths, they are profoundly unaware. Nor do they see, therefore, that such happiness is heavenly happiness and that it is the happiness of genuine neighborly love. Ask the wise of today whether they know that this is heavenly happiness. Because of modern ignorance, many also reject good deeds, believing that no one can do them without seeking to earn something in return. They do not know that people who are led by the Lord want nothing more than to do good deeds and that there is nothing they give less thought to than earning something in return. This characteristic is embedded in a new will that the Lord gives as a gift to people who are being reborn, because the new will is the Lord's in us.

And he will bend a shoulder to take on heavy loads means that they still work with maximum effort. This can be seen from the symbolism of a *shoulder* as all one's might, or maximum effort (discussed in §§1085, 4931–4937), and from that of *taking on heavy loads* as doing good deeds in order to earn credit. *Bending a shoulder to take on heavy loads,* then, means working with maximum effort at doing good deeds in order to earn credit.

This is called taking on heavy loads because such people do good not from devotion to what is good, and therefore not freely, but from devotion to themselves, which is slavery (§6390).

[2] To continue with the discussion of people who want to be rewarded for the efforts they make: Keep in mind that they are never satisfied. They are indignant if they do not receive a greater reward than others; and if they see others more fortunate than themselves, they are pained and criticize them. They do not equate blessing with inner blessing but with the outer blessings of outranking others, controlling them, and being served by angels, so that they are above the angels and consequently are rulers and nobles in heaven. The truth is, though, that heavenly blessedness is not wanting to control or be served by others but wanting to serve others and be least, as the Lord teaches:

> James and John, the sons of Zebedee, came up, saying, "Grant us to sit one on your right and the other on your left in your glory." Jesus said to them, "You do not know what you are asking; to sit on my right and on my left is not mine to give but belongs to those for whom it has been prepared. You know that the ones who are supposed to rule the nations lord it over them and the nobles have authority over them. It shall not be this way among you. But anyone who wants to be great among you must be your attendant, and whichever of you wants to be first must be everyone's slave. For the Son of Humankind did not come to be served but to serve others." (Mark 10:35–45)

[3] And in Luke he teaches that heaven is for people who do good without looking to be repaid:

> All who exalt themselves will be humbled, but those who humble themselves will be exalted. When you make a luncheon or dinner, don't call your friends or your brothers and sisters or your relatives or your rich neighbors, or they might also call you in return and it would become repayment to you. But when you make a banquet, call the poor, the maimed, the lame, the blind; then you will be fortunate, because they have nothing to repay you with. It will be repaid to you in the resurrection of the righteous. (Luke 14:11, 12, 13, 14)

Repayment in the resurrection of the righteous is inner happiness that results from doing good without reward, a happiness that people receive from the Lord when they are doing useful things. When people love to serve without repayment, then the more they love it, the nobler the work they are asked to oversee, and they actually become greater and more powerful than others.

[4] People who do good deeds for the sake of recompense also say that they want to be least in heaven, because they know from the Word [that they ought to]. All the while, though, they are thinking that saying so will make them great, so that same goal is still present. In contrast, people who do good without recompense truly think only about serving, not about their own importance.

[5] On taking credit for one's good deeds, see what was said and shown earlier, such as the following: What these people are like in the other world; they appear to chop wood and mow grass (1110, 1111, 4943); how they are represented (1774, 2027); people who have done good for selfish and materialistic reasons receive nothing in repayment for that goodness in the other life (1835); people who feel they deserve credit for what they do interpret the Word in a literal way that promotes their own interests, and they make fun of its inner content (1774, 1877); genuine neighborly love lacks any sense of merit (2371, 2380, 3816); people who detach faith from neighborly love think their efforts make them deserving (2371 at the end); people who go to heaven discard self-sufficiency and a sense of merit (4007 at the end); many people at the threshold of reformation believe that they do good on their own and that they earn credit for that goodness, but as they are being reborn they shed this belief (4174).

And will serve as tribute, working like a slave means in order to earn credit. This can be seen from the symbolism of *serving as tribute, working like a slave* as being subordinate and serving. People who want to earn credit for their efforts are described as bony donkeys lying down between their burdens and as bending a shoulder to take on heavy loads. So one who works like a slave as tribute also symbolizes people who want to earn credit for what they do. After all, such people are the lowliest slaves, as can be seen above at §6389.

6394

It can be seen in Moses that working like a slave as tribute means being subordinate and serving:

> When you approach a city to fight against it, you shall invite them to peace. But if [the city] should happen to answer you peaceably and open to you, it shall happen that the whole people who is found in it *shall become tribute to you* and *they shall work as slaves to you.* (Deuteronomy 20:10, 11)

In Jeremiah:

> How the city [that was] great with people has sat alone! It has become like a widow [though it was] great among the nations. *The one that ruled over the provinces has become a payer of tribute.* (Lamentations 1:1)

Becoming tribute and a payer of tribute in these passages clearly means serving. In Matthew:

> Jesus said, "How does it seem to you, Simon—*from whom* do the monarchs of the earth *collect tribute or tax,* from their own children or from foreigners?" Peter says to him, "From foreigners." Jesus says to him, "Then the children are free. But to keep us from being a stumbling block to them, making your way to the sea, put in a hook and lift the fish that rises to it first; should you open its mouth you will find a stater. Take and give it for me and you." (Matthew 17:25, 26, 27)

Once again paying tribute or tax means people who serve, so it says that foreigners would pay and the children would be free. Foreigners, you see, were slaves (§1097). The request that Peter take a fish from the sea and find a stater in its mouth with which to pay represented the fact that the lowest part of the earthly level, which is a slave, would [pay]. Fish symbolize the lowest part of the earthly level.

6395   Genesis 49:16, 17, 18. *"Dan will judge his people as one of Israel's tribes. Dan will be a snake on the path, a darting serpent on the track, biting the horse's heels, and its rider will fall off behind it. Your salvation I await, Jehovah!"*

Dan symbolizes people intent on truth but not yet on goodness. *Will judge his people as one of Israel's tribes* means that [this truth] is one of the general categories of truth that the tribes of Israel represent. *Dan will be a snake on the path* symbolizes the faulty way they reason about truth because they are not yet led by goodness. *A darting serpent on the track* means from truth about goodness. *Biting the horse's heels* symbolizes illusions from the lowest level of nature. *And its rider will fall off behind it* symbolizes a consequent backsliding. *Your salvation I await, Jehovah!* means unless the Lord brings help.

6396   *Dan* symbolizes people intent on truth but not yet on goodness. This can be seen from the representation of *Dan* as a good life, as discussed in §§3921, 3923. Here, though, he represents people who do something good in their lives at the urging of truth but not yet out of goodness. That is what happens with people being regenerated by the Lord. At first they are intent on truth rather than on doing anything good in their lives as a result of truth. Later they live a good life at the urging of truth but not yet out of goodness. Still later, when they have been reborn, they live a good life out of goodness. At that point they perceive truth from goodness and make it multiply in themselves. These are the stages of rebirth.

Dan means people who live a good life out of truth but not yet out of goodness. In them, goodness still lies deeply hidden in truth, inspiring them with a desire for truth and driving them to live by the truth.

People like this are in the Lord's kingdom, but what moves them to do good is not goodness but truth—that is, not a new will but their intellect. So they do good not out of love but out of obedience because that is what has been commanded. As a consequence, they live among those in the Lord's kingdom who are in the first or lowest heaven.

These are the people Dan represents, because in this prophecy of Israel's, in its inner meaning, his twelve sons depict the general character of everyone in the Lord's kingdom.

[2] The placement of the people symbolized by Dan in the lowest heaven, or the lowest part of the Lord's kingdom (because they are intent on truth and not yet on goodness), was represented by the following: The lot fell to Dan last when the land of Canaan was being distributed among the tribes as an inheritance (Joshua 19:40–48). And the inheritance they then received was at the farthest edge of that land (Judges 18). The lot was cast in Jehovah's presence (Joshua 18:6), so it fell to each tribe according to that tribe's representation. For the idea that the land of Canaan represented the Lord's kingdom, see §§1607, 3038, 3481, 3686, 3705, 4447, 4454. All its borders were therefore representative (§§1585, 1866, 4116). So the outer bounds of the land represented the outermost attributes of the Lord's kingdom (§4240). Consequently Dan represented people on the lowest levels of that kingdom, because truth is on the outer bounds until it has united with goodness. If truth is totally separated from goodness, though, it does not lie within any border of the Lord's kingdom but outside it. [3] The fact that Dan's inheritance was at the edge of the land of Canaan can be seen from the phrase used to describe the entire extent of that land: *"from Beer-sheba to Dan"* (2 Samuel 3:10; 17:11; 24:15; 1 Kings 4:25). In this phrase Beer-sheba symbolizes the center of the land, since Abraham and Isaac lived there, before Jerusalem and Zion became the center of the land.

[4] The nature of people committed to truth and not yet to goodness was also represented by the Danites sent to scout out the land for a place

to live (Judges 18). They kidnapped a Levite from the household of Micah and stole an ephod, teraphim, and an idol, which symbolizes the worship of people who focus on truth but not yet on goodness because they revere superficialities and do not care about inner depths. Only a person with goodness perceives what lies inside. You can see that this is what the Danites there represented by considering that all Scripture narratives—in both the books of Moses and the books of Joshua, Judges, Samuel, and Kings—represent heavenly and spiritual attributes of the Lord's kingdom. So does this story of the Danites in Judges, then.

In further regard to people intent on truth and not yet on goodness, the inner meaning of the next few phrases about Dan describes their nature.

6397 *Will judge his people as one of Israel's tribes* means that [this truth] is one of the general categories of truth that the tribes of Israel represent, as the following shows: *Judging* symbolizes truth fulfilling its function, as discussed below. A *people* symbolizes individuals devoted to truth (discussed in §§1259, 1260, 2928, 3295, 3581, 4619). Here it symbolizes those devoted to truth and not yet to goodness, because they are meant by Dan, or the people of Dan (§6396). *Israel's tribes* represent all religious truth and goodness in general (dealt with in §§3858, 3926, 3939, 4060, 6335). So *will judge [his] people as one of Israel's tribes* means that the truth represented by Dan is also among the general categories of truth that the tribes of Israel represent.

Judging his people means truth fulfilling its function because the tribes of Israel represent all truth in general (as the sections cited above show), and truth is what passes judgment. So judging his people symbolizes truth fulfilling its function.

[2] The Word says that twenty-four elders will sit on thrones and judge nations and peoples, and that the twelve apostles will likewise sit on thrones and judge the twelve tribes of Israel. Anyone who does not know the Word's inner meaning has to believe this is what will happen. The way to understand it, though, becomes clear when one learns the symbolism from the inner meaning. The twenty-four elders, twelve apostles, and thrones symbolize all truth, taken together, that provides a standard of judgment.

Something similar is meant here by judging the people as one of the tribes of Israel. Not that judgment will be passed by [the people of Dan] or by any elders of theirs but by truth itself, which they symbolize, and consequently by the Lord alone, since all truth emanates from him.

Here is what John says about the twenty-four elders that are to sit on thrones and judge:

> Around the throne *were twenty-four thrones,* and *on the thrones I saw twenty-four elders sitting,* dressed in white clothes, who had golden crowns on their heads. (Revelation 4:4; 11:16)

And in the same author:

> *I saw thrones,* and *people sat,* and *the power of judgment was given to them.* (Revelation 20:4)

Here is what Matthew says about the twelve apostles:

> Jesus said, "You who have followed me—in the rebirth, when the Son of Humankind sits on his glorious throne, *you too will sit on twelve thrones judging the twelve tribes of Israel.*" (Matthew 19:28)

And in Luke:

> I myself am arranging for you—as my Father arranged for me—a kingdom, so that you may eat and drink at my table in my kingdom, *and sit on thrones judging the twelve tribes of Israel.* (Luke 22:29, 30)

[3] Of course this is not about twenty-four elders or twelve apostles but about everything true and good in general, since no human, not even an angel, can judge anyone. None but the Lord alone can know a person's inner depths or the nature of those depths, in the present or in the future, to eternity. (On the point that the twelve apostles, like the twelve tribes, symbolize all truth and goodness taken together, see §§2129, 2553, 3488, 3858 at the end.)

This evidence now shows that "Dan will judge his people as one of Israel's tribes" means that the truth Dan represents is one of the general kinds used for judgment.

Dan will be a snake on the path symbolizes the faulty way they reason about truth because they are not yet led by goodness. This can be seen from the representation of *Dan* as people intent on truth and not yet on goodness (dealt with above at §6396), from the symbolism of a *snake* as faulty reasoning based on sense impressions (dealt with below), and from that of a *path,* [or way,] as truth (dealt with in §§627, 2333). *Dan [will be] a snake on the path* therefore symbolizes the faulty way they reason about truth because they are not yet led by goodness. What follows will talk about the nature of that reasoning and of the truth it produces.

6398

[2] A snake stands for faulty reasoning based on sense impressions because a person's inner capacities are represented in heaven by different kinds of animals and are consequently symbolized in the Word by the same animals. A person's sensory dimension was represented by snakes because sensory information is the lowest plane in a human being, is relatively earthbound, and creeps on the ground, so to speak. This is evident from the structures through which sense impressions flow in, which will be discussed elsewhere, by the Lord's divine mercy. These sense impressions were therefore represented by snakes, and even the Lord's divine sensory plane was represented by the bronze snake in the wilderness (§4211 at the end). The shrewdness and watchfulness itself that comes into play in outward matters was also symbolized by snakes in Matthew:

> Be *shrewd as snakes* and simple as doves. (Matthew 10:16)

[3] However, when a person focuses on the sensory level in isolation from anything inward (like people who concentrate on truth and not yet on goodness) and speaks from the senses, then a snake symbolizes flawed reasoning. So in this case, where the focus is on Dan, the snake symbolizes flawed reasoning about truth, the reasoning being flawed because goodness does not yet lead.

In other passages, malice, cunning, and trickery are also symbolized by snakes, but poisonous snakes, such as vipers and so on. The crooked reasoning of these people is the poison.

For the meaning of a snake as reasoning based on the senses, see §§195, 196, 197. For that of a snake as all evil in general, and for the idea that the evils are distinguished according to the different types of snake, see §§251, 254, 257.

6399 *A darting serpent on the track* symbolizes flawed reasoning from truth about goodness. This can be seen from the symbolism of a *darting serpent* as flawed reasoning about goodness (discussed below) and from that of a *track,* [or way,] as truth (discussed in §§627, 2333, 3477).

A *darting serpent on the track* stands for flawed reasoning from truth about goodness because a snake symbolizes such reasoning, so a darting serpent symbolizes reasoning that hurls itself, namely, from truth at goodness. This is because in the people represented by Dan, truth is down low, goodness up high.

6400 *Biting the horse's heels* symbolizes illusions from the lowest level of nature, as the following shows: *Biting* means inflicting damage by latching on. A *horse's heels* symbolize illusions from the lowest level of nature, because a *heel* symbolizes the lowest part of the earthly and bodily levels (§§259, 4938–4952) and a *horse* symbolizes the intellect (§§2761, 2762, 3217, 5321, 6125). In this case the horse stands for illusions, because it stands for the intellect on the lowest earthly or sensory level.

The fact that people under the sway of truth and not yet of goodness are subject to illusions from the lowest level of nature can be seen from the consideration that truth stands in no light unless it has goodness with it or in it. Goodness is like a flame that radiates light. Where goodness then comes into contact with truth, it not only sheds light on truth but also introduces truth to itself and brings truth into its light. People dedicated to truth and not yet to goodness therefore stand in shadow and darkness, because truth has no light of its own. The light that such people do receive from goodness is weak, like light that fades out. As a result, when they think and reason about truth and from truth about goodness, they are like people seeing ghosts in the dark who believe them to be real and physical. Or they are like people who see flashes of light on a wall in the gloom and conjure them into a picture of a person or an animal, although when day dawns it becomes clear that they are only bits of light, not any kind of picture. That is how matters stand with truth for these people; they see as true what is not true, what should be compared instead to ghosts or to flashes of light on a wall.

What is more, the kind of people who had some truth from the Word but not goodness have created every heresy in the church, because to them the heresy appeared absolutely true. The same is true of false teachings in the church; the people who have promulgated them have been without goodness. This can be seen from the fact that they have rejected charity and the good it does to a position far behind faith and the truth it advocates. As a result some of the ideas they have made up clash directly with charitable goodness.

[2] Because I am saying that people intent on truth and not yet on goodness reason about truth and goodness on the basis of illusions from the lowest level of nature, I ought to define these illusions. Take for example human life after death. People who are subject to illusions from the lowest level of nature (as those with truth and not yet with goodness are) do not believe anything is alive in us but our body. They think that when we die we cannot possibly rise again unless we are given back our body. You can tell them there is an inner self that lives in the body and is revived by the Lord when the body dies. You can tell them that the inner self has the kind of body spirits and angels have and that like a person in

the world it sees, hears, talks, interacts with others, and looks just like a person to itself; but they cannot grasp it. Illusions from the lowest level of nature prevent them from considering such a thing possible, especially since they cannot see it with their physical eyes. [3] When people like this think about the spirit or the soul, they cannot picture it except in the way they picture invisible substances in nature. So they make it out to be like a breath or a gust of wind or a bit of ether or flame. Some imagine it to be pure thought with barely any living quality until it reunites with the body. They think these things because the whole inner realm is shadow and darkness to them. Only the outer realm stands in light. This evidence shows how easily such people can slip into error. They readily backslide from belief in a resurrection merely from thinking about the body (how will it reassemble?), the end of the world (it has been awaited in vain for so many centuries), unreasoning animals (they have a life not unlike ours), the dead (they never appear and tell us about the conditions of their life), and so forth. On many other questions too they readily abandon faith. The reason for their lack of faith is that they do not dwell in goodness and through goodness in light.

As this is their state, the text adds, "And its rider will fall off behind it. Your salvation I await, Jehovah!" symbolizing a consequent backsliding unless the Lord brings help.

6401 *And its rider will fall off behind it* symbolizes a consequent backsliding. This can be seen from the symbolism of *falling off behind it* as backsliding (from truth) and from the symbolism of a *rider* as people enmeshed in illusions from the lowest level of nature. A horse symbolizes those illusions (see just above at §6400), so a rider symbolizes people enmeshed in them. The implications are described above.

Since Dan symbolizes people in the church who are of the type described just above at §6396 and are therefore among the outermost inhabitants of the Lord's kingdom, he also symbolizes people who hatch falsities out of illusions and scatter them around. Their falsities are likewise described as horses and their reasonings about truth and goodness as snakes in Jeremiah:

> *From Dan* was heard the *snorting of its horses;* at the *voice of the whinnyings of its mighty ones,* all the earth trembled, and they came and devoured the earth and its abundance, the city and those residing in it. Because look: I send against you *cockatrice snakes* for which there is no spell, and they will bite you. (Jeremiah 8:16, 17)

Your salvation I await, Jehovah! means unless the Lord brings help. **6402**
This can be seen from the symbolism here of *awaiting salvation* as bringing help. For the fact that *Jehovah* is the Lord, see §§1343, 1736, 2156,
2329, 2447, 2921, 3023, 3035, 5663, 6303.

Here is what needs to be known about the help the Lord brings when
people with truth who are not yet led by goodness backslide (as symbolized by "Its rider will fall off behind it; your salvation I await, Jehovah!"):
Such people look downward, or out toward the surface, because they do
not yet have goodness; but people who have goodness (as people who
have been reborn do) look up, or within. When a person is being reborn,
the pattern shifts in this manner.

Since people devoted to truth and not yet to goodness look downward, or out toward the surface, among them are those who belong to the
region of the skin's surface in the universal human. The surface of the skin
faces outward, away from the inner parts of the body, and takes its sensa-
tions of touch from what lies outside, not in any perceptible way from
what lies inside. This makes it evident that such people are in the Lord's
kingdom, since they are also in the universal human, but in the outermost
parts of it.

About the people who constitute the skin, see §§5552–5559.

Genesis 49:19. *"Gad: a troop will ravage him, and he will ravage their* **6403**
heel."

Gad symbolizes good deeds growing out of truth but not yet out of
goodness. *A troop will ravage him* means that deeds done without good
judgment will drive these people away from the truth. *And he will ravage
their heel* symbolizes consequent disarray on the earthly plane.

Gad symbolizes good deeds growing out of truth but not yet out of **6404**
goodness. This is established by the representation of *Gad* as good deeds,
as discussed in §§3934, 3935. Here he represents deeds growing out of
truth and not yet out of goodness, as is plain from the way he is depicted
in the inner meaning. The symbolism also follows sequentially, because
Dan just above represents people with truth and not yet with goodness
(§6396), and now Gad represents people who perform deeds based on
truth and not yet on goodness.

The next section will tell what those deeds are like.

A troop will ravage him means that deeds done without good judg- **6405**
ment will drive these people away from the truth, as the following shows:
A troop symbolizes good deeds, as discussed at §3934. Here it symbolizes deeds done without good judgment, because people who work from

truth and not yet from goodness have a clouded intellect, but people who work from goodness have an enlightened intellect, because goodness sheds light on it. The light of truth from the Lord flows into the intellect by way of goodness and from there into truth, not into truth directly. The situation is like that of sunlight. It is by means of warmth that sunlight streams into members of the plant kingdom (trees, shrubs, flowers) to make them grow and blossom. The light does not flow directly in, because when light flows in without heat, nothing grows or blooms, as for instance in wintertime. And *ravaging him* means driving such people away from the truth.

[2] I need to say just who the people are that are symbolized here by Gad, however. They are people with delusions about the truth who nevertheless base the deeds they do on truth. Their deeds are therefore not deeds of truth, let alone of goodness. The work they do accordingly drives them away from the truth, because when people with truth and not yet with goodness put some principle into action out of religious conviction, the next thing they do is to defend it as absolute truth. They stand on that principle, and unless they start to adopt goodness, they do not accept correction. By putting a principle into action, they steep themselves in it and grow to love it. So the deeds they do drive them away from the truth. Besides which, they believe what is untrue to be true, because like the people symbolized by Dan, they too make judgments on the basis of sensory evidence, so they lack good judgment.

Take an illustrative example: There are people who accept everyone equally as their neighbor and therefore help the evil just as much as the good; but in helping the evil, they harm others. After putting their principle into action a number of times, they defend it, saying that everyone is their neighbor and that they do not care what the person is like as long as they can be of assistance. So they do what they do without judgment. They also work against the real truth, because the real truth is that everyone is our neighbor to a different degree, and those with goodness are more our neighbor than others (§§2417, 3419, 3820, 5025).

[3] Gad also symbolizes people who locate all salvation in deeds alone, like the Pharisee the Lord described in a parable:

> A Pharisee standing there was praying these things to himself: "God, I thank you that I am not like the rest of the people—greedy, unjust, adulterous—or even like this tax collector. I fast twice a week; I tithe everything I own." (Luke 18:11, 12)

So he took superficialities for absolute truth. People like this are also in the Lord's kingdom, but on its threshold. On this account the Lord says:

I say to you, the tax collector went down to his house more vindicated than the Pharisee. (Luke 18:14)

The Lord implies that the Pharisee too went down vindicated, since he had taken the steps commanded.

In short, Gad represents people who label what is not true as true and base their deeds on this nontruth. Their deeds consequently resemble truth, because deeds are nothing but will and intellect in action. What saves such people is the intent to do good and a measure of innocence in their ignorance.

[4] In Isaiah as well, Gad symbolizes people taken up with outer deeds based on nontruth that they believe to be true:

You are the ones who desert Jehovah, who forget my holy mountain, *who set a table for Gad,* and who fill a libation for Meni. (Isaiah 65:11)

Setting a table for Gad stands for immersing oneself in good deeds alone. And in Jeremiah:

Against the children of Ammon, this is what Jehovah has said to Israel: Does [Israel] have no heir? *Why is its king inheriting Gad* and *[why are] its people residing in his cities?* (Jeremiah 49:1)

Inheriting Gad stands for living a life of deeds based on what is untrue. The children of Ammon mean people who falsify what is true and live by these falsifications (§2468). The prophet applies these words concerning Gad to them.

[And] he will ravage their heel symbolizes consequent disarray on the **6406** earthly plane, as the following shows: *Ravaging* means driving people away from the truth, as just above in §6405, and therefore disrupting what is orderly, or creating disarray. And a *heel* symbolizes the lowest part of the earthly plane, as discussed in §§259, 4938–4952. This explanation shows that *he will ravage their heel* symbolizes disarray on the earthly plane.

People who base their deeds on truth and not yet on goodness cannot help bringing their earthly plane into disarray, because actions have an effect on what is earthly. As a result such people cannot help closing off their inner levels to the same degree, since the plane on which inner levels rest is the earthly dimension. If the earthly dimension is chaotic, the things that flow from deeper within become confused as well. What is more, conditions that are disorganized are dark and dim. As a consequence, these people cannot see what is true but, in that dimness and darkness, seize on nontruth as true and do what they do on the basis of such nontruth.

Furthermore, good works are completely necessary, because that is what neighborly love and faith are when put into effect and expressed in one's life. Who cannot see that without deeds there is no neighborly love? Deeds are simply goodness itself and truth itself in an outward form. After all, when goodness (belonging to the will) and truth (belonging to faith) are put into act, they are called deeds. This line of reasoning shows that the character of the goodness and truth determines the character of the deeds.

6407   Genesis 49:20. *"From Asher: rich with fat is his bread, and he will offer royal delicacies."*

From Asher symbolizes feelings of good fortune. *Rich with fat is his bread* symbolizes the pleasure afforded by goodness. *And he will offer royal delicacies* symbolizes the delight afforded by truth.

6408   *From Asher* symbolizes feelings of good fortune—that is, the blissful heavenly effect of love for the Lord and of charity for one's neighbor. This symbolism can be seen from the representation of *Asher* as the happiness of eternal life and feelings of good fortune, as discussed in §§3938, 3939. Asher was also named for good fortune.

In regard to this good fortune, it cannot easily be described, because it is internal and rarely projects itself into anyone's physical body, so that it rarely comes to anyone's awareness. While we are living in our body we have a distinct sensation of what goes on in our body but a very dim sensation of what goes on in our spirit. Worldly cares stand in the way as long as we are in our body. The inflow of blissful feelings cannot reach our bodily senses, where those cares reside, unless our earthly and sensory dimensions have been reduced to harmony with our inner dimensions—and even then in only a dim way. The inflow arrives as a mere sense of calm that comes of being content at heart. After death, though, the feelings reveal themselves. We experience them as bliss and happiness, and they then affect us both within and without.

In a word, heavenly feelings of good fortune are an inflow from our soul or spirit itself that arrives by an inner route and pushes on toward our body, where it is received so far as the pleasures of earthly and sensory types of love do not block it.

[2] This blessedness is completely impossible in people whose pleasure comes from self-love and love of worldly advantages, because these kinds of love are diametrically opposed to it. So people with these loves also cannot begin to understand that any other kind of blessing exists besides rising to high office, being worshiped as deities, abounding in wealth, and possessing more resources than others. You can tell them that the pleasure rising out of these kinds of love is shallow and dies with the body, and that what remains of it in the lower mind after death turns into something grim and ugly, like the pleasure enjoyed in the hells. You can say that a deep pleasure exists and that it is the prosperous, sunny pleasure of heaven's inhabitants. You can say all this, but such people do not begin to grasp it, because in them the outer realm dominates and the inner realm is shut off.

This discussion shows what is meant by feelings of good fortune, as symbolized by Asher.

Rich with fat is his bread symbolizes the pleasure afforded by goodness. This can be seen from the symbolism of *rich with fat* as pleasure. Fat symbolizes a heavenly quality, or a loving goodness (see §§353, 5943), but when fat is mentioned in connection with *bread,* which symbolizes a loving goodness, the fat then symbolizes the pleasure afforded by that love. For the symbolism of bread as a loving goodness, see §§276, 680, 2165, 2177, 3464, 3478, 3735, 3813, 4211, 4217, 4735, 4976, 5915. **6409**

And he will offer royal delicacies symbolizes the delight afforded by truth. This can be seen from the symbolism of *delicacies* as something delightful and from that of *royalty* as truth (discussed in §§1672, 1728, 2015, 2069, 3009, 4575, 4581, 4966, 5044, 6148). *Offering royal delicacies,* then, means the delight afforded by truth. **6410**

The reason the text refers to both the pleasure afforded by goodness and the delight afforded by truth is that there is the heavenly marriage in every detail of the Word (§6343).

The pleasure afforded by goodness and the delight afforded by truth that constitute the bliss in heaven consist not in leisure but in activity. The pleasure and delight of idleness becomes unpleasant and undelightful, but the pleasure and delight of activity lasts, constantly lifts one up, and blesses one.

Activity among heaven's inhabitants consists in getting useful things accomplished (which is the pleasure that goodness affords them) and in developing a wise grasp of truth in order to be useful (which is the delight that truth affords them).

6411

Genesis 49:21. *"Naphtali is a doe let loose, delivering elegant words."*

Naphtali symbolizes the state that follows times of trial. *Is a doe let loose* symbolizes freedom for earthly desire. *Delivering elegant words* symbolizes a happy mind.

6412

Naphtali symbolizes the state that follows times of trial. This can be seen from the representation of *Naphtali* as times of trial and also the state following them, as discussed in §§3927, 3928. Naphtali was named for wrestlings, which in a spiritual sense are trials.

6413

Is a doe let loose symbolizes freedom for earthly desire. This can be seen from the symbolism of a *doe* as earthly desire (discussed below) and from that of *let loose* as freedom, because when a captive doe is let loose, it gains its freedom.

Being liberated from a state of trial is compared to a doe let loose because a doe is a woodland creature that loves its freedom even more than other animals do. The earthly plane is like this too because it loves to enjoy the pleasure of its desires and consequently to enjoy freedom, since what is done out of desire is free.

A doe symbolizes earthly desires because it is one of the animals that symbolize [positive] desires. Such animals include all the ones that provide food and are useful, such as lambs, sheep, she-goats, kids, and he-goats; and bulls, calves, and cows. These animals symbolize spiritual desires, though, because they were used for burnt offerings and sacrifices. Because does were never used this way, they were symbols of earthly desires. (For the symbolism of animals as desires, see §§45, 46, 142, 143, 246, 714, 715, 719, 776, 1823, 2179, 2180, 3519, 5198. The symbolism of animals as desires results from representations in the world of spirits, §§3218, 5198.)

[2] Earthly desires are also symbolized by does in David:

Jehovah *makes my feet like those of does* and places me on my heights. (Psalms 18:33)

And in Habakkuk:

Jehovih the Lord is my might, who *makes my feet like those of does* and causes me to walk on my heights. (Habakkuk 3:19)

Making one's feet like those of does stands for an earthly level enjoying the freedom of its desires. (For the identification of feet with the earthly level, see §§2162, 3147, 3761, 3986, 4280, 4938–4952, 5328.) Clearly this is what making one's feet like those of does means, since rendering someone's feet as agile and good for running as a doe's is nothing spiritual. Yet the image does involve something spiritual, as is evident from the clauses that follow there, saying that Jehovah places the author—and causes him to walk—on the heights. The heights symbolize spiritual desire, which is higher than earthly desire. The situation is similar with this passage in Isaiah:

> *The lame will spring up like a deer.* (Isaiah 35:6)

A lame person symbolizes someone with goodness but goodness that is not yet genuine (§4302). [3] In David:

> *As a deer cries out for brooks of water,* so my soul cries out to you. (Psalms 42:1)

The deer here stands for a desire for truth. Crying out for brooks of water stands for yearning for truth. (For the identification of water with truth, see §§2702, 3058, 3424, 4976, 5668.) [4] In Jeremiah:

> From the daughter of Zion has departed all her honor. *Her chieftains have become like deer; they have not found pasture.* (Lamentations 1:6)

The daughter of Zion stands for a desire for goodness, which is characteristic of a heavenly religion (§2362). Her chieftains stand for the main truths of such a religion (§§1482, 2089, 5044). These truths are compared to deer, which symbolize desires for earthly truth, and the inability of the deer to find pasture symbolizes earthly desires lacking in truth and truth-based goodness. (For the identification of pasture with truth and truth-based goodness that sustain a person's spiritual life, see §§6078, 6277.) [5] Does have a similar meaning in Jeremiah:

> The earth was shattered that rain did not come on the earth; the farmers were put to shame. They covered their head, *because even the doe in the field gave birth,* but [did so while] abandoning [the fawn], because there was no grass. (Jeremiah 14:4, 5)

The doe stands for a desire for earthly-level goodness. "She gave birth in the field" stands for uniting earthly-level desires with the spiritual desires of religion. These desires came without forms of truth or goodness, though, so the passage says that she abandoned [the fawn] because there was no grass. Anyone can see that this description of a doe contains an inner sense, because without an inner sense, what could it mean that the doe in the field gave birth, but [did so while] abandoning [the fawn] because there was no grass? [6] Likewise these words in David:

> Jehovah's voice has sent the does into labor and strips the forests bare. But in his Temple, everyone says, "Glory!" (Psalms 29:9)

The fact that "Jehovah's voice has sent the does into labor" has an inner meaning, and a spiritual one at that, is quite plain if you consider that the verse follows up directly with the clause "But in his Temple, everyone says, 'Glory!'" In the absence of a spiritual meaning, this clause has no logical connection with the previous ones about does and forests.

6414   *Delivering elegant words* symbolizes a happy mind. This can be seen from the symbolism of *elegant words* as a happy mind, because all words come from the mind, and when the mind is happy and cheerful, it speaks elegantly.

Happiness and pleasure arrive after times of trial; see §§1992, 3696, 4572, 5628.

6415   What Israel says in this prophetic utterance about Dan, Gad, Asher, and Naphtali shows clearly that there is an inner meaning, without which the reader could hardly understand the prophecy at all or know what it is saying. Take the statements that Dan is a snake on the path, a darting serpent on the track, biting the heels of a horse whose rider will fall off behind it; that a troop will ravage Gad and he will ravage their heel; that Asher will have bread rich with fat and that he will offer royal delicacies; and that Naphtali is a doe let loose, delivering elegant words. Who can tell what any of this is about without a key provided by the inner meaning?

The statements are not about Jacob's sons or the tribes, as is clear from the fact that no such thing happened to them at the end of days, even though Israel says in verse 1 that he will tell what will happen to them then. Since the words do not apply to the sons or tribes, it follows that they apply to the kinds of things the sons and tribes represent. What kinds of things those are was explained above.

6416   Genesis 49:22, 23, 24, 25, 26. *"The son of a fertile woman is Joseph, the son of a fertile woman above the spring; daughters [each] stepped onto the wall. [And] he is vexed and shot at and hated by the archers. And he will sit in the sturdiness of his bow. And his arms and hands are strengthened by the hands of powerful Jacob, from whom comes the Shepherd, the Stone of Israel; by the God of your father, who will help you; and with Shaddai, who will bless you with the blessings of the sky from above, with the blessings of* *the abyss lying below, with the blessings of breasts and womb. The blessings of your father will prevail over the blessings of my forebears, even to the desire of the age-old hills. They will be on the head of Joseph and on the crown of the head of the Nazirite among his brothers."*

The son of a fertile woman is Joseph symbolizes a spiritual religion, and in the highest sense, the Lord's divine spirituality. *The son of a fertile woman above the spring* symbolizes the fruitfulness of truth from the Word. *Daughters [each] stepped onto the wall* means for the purpose of combating falsity. *And he is vexed* symbolizes the resistance put up by falsity. *And shot at* means that they use falsities as weapons. *And hated by the archers* means with utter enmity. *And he will sit in the sturdiness of his bow* means being kept safe by doctrinal truth engaged in battle. *And his arms and hands are strengthened* symbolizes the power of the resources used in fighting. *By the hands of powerful Jacob* means received from the omnipotence of the Lord's divine humanity. *From whom comes the Shepherd, the Stone of Israel,* means that from this the spiritual kingdom acquires all its goodness and truth. *By the God of your father, [who will help you,]* means that he is the God of the ancient church. *And with Shaddai* symbolizes the Lord as the one who does good to us after we have been tested. *Who will bless you with the blessings of the sky from above* means with goodness and truth from within. *With the blessings of the abyss lying below* means with knowledge on the earthly level. *With the blessings of breasts* means with desires for goodness and truth. *And womb* symbolizes their union. *The blessings of your father will prevail over the blessings of my forebears* means that this kind of religion receives spiritual goodness from the earthly rather than the rational plane. *Even to the desire of the age-old hills* means to the point of mutual, heavenly love. *They will be on the head of Joseph* symbolizes the receiving of these blessings in their inner form. *And on the crown of the head of the Nazirite among his brothers* symbolizes the receiving of them in their outer form.

The son of a fertile woman is Joseph symbolizes a spiritual religion, and in the highest sense, the Lord's divine spirituality. This is established by the representation of *Joseph* on the highest level as the Lord's divine spirituality, on the inner level as the spiritual kingdom and the goodness that goes with faith, and on the outer level as becoming fruitful and multiplying (discussed in §§3969, 3971). And since Joseph represents goodness becoming fruitful and truth multiplying, the text calls him the *son of a fertile woman.*

6417

The text here treats of the Lord's spiritual kingdom under the figure of Joseph. Earlier it treated of his heavenly kingdom under the figure of

Judah [§§6363–6373]. Heaven is made up of two kingdoms, you see: the heavenly and the spiritual. The inmost or third heaven constitutes the heavenly kingdom, and the middle or second heaven constitutes the spiritual kingdom. To the spiritual kingdom the Lord appears as a moon, but to the heavenly kingdom as a sun (§§1053, 1521, 1529, 1530, 1531, 4060).

I said that in the highest sense Joseph represents the Lord's divine spirituality, but the real situation is that the Lord is nothing but divine goodness. In the Lord's heavenly kingdom, what emanates from his divine goodness and flows into heaven is called divine heavenliness, while in his spiritual kingdom it is called divine spirituality. So the terms *divine spirituality* and *divine heavenliness* relate to the ways his inflow is received.

6418 *The son of a fertile woman above the spring* symbolizes the fruitfulness of truth from the Word, as the following shows: A *son* symbolizes truth, as dealt with in §§489, 491, 533, 2623, 2803, 2813, 3373, 3704. A *fertile woman* symbolizes the fruitfulness of truth, because like delivery and birth, fertility in a spiritual sense is a characteristic of truth and goodness (§§1145, 1255, 3860, 3868, 4070, 4668, 5598). And a *spring* symbolizes the Word, as dealt with in §§2702, 3424, 4861. These explanations show that the *son of a fertile woman above the spring* symbolizes the fruitfulness of truth from the Word.

In the Lord's spiritual church—the church Joseph represents here—truth from the Word teaches people to recognize what is good. So truth initiates them into goodness, which leads to the fruitfulness symbolized by a fertile woman.

6419 *Daughters [each] stepped onto the wall* means for the purpose of combating falsity, as the following shows: A *daughter* symbolizes a religion, as discussed in §§2362, 3963. Here it symbolizes a spiritual religion, because that is the current subject. *Stepping onto the wall* means for the purpose of combating falsity, as is evident from the next few clauses: "He is vexed and shot at and hated by the archers, and he will sit in the sturdiness of his bow." These words symbolize falsity's battle against truth.

[2] The verse says *[each] stepped onto the wall* because the theme of the inner meaning is an attack by falsity on truth and protection for truth against falsity. A spiritual religion, represented by Joseph, is constantly under attack, but the Lord constantly keeps it safe. So the Word compares aspects of a spiritual religion to a city with a wall, bulwark, gates, and bars on the gates. Attacks on that city depict attacks by falsity on truth. As a result, a city symbolizes doctrinal teachings (§§402, 2268, 2449, 2712, 2943, 3216, 4492, 4493). A wall symbolizes truths of faith, which defend

those teachings, and in a negative sense, falsities that are destroyed. The symbolism of a wall as truths of faith that defend theology is evident in Isaiah:

> *A city strong* for us. *He will make its walls and bulwark* its salvation. Open the gates, so that an upright nation keeping faith may walk in. (Isaiah 26:1, 2)

And in the same author:

> You will call *your walls* salvation, and your gates, praise. (Isaiah 60:18)

In the same author:

> Here, now, I have engraved you on my hands; *your walls are always before me.* (Isaiah 49:16)

The walls stand for the truths that constitute faith. In the same author:

> *On your walls,* Jerusalem, I have set up guards; all day and night they will not keep silent, making mention of Jehovah. (Isaiah 62:6)

The meaning is the same. In Jeremiah:

> This is what Jehovah Sabaoth has said: "I myself am turning back the weapons of war by which you are fighting with the king of Babylon [and with the Chaldeans] *besieging you outside the wall.* I myself will fight with you by an outstretched hand." (Jeremiah 21:4, 5)

In the same author:

> Jehovah has thought to *destroy the wall of Zion's daughter.* He has made the *bulwark* and the *wall* mourn; together they droop. Her *gates* have sunk into the earth; he has destroyed and smashed the *bars* on them. (Lamentations 2:8, 9)

In Ezekiel:

> The sons of Arvad and your army were *on your walls all around.* And the Gammadians were in your towers; their shields they hung *on your walls all around,* and they perfected your beauty. (Ezekiel 27:11)

This is about Tyre, which symbolizes a knowledge of goodness and truth.

[3] This symbolism of a city and walls can also be seen plainly from the description of Jerusalem the Holy coming down out of heaven, as seen by John. Every detail shows that it symbolizes a new religion and

that the wall symbolizes divine truth radiating from the Lord. Here is John's description:

> Jerusalem the Holy was coming down out of heaven, *having a wall big and high,* having twelve gates. The *wall of the city* had twelve foundations, and on them the names of the Lamb's twelve apostles. The one who was talking to me was measuring the city and its gates and its *wall. Its wall* was one hundred forty-four cubits, which is the measure of a human, that is, of an angel. *The structure of the wall was jasper,* and the city was pure gold, like pure glass. The *foundations of the city's wall* were adorned with every precious stone. (Revelation 21:10, 12, 14, 15, 17, 18, 19)

[4] The wall means divine truth radiating from the Lord, and therefore religious truth growing out of neighborly kindness. This is clear from everything said about the wall here. For instance, it says the wall had twelve foundations, and on them the names of the Lamb's twelve apostles. Twelve symbolizes everything (§§3272, 3858, 3913), while the wall and its foundations symbolize religious truths, as do the twelve apostles (§§3488, 3858 at the end, 6397). The passage also says the wall was one hundred forty-four cubits. This number symbolizes what twelve does—everything—because it is the product of twelve times twelve. When the number one hundred forty-four is mentioned in reference to a wall, it symbolizes all religious truth and goodness, so the passage adds that this is the measure of a human, that is, of an angel. It also adds that the structure of the wall was jasper and that its foundations were adorned with every precious stone, because jasper and precious stones symbolize religious truth (§114).

[5] The symbolism of a wall in a negative sense as falsity that is destroyed can be seen from the following places. In Isaiah:

> It is a day of upheaval in the Valley of Vision. The Lord Jehovih Sabaoth *has destroyed the wall,* so that people shout toward the mountain, because Elam took up his quiver with a manned chariot [and] riders; riders positioned [themselves] firmly right up to the gate. (Isaiah 22:5, 6, 7)

In the same author:

> The *stronghold of the refuge of your walls* he will lay low, he will cast down, he will level to the earth, even to the dust. (Isaiah 25:12)

In Jeremiah:

> *Climb onto its walls* and throw them down. (Jeremiah 5:10)

In the same author:

> I will light a *fire against the wall of Damascus* that will consume the palaces of Ben-hadad. (Jeremiah 49:27)

In the same author:

> *Against the walls of Babylon* lift a banner; keep guard; set up guards. (Jeremiah 51:12)

In Ezekiel:

> *They will overturn Tyre's walls* and demolish its towers, and I will remove its dirt from it and make it as dry as a rock. (Ezekiel 26:4, 8, 9, 12)

6420   *And he is vexed* symbolizes the resistance put up by falsity. This can be seen from the symbolism of *vexing* as resistance. The current passage is about a struggle, and when there is struggle, then the more resistance there is, the more vexation. The next few phrases show that falsity is what puts up the resistance.

6421   *And shot at* means that they use falsities as weapons. This can be seen from the symbolism of *shooting* as using falsities as weapons. A bow symbolizes theology. Arrows symbolize the tenets of a theology, so in people who subscribe to truth they symbolize true teachings, while in people who subscribe to falsity they symbolize false teachings. See §§2686, 2709. Shooting means using falsity as a weapon here because this verse is about people who subscribe to falsity.

6422   *And hated by the archers* means with utter enmity, as the following shows: *Hatred* symbolizes utter enmity because one who hates another persecutes that other with all possible hostility. And *archers* here symbolize foes of the people in a spiritual religion. An archer means a spiritual person, because a bow symbolizes the teachings of a spiritual religion (§§2686, 2709), so in a negative sense an archer means a person fighting as an enemy against a spiritual person. For the meaning of an archer as a spiritual person, see §§2686, 2709. *Hated by the archers,* then, plainly means that people whose thinking is distorted persecute members of a spiritual religion with utter enmity.

6423   *And he will sit in the sturdiness of his bow* means being kept safe by doctrinal truth engaged in battle, as the following shows: *Sitting* means being kept safe, because someone who sits in the sturdiness of a bow is safe. A *bow* symbolizes a theology, as discussed in §§2686, 2709. The *sturdiness* of theology is truth, because a theology without truth has no strength. On the point that truth possesses strength and moral power, see §§878 at the end, 3091, 4932, 4934, 4937, 6344.

The reason truth has strength is that it provides the means by which goodness acts. Goodness by nature is such that nothing evil or false can go near it. Neither therefore can anyone from the mob in hell, which runs far away when goodness—or an angel with goodness—approaches. But goodness seeks to combat the crowd we have with us from hell and to safeguard us in every way. It wishes to protect spirits newly arrived from the world, too, and the inhabitants of the underground realm. So to gain the ability to do this, goodness acts by means of truth, because it can then approach [hellish spirits].

[2] The amount of power truth contains was made clear to me from sights I was privileged to see in the other world. A spirit who was equipped with earthly-level truth (because he had dealt fairly with others during his life in the world) passed through a number of hells and described them to me by speaking from there. He had so much strength and moral power that the spirits in the hells could not bother him, and he therefore moved safely on from one hell to the next. People without truth cannot possibly do this.

This evidence shows that *he will sit in the sturdiness of his bow* means being kept safe by doctrinal truth. The idea that this truth is engaged in battle follows from the preceding words—that he was shot at and hated by the archers.

6424   *And his arms and hands are strengthened* symbolizes the power of the resources used in fighting. This is established by the symbolism of *arms* and *hands* as powers, as discussed in §§878, 3091, 3387, 4931–4937, 5327, 5328, 5544. Clearly the power is that of the resources used in fighting, since battle is the theme.

6425   *By the hands of powerful Jacob* means received from the omnipotence of the Lord's divine humanity, as the following shows: *Hands* symbolize power, as noted just above at §6424. In the highest sense, which has to do with the Lord, they symbolize omnipotence (§§878, 3387, 4592, 4933 at the end). And *powerful Jacob* symbolizes the Lord's earthly divinity, so it symbolizes his divine humanity (§§1893, 3305, 3576, 3599, 4286, 4538, 6098, 6185, 6276).

The fact that the Lord is the one meant by "powerful Jacob" is also plain in David:

> . . . who swore to Jehovah, *vowed to powerful Jacob:* "If I enter within the tent of my house . . . Until I find the place of Jehovah, the *dwellings of powerful Jacob.*" (Psalms 132:2, 3, 5)

And in Isaiah:

> . . . so that all flesh may know that I, Jehovah, am your Savior and your Redeemer, *powerful Jacob.* (Isaiah 49:26)

In the same author:

> Listen, Jacob, my servant, and Israel, whom I have chosen: I will pour my spirit out on your seed and my blessing on your offspring. This one says, "I am Jehovah's," *and he will call himself by Jacob's name,* and that one will write "Jehovah's" on his hand and *surname himself by Israel's name.* (Isaiah 44:1, 3, 5)

Israel in the highest sense is also the Lord, as in Hosea:

> When *Israel* was a boy, then I loved him, and out of Egypt I called my child. (Hosea 11:1)

The fact that the Lord is the one meant by Israel there can be seen in Matthew:

> Joseph went with the boy into Egypt, so that there would be a fulfillment of the saying by the prophet, "Out of Egypt I called my child." (Matthew 2:14, 15)

From whom comes the Shepherd, the Stone of Israel, means that from **6426** this the spiritual kingdom acquires all its goodness and truth, as the following shows: A *shepherd* symbolizes one who leads people to neighborly kindness through religious truth, as discussed at §§343, 3795, 6044. In the highest sense here, since the passage is about the Lord, the shepherd symbolizes goodness and truth itself. A *stone* symbolizes truth, as dealt with in §§1298, 3720, 3769, 3771, 3773, 3789, 3798. And *Israel* represents a spiritual religion, as dealt with at §§3305, 4286. After all, Israel means spiritual goodness, or the goodness that grows out of truth (§§4286, 4598,

5801, 5803, 5807, 5812, 5817, 5819, 5826, 5833). Truth-based goodness is the essential characteristic of a spiritual religion, so Israel symbolizes a spiritual religion, and in a higher sense, the Lord's spiritual kingdom.

This explanation shows that *from whom comes the Shepherd, the Stone of Israel,* means that from [the omnipotence of the Lord's divine humanity] the Lord's spiritual kingdom acquires all its goodness and truth.

[2] In the highest sense the *Stone of Israel* is the Lord in the role of truth for his spiritual kingdom. The reason for this meaning is that a stone means the Temple generally, and specifically its foundation, and the Temple symbolizes the Lord's divine humanity. This symbolism of the Temple is clear in John 2:19, 21, and this symbolism of its foundation, in Matthew 21:42, 44; Isaiah 28:16.

The meaning of a stone in the highest sense as the Lord in the role of divine truth for his spiritual kingdom can be seen in David:

> A stone that the builders rejected has become the head of the corner; from Jehovah this has happened. [The stone] is miraculous in our eyes. (Psalms 118:22, 23)

The fact that this stone is the Lord can be seen in Luke:

> It has been written, "*The stone that the builders rejected has become the head of the corner;* whoever falls on that *stone* will be shattered, but the one on whom it falls it will pulverize." (Luke 20:17, 18)

The Lord says these things about himself. In Isaiah:

> He is your fear, and he is your dread, since he will become a sanctuary but also a *stone to trip on* and a *rock to stumble over* for the two houses of Israel. Many among them will stumble and fall and be shattered. (Isaiah 8:13, 14, 15)

This is about the Lord. In the same author:

> The Lord Jehovih has said, "Here, I am [the one who] *will lay as a foundation in Zion a stone, a well-tested stone, a precious corner[stone], for a firm foundation.* One who believes will not rush." (Isaiah 28:16)

In Zechariah:

> Jehovah Sabaoth will visit his flock, the house of Judah, and make them like a glorious horse in war; from [Judah] comes the *cornerstone,* from him the nail, from him the *war bow.* (Zechariah 10:3, 4)

[3] In Daniel:

> You were looking, until *a stone was cut out that was not [cut out] by hands,* and it struck the statue on its feet, which were iron and clay, and crushed them. *The stone that struck the statue turned into a great rock* and filled all the earth. The God of the heavens will raise up a kingdom that will not be destroyed to eternity, and their kingdom will not be left to another people. It will crush and consume all those kingdoms, but it itself will stand forever. Because you saw *that a stone was cut out of rock that was not [cut out] by hands,* and it crushed iron, bronze, clay, silver, and gold, . . . (Daniel 2:34, 35, 44, 45)

This stone means the Lord in its highest sense and his spiritual kingdom in a secondary sense. The stone's being cut out of rock means that this kingdom rose out of the true concepts of faith, as that is what rock symbolizes in the Word. Since stone and rock symbolize the true concepts of faith, they also symbolize the Lord's spiritual kingdom, which is intent on such truth and therefore on what is good.

[4] The stone on which Jacob slept and which he then set as a pillar has the same symbolism. Here is the report:

> Jacob woke from his sleep and said, "Surely Jehovah is in this place and I didn't know." And he was afraid and said, "How frightening this place is! *This is nothing but the house of God,* and this is the gate of heaven." And Jacob got up early in the morning and *took the stone* that he had put as his headrest and put it as a pillar and poured oil on its head. He said, "*This stone that I have put as a pillar will be the house of God.*" (Genesis 28:16, 17, 18, 22)

It becomes clear in Joshua too that the ancients took a stone to mean the Lord in the highest sense and his spiritual kingdom in a representative sense:

> *Joshua set up a stone* beneath the oak that was in Jehovah's sanctuary. And Joshua said to the whole people, "Look: *this stone* will serve as a witness to us, *because it* has heard *all Jehovah's speech* that he spoke with us, and it will serve as a witness against us to prevent you from denying your God." (Joshua 24:26, 27)

The explanations above show what kind of content the inner meaning of these two verses holds, but the ideas are necessarily puzzling to one who does not know what the spiritual kingdom is like. The spiritual

6427

kingdom is made up of individuals to whom faith and its truth are important but who make faith's truth part of their life, turning it into goodness. When people live by the truth that composes faith, it becomes goodness and is called truth-based goodness, although in its essence it is truth in action.

Faith's truth varies in the Lord's spiritual church, because what one religion calls untrue another calls true. It depends on the theology of each religion. What these religions refer to as truths, then, are actually doctrines. These are the truths that unite with goodness to become the goodness of a spiritual religion. The goodness consequently takes on the same character as the truth, because truth is what gives goodness its quality.

[2] From this you can see that the goodness of a spiritual religion is impure, and as it is impure, spiritual individuals can gain entrance to heaven only through divine means. The central divine means was the Lord's coming into the world and making the humanity in himself divine. This saved the spiritual.

Since goodness in the spiritual is impure, they cannot help being plagued by evil and falsity and therefore being conflicted. The Lord, however, provides for the impurity in them to be purified gradually through the conflicts they undergo, because he fights for them. That is the symbolism of the words "[each] daughter stepped onto the wall," "he is vexed and shot at and hated by the archers," and "he will sit in the sturdiness of his bow, and his arms and hands are strengthened by the hands of powerful Jacob, from whom comes the Shepherd, the Stone of Israel."

[3] See previous discussions of the people in a spiritual religion: They are somewhat in the dark regarding truth and therefore goodness (2708, 2715, 2718, 2831, 2935, 2937, 3241, 3246, 3833, 6289); their dim conditions are lit by the Lord's divine humanity (2716); before the Lord's Coming there was no spiritual kingdom of the kind that existed afterward (6372); the Lord came into the world to save the spiritual, and they are saved by his divine humanity (2661, 2716, 2833, 2834, 3969).

This evidence also shows that "His arms and hands are strengthened by the hands of powerful Jacob, from whom comes the Shepherd, the Stone of Israel" symbolizes the power of the resources used in fighting, received from the omnipotence of the Lord's divine humanity, which is where the spiritual kingdom acquires all its goodness and truth (§§6424, 6425, 6426).

6428   *By the God of your father, who will help you,* means that he is the God of the ancient church. This can be seen from the representation of Jacob, the *father*, as the ancient church, as treated of in §§4439, 4514, 4680, 4772. The ancient church was a spiritual religion that worshiped the Lord, who is meant here by the God of the ancient church, and he gives help during inner conflict, as noted just above.

And with Shaddai symbolizes the Lord as the one who does good to **6429** us after we have been tested. This can be seen from the symbolism of *Shaddai* as the name applied to the Lord in respect to trials and to the benefits that follow trial (discussed in §§1992, 3667, 4572, 5628).

Who will bless you with the blessings of the sky from above means with **6430** goodness and truth from within, as the following shows: *Blessings* symbolize the multiplication of truth and the fruitfulness of what is good. A blessing in a spiritual sense is nothing else. The *sky from above* means from within, because our sky, [or heaven,] is within us. On the inside, people who live a good life are in company with angels and are therefore in heaven. On the outside they are in company with other people and are therefore in the world. So when we welcome goodness and truth, which come from within as an inflow from the Lord through heaven, we are *blessed with the blessings of the sky from above.*

With the blessings of the abyss lying below means with knowledge on **6431** the earthly level. This is clear from the symbolism of being blessed *with blessings* as receiving the kind of gifts that come from the spiritual world, and from the symbolism of the *abyss lying below* as knowledge on the earthly plane.

The earthly level is called an abyss lying below in relation to inner levels, which are the sky, as noted just above at §6430, and since the abyss lying below symbolizes the earthly level, it also symbolizes knowledge. Knowledge and the pleasure it gives exist on the earthly plane and make up the vital energy there, especially in a spiritual person, who is introduced by knowledge into truth and by truth into goodness. Plainly, then, being blessed *with the blessings of the abyss lying below* means being gifted with knowledge and so with truth on the earthly level.

In Moses' blessing on Joseph as well the abyss symbolizes truth in the form of knowledge on the earthly level:

> A blessing from Jehovah on his land in the precious worth of the sky, in the dew, *and in the underlying abyss.* (Deuteronomy 33:13)

With the blessings of breasts means with desires for goodness and truth. **6432** This can be seen from the symbolism of *breasts* as desires for goodness and truth. The reason breasts have this meaning is that they communicate with the reproductive organs, and because they do, they belong to the province of marriage love. (Concerning this province, see §§5050–5062.) Marriage love corresponds to the heavenly marriage, which is the marriage of goodness and truth (since marriage love descends from the heavenly marriage, §§2618, 2728, 2729, 2803, 3132, 4434, 4835, 6179), so breasts symbolize desires for goodness and truth. A further reason for the symbolism is the fact that breasts are for feeding babies, and through this desire [for nourishing babies] they symbolize the strong link between marriage love and love for offspring.

[2] Breasts symbolize these desires in Isaiah too:

> You will suck the milk of the nations, and *you will suck the breasts of kings.* For bronze I will bring in gold, and for iron, silver. (Isaiah 60:16, 17)

Sucking the breasts of kings stands for sucking goodness from truth, since kings symbolize truth (§§1672, 2015, 2069, 3009, 3670, 4575, 4581, 4966, 5044, 5068, 6148). The milk of the nations and the breasts of kings clearly have some hidden symbolism that is spiritual, since otherwise they would be meaningless words. The fact that they symbolize goodness and truth is plain from the words that follow: "For bronze I will bring in gold, and for iron, silver." Bronze is earthly-level goodness (425, 1551), gold is heavenly goodness (113, 1551, 1552, 5658), iron is earthly-level truth (425, 426), and silver is spiritual truth (1551, 2954, 5658, 6112). [3] In Ezekiel:

> Regarding your growth: I have made you a young shoot in the field, so you have grown and matured and come into [the time of] the most beautiful of ornaments; *your breasts have become firm,* and your hair has grown. (Ezekiel 16:7)

This is about Jerusalem, which here symbolizes the ancient church, a spiritual religion. The firm breasts stand for inner desires for goodness and truth. "Your hair has grown" stands for outer desires belonging to the earthly level. (For the meaning of hair as truth on the earthly level, see §§3301, 5247, 5569–5573.) Obviously these words contain a spiritual meaning that is not visible in the literal text, because without such a meaning, what sense would there be in saying that Jerusalem's breasts had become firm or that its hair had grown? [4] In the same author:

> There were two women, the daughters of one mother, who whored in Egypt; in their youth they whored. *In that place their breasts were squeezed,* and in that place [men] fondled their virgin bosoms. (Ezekiel 23:2, 3, 8, 21)

The two women are Jerusalem and Samaria, as the text there says [Ezekiel 23:4], and in an inner sense they symbolize two churches. Their whoring with Egypt in their youth means that they used knowledge to turn the church's truth into falsity. (For the symbolism of whoring as falsification of truth, see §§2466, 4865; and for that of Egypt as knowledge, §§1164, 1165, 1186, 1462, 5700, 5702.) So "their breasts were squeezed" means that their desire for goodness and truth was corrupted by their falsifications. The fact that this is the symbolism of the women's whoring and of the squeezing of their breasts is clear to readers who look closely into the meaning of the description of the women. [5] In Hosea:

> Strive with your mother. Have her remove her whorings from before her, *and her adulteries from between her breasts,* or else I will strip her naked and make her like a wilderness and cause her to be like a land of drought and kill her with thirst. (Hosea 2:2, 3)

The mother stands for the church (§§289, 2691, 2717, 3703, 4257, 5581). The whorings stand for the falsification of what is true (2466, 4865), the adulteries for adulteration of what is good (2466, 2729, 3399). Adulteries between her breasts, then, stand for desires for goodness and truth that have been adulterated. Stripping her naked stands for depriving the church of all its truth (1073, 4958, 5433). Making her like a wilderness, causing her to be like a land of drought, and killing her with thirst stand for blotting out all truth. [6] In the same author:

> Give them a miscarrying womb and *dry breasts.* (Hosea 9:14)

Dry breasts stand for desires for what is not true or good. In Isaiah:

> Carefree women, stand up; listen to my voice; blithe daughters, perceive my words with your ears. Strip and bare yourself and *wrap your hips [in sackcloth]. They are beating their breasts* because of the fields of unmixed wine and the fruitful grapevine. (Isaiah 32:9, 11, 12)

The daughters stand for desires (§§2362, 3024, 3963). Being bared stands for being deprived of truth (§§1073, 4958, 5433). Wrapping their hips stands for grieving over lost goodness. Beating their breasts stands for grieving over lost goodness-from-truth. This being the symbolism, the passage says "because of the fields of unmixed wine and the fruitful grapevine." A field is the church in regard to goodness and therefore goodness in the church (§§2971, 3196, 3310, 3766), and a grapevine is a spiritual church and consequently goodness-from-truth (§§5113, 6375, 6376). [7] In Revelation:

> I saw seven golden lampstands, and in the middle of the seven lampstands, one like the Son of Humankind, wearing a robe, *and circled at the breasts with a golden band.* (Revelation 1:12, 13)

The golden lampstands are truth-from-goodness. The Son of Humankind is divine truth. His being circled at the breasts with a golden band means a loving goodness. Considering the holiness of the Word, anyone can reach the conclusion that John's visions have to do with phenomena in the Lord's kingdom and in his church, because how holy would it be to make predictions about the kingdoms of the world? It is possible to see, then, that something heavenly is symbolized by the lampstands and by the fact that the Son of Humankind was wearing a robe and was circled at the breasts with a golden band. [8] In Luke:

> A woman raised her voice from among the people; she said of Jesus, "Happy is the belly that carried you *and the breasts that you sucked!*" But Jesus said, "Yet in reality, happy are those who hear God's word and keep it!" (Luke 11:27, 28)

The Lord's answer reveals what the belly that is happy and the breasts symbolize; they symbolize people who hear God's word and keep it. Accordingly, they symbolize the desire for truth felt by people who hear God's word, and the desire for goodness felt by people who keep or do it.

6433   *And womb* symbolizes their union—the union of goodness and truth. This can be seen from the symbolism of the *womb* as the inmost core of marriage love. Since marriage love rises out of the heavenly marriage, which is the union of goodness and truth, the womb symbolizes this union. For the symbolism of the womb as the inmost core of marriage love, see §4918. For the idea that marriage love rises out of the heavenly marriage, or the union of goodness and truth in heaven, §§2618, 2728, 2729, 2803, 3132, 4434, 4835, 6179.

6434   *The blessings of your father will prevail over the blessings of my forebears* means that this kind of religion receives spiritual goodness from the earthly plane, as the following shows: Joseph represents a spiritual religion, as discussed in §6417. Israel, the *father,* represents spiritual goodness on the earthly plane, as discussed in §§5801, 5803, 5807, 5812, 5817, 5819, 5826, 5833. In the highest sense, Isaac and Abraham, the *forebears,* represent the Lord's inner divinity. Isaac represents inner divine humanity, or the Lord's divine rationality (1893, 2066, 2072, 2083, 2630, 3012, 3194, 3210), and Abraham represents the Lord's divinity itself (2010, 3251, 3439, 4615). In a secondary sense, Abraham and Isaac represent the inner part of the Lord's kingdom and church (6098, 6185, 6276).

These remarks to some extent show that *the blessings of your father will prevail over the blessings of my forebears* means that a spiritual religion will receive goodness from the earthly, outer self rather than the rational, inner self. The goodness in a person who is part of a spiritual religion exists on the earthly plane and ventures no further, but the goodness in a heavenly religion exists on the rational plane.

It is impossible to see that this is the meaning unless one knows what Israel represents, what Isaac and Abraham represent, where the goodness in a spiritual religion lies, and where it comes from.

Even to the desire of the age-old hills means to the point of mutual, heavenly love. This can be seen from the symbolism of *age-old hills* as manifestations of mutual love, as discussed below. *Even to the desire of* the age-old hills means in order for the spiritual church to arrive at this love.

6435

First, before using other passages in the Word to demonstrate the symbolism of age-old hills as mutual love, I need to say what is meant by the mutual love a person in a spiritual religion works hard to get—the kind of religion Joseph represents. Numerous earlier discussions and explanations have shown that two kingdoms constitute heaven: a heavenly kingdom and a spiritual one. The difference between the two kingdoms is that the inner goodness of the heavenly kingdom is the goodness that comes of love for the Lord, while the outer goodness there is the goodness that comes of mutual love. Inhabitants of the heavenly kingdom focus on love and goodness, not on the truth people associate with faith. Truth is present in the goodness practiced by that kingdom and in fact cannot be seen separately from goodness. So the inhabitants of that kingdom cannot even use the word "faith" (§§202, 203, 4448). In place of the truth that composes faith they have the goodness that constitutes mutual love.

As for the spiritual kingdom, its inner depths consist in the goodness that comes of charity for one's neighbor, while its outer level consists in the truth taught by faith.

[2] These comments illuminate the difference between the two kingdoms and show that they have a meeting point. The point at which they meet is where the outer aspect of the heavenly kingdom intersects with the inner aspect of the spiritual kingdom through a middle ground called

spiritual heavenliness. As was said above, the outer aspect of the heavenly kingdom is the goodness that comes of mutual love, and the inner aspect of the spiritual kingdom is the goodness that comes of charity for one's neighbor. The goodness that goes with mutual love is deeper than the goodness that goes with charity for one's neighbor, because the former draws on what is rational, the latter on what is earthly. Yet although the goodness that goes with mutual love (the outer aspect of a heavenly religion) is inward, and the goodness that goes with charity for one's neighbor is outward, the Lord still unites the two kinds of goodness through a middle ground, as just mentioned. By uniting the two kinds of goodness he unites the two kingdoms.

[3] In what follows, let me distinguish between the outer goodness of a heavenly religion and the inner goodness of a spiritual religion by calling the former the goodness of mutual love and the latter the goodness of charity for one's neighbor. This is a distinction I have not observed in what precedes.

Once these facts have been established, it is possible to convey the symbolism of *even to the desire of the age-old hills*—one of Israel's blessings concerning this spiritual religion. The symbolism is an intent that the spiritual kingdom climb beyond the goodness of charity all the way to the goodness of mutual love characterizing the heavenly kingdom and that the two kingdoms be intimately united as a result. That is what the phrase symbolizes.

[4] Many passages in the prophetical part of the Word mention mountains and hills, which in an inner sense symbolize the goodness that comes of love. Mountains symbolize the goodness that comes of love for the Lord, which is the inner part of the heavenly kingdom. Hills symbolize the goodness that comes of mutual love, which is the outer part of the same kingdom. Where the theme is the spiritual kingdom, though, mountains symbolize the goodness that comes of charity for one's neighbor, which is the inner part of that kingdom, and hills symbolize the truth espoused by faith, which is its outer part.

Keep in mind that every church of the Lord's has an inner and outer facet and that in consequence both of his kingdoms do too.

[5] This symbolism of hills can be seen from the following passages. In Isaiah:

> In the end of days *Jehovah's mountain* will become the *head of the mountains* and will be loftier *than the hills*. (Isaiah 2:2; Micah 4:1)

Jehovah's mountain, which is Zion, stands for the Lord's heavenly kingdom and therefore for the goodness in that kingdom, which is the goodness that comes of love for the Lord. In the highest sense, then, it means the Lord himself, since all love and all goodness in the heavenly kingdom is the Lord's. [6] Mount Zion has the same symbolism elsewhere in the Word, and its hill symbolizes the goodness belonging to mutual love. In Isaiah, for example:

> Jehovah Sabaoth will come down to do battle *on Zion's mountain* and *on its hill.* (Isaiah 31:4)

The hill here stands for good that is done out of mutual love. Since the hill symbolizes good that is done out of mutual love, and the mountain symbolizes good that is done out of heavenly love, or love for the Lord, the verse says that Jehovah comes down to do battle on that mountain. Jehovah does not do battle on Mount Zion or its hill; but where a loving goodness exists, the Lord (who is Jehovah here) does battle on its behalf. That is, he does battle on behalf of people who have a loving goodness. If he fights for Zion and Jerusalem, it is because they once represented a heavenly religion. That is also why Mount Zion was called holy and why Jerusalem was said to be holy too, even though in itself it was impure (as is evident in the Prophets, where they talk about its abominations). [7] In David:

> The *mountains* will bring peace, as will the *hills,* in righteousness. (Psalms 72:3)

In the same author:

> *Praise Jehovah, you mountains* and *all you hills.* (Psalms 148: [7,] 9)

In the same author:

> The *mountains* leaped like rams; the *hills,* like the offspring of the flock. (Psalms 114:4, 6)

In the same author:

> *Mountain of God, mountain of Bashan. Mountain of hills, mountain of Bashan. Why do you leap up, you mountains, you hills of mountains?* God wants to inhabit *it;* yes, Jehovah will reside [there] to eternity. (Psalms 68:15, 16)

The mountains in these passages stand for heavenly love and the hills for spiritual love. Obviously it is not mountains and hills that are meant, nor the people who lived on mountains and hills. [8] In Isaiah:

> It will be that *on every high mountain* and *on every lofty hill* there will be brooks, channels of water. (Isaiah 30:25)

Channels of water stand for concepts of goodness and truth. Such concepts are said to be on every high mountain and lofty hill because they flow from the goodness belonging to heavenly and spiritual love. [9] In Habakkuk:

> Jehovah stood and measured the earth; he saw and dispersed the nations, because the *eternal mountains* were scattered, and the *age-old hills* humbled themselves. (Habakkuk 3:6)

The eternal mountains stand for a goodness inspired by love that belonged to the earliest church, a heavenly religion. The age-old hills stand for a goodness inspired by the mutual love that belonged to that church. The first formed its core, the second its outer level. When this church is meant in the Word, the adjective "eternal" is sometimes used, because that church was the earliest. The passage above, for instance, mentions eternal mountains, and other passages mention the days of eternity (§6239). The adjective "age-old" is sometimes used as well. The age-old hills here are an example, and so is "to the desire of the age-old hills" in Israel's prophecy. These considerations show that the age-old hills symbolize the goodness of mutual love, which belongs to a heavenly religion, or to the Lord's heavenly kingdom. [10] Likewise in Moses, in his prophetic utterance concerning Joseph:

> Let some of the first fruits of the *eastern mountains* and some of the precious worth of the *eternal hills* come on the head of Joseph. (Deuteronomy 33:15, 16)

In Isaiah:

> The *mountains and hills* will ring with song, and all the trees of the field will clap the palms of their hands. (Isaiah 55:12)

In Joel:

> On that day the *mountains* will shower down new wine and the *hills* will stream with milk and all the brooks of Judah will stream with water. (Joel 3:18; Amos 9:13)

In Ezekiel:

> My sheep wander *in all the mountains* and on *every high hill,* and on the whole face of the earth they have scattered. I will make them—and the *environs of my hill*—a blessing and send down the rain in its season. (Ezekiel 34:6, 26)

In Jeremiah:

> *Over all the hills in the wilderness* have come the destroyers, because Jehovah's sword is devouring. (Jeremiah 12:12)

In these passages the mountains symbolize the goodness of a heavenly love, and the hills symbolize the same thing but on a lower level.

[11] As this is what mountains and hills symbolized, the ancient church held divine worship on mountains and on hills. Later, the Hebrew nation placed altars on mountains and hills, and there they performed sacrifices and burned incense. Where there were no hills, they erected high places. People rendered this type of worship idolatrous by taking the mountains and hills themselves to be holy, obliterating from their minds the holy qualities these symbolized. As a consequence, the people of Israel and Judah were forbidden to engage in such worship, because they leaned far more heavily toward idolatry than other peoples did. Still, Mount Zion was chosen to continue filling this representative role that had existed since ancient times. In the highest sense Zion represented the divine goodness belonging to the Lord's divine love, and in a secondary sense, divine heavenliness and divine spirituality in the Lord's kingdom.

[12] That being the symbolism, Abraham was ordered to sacrifice his son on one of the mountains in the land of Moriah [Genesis 22:2]. The Lord also appeared to Moses on a mountain, and it was from a mountain that the law was issued—the appearance to Moses having taken place on Mount Horeb [Exodus 3] and the issuing of the law on Mount Sinai [Exodus 19–20]. In addition, the Temple of Jerusalem was built on a mountain.

[13] The fact that sacred worship on mountains and hills was an ancient custom later taken up by non-Jewish nations, and that idolaters in Israel and Judah offered sacrifices and incense there, is evident in Jeremiah:

> Your adulteries and your whinnyings, the enormity of your whoredom *on the hills in the field*—I have seen your abominations. (Jeremiah 13:27)

This is about Jerusalem. In Ezekiel:

> . . . when their victims of stabbing lie amid their idols around their altars *on every high hill, on all the heads of the mountains,* and under every green tree, and under every tangled oak. (Ezekiel 6:13)

In Jeremiah:

> *On every high hill* and under every green tree you are going the crooked harlot's way. (Jeremiah 2:20; 3:6)

Additional passages are 1 Kings 14:23; 2 Kings 16:4; 17:10.

[14] Because mountains and hills were the site for idolatrous worship, in a negative sense they symbolize evil that comes of self-love, as in Jeremiah:

> And here, the *mountains* are shaking and *all the hills* are being overthrown. I looked, when there! Not a human! And every bird of the sky had flown away. (Jeremiah 4:24, 25)

In Isaiah:

> Every valley will be raised up, and *every mountain and hill* will be lowered. (Isaiah 40:4)

In the same author:

> Here, I have made you into the sharpest of new threshing boards, equipped with spikes. *May you thresh mountains* and make the *hills* like chaff. (Isaiah 41:15)

In the same author:

> I will devastate *mountains* and *hills,* and all their grass I will wither. (Isaiah 42:15)

In Micah:

> Hear, please, what Jehovah is speaking: "Get up; quarrel *with the mountains,* and *let the hills hear your voice."* (Micah 6:1)

In Jeremiah:

> My people were lost sheep; their shepherds led them astray. *You defiant mountains, they have gone down from mountain onto hill;* they have forgotten their resting place. (Jeremiah 50:6)

There are other passages as well, such as Jeremiah 16:16; Nahum 1:5, 6.

[15] The reason mountains and hills symbolized the doing of good out of heavenly and spiritual love was that they towered above the ground. High, towering places symbolized what belonged to heaven, and in the highest sense, what belonged to the Lord. The land of Canaan, you see, symbolized the Lord's heavenly kingdom (§§1607, 3038, 3481, 3705, 4240, 4447), so everything there had symbolic meaning, and the mountains and hills were symbolic of what is high. When the earliest people, who had a heavenly religion, climbed a mountain, what occurred to them was the idea of height, and height made them think of what was holy. This was because Jehovah (the Lord) was said to live on the highest heights, and because height in a spiritual sense meant a loving goodness (§650).

They will be on the head of Joseph symbolizes the receiving of these **6436** blessings in their inner form. This can be seen from the symbolism of a *head* as inner levels, because everything about us has its starting point in our head. The symbolism of the head as inner levels also comes from correspondence, which gives rise to the symbolism of the neck as a middle ground, the torso as outer levels, and the legs and feet as outermost levels.

This correspondence is a consequence of the fact that heaven resembles a universal human being. The inmost heaven, where the Lord's heavenly kingdom exists, resembles this being's head; the middle or second heaven, where his spiritual kingdom exists, resembles its torso; and the outermost or first heaven resembles its legs and feet. See §§4938, 4939, 5328, 6292.

And on the crown of the head of the Nazirite among his brothers symbol- **6437** izes the receiving of them in their outer form. This can be seen from the symbolism of the *crown of the head of the Nazirite* as outer levels (discussed below) and from the representation of Israel's sons as spiritual truth on the earthly level (discussed at §§5414, 5879, 5951). This kind of truth is also relatively shallow, because a person in a spiritual religion has truth-based goodness, and this goodness is deeper [than truth on the earthly level], since it lies on a deeper earthly plane.

A *Nazirite* symbolizes outer levels because Nazirites represented the Lord's earthly divinity, which is the outer part of his divine humanity. This representation of a Nazirite can be seen from the fact that Naziriteship is hair and that its holiness lay in the Nazirite's hair. Naziriteship consisted in hair for the sake of the representation mentioned, because hair corresponds to the earthly plane and therefore symbolizes what is earthly; see §§3301, 5247, 5569–5573. The same thing can be seen from people making the vow of Naziriteship, who were forbidden to shave their hair during that period (Numbers 6:5). Later, when they had completed the days of their Naziriteship, they would shave their head at the doorway of the tent and put the hair onto the fire under the thanksgiving sacrifice (Numbers 6:13, 18). Still further evidence of the representation is Samson, a Nazirite, whose strength lay in his hair (Judges 13:3, 5; 16:1–end). See §3301. Jeremiah therefore says:

> *Chop off the hair of your Naziriteship* and throw it away and raise a lament on the hills. (Jeremiah 7:29)

All these examples show that the crown of the head of the Nazirite symbolizes outer levels, since the crown of a Nazirite's head is where the Nazirite's hair is.

This is the secret symbolized by Nazirites in the Word.

6438   These predictions of Israel's concerning Joseph demonstrate once again that every detail has an inner meaning and that without the inner meaning hardly anything can be understood.

People who look only at the literal meaning believe that what was said here about Joseph came to pass (as predicted in verse 1) for the descendants he had through Manasseh and Ephraim. However, no such thing is found in the narratives concerning them in the books of Moses, Joshua, Judges, Samuel, or Kings. They were no more blessed than the others, and like the others they too were carried off into captivity and scattered among the surrounding nations. Plainly, then, it is not the apparent message of the literal sense that is the meaning but something else belonging to the inner sense.

Furthermore, without the inner sense it is impossible to see what any of the statements about Joseph mean. Take the words "the son of a fertile woman is Joseph, of a fertile woman above the spring," "daughters, [each] stepped onto the wall," "he is vexed, shot at, and hated by the archers," "he will sit in the sturdiness of his bow, and his arms and hands will be strengthened by the hands of powerful Jacob, from whom comes the Shepherd, the Stone of Israel," "the blessings of [Joseph's] father will prevail over the blessings of [Israel's] forebears, even to the desire of the age-old hills," and "they will be on the head of Joseph and on the crown of the head of the Nazirite among his brothers." Every one of these statements by its very nature is incapable of being understood except from its inner meaning.

6439   Genesis 49:27. *"Benjamin, a wolf, will seize [game] in the morning, eat the spoils, and at evening divide the prey."*

Benjamin symbolizes truth drawn from the goodness of a spiritual religion (this goodness being Joseph). *A wolf* symbolizes eagerness to rescue good people and liberate them. *Will seize [game] in the morning, eat the spoils* means that this will happen when the Lord is present. *And at evening divide the prey* symbolizes a possession for them in the Lord's kingdom while they are still in the dark.

Benjamin symbolizes truth drawn from the goodness of a spiritual religion (this goodness being Joseph). This symbolism can be seen from the representation of *Benjamin* as heavenly spirituality, discussed in §4592. Heavenly spirituality is truth drawn from goodness. Here it is truth drawn from the goodness belonging to a spiritual religion, and in this mystical utterance of Israel's, Joseph represents a spiritual religion. Since Joseph represents a spiritual religion (§6417), he also represents the goodness belonging to that religion, because a religion is a religion on account of what is good in it. The truth growing out of this goodness is Benjamin.

6440

A wolf symbolizes eagerness to rescue good people and liberate them. This is evident from the symbolism of a *wolf* as one who seizes and scatters. Since animals in the Word symbolize appetites, a wolf symbolizes ravenous greed, as is also clear in Scripture passages mentioning a wolf. In Matthew, for instance:

6441

> Beware of false prophets who come to you in sheep's clothes but inwardly are *ravenous wolves*. (Matthew 7:15)

In John:

> The hired servant who is not a shepherd, whose own the sheep are not, *sees the wolf coming* and abandons the sheep and flees, and *the wolf seizes them* and *scatters the sheep*. (John 10:12)

Likewise in other passages, such as Luke 10:3; Jeremiah 5:6; Ezekiel 22:27; Zephaniah 3:3. From this it is plain that a wolf symbolizes rapacious people. Here, though, the wolf symbolizes one who snatches away from hell people who have been seized [and carried there].

The symbolism of a wolf has something in common with that of a lion, which is also a predator. A lion is also said to seize quarry, gather spoils, and hunt prey, as a wolf is said to do here, and yet in a positive sense a lion symbolizes truth-from-goodness in all its might; see §6367. It is the same with other predators, such as leopards and eagles.

Will seize [game] in the morning, eat the spoils means that this will happen when the Lord is present, as the following shows: *Morning* in the

6442

highest sense symbolizes the Lord, as discussed in §§2405, 2780, so *will seize [game] in the morning* means that when the Lord is present, the good will be rescued and liberated. And *eating the spoils* means taking as his own the people he has rescued and delivered. For the symbolism of *eating* as adopting and uniting with, see §§3168, 3513, 3596, 5643. The identification of the *spoils* with the people who have been rescued and freed is plain.

In the Word the Lord is associated with predation, quarry, spoils, and prey because he rescues and liberates the good. This can be seen from the statement about Judah above at verse 9: "A lion's cub is Judah; *fed with prey*, my son, you have risen," symbolizing deliverance from hell by the Lord through what is heavenly (see §6368). It can also be seen from other Scripture passages, as in Isaiah:

Jehovah's roar is like a lion's; he roars like young lions and growls and *captures prey, so that there is no one rescuing.* (Isaiah 5:29)

In the same author:

As the lion roars—and the young lion—*over its quarry,* so Jehovah will come down to do battle on Zion's mountain. (Isaiah 31:4)

In Jeremiah:

I will rescue you on that day; *I will certainly rescue* you, but let your soul be to you *as spoils* because you trusted in me. (Jeremiah 39:17, 18)

In Zephaniah:

"Wait for me," says Jehovah, "*until the day I rise to the prey.*" (Zephaniah 3:8)

In Isaiah:

I will give him a share among many, *so that with the strong he can share the spoils.* (Isaiah 53:12)

The whole of that chapter is about the Lord.

[2] Balaam's prophecy in Moses shows that eating quarry, or spoils, means taking possession of goodness that has been carried off by the evil:

Watch: a people will rise like an old lion and lift itself like a young lion; it will not rest *until it eats its quarry.* (Numbers 23:23, 24)

This makes it clear that quarry, spoils, and prey are the Lord's rescue and liberation of the good.

This role is assigned to the truth represented by Benjamin, because truth is credited with having power (§§3091, 4932), but power that it acquires from what is good (§§6344, 6423).

And at evening divide the prey symbolizes a possession for them in the Lord's kingdom while they are still in the dark. This can be seen from the symbolism of *evening* as darkness (treated of in §§3056, 3833) and from that of *dividing the prey* as giving someone a possession in the heavenly kingdom. After all, *prey* symbolizes people whom the Lord has rescued and freed, so *dividing* the prey means allotting a portion—a portion among heaven's inhabitants, which is the same as a possession for them in the Lord's kingdom.

6443

The reason this is said to happen in the evening is that people who are raised to heaven are in the dark at first. They cannot achieve clarity until they have been in heaven and learned truth from the Lord through the angels in whose company they have been placed. It takes a bit of time to scatter the darkness imposed on them by falsity.

This is the symbolism of Benjamin. Without the inner meaning, though, who can tell what is wrapped up in the statements about him? I am talking about the statements that he is a wolf, that he will seize [game] in the morning, that he will eat the spoils, and that at evening he will divide the prey. The meaning would be totally hidden if the inner sense did not reveal it. (The Prophets contain much that is equally mysterious. If it were viewed literally, little of it would be intelligible, but if it were viewed in terms of the inner meaning, all of it would be.)

6444

This discussion now shows plainly that Jacob's sons and the tribes named for them symbolize attributes of the Lord's church and kingdom.

Genesis 49:28. *All these are the twelve tribes of Israel, and this is what their father spoke to them, and he blessed them; each according to his blessing he blessed them.*

6445

All these are the twelve tribes of Israel symbolizes all truth and goodness collectively. *And this is what their father spoke to them* symbolizes a communication delivered through an inflow of spiritual goodness. *And he blessed them; each according to his blessing he blessed them* symbolizes predictions of what would happen in everyone's spiritual life in a given state.

All these are the twelve tribes of Israel symbolizes all truth and goodness collectively. This is established by the symbolism of the *twelve tribes of Israel* as all truth and goodness collectively (dealt with in §§3858, 3926, 3939, 4060, 6335, 6397).

6446

This symbolism of the tribes is evident from the discussion of them not only in the sections just cited but also throughout the current chapter.

6447   *And this is what their father spoke to them* symbolizes a communication delivered through an inflow of spiritual goodness, as the following shows: *Speaking* symbolizes flowing in, as discussed in §§2951, 5481, 5743, 5797. Here it symbolizes communication through an inflow. And *Israel, their father,* represents spiritual goodness, as discussed in §§4598, 5801, 5803, 5807, 5812, 5817, 5819, 5826, 5833.

6448   *And he blessed them; each according to his blessing he blessed them* symbolizes predictions of what would happen in everyone's spiritual life in a given state. This can be seen from the symbolism of *blessing* as prediction (mentioned in §§6230, 6254) and from that of *each according to his blessing he blessed them* as what would happen to everyone. The fact that the predictions have to do with everyone's spiritual life in a given state is plain from everything said in the current chapter about Israel's sons, or the tribes named for them. After all, they depict all states of the church in regard to goodness and truth and therefore in regard to the spiritual life of everyone in the church.

6449   Genesis 49:29, 30, 31, 32, 33. *And he commanded them and said to them, "I am being gathered to my people. Bury me near my forebears at the cave that is in the field of Ephron the Hittite, in the cave that is in the field of Machpelah, which is before Mamre in the land of Canaan, [the cave] that Abraham bought along with the field from Ephron the Hittite, for the possession of a grave, where they buried Abraham and Sarah his wife, where they buried Isaac and Rebekah his wife, and where I buried Leah—the purchase of the field and of the cave that is in it, from the children of Heth." And Jacob finished commanding his sons and gathered his feet onto the bed and breathed his last and was gathered to his peoples.*

And he commanded them and said to them symbolizes the instillment of an idea. *I am being gathered to my people* means that he will be present in the earthly-level goodness and truth that come from him. *Bury me near my forebears* means that inner and inmost levels are also present. *At the cave* means where it is dim. *That is in the field of Ephron the Hittite* means that it can nonetheless turn clear. *In the cave that is in the field of Machpelah* means within that dimness. *Which is before Mamre* symbolizes its nature and extent. *In the land of Canaan* means where the church exists. *[The cave] that Abraham bought along with the field from Ephron the Hittite* symbolizes redemption. *For the possession of a grave* symbolizes rebirth. *Where they buried Abraham and Sarah his wife, where they buried*

Isaac and Rebekah his wife, and where I buried Leah, symbolizes all inner levels in order within earthly-level goodness and truth. *The purchase of the field and of the cave that is in it, from the children of Heth* symbolizes the redemption of people who accept truth, and through truth, goodness. *And Jacob finished commanding his sons* symbolizes the effect of the idea instilled. *And gathered his feet onto the bed* means that in regard to his lower levels, in which inner aspects were present, [he retreated] to goodness and truth on the lower earthly level. *And breathed his last* symbolizes new life there. *And was gathered to his peoples* means that he was present in the earthly-level goodness and truth that came from him.

And he commanded them and said to them symbolizes the instillment **6450** of an idea, as can be seen from the speech that follows. In his speech Israel talks to his sons about their burying him in the cave in the field of Machpelah, where Abraham and Isaac were buried. This symbolizes the living energy in truth and goodness on an earthly level in which inner and inmost levels are present. Since this is the theme of what directly follows, *commanding his sons and saying to them* symbolizes introducing them to those ideas. *Commanding* symbolizes an inflow (see §§5486, 5732), so it symbolizes the instillment of an idea.

I am being gathered to my people means that he will be present in **6451** the earthly-level goodness and truth that come from him, as the following shows: Israel's sons and the tribes named for them—*his people* here—represent goodness and truth on the earthly plane, as discussed in §§3858, 3926, 3939, 5414, 5879, 5951, 6335, 6337. That they come from him is self-evident. And *being gathered* to his people means being present in those things.

Because it is the focus here and in what follows, I need to explain how to understand the "gathering" or presence of spiritual goodness (Israel) in earthly-level goodness and truth (his sons, or the tribes named for them).

[2] We have an inmost core, inner depths that lie below the inmost core, and an outer level. All these levels, carefully distinguished from each other, follow one another in this order, from inmost core to the very outermost surface. They also flow into each other in the same order in which they stand in relation to one another. Life therefore flows through the inmost core into inner depths and through those into the outer level. So it follows the pattern in which those levels stand in relation to one another and comes to rest only at the outermost plane, where it stops.

Since the inner levels flow into us in order, all the way to the outermost plane, where they stop, clearly the inner levels coexist on the outermost plane. Here is the pattern in which they stand on that plane, though: The inmost inflowing level takes the center of the outermost plane, the inner depths lying below that inmost core surround the center, and the outer levels make up the circumference. This is true not only in general but also in every particular.

The first pattern is called sequential; the second, simultaneous. The second pattern rises out of the first, because everything coexisting on the same level rises out of the sequential series. And once the simultaneous pattern has arisen out of the sequential, it stays the way it is.

[3] Since all deeper levels also coexist on the outermost plane, life appears to exist on that plane—in other words, in the body—when it really exists at an inner level, and not even there but at the highest level, in the Lord, the source of all life.

A consequence is that the life force on outer levels is relatively dim compared to the life force on inner levels. On outer levels it is a general force rising out of numerous or rather countless elements that flow in from inner levels and appear together, coexisting on the same level.

This discussion goes some way toward explaining how to understand the idea that spiritual goodness (Israel) will be present in earthly-level goodness and truth (his sons, or the tribes). The spiritual goodness that is Israel exists on the inner earthly plane, and the goodness and truth that are his sons exist on the outer earthly plane. The fact that spiritual goodness will be present in them is symbolized by *I am being gathered to my people.*

6452   *Bury me near my forebears* means that inner and inmost levels are also present. This can be seen from the representation of Abraham and Isaac, *his forebears,* as inner and inmost levels. Abraham represents the inmost core and Isaac the inner depths that lie below the inmost core, as discussed in §§3245, 6098, 6185, 6276, 6434.

For the idea that the inmost core and inner depths actually coexist on outer levels and consequently within earthly-level goodness and truth (which are the sons and tribes of Israel), see just above at §6451.

6453   *At the cave* means where it is dim. This is indicated by the discussion in §2935 of the symbolism of a *cave* as something dim. For the idea that conditions are dim on the outer earthly level (where the truth and goodness represented by the sons and tribes of Israel reside) because everything is general there, see just above at the end of §6451.

6454   *That is in the field of Ephron the Hittite* means that it can nonetheless turn clear, as the following shows: A *field* symbolizes the church, as touched on at §§2971, 3766. And *Ephron the Hittite* represents people who can accept truth and goodness (dealt with in §§2933, 2940, 2969) and in whom a dim sight of faith can therefore turn clear.

Here is the situation: Anything on the earthly level, and especially on the outer earthly level, is relatively dim in comparison to the contents of the inner earthly level, and even more so in comparison to the contents of the rational level (§§6451, 6453). There are two ways, though, in which clarity is brought to this obscurity. The first is for the outer levels to be reduced to obedience to inner levels and so to correspondence with them. The second is for a person to be able to rise from the outer to the inner realm and in this way view the outer realm from within. The second way can happen with people in the inner part of the church, the first with people in the outer part. However, it is only through being regenerated by the Lord that either is achieved.

These remarks show what it means to say that what is dim can become clear.

In the cave that is in the field of Machpelah means within that dimness. This is evident from the symbolism of a *cave* and of *Machpelah* as something dim. For the symbolism of a cave as something dim, see §§2935, 6453. For that of Machpelah, see §2935—but Machpelah symbolizes the *nature* of the dimness. **6455**

Which is before Mamre symbolizes its nature and extent. This is clear from the symbolism of *Mamre* as the nature and extent of whatever it is connected with, as noted in §§2970, 4613. **6456**

In the land of Canaan means where the church exists. This is established by the symbolism of the *land of Canaan* as the church, as discussed in §§3686, 3705, 4447, 5136. **6457**

[The cave] that Abraham bought along with the field from Ephron the Hittite symbolizes redemption, as the following shows: *Buying* means adopting for one's own, as discussed at §§4397, 5374, 5410, 5426, so it also means redeeming, because what is redeemed is taken as a possession. *Abraham* in the highest sense represents the Lord, as discussed in §§1965, 1989, 2010, 3245, 3251, 3305, 3703, 4615, 6098, 6185, 6276. A *field* symbolizes the church, as discussed in §§2971, 3766. And *Ephron the Hittite* represents people who can accept goodness and truth, as discussed in §§2933, 2940, 2969. This shows that what is meant by these words is the Lord's redemption of people in the church who can accept goodness and truth. **6458**

For the possession of a grave symbolizes rebirth. This can be seen from the symbolism of a *grave* as rebirth, as discussed in §§2916, 2917, 5551. **6459**

6460   *Where they buried Abraham and Sarah his wife, where they buried Isaac and Rebekah his wife, and where I buried Leah,* symbolizes all inner levels in order within earthly-level goodness and truth. This can be seen from the explanations above at §§6451, 6452.

6461   *The purchase of the field and of the cave that is in it, from the children of Heth* symbolizes the redemption of people who accept truth, and through truth, goodness, as the following shows: A *purchase* symbolizes redemption, as mentioned above at §6458. A *field* symbolizes the church, as discussed in §§2971, 3766, so it symbolizes a person in the church, because such a person *is* a church. A *cave* symbolizes what is dim, as discussed at §§2935, 6453. And the *children of Heth* represent a spiritual religion that came from the ancient church, as discussed in §§2913, 2986. Since the children of Heth represent a spiritual religion that came from the ancient church, they represent people who accept truth, and through truth, goodness. That is the origin of a spiritual religion.

From this you can see that the *purchase of the field and of the cave that is in it, from the children of Heth* symbolizes the redemption of people who are in the church but are still in the dark, and who accept truth, and through truth, goodness.

6462   *And Jacob finished commanding his sons* symbolizes the effect of the idea instilled. This can be seen from the symbolism of *commanding his sons* and saying to them as the instillment of an idea, as discussed above at §6450. As it symbolizes the instillment of an idea, *finishing* commanding them stands for the effect of the idea instilled.

6463   *And gathered his feet onto the bed* means that in regard to his lower levels, in which inner aspects were present, [he retreated] to goodness and truth on the lower earthly level, as the following shows: *Gathering his feet* means retreating to lower levels. Since *feet* are lower levels, *gathering* them plainly means retreating there. Feet stand for what belongs to the earthly level (see §§2162, 3147, 3761, 3986, 4280, 4938–4952), so they stand for lower levels (§6436). The fact that they stand for lower levels in which inner aspects were present is clear from the discussion above at §6451. And a *bed* symbolizes the earthly plane (discussed in §§6188, 6226) and therefore goodness and truth on the earthly plane, since goodness and truth constitute the earthly level in a person. The reason the bed means goodness and truth on the *lower* earthly plane is that this is the part of the earthly plane to which inner levels retreat, as explained at §§6451, 6452. For the idea that the earthly plane has a lower and a higher part, or an inner and an outer, see §§3293, 3294, 5118, 5126, 5497, 5649.

Israel represents spiritual goodness *on the earthly level;* Jacob, spiritual truth *on the earthly level;* and his sons, goodness and truth *on the earthly level* distinguished into their general categories. That is why a *bed* is mentioned, since it symbolizes the *earthly level* (§§6188, 6226). This verse, for instance, says that when Jacob finished speaking to his sons, *he gathered his feet onto the bed.* When Joseph came to him, it says "Israel braced himself *and sat up on the bed"* (§6226). And after he spoke with Joseph about being buried in the grave of his ancestors, it says *"Israel bowed over the head of his bed"* (§6188).

That is the reason for the remarkable fact that when someone thinks about Jacob, a bed with a man lying on it appears in the world of spirits. The sight appears far above the head, out in front toward the right. The reason for the appearance is that in heaven, a thought about Jacob turns into a thought about the earthly plane. Rather than perceiving what Jacob is, heaven's inhabitants perceive what he represents, which is the earthly realm, and the earthly realm is also symbolized by a bed.

And breathed his last symbolizes new life there, within goodness and truth on the lower earthly level, represented by the sons and tribes of Israel. This can be seen from the symbolism of *breathing one's last,* or dying, as new life, as dealt with in §§3498, 3505, 4618, 4621, 6036.

6464

And was gathered to his peoples means that he was present in the earthly-level goodness and truth that came from him. This can be seen from comments above at §6451, where similar words appear. See the points cited there about the presence and life of spiritual goodness (Israel) within goodness and truth on the lower earthly plane (his sons and the twelve tribes).

6465

Concerning the presence of inner levels in outer levels, it is important to know that a cumulative formation is what actually brings everything into being, not only in humans but also in the whole of nature. What is later therefore comes into being through formation from what is earlier. As a result, every layer of formation exists separately from the next layer, although what is later still depends on what is earlier. In fact, what is later cannot survive without what is earlier, because the earlier formation maintains the interconnection and integrity of the later formation. Clearly, then, any later level contains all earlier levels in sequence. The same is true of the modes and powers emanating from the later levels as substances. That is how matters stand with the inner and outer planes in a person and also with the different levels of life in us.

[2] People who do not conceive of the inner and outer planes in a person in terms of a cumulative formation cannot have any idea of the outer

and inner self or of the inflow from the one into the other. Still less can they know about the presence and life of the inner self or spirit or about the nature it has when the outer, physical layer is removed through death. Some conceive of outer and inner levels as continuously purer levels and therefore as blending into one another along a scale. So they do not view them as being distinct from one another through the formation of later levels from earlier levels. These people cannot help but think that when the outer part dies the inner part dies as well. They think that the two levels blend into one another and that because they blend continuously, one dies when the other dies, since the one drags the other with it.

These things have been said to show that the inner plane and outer plane are distinct and separate from each other, that inner and outer planes come one after another in order, and that all inner levels are present together in outer levels—in other words, that everything earlier is present together in everything later. That was the focus of this set of verses in its inner meaning.

Spiritual Inflow, and the Interaction of the Soul and Body (Continued)

6466 AT the end of the preceding chapters I have demonstrated that the two kinds of life in us—the life of our thoughts and the life of our will—come to us as an inflow from heaven by way of the angels and spirits with us [§§5846–5866, 5976–5993, 6053–6058, 6189–6215, 6307–6327]. An inflow from heaven, though, should be understood as an inflow from the Lord through heaven. All the life that angels have comes from the Lord, as they themselves unanimously declare; and they live in the perception that it does. Since all the life that angels have comes from the Lord, all the life that people have also comes from him, because he governs us through angels and spirits in particular and through heaven in general.

6467 Clearly, then, none of us has any life on our own. Accordingly, we cannot think or will on our own, as our life consists in thinking and willing. There is only one life, the Lord's life, which flows into everyone. But we receive that life in various ways, according to the character we have stamped on our soul by the way we lived in the world. So in evil people, goodness and truth turn into evil and falsity, but in good people, goodness is received as goodness, and truth as truth.

The situation can be compared to sunlight that flows into objects. The objects modify the light and variegate it according to the form of their parts, lending it colors that are either gloomy or cheerful, according to the nature of the objects. When we are living in the world, we likewise stamp a character on the purest substances of our inner reaches that determines how we receive the Lord's life.

Note that the life from the Lord is a life of love for the entire human race.

When spirits first arrive from the world, before they have received instruction from angels, they are fully convinced that all life inheres in a person, that none of it comes from elsewhere. The reason for this conviction is that they have no detailed knowledge of heaven or consequently of any inflow from heaven. Spirits who are not good do not *want* to learn about it, because they want to have self-originating life. [One time] they told me I had no life, because they heard me saying I did not have life on my own. They also heard me saying I knew so from constant experience, but this they did not want to pay attention to. I was allowed to add that we each have life in keeping with the inner form we have acquired by the way we intend and act, think and speak.

6468

[2] Later I talked with some good spirits about the inflow of life from the Lord. "This life flows into everyone," I said, "as you can tell from heaven and the fact that it resembles a human being. That is why it is called the universal human"—which I have discussed at the end of many chapters, showing that everything in a human being corresponds with it. "This could never happen," I continued, "if life from the Lord did not flow into heaven in general and into every inhabitant in particular.

[3] "You can also tell from the fact that all heaven relates to the Lord, where he is the focus of everyone's gaze. Heaven's inhabitants look up toward him, and hell's inhabitants look down away from him, because he appears as the sun to inhabitants of the heavens. In the heavens the Lord is up above.

"Another way you can tell that all life comes from the Lord," I added, "is by considering that the human soul can form the body in the womb in such a miraculous way, its numerous limbs and organs in such a series, and its inner depths in the image of heaven. This could never happen if all life did not come from the Lord and if heaven were not in this form."

6469   I also had the opportunity through an inflow from the angels to feel the sweet sensation they feel from thinking and willing under the Lord's power rather than their own. Doing so yields them peace, calm, and happiness.

When angels flowed into me perceptibly, I clearly sensed the Lord's presence—a sign that they are awash in the Lord's life, as I have been able to learn from ample experience.

Another time, when I was thinking about the inflow of life from the Lord, while mulling certain doubts, the awareness flowed in from heaven that the thousands of objections and reasonings that [sensory] illusions raise ought to be ignored.

6470   Another piece of evidence showing me that all life comes from the Lord has been the fact that no spirit thinks or speaks on his or her own, only from others, who think and speak from still others, and so on. This fact has been demonstrated many times to spirits who believed that life was innate in them and did not come from elsewhere. From such demonstrations I was able to draw the following conclusion: Since no one's thoughts and words originate in that individual but only in others, eventually they must all originate in one person and therefore in the Lord. If they did not all originate in one, no orderly pattern could possibly be displayed by all the lives in heaven. But in fact heaven does exhibit a pattern under which it is divided into communities with great accuracy according to type of goodness. Things would be entirely different if everyone's actions were powered by that individual's own vital energy.

6471   Once there was a spirit who came not from a bad-hearted group but from a group that imagined they had more religious knowledge than others. These spirits instructed many others, even teaching that everything good and true comes from the Lord and that we humans cannot think or will anything good on our own. This particular spirit was brought into a state devoid of self-originated thought and will (since people can be brought into such states in the other world). When in that state the spirit said, "I cannot live in this state. No, this kind of life is a burden to me."

"Then you do not like living by the truth you taught," I responded. "Angels are in that state, and they are happiest when aware that they have no independent life." My argument carried no weight with the spirit, however. The experience showed me how hard it is to live a life of faith if one does not also practice the goodness urged by neighborly love.

6472   It was by means of revelation that I was allowed to learn how matters stand with the inflow from the Lord of both kinds of life, the life of our thoughts and the life of our will. What happens is that the Lord flows into us in two ways, indirectly through heaven and directly from himself, and the inflow directly from him acts both on our rational capacities, or inner realm, and on our earthly capacities, or outer realm.

What flows in from the Lord is love's goodness, and faith's truth, because what issues from the Lord is divine truth containing divine goodness. However, we receive these qualities in different ways, depending on our character.

[2] The Lord does not force us to accept what flows in from him. Rather, he guides us in our freedom, and so far as we let him, he uses our freedom to guide us to what is good. So the Lord leads us in harmony with our pleasures and also in harmony with our illusions and the assumptions we base on them; but he gradually extracts us. Moreover, it appears to us as though we do it on our own. The Lord does not break our pleasures and illusions, then, since to break them would be to violate our freedom, whereas freedom is a must if we are to be reformed (§§1937, 1947, 2875, 2876, 2881, 3145, 3146, 3158, 4031).

It is a secret so far unknown that the Lord flows into us this way, not only indirectly through heaven, but also directly from himself into both our inner and outer levels.

The Lord is in equal control of what comes last and what comes first **6473** in us. This can be seen from the fact that the overall design comes from the Lord and follows a progression from first to last. This design contains nothing that is not divine, and as a result the Lord is necessarily as fully present in what is last as in what is first. The one follows from the other in keeping with the design's course of progress.

An hour's worth of experience showed me how the Lord governs all **6474** thinking. There was an inflow that was like a very gentle, almost imperceptible river whose current is invisible but still exerts a pull. In just this way the inflow from the Lord guided every train of thought I had along a channel. Although the leading was gentle, it was firm—so firm that I found it impossible to wander off into other channels of thought. I was allowed to try, but it was no use.

Once there were some evil spirits in the world of spirits who were **6475** constantly thinking negatively about the Lord. (To see what goes on with spirits from hell when they are in the world of spirits, consult §5852.) I heard them being told to produce anyone who could honestly claim to know an angel in heaven (or if possible to directly point out a single inhabitant of heaven) who did not acknowledge the Lord, identify him as the life force in everyone, and say, "Anything I have, I have from him." They said not a word because they could not do it.

Some of the evil spirits believed there were heavens somewhere in which the Lord was not acknowledged, and they roamed around inquiring but returned when the effort failed.

"Everyone in hell harbors thoughts against the Lord," they were also told. "No one there ascribes any superhuman quality to him. Most say they acknowledge a Supreme Being, by which they mean the Father, but they still live lives of hatred and revenge, constantly wanting to lift themselves up above others and to be worshiped as gods. So they create their own hell."

The situation is completely different with people who acknowledge the Lord and believe in him from the heart.

This too shows that the Lord flows into everyone, both through heaven in a general way and directly from himself in a particular and universal way. Further, it shows that where neighborly kindness exists he is present, and where its opposite exists he is also present, but only to give life to people and to lead them as much as possible away from evil.

6476 Whenever I have read the Lord's Prayer, I have had a clear sensation of being raised up toward him by a kind of pull. My mind was then receptive, which brought about contact with certain communities in heaven. I was aware of the Lord's inflow into every word of the prayer and therefore into every single thought sparked in my mind by the prayer's message.

This inflow did not occur the same way one time as another but in indescribably varied ways, which showed how infinite the content of each detail was. It also showed that the Lord was present in all the details.

6477 Over many years I have observed the overall environment of the inflows around me. It consisted of a perpetual impetus to do evil coming from the hells on one side, and a perpetual impetus to do good coming from the Lord on the other. I had always been held in balance by these two opposing forces.

Everyone experiences these forces and the resulting equilibrium, which supply us with the freedom to turn in whatever direction we choose. However, the equilibrium varies with the evil or goodness dominant in us.

This too provided evidence that the inflow from the Lord is universal and, because of being universal, is also minutely particular.

I also learned that the negative impetus from hell is nothing but a perversion into evil of the goodness radiating from the Lord.

When angels do good to anyone, they also share with that person **6478**
their good fortune, favor, and sense of grace, which they do from an attitude of wanting to give the other everything and keep nothing back.
When they share this way, goodness comes to them, along with a sense of
favor and grace, in much greater quantity than they give, and with constant increase.

As soon as the thought arises, though, that they might want to share
what they have specifically in order to acquire an inflow of fortune and
favor for themselves, the stream dries up. This is especially so if any thought
occurs of being repaid by the individual to whom they communicate their
blessings. Plentiful experience has taught me this.

Such evidence again shows that the Lord is everywhere, because by
his very nature he longs to give himself to all and increase the fortune and
favor of those who are his images and likenesses.

Less upright spirits who were with me for some time constantly poured **6479**
in doubts (based on sensory illusions) undermining the idea that everything can flow in from a single fount, which is to say, from the Lord. "The
number of doubts you raise cannot be shoved aside quickly," I countered,
"because you have to shake off your sensory illusions first and also because
there is so much you do not know that you need to learn first. In fact,
doubt *cannot* be dispelled in people with a negative attitude—people in
whom negativity governs at every turn. For them, one small objection over-
powers a thousand proofs, because one little objection is like a grain of sand
put right in front of the pupil of the eye: there is only one, and it is tiny, but
it still blocks all vision.

"But people with a positive attitude—people in whom affirmativeness
governs at every turn—reject objections based on illusions that conflict
with truth. If there is anything they do not grasp, they put it off to the
side, saying they do not understand it yet. And despite their puzzlement
they continue to believe in the truth."

The spirits were paying scant attention to these words, though, because
they had a negative attitude.

A more fitting name for what is being discussed here—the Lord's **6480**
indirect inflow through heaven and direct inflow from himself—is providence. After all, he flows not only into human will and thought but also
into the many happenstances of a person's life. So let me refer to it as
providence in what follows next.

Spirits who go to the other world take with them the opinion that **6481**
divine providence is universal but does not apply to particulars. The reason

for the opinion is that they had seen evil people rise to high position, grow rich, and succeed, and had attributed it to those people's own cleverness. They failed to realize that the goal of divine providence is a person's eternal salvation, not the person's temporal good fortune, or wealth and status. While they are living in their body, most people identify these boons with true happiness, when in reality they do not constitute happiness. Status usually gives birth to self-love, and wealth to materialism, and therefore to the diametric opposites of love for God and charity for one's neighbor. Prosperity is granted to the wicked, then, and also to the good as long as it does not make trouble for them or lead them away from heaven. [2] Besides, the Lord uses the evil as well as the good to fulfill his purposes. He employs those very passions [of self-love and materialism] in the evil to make them help their neighbor, their country, and the church. The evil like being honored, they like growing rich, so they like to be viewed as upright and zealous. This craving lights a fiercer fire under them than under honest people to do such deeds.

Evil people are allowed to believe that everything is a result of their own shrewdness and that there is no divine providence (or only a universal providence), because they do not want to see otherwise. Moreover, to ensure that they take steps beneficial to the state, they are also granted what they consider success, and because they attribute success to their own efforts, it inspires them even more.

6482   I talked with some spirits about the Lord's universal governance. A universal quality is completely impossible without specifics, I said. Otherwise it is nothing. A thing is called universal because its specifics taken together are called universal, just as particulars taken together are referred to as general. So to talk about providence in what is universal and not in what is specific is to say nothing.

If anyone takes a universal providence to mean preservation of the whole in keeping with a pattern stamped on all of nature at the moment of its creation, that person is not considering that nothing can remain in being unless it is constantly coming into being. As the scholarly world knows, survival is perpetual emergence; so preservation is perpetual creation. Providence, then, is always in the details.

To prove that what is universal can exist without what is particular, some use the example of a monarch, who reigns overall but not in the details. They fail to consider, though, that royal power lies not only in the sovereign but also in the sovereign's ministers, who discharge the royal duty in matters that are beyond the monarch's abilities. The monarch's universal control is consequently present in the details.

The same is not necessary for the Lord, though. Everything in him is infinite, because it is divine. He has angels for his ministers so that they can live an active and therefore happy life. Still, the ministries they perform come not from them but from an inflow from the Lord, which the angels themselves unanimously confess.

The remarks just above once more show that what is universal is a perfect reflection of its individual parts. The less detailed the parts, the less exalted the whole, and the more detailed the parts, the more exalted the whole, because the individual parts cause the whole to be universal and to be called universal.

6483

From this you can see what divine universality is like. You can see that it exists in the most detailed specifics of all, because, being divine and infinite, it is exalted the highest of all.

There was once a spirit who had confirmed to himself that nothing was a matter of divine providence but that absolutely everything resulted instead from prudence and from luck and chance. He assumed there was such a thing as luck but did not know what it was. He was one of the more subtle evil spirits, because he had indulged more in thinking than in talking or interacting with others.

6484

When he entered the other world, he there continued his previous life, as everyone does. He sought out and absorbed any knowledge (including the magic arts) that he thought could help him in his efforts to ensure his own happiness.

I talked with him, and he said he was in his heaven when he was doing this, and that no other heaven was possible than one he created for himself. But I was allowed to answer that his kind of heaven turns into hell as soon as heaven proper flows into it.

He was then in the world of spirits, and while spirits are there, they enjoy the same pleasures they had loved in the world (§5852). What happened next, though, was that heaven flowed into his pleasure, and suddenly he could feel hell. Shuddering, he said he never would have believed it.

Some good spirits told me he was worse than others because his inflow was subtler.

[2] Later the same spirit was taken back to the state of his childhood. The Lord showed some angels what he had then been like and what kind of future had then been foreseen for him. They were shown that every

moment of his life had been steered by the Lord and that otherwise, if the Lord's constant providence had left off even in the slightest, he would have pitched himself headlong into the most appalling hell. This kind of scene can be presented visually to angels.

The spirit was also asked whether he had ever thought about eternal life. "I did not believe in it," he said. "I rejected all that because I saw so many things that were upside down—that the honest suffered, the ungodly boasted, and so on. What is more, I saw that brute animals had the same senses I did, the same life, the same awareness and cunning, so I believed I would die the way they do. I was floored when I realized I was still alive after death."

6485   I spoke with some good spirits about divine providence and a person's own prudence, and they demonstrated their idea of the matter in an image familiar to them: a thin cloud of dust scattered on the air. In relation to divine providence, they said, our own prudence is like that dust in relation to the entire atmosphere; it is nothing by comparison, and what is more, it falls down.

People who ascribe everything to their own prudence, they added, are like wanderers in shadowy forests who do not know the way out. If they happen upon it, they attribute the success either to their own cleverness or to luck.

All chance is a function of providence, the spirits continued, and providence acts silently and secretly for many reasons. If it acted openly, we could never be reformed.

6486   I heard angels talking to each other about the Lord's providence, but although I understood what they said, I cannot write much of it down. Their words were accompanied by a steady stream of heavenly representations, you see, of which I cannot express more than a tiny fraction.

They spoke with great wisdom, saying that the Lord's providence directs the smallest details of all but that it does not follow the plan we propose to ourselves, because he is both foreseeing and providing for future events. "It is like someone building a palace," they said, "who first assembles all kinds of materials and throws them into piles, where they lie in a jumble. Only the eye of the architect's mind sees what kind of palace will result."

6487   When I spoke with angels about the Lord's divine providence, there were spirits present who had adopted some idea of fate, or absolute necessity. They thought the Lord's course of action was controlled by necessity, because he can proceed only in accordance with certain vital considerations and therefore with the requirements of a perfect plan. The spirits were shown, however, that people have freedom, and if they have free-dom, events are not controlled by necessity. The idea was illustrated by houses under construction. Bricks, clay, sand, stones for bases and columns, boards and beams, and other materials are hauled in, not in the order in which they are needed for building the house but at will. Only the Lord knows what kind of house can be put together from them. All the supplies, which the Lord provides, are vital, but they do not necessarily arrive in order. Rather, they arrive in accord with our free choice.

Predestination was discussed. On the basis of assumptions they had made in the world, many spirits held the opinion that some are predestined for heaven, some for hell. From heaven, though, I heard the answer that no one is ever predestined for hell; everyone is predestined for eternal life.

6488

The case with the Lord's providence is that it is bound up with his foresight. The one is impossible without the other. This is because evil is foreseen but goodness is provided. The Lord in his providence constantly arranges for foreseen evil to be bent in a good direction. He aims at what is good, and this divine aim reigns universally, so nothing is permitted for any purpose except that some good may come of it. Since we have freedom, though, and in order that we can be reformed, we are deflected from evil to goodness so far as we freely allow. We labor tirelessly to plunge ourselves into the direst hell but are constantly being turned from there toward a milder hell, if we cannot be led to heaven.

6489

If the Lord's providence did not concern itself with the smallest details, we could never be saved or even stay alive, because life is from the Lord, and every moment of life has a series of consequences reaching to eternity.

6490

One time I was allowed to sense plainly the aura radiated by the Lord's providential aims.

The Lord's providence is infinite and looks to eternity. This can be seen from the way a fetus forms in the womb. Outlines of features yet to come are constantly being laid down there, so that one element always acts as a foundation for the next, without any deviation, until the fetus is fully formed. Later too, when the baby has been born, each stage in order anticipates and prepares for the next, so that a complete human being—and eventually a person capable of accepting heaven—can emerge.

6491

If these detailed provisions are made for our conception, birth, and maturation, what does that not imply for our spiritual life?

My father appeared to me in a dream. I talked with him, saying that after a son has become his own master, he does not have to acknowledge his father as his father the way he did before. The reason he has to acknowledge

6492

his father during his upbringing is that a father is in place of the Lord at that stage. Unless he receives his father's direction, he does not know what to do. Once he gains adult rights, though, he comes to think for himself and considers himself capable of guiding himself, and the Lord—for whom his earthly father had previously stood in—must then be his father.

I said all this in the dream. Once I had woken I saw coming down from heaven a long scroll attached to some rods and tied with a most gorgeous bright blue braid. Its beauty was indescribable. I was told that angels exchange gifts like these.

6493   I often talked with spirits about fortune, which in the world looks like random chance, because people do not know what causes it. Not knowing, some deny that fortune exists.

When an apparently lucky event happened to me, I was told by angels that it happened because spirits of that type were present, and when something unlucky happened, that the influence of *those* spirits predominated.

In addition, evil spirits have used their skills to discover how to generate a sphere of influence producing misfortunes that look exactly like the results of chance.

I also learned that the Lord's providence directs all events, even the smallest of all events, down to the smallest of the smallest, including our actual footsteps. When anything contrary to providence succeeds, misfortunes happen.

The angels confirmed that there is no such thing as chance and that apparent luck or good fortune is providence on the lowest level of the divine design, where everything is relatively unpredictable.

6494   For many years I have carefully observed to see whether luck was anything and discovered that it was, and that prudence accomplishes nothing when luck is at work. Anyone who has mulled the question very long sees and acknowledges this to be the case but does not know why it is. Hardly anyone knows that the spiritual world is responsible, but it is.

Once, when I was in company, playing a common game of chance with dice, the spirits near me were talking with me about luck in game playing. They said that good luck was represented to them by a white cloud, and bad luck by a dark cloud, and further, that when a dark cloud appeared near me, I could not win. From this sign they also predicted my turns of fortune in the game. The experience taught me that what we attribute to luck comes from the spiritual world. This is true even for games but especially true for the changing fortune of events in the course of our life. What we call luck, I learned, results from the inflow of providence into the lowest levels of the divine design, where it emerges in this form.

Providence lies in the most particular details of all, then, as the Lord said: not even one small hair falls from our head without the will of God.

From the evidence cited so far, you can see that the inflow from the Lord is both direct and also indirect through heaven. What flows in from the Lord is a goodness born of heavenly love and therefore of love for one's neighbor. In this love the Lord is present, because he loves the whole human race and wants to save every member of it forever. Since the goodness born of this love comes from him, he is in such goodness, so he is present in a person who possesses it. **6495**

However, when we put ourselves in a state in which we accept an inflow from hell, then a life of self-love and of love for worldly advantages feels pleasant, while a life of neighborly love feels unpleasant, unless we can profit by it.

[2] People in this state crave nothing but evil and think nothing but distorted thoughts about spiritual life. To prevent them from acting as they crave and speaking as they think, then, they are held in chains by those same kinds of love, dreading to be deprived of its objects. So they are fettered by the fear of losing their rank, wealth, reputation, or life. Such fetters make up the lowest plane [of life], and the Lord flows into them, using them to govern such people. As a result, these people seem genuinely moral and civilized, sometimes even resembling angels, and they refrain from harming society or their neighbor. If they do inflict damage, society has laws to punish them.

This plane is absent from the other life, though. We live in a spiritual world there and consequently in the realm of our inner depths. That is, we are the same there as we had been inwardly, not as we had appeared outwardly. Our veneer is taken from us, and when it has been removed it becomes obvious what kind of devil or angel we had been in the world.

This subject continues at the end of the next chapter [§§6598–6626]. **6496**

Genesis 50

1. And Joseph fell on his father's face and wept over him and kissed him.

2. And Joseph commanded his servants the doctors to embalm his father, and the doctors embalmed Israel.

3. And forty days were fulfilled for him, because that fulfills the days for embalming. And the Egyptians wept for him seventy days.

4. And the days of weeping for him passed, and Joseph spoke to the household of Pharaoh, saying, "Please, if I have found favor in your eyes, please speak in Pharaoh's ears, saying,

5. 'My father put me under oath, saying, "Here, now, I am dying. In my grave that I dug for myself in the land of Canaan—there you are to bury me." And now let me go up, please, and bury my father and return.'"

6. And Pharaoh said, "Go up and bury your father, as he made you swear."

7. And Joseph went up to bury his father, and there went up with him all Pharaoh's servants, the elders of his household and all the elders of the land of Egypt,

8. and Joseph's whole household and his brothers and his father's household. Only their little children and their flocks and their herds they left in the land of Goshen.

9. And there went up with him both chariot and riders, and it was a very heavy army.

10. And they came to the threshing floor of Atad, which is at the ford of the Jordan, and they keened there a very great and heavy keening, and he carried out mourning for his father seven days.

11. And the Canaanite resident of the land saw the mourning on the threshing floor of Atad, and they said, "This is [a time of] heavy mourning for the Egyptians." Therefore its name was called Abel-mizraim, which is at the ford of the Jordan.

12. And his sons did so, as he had commanded them.

13. And his sons bore him to the land of Canaan and buried him in the cave of the field of Machpelah, which Abraham had bought along with the field for the possession of a grave, from Ephron the Hittite, before Mamre.

14. And Joseph returned to Egypt—he and his brothers and all those going up with him to bury his father—after he had buried his father.

15. And Joseph's brothers saw that their father was dead, and they said, "Maybe Joseph will hate us and make sure he returns to us all the evil that we rendered to him."

16. And they gave a command to Joseph, saying, "Your father gave a command before he died, saying,

17. 'This is what you are to say to Joseph: "Please forgive, please, the transgression of your brothers and their sin, because they rendered evil to you."' So now forgive, please, the transgression of the servants of your father's God." And Joseph wept as they spoke to him.

18. And his brothers also went and fell before him and said, "Look: we will serve as slaves to you."

19. And Joseph said to them, "Don't be afraid, because am I in place of God?

20. And you thought evil upon me; God thought it for good, in order to do as at this day, to keep a great people alive.

21. And now don't be afraid; I will sustain you and your little children." And he comforted them and spoke to their heart.

22. And Joseph resided in Egypt, he and his father's household. And Joseph lived one hundred ten years.

23. And Joseph saw Ephraim have children of the third generation. In addition, the children of Machir, Manasseh's son, were born on Joseph's knees.

24. And Joseph said to his brothers, "I am dying, and God will unfailingly visit you and bring you up from this land to the land that he swore to Abraham, Isaac, and Jacob."

25. And Joseph put the children of Israel under oath, saying, "God will unfailingly visit you, and you must bring my bones up from this place."

26. And Joseph died, a son of one hundred ten years. And they embalmed him. And he was put in an ark in Egypt.

Summary

NOW that the text has finished with Abraham, Isaac, and Jacob, who in the highest sense represent the Lord, the inner meaning of this final chapter [of Genesis] talks about the church. It tells how the Lord

6497

established a spiritual church after the heavenly church had died. The beginning and development of the spiritual church are described in the inner meaning, and its end is described at the end of the chapter. The message is that a mere representation of a religion was established among Jacob's descendants to replace the spiritual church.

Inner Meaning

6498   GENESIS 50:1, 2, 3. *And Joseph fell on his father's face and wept over him and kissed him. And Joseph commanded his servants the doctors to embalm his father, and the doctors embalmed Israel. And forty days were fulfilled for him, because that fulfills the days for embalming. And the Egyptians wept for him seventy days.*

And Joseph fell on his father's face symbolizes an inflow of inner depth into the desire for what is good. *And wept over him* symbolizes sorrow. *And kissed him* symbolizes initial union. *And Joseph commanded his servants the doctors* symbolizes preservation from evils that would hinder union. *To embalm his father* means in order to prevent contamination. *And the doctors embalmed Israel* symbolizes carrying out the preservation of truth-based goodness. *And forty days were fulfilled for him* symbolizes states of being prepared through times of trial. *Because that fulfills the days for embalming* means that these are states of preservation. *And the Egyptians wept for him* symbolizes grief among items of knowledge possessed by the church. *Seventy days* symbolizes a complete state.

6499   *And Joseph fell on his father's face* symbolizes an inflow of inner depth into the desire for what is good, as the following shows: *Falling on someone's face* symbolizes an inflow. *Joseph* represents the inner dimension, as discussed in §§5805, 5826, 5827, 5869, 5877, 6177, 6224. A *face* symbolizes an emotion, [or a desire,] as discussed in §§4796, 4797, 5102. And Israel, the *father,* represents spiritual goodness, or goodness born of truth, as discussed in §§3654, 4598, 5801, 5803, 5807, 5812, 5817, 5819, 5826, 5833. This shows that *Joseph fell on his father's face* symbolizes an inflow of inner depth into the desire for spiritual goodness.

[2] Why is an inflow of inner depth into the desire for spiritual goodness being symbolized? It is because the inner meaning here treats of the

piritual church established by the Lord. Israel, after all, symbolizes truth-
based goodness, or spiritual goodness, and this kind of goodness constitutes a spiritual religion, so Israel also symbolizes such a religion (§§4286,
6426). If this kind of goodness is to exist, there must be an inflow from
the inner heavenliness represented by Joseph, because without it, spiritual
goodness is not good, since it is devoid of desire.

The inner meaning of the next verses continues to discuss the establishment of a spiritual religion (§6497).

This religion is depicted by an Israel now dead and about to be buried because death in an inner sense does not mean death, nor does burial
mean burial. No, death means new life (§§3498, 3505, 4618, 4621, 6036),
and burial means rebirth (§§2916, 2917, 5551).

And wept over him symbolizes sorrow, as is self-evident.

6500

The inner sense of the sorrow symbolized by this weeping, unlike
the outer sense, does not mean sorrow over death. Rather, it means sorrow that the goodness characterizing a spiritual religion cannot be raised
above the earthly level. The Lord, flowing in through the inner dimension, constantly wants to improve that goodness and bring it closer to
himself, but it still cannot be elevated to the first rung of the goodness in
a heavenly religion (§3833). People in a spiritual religion are somewhat in
the dark, you see. They reason about truth and its validity, or else they
corroborate what is called doctrine, without a feel for whether the teachings they corroborate are true or not. Once they have proved a doctrine
to their own satisfaction, they put full faith in its validity, even if it is
false. There is nothing that cannot be proved, because it is a task requir-
ing cleverness, not understanding, let alone wisdom. Furthermore, falsity
is more amenable to proof than truth is, because it justifies our cravings
and agrees with our sensory illusions.

As that is what people in a spiritual religion are like, they can never
rise above the earthly level. Hence the sorrow symbolized by *Joseph wept
over him.*

And kissed him symbolizes initial union. This can be seen from the
symbolism of *kissing* as union based on desire (discussed in §§3573, 3574,
4215, 4353, 5929, 6260) and in this case as initial union, since what follows
is about a closer union.

6501

And Joseph commanded his servants the doctors symbolizes preservation
from evils that would hinder union. This is clear from the symbolism of
commanding as flowing in (discussed at §5732), from the representation of
Joseph as the inner dimension (noted just above at §6499), and from the
symbolism of *doctors* as preservation from evil. The thread of the story

6502

makes it clear that the evils being warded off are those hindering the union mentioned just above at §6501. Plainly, then, *Joseph commanded his servants the doctors* symbolizes an inflow from the inner dimension concerning preservation from evils that would hinder union.

Doctors symbolize preservation from evil because evil and falsity are the diseases of the spiritual world. Spiritual sickness is nothing else, because evil and falsity rob our inner self of its health. They subject our mind to illness and eventually to anguish, and that is exactly what sickness in the Word symbolizes.

[2] The symbolism in the Word of medical people, the practice of medicine, and medicinal remedies as preservation from evil and falsity is established by passages that mention them. In Moses, for instance:

> If you listen intently to the voice of your God and do what is good in his eyes and give ear to his commandments and keep all his statutes, I will not lay on you *any disease* that I laid on the Egyptians, *because I am Jehovah your physician.* (Exodus 15:26)

Jehovah as physician stands for someone who preserves people from evil, because evil is what the diseases laid on the Egyptians symbolize. The diseases laid on the Egyptians symbolize evil and falsity rising out of reasonings based on bad information concerning religious mysteries, as will be shown in the discussion of them, by the Lord's divine mercy. This verse provides evidence that something spiritual is meant, because it says that if they listened to God's voice, did good, gave ear to his commandments, and kept his statutes, then the diseases would not be laid on them. [3] The Lord also calls himself a doctor in the same sense in Luke:

> *The healthy do not need a doctor,* only those doing poorly; I have not come to call the righteous but sinners to repentance. (Luke 5:31, 32)

Here too the doctor stands for someone who preserves people from evil, because the healthy stand for the righteous, and those doing poorly stand for sinners. In Jeremiah:

> Is there no *balm* in Gilead? *Is there no doctor there?* Then why has the *health* of the daughter of my people not improved? (Jeremiah 8:22)

The doctor stands for preservation from falsity in the church, because "the health of the daughter of my people" means doctrinal truth in the church.

[4] The Word speaks of healings, wellness, cures and medicines not in a physical but in a spiritual sense, as is plain in Jeremiah:

> Why have you struck us *so that there is no cure for us?* Look for peace, but there will not be goodness; for a *time of healing,* but here, terror! (Jeremiah 14:19; 8:15)

In the same author:

> I myself will improve the *health* and *wellness* of [Jerusalem] and *heal* them and reveal a crown of peace to them, and truth. (Jeremiah 33:6)

In the same author:

> There is no one rendering judgment on you *to heal you;* you do not have *restorative medicines.* (Jeremiah 30:13)

In the same author:

> Go up to Gilead and take *balm,* virgin daughter of Egypt! In vain have you multiplied *medicines;* there is no *healing* for you. (Jeremiah 46:11)

[5] In Ezekiel:

> Beside the river, on its bank, on this side and that, grows every food tree, whose leaf does not fall, and its fruit is not used up; month by month it is reborn, because its waters are going out from the sanctuary. So its fruit serves as food, *and its leaf as medicine.* (Ezekiel 47:12)

This part of Ezekiel is about the new house of God, or the new temple, which symbolizes a new religion, and in a deeper sense, the Lord's spiritual kingdom. The *river,* then, on whose bank grows every food tree, symbolizes facets of understanding and wisdom (§§108, 109, 2702, 3051). The *trees* symbolize the perception and knowledge of what is good and true (103, 2163, 2682, 2722, 2972, 4552). The *food* symbolizes goodness and truth itself (680, 4459, 5147, 5293, 5576, 5915). The *water* going out from the sanctuary symbolizes the truth that creates understanding (2702, 3058, 3424, 4976, 5668). The *sanctuary* symbolizes heavenly love, and in the highest sense the Lord's divine humanity, from which that love comes. The *fruit* that serves as food symbolizes the good done by love (913, 983, 2846, 2847, 3146). The *leaf* that serves as medicine symbolizes the truth taught by faith (885). All this shows what *medicine* means. It means something that preserves us from falsity and evil. Religious truth preserves us when it leads to a good life, because it leads us away from evil.

6503　　*To embalm his father* means in order to prevent contamination. This can be seen from the symbolism of *embalming* as a means of preservation from contamination, and from the representation of Israel as the goodness characterizing a spiritual religion (discussed above at §6499). This shows that *to embalm his father* symbolizes a means of preserving the goodness belonging to a spiritual religion from contamination.

　　Embalming symbolizes a means of preservation from contamination because people used embalming to preserve a body from decay.

　　This means of preserving spiritual goodness from contamination is also dealt with below.

6504　　*And the doctors embalmed Israel* symbolizes carrying out the preservation of truth-based goodness, as the following shows: *Embalming* symbolizes a means of preservation from contamination, as discussed just above at §6503. Here it symbolizes the carrying out of that preservation because the text says they did the embalming. *Doctors* symbolize preservation from evils, as discussed above at §6502. And *Israel* represents spiritual goodness, which is the same as truth-based goodness, also mentioned above, at §6499.

6505　　*And forty days were fulfilled for him* symbolizes states of being prepared through times of trial. This can be seen from the symbolism of *forty* as times of trial (discussed in §§730, 862, 2272, 2273) and from that of *days* as states (discussed in §§23, 487, 488, 493, 893, 2788, 3462, 3785, 4850). The preparatory nature of the states is symbolized by *those days were fulfilled for him.* Through the fulfillment of those days, after all, preparations for the preservation of bodies from decay were being carried out, and in a spiritual sense, for the preservation of souls from contamination by evil.

　　The trials we undergo remove evil and falsity from us and prepare us to accept truth and goodness; see §§868, 1692, 1717, 1740, 2272, 3318, 4341, 4572, 5036, 5356, 6144.

6506　　*Because that fulfills the days for embalming* means that these are states of preservation. This can be seen from the fact that *days* symbolize states (noted directly above at §6505) and being *embalmed* symbolizes a means of preservation (also noted above, at §6503).

6507　　*And the Egyptians wept for him* symbolizes grief among items of knowledge possessed by the church. This is indicated by the symbolism of *weeping* as the pinnacle of grief and a sign of inward mourning (dealt with at §§3801, 4786) and from the representation of *Egyptians* as items of knowledge possessed by the church (dealt with at §§4749, 4964, 4966).

The grief among items of knowledge possessed by the church symbolized by *the Egyptians wept for Israel* does not mean grief over his death.
This meaning is the literal one. Instead, the grief here means grief that
goodness in the church, represented by Israel, left knowledge behind when
it moved up from knowledge, which is the outer level of the church, to
truth-based goodness, the church's inner core. At that point goodness in
the church does not regard knowledge as existing alongside it, the way it
did before, but as lying below it. When truth known to a spiritual religion
turns into goodness, a change takes place. Goodness no longer views truth
from the standpoint of truth but from the standpoint of goodness. This
reversal has already been discussed a number of times. The change causes
grief, and so does the emergence of a new hierarchy among items of knowledge, which also cannot happen without anguish.

Seventy days symbolizes a complete state. This can be seen from the
symbolism of *seventy,* which has the same meaning as seven. Seven symbolizes a whole time span from start to finish, so it symbolizes a complete
state (§§728, 2044, 3845). For the fact that numbers in the Word have
symbolic meaning, see §§1963, 1988, 2075, 2252, 3252, 4264, 4495, 4670,
5265, 6175; and that multiples have the same symbolism as their factors,
§§5291, 5335, 5708. So seventy has the same meaning as seven.

[2] The following passages also clarify that seventy means a whole time
span and therefore a complete state. In Isaiah:

> It will happen on that day that Tyre will be forgotten *for seventy years,*
> corresponding to the days of one king. *At the end of seventy years,* the
> harlot's song will be Tyre's. For it will happen *at the end of seventy years*
> that Jehovah will visit Tyre. (Isaiah 23:15, 17)

Tyre stands for concepts of goodness and truth known to the church (§1201),
which will be forgotten. Seventy years stands for the whole span of time
from beginning to end. "Corresponding to the days of one king" stands for
a state of truth within the church, since days mean states (§6505), and a king
means truth (§§1672, 2015, 2069, 3009, 5044, 5068, 6148). Anyone who
thinks it through can see that Tyre does not mean Tyre here. Such a person
can see that without the inner sense it is impossible to grasp the meaning
of the statements that Tyre will be forgotten for seventy years, that this corresponds to the days of one king, and so on. [3] In Jeremiah:

> The whole land will become a ruin, a wasteland, and these nations will
> serve the king of Babylon *seventy years,* and it will happen, when the

seventy years have been fulfilled, that I will inflict punishment on the king of Babylon and on this nation for their wickedness. (Jeremiah 25:11, 12; 29:10)

The seventy years stand for a full state of desolation and devastation. That was the symbolism of the seventy-year captivity the people of Judah endured. [4] In Daniel:

Seventy weeks have been decreed upon your people and upon your holy city, to bring an end to transgression, and to seal up sin, and to atone for wickedness, and to introduce everlasting righteousness, and to seal up vision and prophet, and to anoint the Holiest Place. (Daniel 9:24)

Seventy clearly stands for a complete state and accordingly for the entire span of time before the Lord was to come, which is why it is said that he came in the fullness of time [Galatians 4:4]. The fact that seventy weeks means a complete state is plain in Daniel 9:24 from everything the seventy weeks was decreed for: bringing an end to transgression, [sealing up sin,] atoning for wickedness, introducing everlasting righteousness, sealing up vision and prophet, and anointing the Holiest Place. Each of these acts involves something brought to completion.

The same is true for the next verse in Daniel 9:

Know therefore and perceive that from the issuing of the Word to restore and rebuild Jerusalem up to the time of Messiah the prince, there will be *seven weeks*. (Daniel 9:25)

Seven here stands for a complete state. See just above for the idea that seven is as much a symbol for such a state as seventy is. Jerusalem obviously stands for a new religion in this instance, because rather than being rebuilt at that time, Jerusalem was actually destroyed.

6509   Genesis 50:4, 5, 6. *And the days of weeping for him passed, and Joseph spoke to the household of Pharaoh, saying, "Please, if I have found favor in your eyes, please speak in Pharaoh's ears, saying, 'My father put me under oath, saying, "Here, now, I am dying. In my grave that I dug for myself in the land of Canaan—there you are to bury me." And now let me go up, please, and bury my father and return.'" And Pharaoh said, "Go up and bury your father, as he made you swear."*

And the days of weeping for him passed means that the states of sorrow reached their end. *And Joseph spoke to the household of Pharaoh* symbolizes an inflow from the inner dimension into the earthly mind. *Saying, "Please, if I have found favor in your eyes,"* means in order to be warmly received. *Please speak in Pharaoh's ears, saying,* symbolizes an appeal for consent. *My father put me under oath* means taking the church to heart. *Saying, "Here, now, I am dying,"* means that it ceased to exist. *In my grave that I dug for myself in the land of Canaan—there you are to bury me* means that it needed to be revived where it had existed before. *And now let me go up, please, and bury my father* symbolizes revival of the church there by the inner dimension. *And return* symbolizes [the inner dimension's] presence in the earthly mind. *And Pharaoh said, "Go up and bury your father,"* symbolizes agreeing to revival of the church. *As he made you swear* means because of taking the church to heart.

And the days of weeping for him passed means that the states of sorrow reached their end. This is evident from the symbolism of *they passed* as reaching their end and from that of *days of weeping* as states of sorrow (discussed above at §6500; for the symbolism of days as states, see §6505).

6510

And Joseph spoke to the household of Pharaoh symbolizes an inflow from the inner dimension into the earthly mind, as the following shows: *Speaking* symbolizes an inflow, as noted in §§2951, 5481, 5743, 5797. *Joseph* represents the inner dimension, as noted above at §6499. A *household* symbolizes the mind, as discussed in §§4973, 5023. And *Pharaoh* represents the earthly plane, as dealt with at §§5160, 5799, 6015. This shows that *Joseph spoke to the household of Pharaoh* symbolizes an inflow from the inner dimension into the earthly mind.

6511

Saying, "Please, if I have found favor in your eyes," means in order to be warmly received. This is clear from the symbolism of *finding favor in someone's eyes* as an ingratiating turn of phrase seeking a warm reception for the speaker; see §§4975, 6178.

6512

Please speak in Pharaoh's ears, saying, symbolizes an appeal for consent. This can be seen from the symbolism of *please speak* as an appeal and from that of *ears* as obedience (discussed at §§2542, 3869, 4551, 4652–4660). In this case the ears symbolize consent, because a monarch is being addressed. Obedience too involves consent, but one speaks of obedience in regard to the lowly and of consent in regard to the high-ranking.

6513

My father put me under oath means taking the church to heart, as the following shows: Israel, the *father,* represents a spiritual church, as discussed in §§4286, 6426. *Putting someone under oath* means laying oneself under an inward obligation, and here, taking something to heart. When we lay ourselves under an inward obligation—lay a demand on our conscience—we do so because we have taken something to heart. So that is what putting Joseph under oath symbolizes here.

6514

6515   *Saying, "Here, now, I am dying,"* means that it—the church—cease̶d to exist. This is indicated by the symbolism of *dying* as no longer existing (discussed in §494) and as the final days of the church, when it is passing away (§§2908, 2917, 2923).

6516   *In my grave that I dug for myself in the land of Canaan—there you are to bury me* means that it (the church) needed to be revived where it had existed before. This can be seen from the symbolism of a *grave* and being *buried* as revival (discussed in §5551) and from that of the *land of Canaan* as the Lord's kingdom and church (discussed in §§1413, 1437, 1607, 1866, 3038, 3481, 3705, 4240, 4447).

Jacob wanted to be buried in the land of Canaan (where Abraham and Isaac were buried) and not anywhere else because his descendants were going to possess the land and he would therefore lie among his own people. In an inner sense, though, it was not this but something else that was being symbolized, namely, rebirth and resurrection, because Canaan is where the church was. Burial in an inner sense symbolizes rebirth and resurrection (§§2916, 2917, 4621, 5551), and the land of Canaan symbolizes the church (as the sections cited above here show). Abraham, Isaac, and Jacob symbolize the Lord's divinity itself and divine humanity, and in a secondary sense, the inner and outer part of the Lord's kingdom (§§1965, 1989, 2010, 3245, 3305 at the end, 4615, 6098, 6185, 6276). The meaning given, then, is the inner-level symbolism of their burial in that land. Jews who believe in resurrection still believe they will rise again in Canaan, even if they have been buried elsewhere.

[2] The reason for saying that the church needed to be revived *where it had existed before* is that the Lord's church had existed in Canaan since earliest times (see §§3686, 4447, 4454, 4516, 4517, 5136). That is consequently the place that Abraham was ordered to go to and Jacob's descendants were led into. This was not because it would be holier than any other lands but because since earliest times all the sites there—the regions, cities, mountains, and rivers—served to represent attributes of the Lord's kingdom. Even the names given to them signaled those attributes. Every name bestowed by heaven on a place or a person involves what is heavenly and spiritual. When a name has been assigned by heaven, its meaning is perceived there. And it was the earliest church, which was heavenly and was in contact with heaven, that had given the names [to sites in Canaan].

The purpose in having the church return there, then, was for a Word to be given in which the whole and every part would serve to represent and symbolize something spiritual and heavenly. This would mean that the Word would be understood as readily in heaven as on earth, which could never have happened if the names of the places and people had not also been symbolic. That is why Jacob's descendants were brought into the land, why prophets were raised up there to write the Word, and why the representation of a religion was established among Jacob's descendants. You can see, now, why I said the church needed to be revived where it had existed before.

[3] For the idea that names in the Word have symbolic meaning, see §§1224, 1264, 1876, 1888, 4442, 5225, not to mention many other sections explaining what that meaning is. However, the fact that heaven's inhabitants perceive the symbolism of scriptural names, without training, is a secret no one knows yet, so I need to tell it.

When we read the Word, the Lord flows in and teaches us. What is more—and what is amazing—there are writings in the spiritual world that I have sometimes seen and been able to read but not to understand. Good spirits and angels understand them clearly, because the writing harmonizes with their universal language. I had the privilege of learning that every word there, down to individual letters, holds in it the kinds of ideas that belong to that world—in other words, spiritual ideas. The spiritual meaning is perceived from the aspiration behind the words and from the feeling evoked by the way they are pronounced, whether softly or harshly. But there may not be many at all who will believe it.

I have revealed this secret to show that the names in the Word have been recorded in heaven and that their symbolism is therefore instantly perceived there.

And now let me go up, [please,] and bury my father symbolizes revival of **6517** the church there by the inner dimension. This can be seen from the symbolism of being *buried* as being revived (discussed right above at §6516), from the representation of Israel, the *father*, as the church (also mentioned above, at §6514), and from that of Joseph, who says this about himself, as the inner dimension (noted at §6499).

And return symbolizes [the inner dimension's] presence in the earthly **6518** mind. This can be seen from the symbolism of *returning* as presence. In an inner sense, setting off and going symbolizes living (§§3335, 4882, 5493, 5605), so coming back or returning means the presence of life at the point where the journey began, since the mind is still present there. Presence in the earthly mind is what is meant because the land of Egypt, to which Joseph was to return, symbolizes the earthly mind (§§5276, 5278, 5280, 5288, 5301).

6519 *And Pharaoh said, "Go up and bury your father,"* symbolizes agreeing to revival of the church. This is evident from the remarks just above at §6517, where similar words appear. Plainly agreement is meant.

6520 *As he made you swear* means because of taking the church to heart. This is evident from the symbolism of *making swear,* [or putting under oath,] as taking something to heart, which is discussed above in §6514.

6521 Genesis 50:7, 8, 9. *And Joseph went up to bury his father, and there went up with him all Pharaoh's servants, the elders of his household and all the elders of the land of Egypt, and Joseph's whole household and his brothers and his father's household. Only their little children and their flocks and their herds they left in the land of Goshen. And there went up with him both chariot and riders, and it was a very heavy army.*

And Joseph went up to bury his father symbolizes the inner dimension at the time when the church was established. *And there went up with him all Pharaoh's servants* means that it attached earthly-level items of knowledge to itself. *The elders of his household* symbolizes those that would harmonize with goodness. *And all the elders of the land of Egypt* symbolizes those that would harmonize with truth. *And Joseph's whole household* symbolizes heavenly qualities of a spiritual type. *And his brothers* symbolizes truth derived from those qualities. *And his father's household* symbolizes spiritual goodness. *Only their little children* symbolizes innocence. *And their flocks* symbolizes neighborly love. *And their herds* symbolizes the exercise of neighborly love. *They left in the land of Goshen* means that these lie at the core of religious knowledge. *And there went up with him both chariot* symbolizes religious teachings. *And riders* symbolizes matters of intellect. *And it was a very heavy army* symbolizes truth and goodness united.

6522 *And Joseph went up to bury his father* symbolizes the inner dimension at the time when the church was established, as the following shows: *Joseph* represents the inner dimension, as mentioned above at §6499. Being *buried* symbolizes being revived, as dealt with in §6516, so because the term is being used in reference to the church, it symbolizes being established. And Israel, the *father,* represents the church, as treated of in §§4286, 6426.

6523 *And there went up with him all Pharaoh's servants* means that it had attached earthly-level items of knowledge to itself, as the following shows: *Going up with him* symbolizes his attaching something to himself. It was by [Joseph's] command that they went up, so he attached them to himself. And *Pharaoh's servants* symbolize earthly-level items of knowledge. After all, *Pharaoh* represents the earthly plane in general (§§5160

5799, 6015 at the end), and since the earthly plane contains items of knowledge, that is what his *servants* symbolize, as do Egyptians (§§1164, 1165, 1186, 1462, 4749, 4964, 4966, 5700, 5702, 6004).

The elders of his household symbolizes those that harmonize with goodness. This can be seen from the symbolism of *elders* as the leading elements of wisdom and therefore as something that harmonizes with goodness (discussed below) and from that of a *household,* [or house,] as goodness (dealt with in §§2559, 3652, 3720, 4982).

6524

Elders mean the leading elements of wisdom because old people in the Word symbolize the wise and, in an abstract sense, wisdom. Since the twelve tribes of Israel symbolized all truth and goodness as a whole, they had chieftains placed over them, and elders as well. The chieftains symbolized the main truths that constitute understanding. The elders symbolized the leading elements of wisdom and therefore aspects of goodness. [2] For the symbolism of chieftains as the main truths that constitute understanding, see §§1482, 2089, 5044. The symbolism of elders as the leading elements of wisdom, on the other hand, and of old people as wisdom, is plain from the following passages. In David:

They will exalt Jehovah in the assembly of the people, and *in the council of the old* they will praise him. (Psalms 107:32)

The assembly of the people stands for individuals possessing the truth that leads to understanding, because an assembly is mentioned in connection with truth (§6355), as is a people (§§1259, 1260, 2928, 3295, 3581). The council of the old stands for individuals possessing the goodness that constitutes wisdom. Wisdom is a matter of life and so of goodness, but understanding is a matter of knowledge and so of truth (§1555). In the same author:

I am wiser than the old, because I have kept your requirements. (Psalms 119:100)

The old plainly stand for someone wise. Likewise in Job:

Among the old there is wisdom; in length of days there is understanding. (Job 12:12)

In Moses:

Before white hair you shall get up, and you shall honor the presence of an old person. (Leviticus 19:32)

This command was given because the old represented wisdom. [3] In John:

> On the thrones I saw *twenty-four elders sitting,* dressed in white clothes, who had golden crowns on their heads. (Revelation 4:4)

The elders stand for different aspects of wisdom and consequently of goodness. This symbolism is clear from the description of the elders as sitting on thrones, wearing white clothes, and having golden crowns on their heads. Thrones mean the truth that constitutes understanding, born of the goodness that constitutes wisdom (§5313). White clothes have a similar meaning. (On the point that clothes mean truths, see §§1073, 4545, 4763, 5248, 5954; and that white is mentioned in connection with truth, see §§3301, 5319.) Golden crowns on their heads mean wise goodness, because gold means a loving goodness (113, 1551, 1552, 5658), and the head means the heavenly plane, where wisdom resides (4938, 4939, 5328, 6436). Inhabitants of the third or inmost heaven, who are closest to the Lord, are called wise, but inhabitants of the middle or second heaven, who are not as close to the Lord, are described as having understanding. [4] In the same author:

> All the angels stood around the throne and the *elders* and the four living creatures. (Revelation 7:11)

The elders again stand for facets of wisdom, as they also do in the following passages. In Isaiah:

> Youths will vaunt themselves *against the old,* and the despised against the honored. (Isaiah 3:5)

In the same author:

> Jehovah Sabaoth will rule on Mount Zion and in Jerusalem, and *before his elders,* his glory will rule. (Isaiah 24:23)

In Jeremiah:

> My priests and *my elders* expired in the city, for they had tried to find food for themselves with which to revive their soul. (Lamentations 1:19)

In the same author:

> Her monarch and *her chieftains* live among the nations; there is no law. The *elders of Zion's daughter* sit on the earth and keep quiet. (Lamentations 2:9, 10)

In the same author:

> They have raped women in Zion; young women in the cities of Judah. *Chieftains* have been hung by their hands; *the presence of the old has not been honored; elders* have ceased from the gate. (Lamentations 5:11, 12, 14)

In Ezekiel:

> There will come misery upon misery, and there will be rumor upon rumor, so they will seek a vision from the prophet, but the law has perished from the priesthood, and *counsel from the elders.* The monarch will mourn and the *chieftain* will be clothed in shock. (Ezekiel 7:26, 27)

In Zechariah:

> *Old men* and *women* will still live on the streets of Jerusalem—as will the man who has his staff in his hand—because of the multitude of their days. (Zechariah 8:3, 4)

In order that *elders* might represent aspects of wisdom, some of Moses' spirit was taken and given to them, so that they prophesied (Numbers 11:16 and following verses).

In a negative sense elders stand for what is the opposite of wisdom (Ezekiel 8:11, 12).

And all the elders of the land of Egypt symbolizes those that harmonize with truth, as the following shows: *Elders* symbolize the leading elements of wisdom and therefore something that harmonizes with goodness, as discussed just above at §6524. Here they symbolize something that harmonizes with truth, because what harmonizes with goodness also harmonizes with truth. And the *land of Egypt* symbolizes the earthly mind, where knowledge resides (discussed in §§5276, 5278, 5280, 5288, 5301), and consequently where truth resides as well. Knowledge is the truth of the earthly mind, and when it is genuinely true it is called truth in the form of knowledge. **6525**

And Joseph's whole household symbolizes heavenly qualities of a spiritual type. This is evident from the representation of *Joseph* as spiritual heavenliness, as discussed in §§4286, 4592, 4963, 5307, 5331, 5332. Joseph's *household,* then, symbolizes heavenly qualities of a spiritual type. **6526**

And his brothers symbolizes truth derived from those qualities. This can be seen from the representation of Israel's sons, *Joseph's brothers,* as spiritual truth, as dealt with in §§5414, 5879, 5951. This truth actually grows **6527** out of the inner heavenliness that is Joseph, though by way of the spiritual goodness that is Israel.

6528   *And his father's household* symbolizes spiritual goodness, as is evident from the representation of Israel, the *father*. He represents spiritual goodness, as discussed in §§3654, 4598, 5801, 5803, 5807, 5812, 5817, 5819, 5826, 5833, so his *household* means everything connected with that kind of goodness, taken together.

6529   *Only their little children* symbolizes innocence. This is established by the discussion in §§430, 3183, 5608 of the symbolism of *little children* as innocence.

6530   *And their flocks* symbolizes neighborly love. This can be seen from the symbolism of *flocks* as inward neighborly kindness, as discussed in §§5913, 6048.

6531   *And their herds* symbolizes the exercise of neighborly love. This can be seen from the symbolism of *herds* as a more outward sort of neighborly kindness, as discussed in §§2566, 5913, 6048, and therefore as the exercise of neighborly love. After all, the exercise of that love is a more outward form of neighborly kindness.

6532   *They left in the land of Goshen* means that these lie at the core of knowledge. This can be seen from the symbolism of the *land of Goshen* as the center or inmost part of the earthly plane, where religious knowledge resides, as discussed in §§5910, 6028, 6031, 6068. The idea that innocent goodness along with inward and outward neighborly kindness (§§6529, 6530, 6531) lay at that core is symbolized by the leaving of the children, flocks, and herds in the land of Goshen, because what is left somewhere continues to be there. So in the inner meaning here, *they left* is not about leaving anything but about its being in that place—at the core of religious knowledge, which is the land of Goshen.

6533   *And there went up with him both chariot* symbolizes religious teachings. This can be seen from the discussion in §§5321, 5945 of the symbolism of a *chariot* as religious teachings.

6534   *And riders* symbolizes matters of intellect, as can be seen from the symbolism of *riders*. Horse riders symbolize intellectual matters, because a horse symbolizes the intellect (§§2760, 2761, 2762, 3217, 5321, 6125).

The symbolism of riders as matters of intellect can be seen further from the following passages. In Moses:

> Jehovah alone led them; *he made them ride on the heights of the earth.* (Deuteronomy 32:12, 13)

This is about the ancient church. Making them ride on the heights of the earth stands for gifting them with higher intellect. [2] In David:

> In all your honor, mount *and ride on the word of truth* and gentleness and justice, and your right hand will teach you marvelous things. (Psalms 45:4)

This is about the Lord. Riding on the word of truth stands for having the quintessential understanding of what is true. In the same author:

> Sing to God; praise his name! Extol the *one riding on the clouds* by his name, Jah! (Psalms 68:4)

This too is about the Lord. The clouds stand for the Word's literal meaning (preface to Genesis 18, §§4060, 4391, 5922, 6343 at the end). Riding on the clouds stands for focusing on the inner meaning, where truth resides with all the understanding and wisdom it confers. [3] In Zechariah:

> On that day I will strike *every horse* with bewilderment and *its rider with madness,* and on the house of Judah I will open my eye. *But every horse of the peoples I will strike with blindness.* (Zechariah 12:4)

The horse stands for intellectual activity and the rider for the intellect. Who can fail to see that the horse here is not a horse nor the rider a rider? No, something is being symbolized that can be struck with bewilderment and madness and with blindness. That something is obviously the intellect. [4] Horses and riders symbolize what belongs to true intellect, and in a negative sense they symbolize rationalizations and the resulting falsity. Both senses can be seen in John:

> I looked, when there! A *white horse!* And *one sitting on it,* having a bow, who was given a crown. He went out conquering. Then there went out *another horse, red,* and the *one sitting on it* was granted to take peace away from the earth and to [make people] kill each other; so a large blade was given to this one. I looked, when there! A *black horse!* And *one sitting on it,* having a balance in his hand. So I looked, when there! A *pale horse!* And *one sitting on it* whose name was death. (Revelation 6:2, 4, 5, 8)

The horses here and the people sitting on them have a symbolism connected with understanding truth and in a negative sense with falsity, as the details show. The white horse and the one sitting on it stand for the ability to understand truth from the Word. The one sitting on the white horse is the Lord as the Word, and Revelation 19:11, 13, 16 says as much.

The red horse and the one sitting on it stand for rationalizations produced by cravings for evil, which inflict violence on truth from the Word. The black horse and the one sitting on it stand for an obliterated capacity for understanding truth. And the pale horse and the one sitting on it stand for the resulting damnation.

[5] Once again in Ezekiel horses and riders in a negative sense stand for a corrupt intellect and the falsity it spawns:

> Oholah whored against me and doted on her lovers—rulers and leaders, desirable young men all, *riders riding horses.* Her sister Oholibah lusted after the sons of Assyria—rulers and leaders, neighbors, dressed in perfect finery, *riders riding horses,* desirable young men all. (Ezekiel 23:5, 6, 12)

Oholah stands for a corrupted spiritual church, or Samaria, and Oholibah for a corrupted heavenly church, or Jerusalem. Israelites in Samaria represented the spiritual church, and Jews in Jerusalem represented the heavenly church. Assyrians and the sons of Assyria stand for reasoning that opposed religious truth (§1186). Riders riding horses stand for a corrupt intellect, which is a source of falsity. [6] In Habakkuk:

> I am rousing the Chaldeans, a nation bitter and rash, invading the breadth of the land to inherit dwellings that are not theirs—its *horses* being *nimbler* than leopards, [keener] than wolves at evening—*in order that its riders can spread in all directions,* so that *its riders* come from a distance. (Habakkuk 1:6, 8)

The Chaldeans stand for people who subscribe to falsity but look on the outside as though they subscribe to truth. Consequently they stand for profanation of truth, although Babel stands for profanation of what is good (§§1182, 1368). Invading the breadth of the land stands for destroying truth, the breadth of the land meaning truth (see §§3433, 3434, 4482). This shows that riders who spread in all directions and approach from a distance mean the contents of a corrupted intellect, and therefore falsity.

6535   *And it was a very heavy army* symbolizes truth and goodness united. This can be seen from the symbolism of an *army* as truth and goodness, as discussed at §3448. Since there was a coming together of the true ideas and good qualities symbolized here by the elders of Pharaoh's household and the elders of the land of Egypt, by Joseph's household and his brothers, and by their father's household, the *very heavy army* symbolizes truth and goodness united.

Genesis 50:10, 11. *And they came to the threshing floor of Atad, which* **6536** *is at the ford of the Jordan, and they keened there a very great and heavy keening, and he carried out mourning for his father seven days. And the Canaanite resident of the land saw the mourning on the threshing floor of Atad, and they said, "This is [a time of] heavy mourning for the Egyptians." Therefore its name was called Abel-mizraim, which is at the ford of the Jordan.*

And they came to the threshing floor of Atad symbolizes a first state. *Which is at the ford of the Jordan* means which is a state of initiation into the knowledge of what is good and true. *And they keened there a very great and heavy keening* symbolizes grief. *And he carried out mourning for his father seven days* symbolizes the end of grief. *And the Canaanite resident of the land saw the heavy mourning on the threshing floor of Atad* means that goodness in the church sensed the grief. *And they said, "This is [a time of] heavy mourning for the Egyptians,"* means that knowledge grieves until it has been initiated into the truth known to the church. *Therefore its name was called Abel-mizraim* symbolizes the quality of the grief.

And they came to the threshing floor of Atad symbolizes a first state, as **6537** the following shows: A *threshing floor* symbolizes [a state] in which there is truth-based goodness because it is a place for grain, and grain symbolizes goodness-from-truth (§§5295, 5410) and also truth-from-goodness (§5959). And *Atad,* like the names of other places, symbolizes the quality of that state. The reason the threshing floor of Atad symbolizes a [first] state, on the way to religious goodness and truth, is that it stood at the ford of the Jordan, which symbolizes initiation into the knowledge of goodness and truth (discussed just below). The Jordan was the first border on the way to the land of Canaan, and Canaan symbolizes the church. So the Jordan symbolizes the first steps of religion, or that which opens the door to the church. That is why the threshing floor of Atad symbolizes a first state. As the threshing floor symbolized a first state, the mourning took place beside it, because it was on the near side of the Jordan, and the land of Canaan, which symbolizes the church, lay in sight of it.

[2] The symbolism of a threshing floor as [a state] in which there is goodness-from-truth and truth-from-goodness and therefore in which religious traits exist is clear in Joel:

> Children of Zion, rejoice and be glad in Jehovah your God. *The threshing floors are full of grain,* and the presses overflow with new wine and oil. (Joel 2:23, 24)

Children of Zion stand for truth-from-goodness. Threshing floors full of grain stand for abounding truth and goodness. [3] In Hosea:

> Do not be glad, Israel, because you whored against your God; you delighted in the wage you earned as a harlot *on all the grain-threshing floors. Threshing floor* and winepress will not feed them, and the new wine will prove false to [that land]. (Hosea 9:1, 2)

Whoring and delighting in a harlot's wage stand for turning truth into falsity and loving what results. Grain-threshing floors stand for truth-from-goodness turned into falsity.

[4] Since a threshing floor symbolized goodness and also truth, the people celebrated the Feast of Booths when they were gathering produce from the threshing floor. This is what Moses says about it:

> A Feast of Booths you shall make for yourself for seven days *when you gather [produce] from your threshing floor* and from your winepress. (Deuteronomy 16:13)

The Feast of Booths symbolized sacred worship and therefore worship inspired by goodness and truth (§§3312, 4391).

6538   *Which is at the ford of the Jordan* means which is a state of initiation into the knowledge of what is good and true. This is established by the symbolism of the *Jordan* as initiation into the knowledge of what is good and true and therefore as the first step on entering the Lord's kingdom and the church, and the last step on leaving, as discussed at §4255. The rivers that formed the borders to the land of Canaan served to represent the outermost parts of the Lord's kingdom; see §§1585, 4116, 4240. That is why the *ford of the Jordan* symbolizes initiation into the knowledge of goodness and truth, because learning to recognize goodness and truth is the first step initiating a person into the realm of religion.

6539   *And they keened there a very great and heavy keening* symbolizes grief, as is evident from the symbolism of *keening* as grief. The grief symbolized here is grief over the initiation discussed just above at §6538. Concepts of what is good and true, which serve to initiate, need to be grafted onto goodness and in this way become the kind of goodness that marks the church, and until this can be accomplished, there is grief. A new state needs to be imposed on our earthly self, and the knowledge it has needs to be reorganized. What we used to love therefore has to be destroyed, and as a result we also have to undergo trials. That is the reason for the grief represented by the heavy keening the people keened.

And he carried out mourning for his father seven days symbolizes the end **6540**
of grief, as the following shows: *Mourning* symbolizes the grief that lasts
until concepts of goodness and truth have been grafted on, as described
just above at §6539. And *seven days* symbolize a whole time span from
start to finish, as discussed in §§728, 2044, 3845, 6508. In this case, then,
they symbolize the end, since the mourners crossed the Jordan once those
days were over.

And the Canaanite resident of the land saw the heavy mourning on **6541**
the threshing floor of Atad means that goodness in the church sensed the
grief, as the following shows: *Seeing* means perceiving, [or sensing,] as
dealt with in §§2150, 3764, 4723, 5400. A *resident* symbolizes goodness,
as dealt with in §§2268, 2451, 2712, 3613. The *land*—here, the land of
Canaan, where the *Canaanite resident* lived—symbolizes the church, as
dealt with in §§1413, 1437, 1607, 1866, 3038, 3481, 3705. *Mourning* symbolizes grief, as dealt with just above in §§6539, 6540. And the *threshing
floor of Atad* symbolizes a first state, or a state of initiation, as dealt with
in §§6537, 6538. Plainly, then, *the Canaanite resident of the land saw the
heavy mourning on the threshing floor of Atad* means that goodness in the
church sensed the grief.

And they said, "This is [a time of] heavy mourning for the Egyptians," **6542**
means that knowledge grieves until it has been initiated into the truth
known to the church. This can be seen from the comments above at §6539,
where these words are explained.

Therefore its name was called Abel-mizraim symbolizes the quality of **6543**
the grief. This can be seen from the symbolism of a *name* and *calling* a
name as the quality of a thing, as discussed in §§144, 145, 1754, 1896,
2009, 2724, 3006, 3421. Consider also that in ancient times people gave
names symbolizing inner conditions and states and therefore the quality
of a thing (§§1946, 3422, 4298). *Abel-mizraim,* a name meaning "mourning of the Egyptians" in the original language, therefore symbolizes that
very quality.

Genesis 50:12, 13. *And his sons did so, as he had commanded them.* **6544**
*And his sons bore him to the land of Canaan and buried him in the cave
of the field of Machpelah, which Abraham had bought along with the field
for the possession of a grave, from Ephron the Hittite, before Mamre.*

And his sons did so, as he had commanded them, symbolizes the carrying
out of the inflowing message. *And his sons bore him to the land of Canaan*
means that the church was transferred there. *And buried him* symbolizes
revival there. *In the cave of the field of Machpelah* symbolizes the start of

rebirth. *Which Abraham had bought along with the field* symbolizes people whom the Lord had redeemed. *For the possession of a grave, from Ephron the Hittite* symbolizes people who accept religious truth and goodness and let themselves be reborn. *Before Mamre* symbolizes its nature and extent.

6545   *And his sons did so, as he had commanded them,* symbolizes the carrying out of the inflowing message. This can be seen from the symbolism of *they did* as a carrying out and from that of *commanding* as an inflow, as discussed at §§5486, 5732.

6546   *And his sons bore him to the land of Canaan* means that the church was transferred there. This can be seen from the symbolism of *they bore* as being transferred—the church's being transferred, since the church is what the *land of Canaan* symbolizes (§§1413, 1437, 1607, 1866, 3038, 3481, 3705).

The reason for transferring the church there may be seen above at §6516.

6547   *And buried him* symbolizes revival there. This can be seen from the discussion in §§5551, 6516 of the symbolism of being *buried* as being revived.

6548   *In the cave of the field of Machpelah* symbolizes the start of rebirth. This can be seen from the symbolism of the *cave of the field of Machpelah* as dimly lit faith (discussed in §2935) and of *Machpelah* as rebirth (§2970). The phrase consequently symbolizes the start of rebirth, since that is when faith is dim.

6549   *Which Abraham had bought along with the field* symbolizes people whom the Lord had redeemed, as the following shows: *Buying* symbolizes redemption, as treated of in §§6458, 6461. And *Abraham* represents the Lord, as treated of in §§1965, 1989, 2010, 2172, 2198, 3245, 3305 at the end, 3439, 3703, 4615, 6098, 6185, 6276. And a *field* symbolizes the church, as treated of in §§2971, 3766. From this it is evident that *which Abraham had bought along with the field* symbolizes people belonging to the church, whom the Lord had redeemed.

6550   *For the possession of a grave, from Ephron the Hittite* symbolizes people who accept religious truth and goodness and let themselves be reborn. This can be seen from the symbolism of a *grave* as rebirth (discussed in §§2916, 2917, 5551, 6459) and from the representation of *Ephron the Hittite* as people who can accept goodness and truth (discussed at §6458).

6551   *Before Mamre* symbolizes its nature and extent. This can be seen from the symbolism of *Mamre* as the nature and extent of whatever it is connected with, as noted in §§2970, 4613, 6456.

Obviously there is particular meaning to the fact that Abraham had bought the cave of the field of Machpelah, which is before Mamre, from Ephron the Hittite, since the statement is repeated so often, as in Genesis 23:

> The field of Ephron that was in Machpelah, which is before Mamre, was established [for Abraham]. (verse 17)

> After this, Abraham buried Sarah his wife *at the cave of the field of Machpelah before Mamre.* . . . The *field and the cave* that was in it was established for Abraham as the *possession of a grave from the children of Heth.* (verses 19, 20)

In Genesis 25:

> They buried Abraham *at the cave of Machpelah, at the field of Ephron,* son of Zohar the *Hittite, which is before Mamre—the field that Abraham bought from the children of Heth.* (verses 9, 10)

In Genesis 49:

> Bury me *in the cave* that is *in the field of Machpelah, which is before Mamre* in the land of Canaan, *[the cave] that Abraham bought along with the field from Ephron the Hittite,* for the possession of a grave, the *purchase of the field and of the cave* that is in it, *from the children of Heth.* (verses 30, 32)

And in the current chapter:

> They buried him *in the cave of the field of Machpelah, which Abraham had bought along with the field* for the possession of a grave, *from Ephron the Hittite,* before Mamre. (verse 13)

The particular meaning of this frequent repetition in almost the same words is due to the fact that Abraham, Isaac, and Jacob represent the Lord; their burial represents rising again and being revived; the cave of the field of Machpelah represents the start of rebirth; Ephron the Hittite represents people who accept the goodness inherent in faith and let themselves be reborn; and the children of Heth represent a spiritual religion. It is because these words as a whole symbolize the establishment of a spiritual religion that they are repeated the same way so many times.

　　　Genesis 50:14. *And Joseph returned to Egypt—he and his brothers and all those going up with him to bury his father—after he had buried his father.*

6552

And Joseph returned to Egypt—he and his brothers means that inner heavenliness and religious truths lived among knowledge. *And all those going up with him to bury his father* symbolizes everything that contributes to rebirth. *After he had buried his father* means in order to revive the church.

6553   *And Joseph returned to Egypt—he and his brothers* means that inner heavenliness and religious truths lived among knowledge, as the following shows: *Returning* means living, as discussed in §§5614, 6518. *Joseph* represents inner heavenliness, as discussed in §§5869, 5877, 6177. Israel's sons, to whom *his brothers* refers here, represent religious truths collectively, as discussed in §§5414, 5879, 5951. And *Egypt* symbolizes knowledge, as discussed in §§1164, 1165, 1186, 1462, 4749, 4964, 4966.

The life that inner heavenliness and religious truths spent among knowledge was dealt with in the chapters treating of the following: Joseph's appointment as lord over the land of Egypt and officer over Pharaoh's household [Genesis 41, as discussed in §§5191, 5192, 5288, 5311–5313, 5315–5329]; the journey by Jacob's sons to Joseph [Genesis 42–45, as discussed in §§5398, 5417–5428, 5510, 5637, 5638]; and their arrival and the arrival of Jacob their father in Egypt [Genesis 46–47], as discussed in §§6004, 6023, 6052, 6071, 6077.

6554   *And all those going up with him to bury his father* symbolizes everything that contributes to rebirth. This is evident from the symbolism of being *buried* as rebirth and resurrection (discussed in §§2916, 2917, 4621, 6516) and as the revival and establishment of the church (5551, 6516). Everything that contributes to this is symbolized by *all those going up with him,* which included Joseph's whole household, his father's household, the elders of Pharaoh's household, and the elders of the land of Egypt. Joseph's household symbolizes heavenly qualities of a spiritual type (6526). His father's household symbolizes everything connected with spiritual goodness (6528). The elders of Pharaoh's household symbolize what would harmonize with goodness (6524), and the elders of the land of Egypt, what would harmonize with truth (6525). Plainly, then, *all those going up with him to bury* symbolizes everything that contributes to rebirth.

Why does *burying* symbolize rebirth, resurrection, and the revival and establishment of the church? It is because these symbolic meanings are alike. Rebirth is resurrection, because when we are reborn, we come to life after being dead and therefore rise again. The same thing happens when the church is revived and established in us, because this is accomplished through rebirth and so through resurrection from death to life.

After he had buried his father means in order to revive the church. This can be seen from the symbolism of being *buried* as revival of the church, as pointed out just above at §6554, and from the representation of Israel as a spiritual church, as discussed in §§4286, 6426, 6514, 6517, 6522.

6555

Genesis 50:15, 16, 17, 18, 19, 20, 21. *And Joseph's brothers saw that their father was dead, and they said, "Maybe Joseph will hate us and make sure he returns to us all the evil that we rendered to him." And they gave a command to Joseph, saying, "Your father gave a command before he died, saying, 'This is what you are to say to Joseph: "Please forgive, please, the transgression of your brothers and their sin, because they rendered evil to you."' So now forgive, please, the transgression of the servants of your father's God." And Joseph wept as they spoke to him. And his brothers also went and fell before him and said, "Look: we will serve as slaves to you." And Joseph said to them, "Don't be afraid, because am I in place of God? And you thought evil upon me; God thought it for good, in order to do as at this day, to keep a great people alive. And now don't be afraid; I will sustain you and your little children." And he comforted them and spoke to their heart.*

6556

And Joseph's brothers saw that their father was dead symbolizes a perception that the church had been revived. *And they said, "Maybe Joseph will hate us,"* means that they rejected the inner dimension. *And make sure he returns to us all the evil that we rendered to him* means that a deserved punishment therefore threatens. *And they gave a command to Joseph, saying,* symbolizes an inflow from the inner dimension and a resulting perception. *Your father gave a command before he died, saying,* means according to the church's commandment. *This is what you are to say to Joseph* symbolizes a perception of what to do, received from within. *Please forgive, please, the transgression of your brothers and their sin* symbolizes pleading and repentance. *Because they rendered evil to you* means that they had turned their back on inflowing goodness and truth. *So now please forgive, please, the transgression of the servants of your father's God* symbolizes repentance and acknowledgment of what is God's in the church. *And Joseph wept as they spoke to him* symbolizes a loving reception. *And his brothers also went and fell before him* means making the contents of the earthly plane subordinate to the inner dimension. *And said, "Look: we will serve as slaves to you,"* means that they will not be in charge of themselves. *And Joseph said to them, "Don't be afraid,"* symbolizes being revived by the inner dimension. *Because am I in place of God?* means that God will provide. *And you thought evil upon me* means that the estranged elements intend nothing but evil. *God thought it for good* means that the Divine turns it to good.

In order to do as at this day means that this has been the orderly way from eternity. *To keep a great people alive* symbolizes consequent life for people dedicated to truth-from-goodness. *And now don't be afraid* means that they should not worry. *I will sustain you and your little children* means that they will receive life from the Divine through the inner dimension by means of truth in the intellect and goodness in the will. *And he comforted them* symbolizes hope. *And spoke to their heart* symbolizes reassurance.

6557   *And Joseph's brothers saw that their father was dead* symbolizes elements estranged from truth and goodness, and a perception that the church had been revived, as the following shows: *Seeing* means understanding and perceiving, as discussed in §§2150, 2325, 2807, 3764, 3863, 4403–4421, 4567, 4723, 5400. Jacob's sons, the *brothers,* represent elements estranged from truth and goodness. When they wanted to kill Joseph and sold him [Genesis 37:17–28], they represented something estranged from truth and goodness. That state is symbolized here, as is clear from their words: "They said, 'Maybe Joseph will hate us and make sure he returns to us all the evil that we rendered to him.'" That is why they then had a negative representation. *Being dead* symbolizes being revived—the church's being revived—as discussed in §§3326, 3498, 3505, 4618, 4621, 6036, 6221. And Israel, the *father,* represents the church, as discussed in §§4286, 6426. This shows that *Joseph's brothers saw that their father was dead* symbolizes an awareness by elements estranged from truth and goodness that the church had been revived.

6558   *And they said, "Maybe Joseph will hate us,"* means that they rejected the inner dimension. This is clear from the symbolism of *hating* as opposing and rejecting, and from the representation of *Joseph* as the inner level (referred to at §§6177, 6224)—not that Joseph rejected them, but that they rejected Joseph. It is in keeping with appearances that something done by the outer dimension (meant by Joseph's brothers) is attributed to the inner dimension (meant by Joseph). Hatred and vengefulness are ascribed to Jehovah, for instance, when they really belong to us.

6559   *And make sure he returns to us all the evil that we rendered to him* means that a deserved punishment therefore threatens. This can be seen from the symbolism of *returning the evil that we rendered to him* as a deserved punishment. Evil that rebounds on anyone comes as punishment earned.

I need to tell about the rebound of evil in the spiritual world, or punishment there, because doing so will show what the inner meaning of these words is. In the world of spirits, evil spirits sometimes do evil above and beyond what they had adopted by the way they lived in the world. When they do, punishers immediately appear and discipline them for the exact degree of their excess. In the other life there is a law that forbids anyone to become worse than she or he had been in the world. The spirits receiving the punishment are totally puzzled as to how these disciplinarians know that the evil goes beyond what they have adopted. They are taught, though, that the way the other life is set up, evil carries its own punishment with it. As a result, the evil done is directly connected to the evil inflicted as punishment; that is, evil itself contains its own punishment. It is part of the arrangement, then, that avengers instantly become present.

That is what happens when evil spirits do wrong in the world of spirits, but in their hell they punish one another according to the evil they had actively adopted in the world. This is because they take such evil with them to the other life.

This information shows how to understand the idea that a deserved punishment therefore threatens, as symbolized by *he will make sure he returns to us all the evil that we rendered to him.*

As for good spirits, on the other hand, if they happen to say or do something wrong, they are pardoned and excused rather than punished, because their aim is not to say or do anything wrong. Good spirits know that these errors have been triggered in them by hell, so that it was not their fault the words and deeds came out. This can be discerned from the spirits' resistance and from their distress after the fact.

And they gave a command to Joseph, saying, symbolizes an inflow from the inner dimension and a resulting perception. This can be seen from the symbolism of *commanding* as an inflow (dealt with in §§5486, 5732), from the representation of *Joseph* as the inner level (dealt with in §§6177, 6224), and from the symbolism of *saying* as a perception (dealt with many times). *They gave a command to Joseph, saying,* then, symbolizes an inflow from the inner level and a resulting perception.   **6560**

The reason "they gave a command to Joseph" means an inflow from the inner dimension into the outer, not from the outer dimension into the inner, is that all inflow comes from within, never from outside; see §6322.

Our father gave a command before he died, saying, means according to the church's commandment, as the following shows: Israel, the *father,* represents the church, as discussed in §§4286, 6426. And *commanding* symbolizes an inflow, as noted just above in §6560, though here it symbolizes a commandment, because it is intended for the church and therefore comes from the Divine. And *before he died* means while it was still a church.   **6561**

The church has a commandment that we are to forgive our brother or sister—in other words, our neighbor—as the Lord's words in Matthew make clear:

> Peter said to Jesus, "Lord, how often will my brother sin against me and I have to forgive him? Up to seven times?" Jesus said to him, "I don't say this, up to seven times, but up to seventy times seven times." (Matthew 18:21, 22)

It was ingrained in the people of the Jewish nation, though, never to forgive but to hold as an enemy anyone who wounded them in any way. They then considered it legitimate to hate these enemies, treat them any way they wanted, and kill them. This was because that nation concentrated solely on what is external, devoid of any inner dimension, so they possessed no commandment of a religion with depth. That is why Joseph's brothers were so fearful that Joseph would hate them and repay them evil.

6562   *This is what you are to say to Joseph* symbolizes a perception of what to do, received from within. This is established by the symbolism of *saying* in the Word's narratives as a perception (discussed in §§1791, 1815, 1819, 1822, 1898, 1919, 2080, 2619, 2862, 3509, 5687, 5743) and from the representation of *Joseph* as the inner level (mentioned in §§6177, 6224, 6560). The fact that the perception is about *what to do* is symbolized by "*This is what* you are to say."

6563   *Please forgive, please, the transgression of your brothers and their sin* symbolizes pleading and repentance. This can be seen from the symbolism of *please forgive, please,* as pleading. Obviously it symbolizes repentance too, since the brothers confessed they had transgressed and sinned. The same thing can be seen from the next verse, since the brothers offer themselves to Joseph as slaves.

The text mentions both transgression and sin for the sake of the marriage between truth and goodness, which exists at every point in the Word. Transgression symbolizes evil inflicted on truth, which is lesser, and sin symbolizes evil inflicted on goodness, which is greater. That is why both are mentioned, as they are in other places too, such as Genesis 31:

> Jacob said to Laban, "What is *my transgression?* What is *my sin,* that you pursued after me?" (Genesis 31:36)

In Isaiah:

> I will wipe out *your transgressions* like a cloud and *your sins* like a cloud. (Isaiah 44:22)

In Ezekiel:

> *In their transgression* that they *transgressed,* and *in their sin* that they *sinned,* in these they will die. (Ezekiel 18:24)

In the same author:

> . . . when *your transgressions* are revealed, so that *your sins* become visible in all your deeds, . . . (Ezekiel 21:24)

In David:

> Happy is the one whose *transgression* is forgiven, whose *sin* is covered over. (Psalms 32:1)

Because they rendered evil to you means that they had turned their back on inflowing goodness and truth. This is evident from the symbolism of *evil* as a turning away, as discussed in §5746. The fact that inflowing goodness and truth were what was turned away from is symbolized by *they rendered [evil] to you,* since Joseph stands for inner heavenliness and deep goodness (§§5805, 5826, 5827, 5869, 5877), through which goodness and truth flow in from the Lord.

6564

Here is the situation with the inflow through the inner dimension: The Lord constantly flows in through our inner dimension with goodness and truth. The goodness gives us life and its warmth, which is love. The truth gives us enlightenment and its illumination, which is faith. However, when this inflow in evil people travels further, into their outer dimensions, they resist and reject it, or else they corrupt or smother it. The more they reject, corrupt, or smother it, the more their inner reaches close off. The only thing left open is a point of entry here and there, through cracks all around. These openings enable them to keep their capacity for thought and intention, but only for thoughts and intentions that oppose truth and goodness. The more they live a life of evil and consequently persuade themselves of what is false, the further and further outward the closing-off extends. Eventually it reaches the sensory level of their mind, which is where their thinking then originates. Afterward, physical pleasures and appetites rob them of everything.

This state is the state of hell's inhabitants. The evil sometimes have insight into behavior that is honorable and good, because of the wealth, honors, and reputation they can gain by it, but when they arrive in the other world those insights are taken from them. They then operate on a sensory level.

6565   *So now please forgive, please, the transgression of the servants of your father's God* symbolizes repentance and acknowledgment of what is God's in the church, as the following shows: *Please forgive, please, the transgression* symbolizes a confession that they had transgressed, and repentance. The *servants of your father's God* symbolize an acknowledgment of what is God's in the church, because in calling themselves the servants of his father's God they acknowledge that they serve the church's God and therefore acknowledge what is divine there. After all, Israel, the *father,* symbolizes the church (§§4286, 6426).

6566   *And Joseph wept as they spoke to him* symbolizes a loving reception, as the following shows: *Weeping* means a symbol of both sorrow and love, as discussed in §§3801, 5480, 5873, 5927, 5930. *Joseph* represents inner heavenliness, as discussed in §§5805, 5826, 5827, 5869, 5877, 6177, 6224. And *speaking* symbolizes an inflow and therefore reception, as discussed at §5797. The inflow comes from inner heavenliness, or Joseph, and is received by truths on the earthly plane, or his brothers. Clearly, then, *Joseph wept as they spoke to him* symbolizes a loving reception.

6567   *And his brothers also went and fell before him* means making the contents of the earthly plane subordinate. This can be seen from the representation of Israel's sons, the *brothers,* as spiritual truth on the earthly plane (discussed in §§5414, 5879, 5951), from the symbolism of *they fell before him* as subordination, and from the representation of Joseph as the inner dimension (mentioned at §6499). This explanation shows that *his brothers went and fell before him* means making the contents of the earthly plane subordinate to the inner dimension.

The theme of the chapter is the establishment of a spiritual religion, and at this point, subordination of the earthly level's contents to the inner dimension. Regarding this subordination, it needs to be known that a spiritual religion is completely unable to be established in anyone unless what belongs to the earthly, outer self has been made subordinate to the spiritual, inner self. As long as faith's truth alone dominates in us, and not neighborly goodness, our earthly, outer self is not subordinate to our spiritual, inner self. As soon as goodness does take control, though, our earthly, outer self surrenders and we become a spiritual church.

[2] The validity of this statement can be recognized from the fact that inclination then leads us to do what truth teaches us to do; we do not violate that inclination, no matter how intensely our earthly plane wants us to. Genuine desire and consequent rationality rule us, subduing the pleasures of self-love and materialism present on our earthly plane, as

well as the illusions that have permeated the knowledge stored there. The conquest is eventually so complete that we count it as one of our greater satisfactions, at which point our earthly dimension quiets down and then comes into harmony. When it comes into harmony, it shares the inner dimension's sense of satisfaction.

This shows what is meant by making the earthly level's contents subordinate to the inner level, as symbolized by "His brothers went and fell before him and said, 'Look: we will serve as slaves to you.'"

And said, "Look: we will serve as slaves to you," means that they will not be in charge of themselves. This can be seen from the symbolism of *slaves* as being without the freedom of self-rule and therefore not being in charge of oneself and in control of one's own affairs, as discussed in §§5760, 5763.

6568

And Joseph said to them, "Don't be afraid," symbolizes being revived by the inner dimension. This is clear from the representation of *Joseph* as the inner dimension (noted above at §6499) and from the symbolism of *don't be afraid* as not worrying. In the speech that follows, Joseph relieves his brothers of their worry, comforting them and speaking to their heart, so *don't be afraid* here symbolizes having their spirits revived.

6569

Because am I in place of God? means that God will provide. This can be seen from the symbolism of *am I in place of God?* as meaning that he is not God but that God will provide.

6570

And you thought evil upon me means that the estranged elements intend nothing but evil, as the following shows: Jacob's sons, *you,* represent elements estranged from truth and goodness (as explained above at §6557), because when they thought evil against Joseph they represented what was estranged. *Thinking evil upon me* means intending evil, because the evil we think against anyone is evil we intend. Since something that is estranged cannot intend good, the explanation says that *nothing but* evil is intended.

6571

[2] To address the idea that elements estranged from truth and goodness intend nothing but evil: People who have become estranged from goodness and truth intend nothing but evil because intending something good is out of the question. What they intend reigns supreme in them, so it is present in all their thoughts, down to the slightest. After all, our intention or goal is our very life, because our goal is what we love, and love is life. What is more, our character is exactly the same as the purpose we hold, and our outward appearance in heaven's light is exactly the same as well. Surprisingly, perhaps, our appearance overall is reflected in the appearance of the slightest urges of our will. We therefore *are* our

purpose through and through. From this you can see that a person who is an evil purpose cannot possibly live among people who are good purposes, which means that one who is in hell cannot possibly live in heaven. The aims clash, and good aims win, because they come from the Divine.

[3] You can also see that to believe that anyone at all can be introduced into heaven out of pure mercy is to think wrongly. If those who are evil purposes go to heaven, they struggle to remain alive, like a person lying dreadfully tormented in the throes of death. Besides which, in heaven's light they look like devils.

This shows that people who have become alienated from truth and goodness cannot think anything but evil. The fact that evil is present in their slightest thoughts and intentions is obvious from the aura they give off far and wide, because from it others sense what they are like. The aura is like a spiritual vapor seeping from every pore of their life.

6572 *God thought it for good* means that the Divine turns it to good. This can be seen from the symbolism of *thinking something for good* as so intending, which is discussed just above at §6571. Since it is said of *God,* though, it means turning something to good. What the Lord intends, he does.

6573 *In order to do as at this day* means that this has been the orderly way from eternity, as the following shows: *Doing,* when ascribed to the Divine symbolizes order, because whatever the Divine does is orderly. And *as at this day* means from eternity, as discussed in §§2838, 3998, 4304, 6165, 6298.

6574 *To keep a great people alive* symbolizes consequent life for people dedicated to truth-from-goodness, as the following shows: *Keeping someone alive* symbolizes spiritual life, as discussed in §§5890, 6032. A *people* symbolizes truth, as discussed in §§1259, 1260, 3295, 3581, 4619, and here it symbolizes truth-from-goodness, because the text speaks of a *great people.* Truth rising out of goodness is greater than truth that gives rise to goodness, because the former kind—truth rising out of goodness—*is* essentially goodness. It is formed from goodness, so it is goodness in a form—the form proper to goodness.

[2] The words Joseph has just spoken to his brothers—"You thought evil upon me; God thought it for good, in order to do as at this day, to keep a great people alive"—are words that contain one of heaven's secrets, and the secret is this: The Lord allows hellish spirits in the other world to subject the good to trials, which means flooding the good with falsity and evil. The hellish put all their effort into this endeavor because when they do they are in their element, enjoying life to the utmost. At the same time though, the Lord himself is present directly with the people undergoing

hese trials, and he is present indirectly too, through angels. He puts up
esistance, refuting the lies of the hellish spirits and dissipating their malev-
lence, which brings renewal, hope, and victory to the sufferers. In this
vay, faith's truth and charity's goodness are more deeply implanted and
nore firmly strengthened in people who possess truth-from-goodness. It is
he means by which they receive the gift of spiritual life.

[3] This evidence shows what the words of the current verse mean in
n inner sense. They mean that people who have become estranged from
ruth and goodness—as spirits who inflict times of trial have—intend
othing but evil, but the Divine turns that evil to good, in what has been
he orderly way from eternity, and the result is life for people dedicated to
ruth-from-goodness.

It is important to realize that hellish spirits who are permitted to attack
he good in this way intend nothing but evil, since they want to drag the
;ood down from heaven as forcefully as possible and throw them into hell.
To destroy anyone's soul—that is, to destroy anyone forever—is the cen-
ral pleasure of their life. The Lord does not yield them an inch, though,
xcept in order to bring good out of it. The good he seeks is to firm up
nd strengthen truth and goodness in people undergoing times of trial.

The Lord has a purpose radiating from him that reigns supreme
hroughout the spiritual world, and that purpose is for something good
o come out of absolutely everything that happens, even the most minor.
'or this reason the Lord's kingdom is called a kingdom of purpose and
isefulness.

And now don't be afraid means that they should not worry, as is self-
vident.

I will sustain you and your little children means that they will receive
ife from the Divine through the inner dimension by means of truth in
he intellect and goodness in the will, as the following shows: *Sustain-
ng* symbolizes an inflow of goodness and truth, as discussed at §6106, so
t symbolizes life received through truth and goodness. Joseph represents
he inner dimension, as noted at §6499, but since spiritual life comes not
rom the inner level but from the Lord by way of the inner level, the explanation is "from the Divine through the inner dimension." *You and your
little children* symbolize spiritual truth on the earthly level and the innocence it contains, both of which will receive life from the Divine through
he inner dimension by means of truth and goodness.

Sustaining stands for life received by means of truth and goodness
because spiritual food is knowledge, understanding, and wisdom and

therefore truth and goodness; see §§56–58, 681, 4792, 5293, 5340, 5342, 5576, 5579.

The reason for speaking of truth *in the intellect* and goodness *in the will* is that all truth belongs to the intellect and all goodness to the will. The intellect holds truth, and the will holds goodness.

6577   *And he comforted them* symbolizes hope. This can be seen from the symbolism of *comforting* as calming an agitated mind with hope, as mentioned at §3610.

6578   *And spoke to their heart* symbolizes reassurance. This can be seen from the symbolism of *speaking to their heart* as giving reassurance—reassurance that nothing bad would happen to them. *Speaking* means an inflow (§§2951, 5481, 5797), and the *heart* means the will (§§2930, 3888), so speaking to someone's heart stands for an inflow into the person's will resulting in reassurance.

These points also show that every detail of the Word contains a marriage between truth in the intellect and goodness in the will, because comforting has to do with the intellect and speaking to someone's heart has to do with the will. So comforting them symbolizes hope, because truth brings hope to the intellect, while speaking to their heart symbolizes reassurance, because goodness offers reassurance to the will. Genuine assurance is not possible except in people who do good out of love for their neighbor, nor genuine hope except in people who do good out of faith.

6579   Genesis 50:22, 23. *And Joseph resided in Egypt, he and his household. And Joseph lived one hundred ten years. And Joseph saw Ephraim have children of the third generation. In addition, the children of Machir, Manasseh's son, were born on Joseph's knees.*

And Joseph resided in Egypt symbolizes the life that religious knowledge receives from the inner dimension. *He and his household* means from the inner dimension and the goodness there. *And Joseph lived one hundred ten years* symbolizes its state and nature. *And Joseph saw Ephraim have children of the third generation* symbolizes establishment of the church, specifically its intellect and what developed out of this. *In addition, the children of Machir, Manasseh's son,* means and specifically its will and what developed out of this. *Were born on Joseph's knees* means that it comes from goodness united with truth, received from the inner dimension.

6580   *And Joseph resided in Egypt* symbolizes the life that religious knowledge receives from the inner dimension. This can be seen from the symbolism of *residing* as life (discussed in §§1293, 3384, 3613, 4451, 6051), from the representation of *Joseph* as the inner dimension (mentioned above at §6499), and from the symbolism of *Egypt* as religious knowledge (discussed in §§4749, 4964, 4966, 6004).

The preliminaries to this chapter [§6497] talk about a spiritual church that was to be established. By now Joseph's brothers have fallen before him and offered themselves to him as slaves, symbolizing the fact that the outer, earthly plane became completely subordinate to the inner, spiritual plane. So the focus switches to the now-established church, which is depicted in the current verses by Joseph's residence in Egypt and by the birth of sons to Ephraim and to Machir, Manasseh's son.

In a person who is part of the spiritual church, religious knowledge contains life received from the inner plane. It contains life because in such a person, items of knowledge are subordinate and have been so far reduced to order that they are open to an inflow of goodness and truth. This makes them recipients of inflow from the inner dimension.

Not so with people who are not part of the church. In them, items of knowledge are arranged in a pattern that casts any evidence confirming what is true and good off to the edges, far from heaven's light. The remaining knowledge, then, is open to falsity and evil.

He and his household means from the inner dimension and the good- **6581** ness there. This can be seen from the representation of Joseph, *he,* as the inner dimension (noted at §6499) and from the symbolism of a *household* as goodness (discussed in §§2048, 3720, 4982).

Joseph lived one hundred ten years symbolizes its state and nature. This **6582** is evident from the symbolism of numbers in the Word as realities (discussed in §§575, 1963, 1988, 2075, 2252, 3252, 4264, 5265, 6175) and in fact as the state and nature of a reality (§4670). The same for the number *one hundred ten,* which contains the state and nature of the life that items of knowledge receive from the inner plane.

And Joseph saw Ephraim have children of the third generation symbolizes **6583** establishment of the church, specifically its intellect and what developed out of this, as the following shows: *Ephraim* represents the church's intellect, as discussed in §§3969, 5354, 6222, 6234, 6238, 6267. And *children of the third generation* symbolize further developments, because children and grandchildren, as the descendants of a parent, stand for whatever develops out of the reality their parent represents. The establishment of the church by the inner dimension, or rather by the Lord through the inner dimension, is symbolized by *Joseph saw.* (For a definition of the church's intellect, represented by Ephraim, see §6222.)

6584   *In addition, the children of Machir, Manasseh's son,* means and specifically its will and what developed out of this, as the following shows
Manasseh represents the church's will, as discussed in §§5351, 5353, 5354
6222, 6238, 6267, 6296. And his children and grandchildren, the *childre*
of Machir, symbolize further developments, as above at §6583.

The offshoots of the church's will symbolized by Machir's children ar
good desires united with true ideas, and therefore also true ideas that grov
out of goodness, because truths that develop from goodness are forms o
goodness.

The role of Machir's children as good desires united with true idea
is symbolized by their having been born on Joseph's knees, as the nex
phrase says. Their role as truth that grows out of goodness is symbolize(
in Judges:

> *From Machir,* lawgivers will descend. (Judges 5:14)

Lawgivers stand for truth based on goodness (§6372).

6585   *Were born on Joseph's knees* means that it comes from goodness unite(
with truth, received from the inner dimension. This is indicated by th
symbolism of *giving birth on someone's knees* as a union of goodness an(
truth (discussed at §3915) and from the representation of *Joseph* as th
inner dimension (mentioned at §6499).

The statement that Machir's children were born on Joseph's knee
implies that Joseph acknowledged them as his. When that figure of speec
is used, it means the children are adopted as one's own. This is clear fron
the sons born to Bilhah, Rachel's maid, of whom Rachel says, "Look—
my maid, Bilhah; come to her, and *let her give birth on my knees,* and I, ye
I, will be built up from her" (Genesis 30:3). Joseph acknowledged Machir'
children as his because Manasseh represents the church's will and there
fore its goodness. The inner plane, represented by Joseph, flows in witl
goodness, but not with truth except by way of goodness. That is why th
text says they were born on Joseph's knees.

6586   Genesis 50:24, 25, 26. *And Joseph said to his brothers, "I am dying, an(*
God will unfailingly visit you and bring you up from this land to the lan(
that he swore to Abraham, Isaac, and Jacob." And Joseph put the children o
Israel under oath, saying, "God will unfailingly visit you, and you must brin
my bones up from this place." And Joseph died, a son of one hundred ten years
And they embalmed him. And he was put in an ark in Egypt.

And Joseph said to his brothers, "I am dying," symbolizes a predictio
that the inner dimension of the church will come to an end. *And God wi*

unfailingly visit you means that the last days will arrive. *And bring you up from this land to the land that he swore to Abraham, Isaac, and Jacob* means that they will achieve the state of religion that characterized the ancients. *And Joseph put the children of Israel under oath* symbolizes an obligation. *God will unfailingly visit you* means when the last days of the church arrive. *And you must bring my bones up from this place* means that there will be a presentation of a religion but not a representative religion, since a representative religion is awake to the inner dimension as well [as the outer]. *And Joseph died* means that the inner plane of the church ceased to exist. *A son of one hundred ten years* symbolizes its state then. *And they embalmed him* symbolizes preservation nonetheless. *And he was put in an ark in Egypt* symbolizes concealment within religious knowledge.

And Joseph said to his brothers, "I am dying," symbolizes a prediction **6587** that the inner dimension of the church will come to an end, as the following shows: *Joseph* represents the inner dimension, as noted at §6499. Here he represents the inner dimension of the church, because the theme above has been the establishment of the church by the inner dimension, or rather by the Lord through the inner dimension. And *dying* means something's ceasing to be what it was, as discussed at §494, and therefore its coming to an end. Dying also symbolizes the last days of the church (§§2908, 2912, 2917, 2923). A prediction of those days is symbolized by *Joseph said to his brothers,* because from here to the end of the chapter the topic is the subsequent state of the church. Plainly, then, *Joseph said to his brothers, "I am dying,"* means that the inner dimension of the church will come to an end.

[2] Here is the situation: In order for the church to exist, it has to have an inner part and an outer part, because there are people who belong to the inner part and people who belong to the outer part. There are few of the former but many, many of the latter. Yet people who have the inner church in them must also have the outer church, because the inner part cannot be separated from the outer part. People who have the outer church in them likewise must have the inner church as well, but with them the inner church is hard to see.

[3] The inner dimension of religion consists in wishing well from our heart and being affected by what is good. The outer dimension of this is to do good and to base our good deeds on the religious truth we have learned at the hand of goodness. But the outer dimension of religion is to observe sacred rituals and to do charitable deeds in keeping with the church's commandments.

You can see, then, that the inner dimension of religion is charitabl goodness in the will. When it comes to an end, the church itself comes t an end, because charitable goodness is its very essence. Outward worshi does linger on, after the end as before, but at that point it is ritual rathe than worship—ritual that has been preserved as an institution. It look like worship, so it is like a nutshell without the nut. It is a facade wit nothing inside. When the church reaches this stage, it is defunct.

6588   *And God will unfailingly visit you* means that the last days will arriv This is clear from the symbolism of being *visited* as the last days. In th case it is the last days of oppression for the children of Israel in Egypt. I an inner sense it means the last days of an old church and the first day of a new one. The Word calls these last days a visitation, and the terr applies to the church in general and to people in the church in particula It also applies to a new religion being born and to an old religion pass ing away, and in particular to a person in the church who is being eithe saved or damned.

[2] This scriptural symbolism of visitation and of a day of visitatio can be seen in the following places. In Luke:

> A blessing on the Lord God of Israel, because he has *visited* his people and secured their deliverance, through the visceral mercies of our God, with which the sunrise from above has *visited us,* to show himself to people who sit in the dark and the shadow of death. (Luke 1:68, 78, 79)

This is Zechariah's prophetic utterance about the Lord's birth. Being vis ited stands here for the revival of a new religion and the enlightenmen that would then be enjoyed by people lacking any knowledge of religiou truth and goodness. It accordingly stands for their deliverance. That i why the passage says, "He has visited his people and secured their deliver ance, he has visited to show himself to people who sit in the dark and th shadow of death." [3] In Moses:

> Jehovah to Moses: "Gather the elders of Israel and say to them, 'Jehovah, the God of your ancestors, has appeared to me—the God of Abraham, Isaac, and Jacob—saying, *"I will unfailingly visit you* and what has been done to you in Egypt."'" (Exodus 3:16)

In the same author:

> The people believed and heard that *Jehovah had visited the children of Israel.* (Exodus 4:31)

In this case being visited stands for the last days of the church, when it has come to an end, and for the first days, when it begins. It stands for the church's last days among the Egyptians and for its first days among the children of Israel, so it also stands for the deliverance of the latter. [4] In Jeremiah:

> They will be taken to Babylon and be there *until the day when I visit them.* Then I will bring up the vessels of the House of God and return them to their place. (Jeremiah 27:22)

In the same author:

> When seventy years have been fulfilled for Babylon, *I will visit you* and establish my good word concerning you and return you to this place. (Jeremiah 29:10)

Visiting them stands for freeing them, and in general for captivity and desolation in the last days.

[5] Visitation and a day of visitation stand for the last days of the church in Isaiah:

> What will you do *on the day of visitation* and devastation, [which] will come from far away? To whom will you flee for help? (Isaiah 10:3)

In the same author:

> Look—the *day* of Jehovah comes as a cruel one, and one of outrage and of wrath and of anger, to make the earth a wasteland; *I will visit evil on the world* and their wickedness on the ungodly. (Isaiah 13:9, 11)

In Jeremiah:

> They will fall down among those who fall, and *at the time of their visitation* they will stumble. (Jeremiah 8:12)

In Hosea:

> The *days of visitation* have come; the days of retribution have come. (Hosea 9:7)

In Moses:

> Jehovah to Moses: "Nevertheless go lead this people into [the land] that I spoke of to you. Here, now, my angel will go before you, but *on the day of my visiting I will visit* their sin on them." (Exodus 32:34)

In Luke:

> Jesus, concerning Jerusalem: "They will not leave in you stone upon stone, because you did not recognize the *time of your visitation.*" (Luke 19:44)

The day of visitation stands for the Lord's Coming and enlightenment at that time. In relation to the Jewish nation, though, because its people did not recognize the end, the day of visitation stands for the last days of practices they had that represented a religion. After all, once Jerusalem was destroyed, sacrifices ceased and the nation was dispersed. [6] In Ezekiel:

> A loud voice shouted in my ears, "The *city's visitations* have come near, and a man has his weapon of destruction in his hand." (Ezekiel 9:1)

The meaning is similar. In Isaiah:

> The Rephaim will not rise again, *because you visited them,* you obliterated them. (Isaiah 26:14)

The Rephaim stand for descendants of the earliest church, which predated the Flood. They were also called Nephilim and Anakim. For more about them, see §§567, 581, 1673. "You visited and obliterated the Rephaim" stands for the final days of that church and for the casting of those people into hell. On this subject, see §§1265–1272.

Visitation stands for retribution and consequently for damnation, in Jeremiah:

> *Should I not for this reason visit them?* Or on a nation that is like this one should my soul not take revenge? (Jeremiah 5:9)

In the same author:

> Esau's calamity I will bring on him *at the time I visit him.* (Jeremiah 49:8)

In Hosea:

> *I will visit their ways on them,* and their deeds I will repay. (Hosea 4:9)

6589   *And bring you up from this land to the land that he swore to Abraham, Isaac, and Jacob* means that they will achieve the state of religion that characterized the ancients, as the following shows: The land of Egypt, from which they would *go up,* symbolizes the church after it has been devastated. That is what the Egyptians represented in oppressing the children of Israel. The death of the church was represented when they were drowned in the Suph Sea [Exodus 14:21–28]. And the land of Canaan, to which the children of Israel were about to go up, symbolizes the Lord's kingdom and

he church, as discussed in §§1607, 3038, 3481, 3705, 4447, 4517. [2] The
hurch in question is the ancient church, or the state of religion that char-
cterized the ancients, as is symbolized by the statement that God *swore
o give* that land *to Abraham, Isaac, and Jacob*. These three stand in the
ighest sense for the Lord and in a representative sense for his kingdom
n the heavens and his kingdom on earth, which is the church (§§1965,
989, 2010, 3245, 3305 at the end, 6098, 6185, 6276). Swearing that land to
hem, then, means confirming that they would achieve the state of reli-
;ion that characterized the ancients. This does not refer to Jacob's descen-
lants, because they were unable to achieve that state of religion. The most
hey could manage was the outward show—the representative practices—
»f religion, and then just barely. No, it refers to people symbolized by the
:hildren of Israel, meaning everyone in the spiritual church, both then
.nd in the future. [3] (On the point that *swearing* means confirmation by
he Divine, see §§2842, 3375. On the point that the land of Canaan was
»romised and given to Jacob's descendants so that they could represent a
:hurch—because the church had existed in that land since ancient times,
vhen all its sites received names and took on representative roles—see
§§3686, 4447, 4516, 4517, 5136, 6516.)

And Joseph put the children of Israel under oath symbolizes an obliga- **6590**
ion, as needs no explanation.

God will unfailingly visit you means when the last days of the church **6591**
urrive. This can be seen from the symbolism of *visiting* as the last days of
he church, discussed just above at §6588.

And you must bring my bones up from this place means that there will **6592**
>e a representation of a religion [but] not a [representative] religion, since
ι representative religion is awake to the inner dimension as well [as the
»uter]. This can be seen from the representation of Joseph as the inner
limension of the church, which is discussed above at §6587. As he rep-
esents the church's inner dimension, his *bones* symbolize the lowest
ιspect of the church, or its outermost facet, and therefore its represen-
ative role. Representative practices in the ancient church, which were
ιlso established among Jacob's descendants, were the outermost aspect
»f the church. The qualities they symbolized and represented were the
nner aspect. The inner aspect is symbolized by flesh in which there is
pirit, and the outermost aspect by bones. From this you can see what
he church is like when it focuses solely on outward observance, without
ιny inward content: it is like a person's bony frame without the flesh.
Among the people of Israel and Judah there was not an actual religion,
»nly a representation of a religion; see §§4281, 4288, 4307, 4500, 4680,

4844, 4847, 4903, 6304. The representation of a religion was not established among them until after they had been thoroughly purged of any
inner dimension, and if it had been established earlier they would have
profaned what was holy; §4289.)

6593   *And Joseph died* means that the inner plane [of the church] ceased to
exist. This is established by the symbolism of *dying* as something's ceasing
to be what it was (discussed in §§494, 6587) and from the representation
of *Joseph* as the inner plane (mentioned at §6499). For a discussion of the
church's nature when any inner depth has come to an end, see §§6587,
6592 above.

6594   *A son of one hundred ten years* symbolizes its state then. This can be
seen from the symbolism of *one hundred ten years* as the state and nature
of the life that items of knowledge receive from the inner plane, as discussed at §6582. For the meaning of *years* as states, see §§487, 488, 493.

6595   *And they embalmed him* symbolizes preservation nonetheless. This can
be seen from the symbolism of *embalming* as preservation from contamination by evil, as dealt with in §§6503, 6504.

As the theme here is the end of the church, I need to say what is
meant by preservation nonetheless when the church has ceased to exist,
which happens when its inner dimension comes to an end in us (§§6587,
6592). Even then, the outer dimension remains. The outer dimension is
such that it contains an inner dimension, but this inner plane is not there
present with us, because we do not think about it, and even if we were to
think about it we would not be affected by it. The inner plane *is* present
with the angels who accompany us. Since people in a devastated religion
never think about the inner plane, are not affected by it, and usually do
not know it exists, they cannot injure it. When we know about something, and especially once we believe in it, we can damage it, but we cannot hurt what we neither know about nor believe in. This *preserves* the
church's inner depths from harm by any evil.

That is how the inner depths of the church were preserved among
Jacob's descendants. These people were so involved in what is external,
apart from any inner dimension that they did not even want to hear
about anything deep. For that reason, the church's inner knowledge was
not revealed to them.

On the point that inner knowledge was not disclosed to Jacob's pos-
terity out of concern that they would injure it by profanation, see §§3398,
3479. On the point that the church's inner knowledge cannot be profaned
by people who do not believe in it, let alone people who are ignorant of
it, see §§593, 1008, 1059, 2051, 3398, 3402, 3898, 4289, 4601. On the point

that inner religious knowledge is not revealed until the church has been devastated, because then people no longer believe in it and consequently cannot profane it either, see §§3398, 3399.

All this is what preservation means.

And he was put in an ark in Egypt symbolizes concealment within religious knowledge. This can be seen from the symbolism of an *ark* as that in which something is stored away or hidden and from the symbolism of *Egypt* as religious knowledge (discussed in §§4749, 4964, 4966). The church's knowledge at that time consisted in knowledge of the representations and symbolisms used in the ancient church. This was the place of concealment for the inner dimension symbolized by the current clause. Concerning the concealment of the church's inner dimension and its resulting preservation from harm, see just above at §6595.

The meaning of an *ark* as that in which something is stored away or hidden can be seen from the *ark of the testimony,* which was called an ark because the testimony, or the law, was stored away in it. **6596**

With this I finish discussing the inner meaning of the subject matter in Genesis. The contents of Genesis are all narratives (except chapters 48 and 49, which contain prophetic passages), so it may be almost impossible to see that the explanation given actually is the inner meaning. Stories bog the mind down in the literal meaning, distracting it from any inner meaning, especially because the inner meaning is radically different from the literal. The inner meaning deals with spiritual and heavenly matters, the literal meaning with worldly and earthly matters. **6597**

The inner meaning really is as I have explained, however. This is evident from the detailed exposition and above all from the fact that the inner meaning was dictated to me from heaven.

Spiritual Inflow, and the Interaction of the Soul and Body (Continued)

PEOPLE recognize that one individual has greater ability than another to understand and perceive what is honorable in private life, fair in public life, and good in spiritual life. The reason some excel is that they **6598** raise their minds to heavenly considerations, which draws their thought away from the outer senses. People who base their thinking on sensory information alone cannot begin to see what is honorable, fair, and good. As a consequence, they rely on [the judgment of] others and speak at length [on the subject] from rote memory. In their own eyes, this makes them wiser than others.

However, people who can lift their thinking above their senses possess a greater ability than others to understand and perceive, as long as they put memorized knowledge in its proper place. The more inward the level from which they view an issue, the more ability they have.

6599   Let me pass along what I have learned from experience about the situation of people whose minds work on the level of the senses and of people whose minds operate above that level, and about the kind of inflow into each group.

First, however, it is important to know that our thinking as a whole is divided up into individual thoughts and that one thought follows another the way one word follows another in speech. Individual thoughts follow one another so quickly, though, that while we are living in the body our thinking appears continuous; we see no partitioning. But in the next life it becomes clear that our thinking is split up into individual thoughts because the units of speech there are thoughts (§§2470, 2472).

Now it is time to say how matters stand with thinking and individual thoughts. First, *thought spreads out to communities of spirits and angels all around,* and one's capacity for understanding and perceiving matches the reach of one's thoughts into those communities; that is, it matches the inflow from those communities. Second, *a single individual thought holds countless elements,* and an aggregate idea composed of individual thoughts holds even more.

6600   *The thoughts of a person, of spirits, and of angels spread out to numerous communities in the spiritual world,* as I was shown quite plainly; but one individual's thinking spreads differently than another's. So that I could know this for sure, I was allowed to talk with some communities to which my thinking had penetrated. From them I was able to learn what inflow had affected my thinking, what community it had come from, where the community was, and what the community was like, with such certainty that I could not be mistaken.

The reach of one's thoughts and feelings into various communities brings about the capacity a person, spirit, or angel has for understanding and perceiving.

[2] People devoted to a goodness inspired by neighborly love or a goodness inspired by faith have a reach that extends to heavenly communities. The greater their degree of devotion to these kinds of goodness, and the more genuine the goodness is, the farther their reach. Both kinds of goodness harmonize with heaven and consequently flow there spontaneously, far and wide. There are two kinds of communities, though: those that can be reached by a desire for truth and those that can be reached by a desire for goodness. A desire for truth makes its way to communities of spiritual angels, and a desire for goodness to communities of heavenly angels.

On the other hand, the thoughts and feelings of people devoted to evil and falsity extend into hellish communities, likewise in proportion to the degree of evil and falsity with them.

[3] I said that the thoughts and feelings of a person, spirit, or angel spread out to various communities, and that understanding and perception result, but be aware that this is said in keeping with the appearance. Thoughts and feelings do not flow to these communities but from them, through the angels and spirits we have with us. As was shown at the end of earlier chapters, all inflow comes from within. So with the good it comes from heaven, or rather from the Lord through heaven, and with the evil, it comes from hell.

One morning I was given a clear demonstration that every individual thought and every little feeling of mine held countless elements and that the thoughts and feelings made their way to various communities. I was kept for a time in a certain emotion and its accompanying thoughts, and while there I was shown how many communities joined me in the sentiment. There were five communities that revealed themselves by speaking out loud. They told me what they were thinking and said they could tell I was entertaining the same thoughts. They also knew both the direct causes and the ultimate purposes behind the subjects I was thinking about, which I had not bothered noticing. The other communities my thinking reached—of which there were many—did not reveal themselves this way, and they were more remote.

6601

[2] The case with the extension of thought from its objects, or from the subjects one is thinking about, resembles the case with objects of sight. Visual objects bristle with rays of light that stream great distances to fall on the human eye. The distance they radiate is longer or shorter depending on the glow and fieriness of the object. If it is fiery, it is visible much farther away than something cloudy and dark. The same holds

true for the extension of inner sight (or the ability to see in thought) from its objects. The objects of this kind of sight are not made of matter, as objects in the world are, but instead are spiritual. So they radiate to the kinds of things that exist in the spiritual world—that is, to truth and goodness there, and therefore to communities that exhibit truth and goodness. Just as something fiery in the world radiates great distances, so do goodness and the desire for goodness in the spiritual world, since fire corresponds to a desire for goodness.

This evidence shows that the quality of the life we have depends entirely on the communities to which our thoughts and feelings reach and on the nature and extent of that reach.

6602   Thoughts and feelings have a sphere of influence that extends all around into the spheres of influence from communities far away. This became clear to me from the fact that when some emotion inspired me to think about subjects that were particularly moving for some distant community, the inhabitants there talked with me about the subject, giving me their opinion. This happened a number of times. One community was fairly far off to the right, on a level with the lower part of my chest. Another, also off to the right but closer, was on a level with my knees.

The perception of distance arises from states of desire for truth and goodness. The distance that appears to separate any two communities equals the extent to which the state of one differs from the state of the other.

6603   It needs to be known, though, that the thoughts and feelings that reach other communities do not specifically move those communities to think and will the same way as the person, spirit, or angel in whom the thoughts and feelings originate. Rather, they enter the overall field of feeling and consequent thought already present in those communities. The communities themselves therefore are unaware of the inflow. After all, there is a spiritual environment surrounding all communities that varies for every one of them. When thoughts and feelings enter this environment, the communities are not noticeably affected.

All thoughts and feelings penetrate the environment of communities with which they agree.

That is why the outreach [of thoughts and feelings] extends freely in all directions, like the radiation of light from objects in the world, which shoots out profusely on all sides, reaching the eyes of every bystander all around. The range varies with the sharpness or dullness of the bystanders' vision and also with the clarity or haziness of the air. In the spiritual world, clear air corresponds with a desire to know what is true and good

Several times I saw an angel whose face was clearly visible to me. His face was constantly changing with the quality of the emotions that followed one after another in order with him, from one extreme to the other. Yet his all-pervasive, dominant passion remained, from which he could be recognized as being the same angel. I was taught that his changes of face came from the different communities with which he had contact and occurred as he came into closer contact with one community or another in succession.

6604

Feelings and thoughts have limitations to their reach, which peters out in the farthest outlying communities, and fails, the way eyesight fails when directed out into the universe. Within the limits of that overall sphere of influence, thoughts and feelings can vary, moving closer to one community at one time and to another community at another. When they are centered in one community, the other communities are relatively marginal. And so on, with all the variations possible within those limitations.

It is worth noting that just as heaven in its entirety resembles a single human being, which is accordingly called the universal human (discussed at the ends of many chapters), so every community likewise resembles a human being. The image of the whole heaven flows into communities—making them like itself—and not only into communities but also into everyone in a community. This gives individuals their human form, because everyone in an angelic community is a heaven in miniature. Differences in their human form reflect the nature of the goodness and truth they possess.

6605

That is why every spirit and angel appears in a form perfectly reflecting the communication that individual's thoughts and feelings have with various communities. The more these individuals immerse themselves in goodness and truth, then, the more beautiful their human form. If their thoughts and feelings communicate with various communities indiscriminately, rather than reflecting a heavenly pattern, to that extent their form lacks beauty.

If their thoughts and feelings communicate with the communities of hell, though, their form is that of a devil, and ugly. And anyone who is diametrically opposed to goodness and truth—because of being opposed to the heavenly form, which is the human form—looks like a monster rather than a person in heaven's light. That is what hell as a whole looks like, and what its communities look like, and what every member of its communities looks like. This too varies, depending on the degree of opposition evil puts up to goodness, and falsity therefore puts up to truth.

6606   When talking with angelic spirits, I have observed that the feeling and thoughts involved looked like a flowing stream all around us an that the matter we were considering stood in the middle, surrounded b the flowing stream, which spread out from there in every direction. Thi too made it plain that thoughts and feelings reach out to communitie on all sides.

6607   I was shown that when thoughts together with feelings spread abroad they swirl around in almost the same pattern that the folds of gray matte take in the human brain. I watched their convolutions for a long time They circled, bent, wove their way inward, and reemerged the same wa as the aforementioned gray matter in the brains.

The patterns of heaven are even more amazing, though, and beyon all comprehension, even by angels. Angelic communities in the heaven follow this pattern. Angels' thoughts also flow into the same pattern, an reach great distances almost instantly, because they follow an infinitel perfect pattern.

6608   In my thinking, speaking, and writing, intellectual light has been give to me, taken from me, lessened, and modified, over and over, and I hav been allowed to distinguish the different types and varieties. I perceive the light itself as an illumination that lit up the mechanism of inner sight just as the light of the sun lights up the organs of physical sight. Thi general illumination always made objects of thought visible, as objects o earth are visible to an eye that receives light. I was instructed that th variations I experienced reflected all the contact I had with various heav enly communities.

6609   The thoughts and conversation of the communities in which my ow thoughts lived were represented to me a number of times as clouds risin and falling in the blue. From the shape, color, and thinness or thicknes of the clouds I was able to recognize the identity of the inflow. True idea were represented by the color blue mixed with an indescribably beauti ful white. Seeming truth was represented by a dull white, and false idea by black clouds. This too was a clue to [the nature of] the inflowin thoughts and feelings.

6610   The whole time we are living, the ideas that compose our thinkin are changing, specifically by dividing and multiplying, and in the pro cess are reaching out to new and different communities. People unde the sway of evil have thoughts that reach out to communities in hell, a do people persuaded of falsity.

People who have convinced themselves that such and such is true—that is, people with a dogmatic faith—have thoughts that are severely restricted. The thoughts and feelings of people who are being reborn, however, are constantly wending their way to new heavenly communities and increasing their outreach. Such people's previous thoughts and feelings subdivide, too, and the subdivisions tie in with ideas that communicate with yet other new communities. In particular, their general ideas become filled in with specifics, and the specifics with even smaller details. In other words, their ideas become filled with new truth, which increases their enlightenment.

I have talked with spirits about the changes of state our life undergoes, describing that state as unpredictable and saying that we are carried up and down, toward heaven and toward hell. But those of us who allow ourselves to be reborn are constantly carried upward, into more inward heavenly communities. The Lord allows our sphere of influence to extend into those communities when we are being reborn, especially when being reborn through trials in which we resist evil and falsity. At those times, you see, he uses angels to battle evil and falsity, which introduces us into the inner communities of those angels. Once we have been introduced into them, we stay there. As a result, we also receive a broader, loftier capacity for perception. **6611**

You can see from this too, then, that the shallower our thinking, the narrower our reach, and the deeper our thinking, the broader our reach. People who think shallowly, on the level of the senses, communicate only with relatively coarse spirits, while those who think deeply, using rationality, have communication with angels. The difference between the two is evident from the density of the aura around sense-oriented spirits and the purity of the aura around the angels of heaven. It is like the difference between the range of sound and the range of light—and scientists know how big that difference is. **6612**

A single individual thought holds countless elements, and an aggregate idea composed of individual thoughts holds even more. This I was able to learn from much experience. Let me relate some of that experience here. **6613**

Personal experience showed me how the ideas of angels flow into the lower-level ideas of spirits and therefore into a more blunted kind of thinking. A wealth of thoughts from heaven and its angels was presented in visible form as a white cloud distinguished into little masses. Each mass, which consisted of countless elements, produced a single simple **6614** idea in a spirit. It was then shown that the idea contained thousands and thousands of elements, which were also represented as a cloud of words spoken by spirits.

Afterward I talked with the spirits about it, and said that the phenomenon can be illustrated by objects of sight. Examining one simple-looking object with a magnifying glass reveals thousands of previously invisible parts. Take tiny little worms, for example, which look like a single indistinct object. When they are inspected with a microscope, not only are they numerous, each is in the shape of a worm. If each shape is examined at even higher magnification, one sees organs, parts, viscera, and even vessels and fibers.

The situation is the same with thoughts. Each thought contains thousands upon thousands of considerations, even though all these components of the thought, taken together, look like a simple unit.

However, one person's thinking contains more individual thoughts than another's. The richness of component thoughts reflects the breadth of outreach to various communities.

6615   When the thinking of angels filters down to lower levels, it looks like a white cloud, as noted just above. When the thinking of angels in the higher heavens filters down, though, it looks like a fiery light giving off shimmering radiance. The white cloud and the fiery light are actually the innumerable components of the angels' thinking. When these components flow into the thinking of the spirits below, they are presented there as a single unit. The radiance of the light flows into the spirits' thoughts, and the flame flows into their feelings of love, which guide and unite their thoughts. The fiery light and its shimmering radiance is not visible to them, but both were made visible to me, to teach me that what is higher flows into what is lower and that what is perceived as a single unit is multiple.

6616   The fact that one idea contains so much was also evident to me from listening to spirits talk with me. Just from the sound of their voice I could tell whether their words were disingenuous, sincere, friendly, or full of loving kindness. We can see this in another's face and to some extent hear it in another's speech. When we see a face smiling at us or hear words encouraging us, we can sense the presence of pretense, deceit, good cheer (whether innate or as a response to some event), shyness, friendliness, insanity, and so on. This too is a sign that every thought holds immeasurable content.

When I talked with spirits about it, some of them were skeptical, so they were taken up into a higher region. Speaking to me from there, the said they saw an immense amount in every one of my thoughts, and in this way they were convinced.

Another piece of evidence demonstrating that one thought contains myriad factors was this: that angels can tell instantly what kind of life a spirit or person leads when they simply hear that individual talking or look at what that individual is thinking. The angels of a lower heaven can see it, and the angels of a higher heaven see even more.

6617

A good spirit was once lifted up to the first heaven and spoke to me from there. "I see infinite layers in what you are reading in the Word," the spirit said, although I myself had only one simple concept of the subject. Next the spirit was raised to a more inward heaven. "Now I see even more," the spirit said from there. "In fact, I see so much that what I saw before seems relatively coarse." From there the spirit rose even farther within, where there were heavenly angels, and said, "What I saw before is almost nothing compared to what I am seeing now."

While this experience lasted, various qualities were flowing into me and affecting me in various ways.

Some spirits once boasted that they knew everything. (In the universal human these spirits correspond to the memory.) They were told, though, that what they do not know is boundless. In fact, one thought can be filled with unlimited information and still appear unitary. If their thoughts were filled with more information every day forever, they were told, they could not encompass even the broadest categories of knowledge, and from this they could judge how much there is that they do not know.

6618

This fact was demonstrated to them to the point where they could acknowledge it. An angel spoke to them while undergoing changes of state, but they could not understand what the angel said. They were told that every change of state contained unlimited material but that they were not even aware of it, because not only did they fail to understand it, they were not interested in it.

The fact that individual thoughts have numberless facets, and that any properly arranged contents of a thought come from within, also became clear to me when I said the Lord's Prayer morning and evening. Whenever I said the prayer, my thoughts opened up toward heaven, and countless ideas flowed in. As a result, I noticed plainly that the ideas I gleaned from the contents of the prayer were filled in from heaven. Some of what was poured in was by nature incapable of being verbalized, and some was beyond my comprehension, so that I merely sensed the resulting general

6619

feeling. Surprisingly, the inflowing thoughts and feelings were different every day.

All this enabled me to see the following: The contents of the Lord's Prayer hold more than all heaven is capable of understanding; the more we open our mind toward heaven, the more the prayer holds for us; and conversely, the more we close our mind, the less it holds. In people with closed minds, nothing more is visible in the prayer than the literal meaning, or the meaning closest to the words.

6620　This evidence reveals what unlimited content also resides in *every* concept in the Word—since the Word comes down from the Lord through heaven—even though Scripture appears utterly lacking in complexity to people whose thinking is closed off.

One time I discussed this matter with some spirits who denied that anything lay hidden inside the Word. I replied that the Word held infinite, indescribable content that cannot be perceived by closed-minded people. The only meaning the closed-minded accept, as a consequence, is the literal one, which they interpret in favor of their own assumptions and compulsions. In this way they shut off any access they might have to its hidden stores and either drain any real thoughts from their mind or lock them tightly away.

I was also shown what a thought looks like when it is closed and when it is open. (In heaven's light this is done easily.) The closed-off thought looked like a black spot with nothing visible inside. The open thought looked like a patch of light with a kind of flame inside, and everything there turned to face it. The flame represented the Lord, and what turned to face him represented heaven. I was told that every thought from the Lord contains an entire image of heaven because it comes from him who *is* heaven.

6621　Some people reading the Word during bodily life put all their effort into textual criticism, without much concern for the meaning. Their thinking has been represented as lines that come to a dead end instead of standing open, and as a weaving together of those lines.

On one occasion some spirits of this sort were with me, and then everything I thought or wrote became confused. It was as though my mind was imprisoned, because they focused my thoughts solely on the words, distracting my attention from the meaning with such energy that they completely wore me out. And yet they still considered themselves wiser than others.

6622　Conversing with some spirits about the inflow into a person's thoughts, I said that no one could believe the vast amount of material a thought holds. All we take in is a simple, solitary entity, which means that we judge by our outer senses.

The spirits I was addressing held the opinion—of which they had persuaded themselves during bodily life—that there was nothing inside a thought. However, to help them understand that what they perceive as a single unit holds huge quantities, I was inspired to say that a single physical motion requires the cooperative action of millions of motor fibers. Moreover, every part of the body together, in general and particular, harmonizes its movements and adapts to produce the same action. Yet that tiny little motion looks simple and solitary, as if all this activity were not present inside it.

Again, to pronounce one word requires the cooperation of many, many parts simultaneously. The lips twist, along with all their surrounding muscles and fibers, and the tongue, throat, larynx, trachea, lungs, and diaphragm also [move], along with all their muscles in general and particular. Considering that we perceive the one resulting word merely as a simple sound, with nothing more in it, you can see how coarse our sensory perception is. What then about sensory perception concerning the individual thoughts that make up our thinking? After all, these lie in a purer realm and are therefore more remote from the sensory plane.

Because individual thoughts contain so much, just a single word produced by thought reveals to angels what a spirit or a person is like. This too was confirmed by experience. When the mere word *truth* was spoken (which was done by a large number of spirits one after another), I could instantly hear whether the word was hard, rough, soft, childlike, treasured, innocent, full, empty, unsound, insincere, closed, or open, and to what extent. In short, the actual quality of the underlying thought was audible. And this was only at a general level. What about at the level of detail that angels perceive?

6623

Since people think from their senses, this information is obscure to them—so obscure that they do not even know what a component thought is. They especially fail to realize that one's thinking is divided into individual thoughts the same way speech is divided into words, because thinking seems continuous to them, not subdivided. In reality, though, individual thoughts are the words spirits use, and individual thoughts on an even deeper level are the words angels use.

6624

As thoughts are the words used in speech, they are also audible among spirits and angels. Our silent thoughts can therefore be heard by spirits and angels when the Lord pleases.

Thoughts are much more perfect than spoken words, as can be seen from the fact that we are able to think more in a minute than we can verbalize or write in an hour. Evidence was also supplied to me by conversations I had with spirits and angels, during which I filled in a general idea with specifics and brought in the emotion too, all in a moment. From this the angels and spirits distinctly grasped everything I was saying, and much more besides, which appeared as a bright cloud around the main subject.

6625   All this now indicates what kinds of thoughts are entertained by people who live badly and therefore think badly. Such people's thoughts harbor hatred, vengefulness, envy, deceit, adultery, arrogance, an outward decency that mimics honor, a show of chastity, and friendship for the sake of rank and monetary gain that is no friendship, besides unmentionable foulness and filth. In addition, their minds contain a handful of religious teachings that justify their cravings, or in the absence of these, cynicism and ridicule. Such traits and others like them fill the thoughts of people who live wicked lives and therefore think wicked thoughts.

If people like this fill their thoughts with ideas like these, then when they go to the other world they are inevitably separated and distanced from heaven, where such things cause horror.

6626   I will also mention an astonishing phenomenon. The Lord alone is human, and angels, spirits, and the inhabitants of the earth are called human from him. By his inflow into heaven, he causes the whole of heaven to represent and replicate a single human being. Moreover, by his inflow both through heaven and directly from himself into every individual there, he gives everyone a human appearance; and he gives angels a form too beautiful and too radiant to describe. His inflow into the spirit of a person on earth has the same effect. In fact, in angels, spirits, and people who live lives of charity for their neighbor and of love for the Lord, the very slightest bits of their thought also resemble a human being. That is because such charity and love come from the Lord, and whatever comes from the Lord resembles a human being. These are the same qualities that make us human.

Hell's inhabitants, on the other hand, adopt qualities opposed to charity and heavenly love, so although they look human in their own illumination, in heaven's light they resemble dreadful monsters. Some of these monsters display almost no sign of the human form. That is because the inhabitants there do not accept what flows in from the Lord through heaven but reject, snuff out, or corrupt it. That is why they look the way they do. The slightest bits of their thought, or their individual ideas, likewise display a monstrous shape, because everyone is the same in part as in whole. The part and the whole are of the same type and nature.

The form in which hell's inhabitants appear is also the form of the hell they inhabit. Every hell has its own form, which in heaven's light resembles a monster. When the inhabitants of a hell appear, the identity of the hell they come from is recognized from their form. I saw them standing in some gates that lay open to the world of spirits, and they resembled a wide variety of monsters. (On the point that the gates of hell open into the world of spirits, see §5852.)

END OF GENESIS

Biographical Note

EMANUEL SWEDENBORG (1688–1772) was born Emanuel Swedberg (or Svedberg) in Stockholm, Sweden, on January 29, 1688 (Julian calendar). He was the third of the nine children of Jesper Swedberg (1653–1735) and Sara Behm (1666–1696). At the age of eight he lost his mother. After the death of his only older brother ten days later, he became the oldest living son. In 1697 his father married Sara Bergia (1666–1720), who developed great affection for Emanuel and left him a significant inheritance. His father, a Lutheran clergyman, later became a celebrated and controversial bishop, whose diocese included the Swedish churches in Pennsylvania and in London, England.

After studying at the University of Uppsala (1699–1709), Emanuel journeyed to England, the Netherlands, France, and Germany (1710–1715) to study and work with leading scientists in western Europe. Upon his return he apprenticed as an engineer under the brilliant Swedish inventor Christopher Polhem (1661–1751). He gained favor with Sweden's King Charles XII (1682–1718), who gave him a salaried position as an overseer of Sweden's mining industry (1716–1747). Although Emanuel was engaged, he never married.

After the death of Charles XII, Emanuel was ennobled by Queen Ulrika Eleonora (1688–1741), and his last name was changed to Swedenborg (or Svedenborg). This change in status gave him a seat in the Swedish House of Nobles, where he remained an active participant in the Swedish government throughout his life.

A member of the Royal Swedish Academy of Sciences, he devoted himself to studies that culminated in a number of publications, most notably a comprehensive three-volume work on natural philosophy and metallurgy (1734) that brought him recognition across Europe as a scientist. After 1734 he redirected his research and publishing to a study of anatomy in search of the interface between the soul and body, making several significant discoveries in physiology.

From 1743 to 1745 he entered a transitional phase that resulted in a shift of his main focus from science to theology. Throughout the rest of his life he maintained that this shift was brought about by Jesus Christ, who appeared to him, called him to a new mission, and opened his perception to a permanent dual consciousness of this life and the life after death.

He devoted the last decades of his life to studying Scripture and publishing eighteen theological titles that draw on the Bible, reasoning, and his own spiritual experiences. These works present a Christian theology with unique perspectives on the nature of God, the spiritual world, the Bible, the human mind, and the path to salvation.

Swedenborg died in London on March 29, 1772 (Gregorian calendar), at the age of eighty-four.